UNEDITING
THE RENAISSANCE

Many readers of Shakespeare, Milton, Marlowe and other Renaissance authors do not recognize the extent to which those texts have been filtered through eighteenth-century and Victorian sensibilities. To "unedit" these texts is to discover a vast array of possibilities suppressed or neglected in modern editions: a Shakespearean Katharine who may not end up tamed after all; a Sycorax with blue eyes and a potential for sexual allure that is foreclosed in modern editions of *The Tempest*; a Dr Faustus who alters his transgressive activities in keeping with changes in his audience; a Milton who loses part of himself as he relinquishes traditional oral forms and adapts to the new demands of literate print culture.

By using ethnographic modelling to explore typical features of modern editorial practice, Leah Marcus demonstrates how much modern texts of early modern authors have altered and rigidified over time, and how much modern interpretation and performance of their work can be energized by a recognition of the range of potential meanings closed off by modern editions.

Unediting the Renaissance is a provocative and lively work in which students and scholars of the Renaissance will find much material for debate and new understanding of textual editing. General readers who wish to learn more about what goes on behind the "barbed wire" of textual apparatus in modern editions will also find it fascinating reading.

Leah S. Marcus is Blumberg Centennial Professor in English at the University of Texas, Austin. Her previous books include *Childhood and Cultural Despair*, *The Politics of Mirth* and *Puzzling Shakespeare*.

UNEDITING
THE RENAISSANCE

Shakespeare, Marlowe, Milton

Leah S. Marcus

London and New York

First published 1996
by Routledge
11 New Fetter Lane, London EC4P 4EE

Simultaneously published in the USA and Canada
by Routledge
29 West 35th Street, New York, NY 10001

Typeset in Baskerville by
Keystroke, Jacaranda Lodge, Wolverhampton
Printed and bound in Great Britain by
Biddles Ltd, Guildford and King's Lynn

British Library Cataloguing in Publication Data
A catalogue record for this book is available from the British Library

Library of Congress Cataloguing in Publication Data
Marcus, Leah S.
Unediting the Renaissance : Shakespeare, Marlowe, Milton / Leah S.
Marcus.
Includes bibliographical references and index.
1. English literature—Early modern, 1500–1700—Criticism,
Textual. 2. Shakespeare, William, 1564–1616—Criticism, Textual.
3. Marlowe, Christopher, 1564–1593—Criticism, Textual. 4. Milton,
John, 1608–1674—Criticism, Textual. 5. Shakespeare, William,
1564–1616—Editors. 6. Marlow, Christopher, 1564–1593—Editors.
7. Milton, John, 1608–1674—Editors. 8. Transmission of texts.
9. Renaissance—England. 10. Editing. I. Title.
PR418.T48M37   1996
820.9′003—dc20   96-7263

ISBN 0–415–09934–X
0–415–10053–4 (pbk)

For Lauren

CONTENTS

ILLUSTRATIONS

PREFACE AND ACKNOWLEDGEMENTS

This project is one year older than its dedicat⸜ ⸝, and has altered over time almost as much as she has. Like any book that a empts to mediate between disciplines, it has required a delicate balance between them and runs the risk of being condemned by both. I have, I ⸜   ⸝ included far too few textual details to satisfy most bibliographe⸜   ⸝v to be palatable to other readers still laboring under the ⸜   ⸝at such matters are of no consequence. These latter, I ferve⸜ convert. Throughout the book, I have been quite speculativ⸜ interested in suggesting directions for further inquiry than in ofte definitive statements. As will be fairly obvious to my readers, I am mo⸜ excited about the newest material – on memory, oral/aural modes of communication, and seventeenth-century anxieties about lost oral presence – as treated in chapters 5 and 6. Some segments of the argument have appeared elsewhere, usually in markedly different form. Part of chapter 2 is reprinted by kind permission of Northwestern University Press and Mary Beth Rose, editor of *Renaissance Drama*, from "Textual Indeterminacy and Ideological Difference: The Case of *Doctor Faustus*," *Renaissance Drama* new series 20 (1989): 1–30, but appears here with much additional evidence and consideration of yet a third variant form of the play. Part of chapter 4 is reprinted by kind permission of Arthur Kinney, editor of *English Literary Renaissance*, from "The Shakespearean Editor as Shrew-Tamer," *English Literary Renaissance* 22 (1992): 177–200, and is offered here in much revised and expanded form. One- to four-page snippets of chapters 3 and 6 have appeared respectively in "Levelling Shakespeare: Local Customs and Local Texts," *Shakespeare Quarterly* 42 (1991): 168–78; "Robert Herrick," Thomas N. Corns, ed., *The Cambridge Companion to English Poetry: Donne to Marvell* (Cambridge: Cambridge University Press, 1993), pp. 171–81; and "Milton as Historical Subject: Milton Banquet Address, Chicago, 1990," *Milton Quarterly* 25 (1991): 120–27, and are reprinted here with permission of the editors and of Cambridge University Press. But the argument of the book is progressive: readers who read it through in old-fashioned linear fashion will, I trust, find it more convincing than those who plunge into one or two chapters that happen to be of particular interest without considering the rest. There is a pleasant irony about hoping for such fidelity to time-honored traditions of book perusal in a study that aims to destabilize the holistic, organic image of authorship that has traditionally been recommended along with the quaint old habit of linear reading. But that is only one of many strange contradictions that I, among many others, have come not only to accommodate but actually to enjoy in our present climate of methodological ferment and experimentation. Despite the (sometimes) gnarled and tangled thickets of evidence offered in the chapters that follow, I hope the book will give as much pleasure to readers as it has to me in the writing.

Like any project that has been years in the making, this one has accumulated a load of debt, some acknowledged in the notes, some too pervasive to be adequately acknowledged anywhere. I owe a strong debt to my students, first at the University of Wisconsin, then at the University of Texas (especially Jeanne McCarthy), and to my colleagues in both institutions, especially Andrew Weiner, Wayne Rebhorn, Frank Whigham, Eric Mallin, John Velz, John Rumrich, Michael Winship, Terry Kelley, and most of all, Dolora Wojciehowski. In addition, David Wallace, Rita Copeland, Lynda Boose, Mary Beth Rose, Margaret Downs-Gamble, Ernest Sullivan, Ted-Larry Pebworth, John Shawcross, Michael Warren, Steven Urkowitz, Janel Mueller, Patricia Fumerton, Alan Liu, Jerome J. McGann, Randall McLeod (alias Random Cloud or Clod, Claudia Nimbus, Sir Greg Walters, etc.), Laurie Maguire, Thomas Berger, Dan and Jean R. Brink, Kathi Irace, and many others contributed ideas and/or enthusiasm for one or another element of the project. The University Research Institute of the University of Texas contributed travel funds and a semester of leave in 1992; though the time was short, it was very welcome. The staffs of the Huntington Library, especially Alan Jutzi; the Newberry Library; the Folger Shakespeare Library, especially Georgianna Ziegler; Cambridge University Library; the Bodleian; and the British Library have all been helpful beyond measure, but the heaviest burden of assistance with my research has gone, perforce, to the Harry Ransom Humanities Research Center of the University of Texas and its past and present staff – particularly Ken Craven, John Chalmers, Pat Fox, John Thomas, and Richard Oram – and to my research assistant Ioannis Vassiliou, who cheerfully endured the ordeal of checking all the notes (well, almost all of them!). The British Library, Bodleian, Huntington, Folger, and Harry Ransom HRC all supplied photos for the illustrations.

More generally, the book has been enriched by the responses of the many audiences in the United States and Britain before whom I have presented segments of it, and by the perspectives offered by visiting scholars to the University of Texas like Ian Willison, Robin Alston, and even more, D. F. McKenzie, whose charismatic time in Austin during 1988, I now realize in retrospect, helped to spark my enthusiasm for bibliography and the history of the book. My strongest intellectual debt is undoubtedly to my colleague emeritus Warner Barnes, who sat me down one day, inquired courteously whether it might not be time that I learned a little bibliography, and has shared expertise and wise counsel ever since. But as always, I owe most of all to my family – to my computer-wizard husband David who insisted that I upgrade and extricated me from many online crises when I did, and to my daughters Emily and Lauren, who sacrificed much quality time with their mother so that the project could reach completion. None of the above-mentioned scholars, friends, or family is to be held responsible for the book's deficiencies, which my perverse brain is, alas, quite capable of generating by itself. I will be happy if the weaknesses in what follows prove less memorable for readers than its strengths.

ABBREVIATIONS

A   The A text of *Doctor Faustus*, cited from W. W. Greg, ed., *Marlowe's Doctor Faustus, 1604–1616: Parallel Texts* (Oxford: Clarendon, 1950).

B   The B text of *Doctor Faustus*, cited from Greg, ed., as above.

C   *The Works of John Milton*, Columbia edition, ed. Frank Allen Patterson, 18 vols in 21 (New York: Columbia University Press, 1931–38).

F   *The First Folio of Shakespeare*, Norton Facsimile edition, ed. Charlton Hinman (London and New York: Paul Hamlyn, 1968).

G   Greg, ed., as cited in A above

H   *The Three-Text Hamlet: Parallel Texts of the First and Second Quartos and First Folio*, ed. Paul Bertram and Bernice W. Kliman (New York: AMS Press, 1991).

M   *The Poetical Works of Robert Herrick*, ed. L. C. Martin (Oxford: Clarendon Press, 1956).

Q   *Shakespeare's Plays in Quarto: A Facsimile Edition of Copies Primarily from the Henry E. Huntington Library*, ed. Michael J. B. Allen and Kenneth Muir (Berkeley and London: University of California Press, 1981).

S   *A Pleasant Conceited Historie, called The taming of a Shrew* (London: for Cuthbert Barbie, 1594). Signature numbers in text are to this edition; page numbers are to Graham Holderness and Bryan Loughrey, eds, *The Taming of a Shrew* (Hemel Hempstead, UK: Harvester Wheatsheaf, 1992).

TLN   Through Line Number to Charlton Hinman's Norton Facsimile edition cited in full above under F.

1

INTRODUCTION
The blue-eyed witch

What is it that we hope to experience when we read a literary text from an earlier era? Are we looking for unimpeded access to a culture far removed from our own, for contact with the mind of a writer far distant in time? Are we looking for amusement or instruction or moral elevation or escape? For an encounter with transcendence, for visceral engagement with past conflicts, for a glimpse of something alien, or for some or all of the above, mutually exclusive though they may appear to be? What we want out of our reading will depend greatly on the genre, type, and specific subject matter of the work we happen to choose: most of us would not go to the poetry of the Earl of Rochester for moral elevation, nor to the *Enneads* of Plotinus for light entertainment. But what we want from a given text will also depend on the social and intellectual baggage we ourselves bring to it, on the specific coordinates of our individual lives, on the shared assumptions that characterize our particular cultural affiliations and our broader historical situation.

As readers most of us have become quite comfortable with at least some of these forms of relativism. Yet unless we are trained textual scholars or bibliographers, we probably do not occupy ourselves unduly with another form of relativism at least as significant as those listed above – the variability over time and space of any given work itself. The work's material history since its inception, the vast and largely uncharted alterations imposed by that history and by the mediation of generation upon generation of printers, editors, publishers – this is a relativism we are prone to ignore, but ignore at our peril. The approach and critical interests we wish to bring to a given piece of writing may be facilitated, discouraged, or even blocked altogether by the specific version in which we receive it.

The present study is designed with at least two audiences in mind. It is aimed first at readers who already have an active interest in textual studies, in the myriad subtle ways in which literary works are altered by their histories, and by the shaping hands of scholars who transform them in the very act of editing them to make them accessible to a broader community of readers. From at least the 1950s until the mid- to late 1970s, scholarly

1

editors and literary critics lived for the most part in divided and distinguished worlds. There was a fruitful division of labor between them: scholars who identified themselves primarily as editors and bibliographers worked to produce authoritative critical editions of the standard authors; serious lay readers and scholars who identified themselves primarily as literary critics made use of these authoritative editions as a reliable basis for interpretation. Some editors and bibliographers looked with mingled amusement and scorn upon the ephemeral pursuits of the madding crowd of literary critics, who could be relied upon year after year to produce new "definitive" readings of the symbolism of the white whale in *Moby Dick* or the madness of King Lear. By contrast, their own bibliographical efforts – the establishing of a given author's canon, the compilation of a definitive descriptive bibliography, the creation of a standard edition – would endure over time because such work was scientifically based.

On the other side of the divide, literary critics sometimes looked ruefully upon the embarrassing plenitude of their own interpretive efforts, but tended to view them as incremental steps toward some definitive conclusion or larger synthesis: at some point, the "truth" about Melville's novel or Shakespeare's play would finally be attained. Literary critics and lay readers tended to look with considerable scorn upon the "dry as dust" labors of the editors and bibliographers, even while relying heavily upon their work. When I was in graduate school at Columbia University in the late 1960s, most students avoided the bibliography courses like a plague: to specialize in such mechanical matters, we felt in what then passed for wisdom, was to give evidence of some grave defect of personality or imagination. The stereotyped image of the bibliographer among literary critics in the late 1960s is nicely captured in Frederick Crews' caricature, Smedley Force, the impossibly pompous editor of *The Watermark* and Professor of English at the University of Texas. Mr Force insists that criticism cannot possibly begin until he and his ilk have established sufficient appendices, concordances, and (in the case of Shakespeare) accurate scale models of the Blackfriars Theater.[1] And yet, we felt obliged to heed Mr Force and use the "correct" edition – which was, for my period, usually bound in dark blue and labelled "Clarendon" – or risk the solecism of an interpretation based on a non-authoritative text.

More recently, however, the division of labor between critics and bibliographers has broken down, as has some of the mutual distrust that kept the two groups divided. Bibliographers with the profound scholarship, daring, and imagination of D. F. McKenzie have challenged their own discipline's positivist underpinnings by demonstrating the degree to which, for example, the investigation of seventeenth- and eighteenth-century printinghouse practices has been skewed by our twentieth-century author-bound presuppositions about how printed books must have been put together. Scholars like McKenzie, Philip Gaskell, and Jerome J. McGann, among many others, have chipped away at some of the insufficiently historicized assumptions behind the "New Bibliography" (as represented in the work of Alfred Pollard, W. W. Greg, Fredson Bowers, and others) and its standardization of editorial practice. Textual critics like McGann and D. C. Greetham have sought for a rapprochement between the field of textual studies and recent critical theory, so that editors and their readers alike would become more aware of the constructed nature of even the most "definitive" edition. The area of Renaissance literature has been at the forefront of this vital revisionism. In arguing for two texts of *King Lear* rather than a single conflated text, Steven Urkowitz, Gary Taylor, Michael Warren, and others have unleashed a torrent of questions about the reliability of all twentieth-century editions of Renaissance authors. From a different angle of vision, Elizabeth Eisenstein has reinterpreted the meaning of the set of historical shifts we call the "Renaissance" in terms of the development of print culture. And all the while, the vast interdisciplinary project entitled "The History of the Book," under the international leadership of scholars like Henri-Jean Martin, Robert Darnton, Roger Chartier, McKenzie, Ian Willison, David McKitterick, and Asa Briggs, has gathered its energies toward the task of discovering how material texts of all kinds have been conceptualized, produced, marketed, and consumed at specific moments in history.[2]

The present study is designed as a contribution to the newly active field of textual studies, but I also have a second audience in mind – those readers and critics who are as yet unconverted, who are either unaware of the new developments or consider them a tempest in a teapot that can be safely overlooked. As part of our interpretive activity, those of us who read or "profess" literature need to consider the subtle, pervasive rhetorical power exerted by the editions we use. From among the many forces and institutions that may shape a given work, the present study will concentrate on printed books in the Renaissance (as opposed to manuscripts and other materials) and on ways in which their texts are transformed, often dis-figured, by the twentieth-century editorial processes to which they have been subjected. No single version of a literary work, whether Renaissance or modern, can offer us the fond dream of unmediated access to an author or to his or her era; the more aware we are of the processes of mediation to which a given edition has been subject, the less likely we are to be caught up in a constricting hermeneutic knot by which the shaping hand of the editor is mistaken for the intent of the author, or for some lost, "perfect" version of the author's creation.

Until recently, of course, it has been the business of editors to accomplish those very things: to give us the work insofar as possible as the author intended it, or at least in its "original" written form. Editors usually do, and should, strive for objectivity in their labors, but they are, as we all are, creatures of their times: what looks like objectivity to one generation may well look like distortion to another. The present study is dependent on recent critiques of scientific method that demonstrate the rhetorical and socio-political nature of scientific explanation. What we consider the factual basis for our conclusions may well alter its truth-bearing status over time: the human power to elucidate or otherwise account for a phenomenon is always limited by the local parameters of the man or woman doing the elucidation.

Until recently, the successful edition of a literary work was one that created for its readers an aura of near transparency, or unmediated access to the author and his or her achievement. From our present relativist point of view, such an edition was successful not because it had uncovered the "true" version of the literary work (although it might well be based on brilliant scholarship and meticulous analysis of the requisite historical materials), but because it successfully met reader expectations about the author and work in question. The editor's own taste and sensibility were sufficiently at one with that of his audience for his edition to achieve the illusion of transparency. In very recent editions influenced by post-structuralist theory and by the new textual studies, the editor's shaping hand is likely to be much more obvious – we may think, for example, of Hans Gabler's controversial version of *Ulysses* or of the almost equally controversial new single-volume Oxford Shakespeare. Whether we like it or not, scholarly editing is becoming a very different activity than it was even two decades ago: it is revealing, even flaunting, its own plastic energies rather than striving to conceal them; it is coming to be understood as a form of cultural practice. What, then, might be the specific cultural practice behind the standard editions many of us still accept unquestioningly?

We have much to lose by "Unediting the Renaissance." If modern scholars, students, and general readers were suddenly deprived of all the historical, linguistic, and literary investigation that lies behind the average standard edition, we would find ourselves crippled and disoriented. We might well find ourselves repeating the past – assembing new standard editions if only to have a stable reference point for future departures from them. Despite the agenda encapsulated in its title, the present study will by no means contend that editing has become unnecessary. Our discussion here will regularly depend on edited versions of works that are not at the forefront of our analysis. *Ars longa, vita brevis*: there is only so much primary textual investigation that any given scholar can be expected to accomplish. Adopting the purist position that all previous editions must be avoided would bring scholarly writing and research to a halt. It would also have a devastating effect on our ability to teach literature from past centuries or, indeed, to read such literature at all. To call for an investigation of past editorial practice is by no means to throw its achievements out the window – only to suggest that we need to be aware of its dynamics and limitations in the same way that we train ourselves to be attentive to the other implements available to us in the jumbled toolbox we bring to the activity of textual interpretation.

If there is much to be lost by "Unediting the Renaissance," there is also much to be gained. Because of the sheer weight of erudition involved, if for no other reason (and I will suggest a few more later on), editing has tended to be a profoundly conservative activity. To an extent that few of us recognize, our standard editions are shaped by nineteenth-century or even earlier assumptions and ideologies. Even the new, more experimental editions sometimes collapse back into received orthodoxy at moments that are crucial for interpretation. "Unediting the Renaissance" is proposed not as a permanent condition, but as an activity that all editors should engage in as part of their own revisionary efforts, that all readers should practice mentally even as they make use of edited texts. It requires a temporary abandonment of modern editions in favor of Renaissance editions that have not gathered centuries of editorial accretion around them. It requires a questioning of the origins of even the most standard glosses and emendations. To illustrate the value of this process for the benefit of the unconverted, I offer as an example the mysterious case from *The Tempest* of the blue-eyed witch, a crone whose physical demeanor has altered curiously over the centuries along with prevailing attitudes toward women, sexuality, and race.

GRAY EYES, BLACK EYES, BLUE EYES

In Act 1, scene 2 of *The Tempest*, Prospero describes Caliban's mother Sycorax as a "damn'd Witch" condemned to death in "*Argier*" on account of her "mischiefes manifold" and "sorceries terrible." I quote here from the First Folio, the only early text of the play, although most modern edited versions introduce only minor changes to the lines in question.[3] Because of "one thing" Sycorax "did / They wold not take her life" but banished her instead: "This blew ey'd hag, was hither brought with child" – her child being Caliban, born somewhat later on the island where he, Prospero, Miranda, and the others presently reside (TLN 391–96).

Our discussion will focus on the witch's blue eyes, but we may wish to pause briefly over her crime. What was it that Sycorax did to avoid execution? Until the second half of the nineteenth century, readers and editors were in a quandary over this matter. Charles Lamb found the passage puzzling "beyond measure." It aroused "infinite hopeless curiosity" in him until he read of the infamous career of an actual Algerian witch (unnamed in his source) who had earned a reprieve from death by delivering Algiers from the siege of Emperor Charles V.[4] Staid Victorian editions tended to avoid what now appears the obvious explanation, while displaying unease over the passage's sexual innuendo. The matter remained in debate until the early twentieth century; since then, editors have regularly noted that the "one thing" Sycorax did to avoid execution was become pregnant, as actual female convicts sometimes did in early modern England to postpone execution.

This is an example of a genuinely helpful editorial intervention, but it leaves open the question of Caliban's parentage. Was Sycorax pregnant by the devil, as Prospero repeatedly asserts, or by some other father? At some point in her history, Sycorax "with Age and Envy / Was growne into a hoope" (TLN 384–5), and she died sometime before Prospero's and Miranda's arrival on the island. But that deformity was the effect of age and malice: what was she like before that? In this passage and throughout the play, Sycorax is a shadowy figure, and even here, the seemingly specific information we are offered is Prospero's recounting of a story Ariel had apparently told him previously, a narration of events even Ariel had in all likelihood not witnessed himself. Nearly everything we know about Sycorax we know only through Prospero's secondhand information, which may or may not be accurate but is certainly not without prejudice: he has supplanted her son on the island and his magic has rivalled and exceeded hers. To what degree might he, or even Ariel, have "edited" her story? To what extent, if we were editing *The Tempest*, would we want to align ourselves with his perceptions?

Let us return to Sycorax's blue eyes – "blew" in the First Folio, but regularly modernized to "blue" in recent editions. Why has so little been made of their color in recent critical studies of the play? The mention of eye color in Shakespeare is rare, and blue eyes are particularly rare. Why are the witch's eyes blue? Much of the interpretive energy surrounding *The Tempest* in the late twentieth century has gone toward the deconstruction of the play's apparent opposition between the properly European (Prospero, Miranda, Ferdinand) and the colonial or otherwise alien stranger (Caliban, Sycorax). We might have supposed that Sycorax's eye color would be a prominent piece of evidence in such critical revisionism, since blue eyes, in our culture at least, are associated with the Anglo-American imperialist and with the "self," rather than with the colonized peoples and with the "other." As a blue-eyed Algerian, Sycorax would fail to fit our racial stereotypes in a number of interesting ways. We tend not to think of Africans as blue eyed, even though North Africans of "Argier" and elsewhere sometimes are. But the witch's blue eyes scarcely surface in the critical discussions I have read: the critics have dutifully read the explanatory notes to the play in the editions they have used, and modern editions overwhelmingly reject the possibility that "blue-eyed" in this instance can possibly mean blue eyed.

In nearly all modern editions, "blew ey'd," "blue-ey'd," or "blue-eyed" is glossed in a way that cancels out its potential for disrupting the self/other binary that has characterized most readings of the play. Among popular teaching editions of the complete works of Shakespeare, the Riverside glosses "blue-ey'd" as "with dark circles around the eyes"; the Bevington fourth edition suggests, "with dark circles under the eyes or with blue eyelids, implying pregnancy", the Signet edition offers, "referring to the livid color of the eyelid, a sign of pregnancy."[5]

Standard single-play editions are only slightly more informative. Frank Kermode's Arden edition glosses "blue-ey'd" as "Alluding to the eyelid; blueness there was regarded as a sign of pregnancy." G. L. Kittredge suggests, somewhat more creatively, "with blueish settled streaks (often called *circles*) under and partly surrounding her eyes – a sign of exhaustion or debility" and follows the suggested reading with a long list of analogues from other Renaissance texts. John Dover Wilson's notes to the New Shakespeare offer paleographical evidence for a possible emendation of "blew-ey'd" to "blear-ey'd": in the passage of *Sir Thomas More* which had been suggested only a few years before Dover's edition as a sample of Shakespeare's handwriting, final *r* and final *w* are almost indistinguishable. Wilson suggests that Shakespeare may have written "bler-ey'd" and been misread by the compositor.[6] In the hand of the *Sir Thomas More* passage, the two letters are indeed easily confused, but we have no conclusive evidence that the hand in *Sir Thomas More* is Shakespeare's. As Paul Werstine has pointed out, a recent volume of essays on the subject succeeds in demonstrating only that none of the contributors is willing to rule out Shakespeare as possible author of the *More* passage.[7] In most Renaissance hands, final *r* and final *w* are quite easy to distinguish. Wilson's argument is cogent only if we have already accepted his assumption that Sycorax could not possibly be blue eyed. Only a few twentieth-century single-volume editors of *The Tempest* have left the line unannotated: most notably, Northrop Frye and Alfred Harbage in the Pelican Shakespeare. Most editions that do not annotate the line supply the requisite information in a glossary: "blue-eyed" in Shakespeare means with "a dark circle round the eye" or "with blueness about the eyes."[8]

Why are twentieth-century editors so relatively uniform in their interpretation of the line, which would seem, on the face of it, to be receptive to a wide range of explications? In this, as in many other editorial matters, they have followed the lead of William Aldis Wright's prestigious Clarendon edition of *The Tempest* (1874), which contended that "'blue-eyed' does not describe the colour of the pupil of the eye, but the livid colour of the eyelid, and a blue eye in this sense was a sign of pregnancy. See Webster, *Duchess of Malfi*, ii, I, 'The fins of her eyelids look most teeming blue.'"[9] But nineteenth-century editors were by no means so formulaic as their successors have been in their interpretation of the witch's startling blue eyes. In fact, the idea that Sycorax could not possibly be blue eyed in our usual sense of the term seems to have been hatched around mid-century along with the dissemination of Charles Darwin's theory of evolution.

Surprisingly enough, the phrase "blue-eyed hag" went unannotated in editions of Shakespeare from the early folios (which were, of course, not annotated), through all of the eighteenth- and early nineteenth-century annotated editions, until the late 1850s. Even Thomas Bowdler's *Family Shakespeare* (1818) left the description of the pregnant, blue-eyed Sycorax intact, despite his resolve to remove words and expressions "which cannot with propriety be read aloud in a family."[10] The first edition of *The Tempest* to take issue with Sycorax's eye color was the Gilbert Shakespeare (1858–60), edited by Howard Staunton. Staunton suggested emendation of "blew-ey'd" to "blear-ey'd" as a more appropriate epithet for the "damn'd witch." His edition also happened to anticipate Darwin's *Descent of Man* by depicting Caliban as a "missing link" between primate and human. In one of Sir John Gilbert's illustrations, a simian Caliban is attended by his close cousin, the monkey (Figure 1.1). The page on which Sycorax is described is adorned with a portrait of her in standard witch-like garb. She is apparently on the point of imprisoning Ariel, who recoils from the hunched forms of the witch and her half-human son (Figure 1.2).[11] A decade and a half later, Daniel Wilson's *Caliban: The Missing Link* (1873) accepted the emendation as settled, referring several times to the "blear-eyed" Sycorax as part of his discussion of Caliban's borderline status between the animal and the human. Wilson contended:

> Sycorax is spoken of with every term of loathing: as a "foul witch," a "hag," a "damned witch," &c. There seems no propriety in coupling with these the term *blue-eyed* – one of the tokens, according to Rosalind, in "As You Like It," whereby to know a man in love.

Some Victorian stage Calibans followed Gilbert and Wilson, modelling their portrayals of the savage on the behavior patterns of great apes.[12]

Although Staunton's and Wilson's textual emendation was not followed by later editors, who at most admitted it into their notes as conjectural, the rationale behind the suggested emendation was generally accepted. In nineteenth-century literature and culture, blue eyes were commonly associated with beauty, innocence, and transcendence, as in Keats' "beauteous woman's large blue eyes" or Shelley's eyes "like the deep, blue, boundless heaven" or Arnold's "eyes, so blue, so kind."[13] Blue eyes were also associated, at a time of expanding colonization and racial consciousness, with British culture and national heritage, with the "white man's burden," and with the superior moral elevation attained by English-speaking peoples. To imagine Sycorax as "blue-eyed" in any positive sense of the term was to violate deeply engrained cultural assumptions.

Some nineteenth-century editors searched for ways of associating "blue" with malevolence: Sycorax's eyes might be a blue like that "cold, startling blue which suggests malignity so strongly," or like the "pale-blue, fish-like, malignant eye, which is often seen in hag-like women."[14] As Charles and

Figure 1.1 Sir John Gilbert's Caliban
Reproduced by permission of the Harry Ransom Humanities Research Center,
University of Texas, Austin

Mary Cowden Clarke explained in their popular edition designed to elevate Shakespeare for families and purge his texts of phrases "coarse and unfit for modern utterance," the "epithet [blue-eyed], as applied by Shakespeare; is far from being commendatory, as at present. He uses it here to describe the dull, bleared, neutral colour seen in the eyes of old crones."[15] Charles Cowden Clarke was a noted lecturer on literary subjects; he had been intimate with several of the Romantics and had tutored John Keats. He, as much as any other single person, helped to popularize the strict separation in late nineteenth-century editions of *The Tempest* between the heavenly blue eyes of the English cultural ideal and the malignant eyes of the she-demon Sycorax.

The main piece of cultural business performed by annotations of "This blue-eyed hag" in nineteenth-century editions was the policing of boundaries between the acceptably civilized and the loathsomely, dangerously alien. But the range of suggested interpretations during that period was free and wide-ranging by comparison with that of twentieth-century editions, which have frozen earlier editorial speculation into dogma. The only annotated edition since the Pelican to depart from reigning orthodoxy

Figure 1.2 Sir John Gilbert's Sycorax
Reproduced by permission of the Harry Ransom Humanities Research Center,
University of Texas, Austin

on the subject of the "blue-eyed" witch (at least among the editions that I
have encountered) is Stephen Orgel's recent Oxford edition (1987), which
repeats the usual explanations but offers them more as hypothesis than as
self-evident truth.

Having indicated some of the cultural pressures underlying the typical
annotation of "blue-eyed hag," however, we have by no means completed
our task. Editors have not only registered discomfort with the idea of a
witch who is blue eyed, they have also done exhaustive historical research
into the meaning of "blue-eyed" in the Renaissance to support their annotation of the line. They have, in fact, uncovered considerable evidence that
the phrase in English Renaissance culture could be used in senses very
different from our own. If twentieth-century editions may be said to be
impoverished in terms of their interpretation of the line, they are often
copious in providing historical evidence to support the reigning dogma.
And indeed, if they are correct in concluding, as they have, that "blue-
eyed" could not possibly refer simply to eye color in Shakespeare's culture,
then perhaps their intervention is helpful rather than obfuscating.

We in the twentieth century have inherited the nineteenth century's
marked cultural emphasis on blue eyes, particularly insofar as they are
found in young women and accompanied by the requisite blond hair and
an aura of combined innocence and sexual availability, as in Marilyn
Monroe, blond-haired Barbie dolls, and so on. If Shakespeare's "blew-ey'd"
did not resonate for his culture in the ways that "blue-eyed" tends to

10

resonate in ours, then perhaps the editorial intervention is justified. We will note, however, that twentieth-century explications of the line, like their forebears from the previous century, serve to smooth out an apparent incongruity. The witch cannot have blue eyes, because the cultural image of blue eyes is overwhelmingly positive and Sycorax has to be understood as negative.

Part of the purpose of a good edition has traditionally been to bridge historical distance – to make a text and its cultural milieu accessible to people with different practices and assumptions. But that process always involves the risk of over-normalization, of making the past over to accommodate one's own, and one's readers', sense of what constitutes acceptable meaning. Particularly in our own poststructural critical climate, an edition allowing for cultural dissonance and distance might well be more desirable than one that consistently irons out interpretive difficulties. At what point does editorial assistance become unwanted intrusion? We plunge to the heart of the matter when we investigate the range of signification carried by blue eyes in the Renaissance. No doubt many of the unfortunates hanged as witches in early seventeenth-century England had eyes of a color that we would now describe as blue, but the naming of eye colors, then as now, was as much cultural construction as perception. What perceptions matched the phrase "blue-eyed" in England of the early modern era?

According to Wright and most subsequent editors, "blue-eyed" refers not to the iris of the eye, but to the area around the eye. And there are indeed many instances of such usage in the Renaissance. Kittredge cites Shakespeare's *Lucrece* (1587): "And round about her tear-distained eye / Blue circles stream'd" and Davenant's *The Cruel Brother*: "His eyes . . . Encircled with the weakly colour blue" (Kittredge p. 96; see n. 6 below). But much more commonly cited is the example from *The Duchess of Malfi*, already quoted above from Wright's edition, which brings in the association with pregnancy: "The fins of her eyelids look most teeming blue." Although each of these examples refers explicitly to the area around the eye while the Shakespearean passage does not, there are other contemporary instances in which the phrase "blue eyes" seems clearly to mean what we would call "black and blue eyes" or "eyes with dark circles around them." Kittredge cites Dekker's *Honest Whore*, Part II, "Out, you blue-eyed Rogue" and, following Wright, Davenant's *The Playhouse to be Let*: "Her eyes look blue; pray heav'n she be not breeding!" (pp. 96–97). The examples do not all support the same precise reading of the origin of Sycorax's "blue-eyed" demeanor: some imply pregnancy, while others suggest grief or physical bruising. But all of them together demonstrate fairly conclusively that in late sixteenth- and early seventeenth-century England, "blue-eyed" did not necessarily mean what we mean by blue eyed.

The case against the standard emendation is not yet lost, however. To pursue it further, we need to probe into the cultural construction of eye color. For if editors are to be allowed to annotate the line with the interpretive assurance conveyed by most twentieth-century editions, they need to demonstrate not only that "blue-eyed" *could* mean "blue circled" as a result of pregnancy or some other debility; they should be willing to demonstrate an overwhelming likelihood that it meant "blue circled" as opposed to "blue." As we have noted, by no means did all nineteenth-century editors agree about the eyes of Sycorax – some of them opted for eyes of a baleful or malignant blue. Horace Howard Furness queried in his *New Variorum Edition* of *The Tempest* (1892):

> Is it not possible to accept the blueness as referring not only to the dark eyelids and circles round the eyes, but also to the pupil itself, where the *arcus senilis*, as the ophthalmologists call it, is wont to give the baleful expression which we associate with witches?

Following an earlier hint by Edmund Malone, Furness made the interesting suggestion that some of the positive connotations associated with blue eyes in recent Anglo-American culture were in Shakespeare attached to gray eyes:

> Instances are as plenty as blackberries where what we now call blue eyes were by Shakespeare called grey eyes. There are two in *Rom. & Jul.*, where the Friar speaks of "The grey-ey'd morn," and Mercutio of "Thisbe, a grey eye or so." Since, then, our "blue eyes" and Shakespeare's "blue eyes" are not the same, I think we are at liberty to include, in the present phrase, whatsoever tends to add abhorrence to the repulsive witch.[16]

If we combine all of these suggestions about historical differences in meaning, a Shakespearean taxonomy of eye-color would run something like this: his blue eyes = our dark circled eyes, his gray eyes = our blue eyes. And in fact, in pre-Shakespearean literature the eyes of the desired woman are often gray rather than blue. In Chaucer, for example, the desirable woman typically has "eyen greye as glas" or at least "greye." John Skelton gives her "eyen grey and steep."[17] "The phrase "grey as glasse" occurs in *Two Gentlemen of Verona* 4.4.196 (F TLN 2010), Olivia has grey eyes in *Twelfth Night* 1.5.256 (F TLN 538), and there are similar references in *Romeo and Juliet* 2.4.45 and 3.5.19. The *OED* confirms that "blue eye" gradually migrated in signification from what we would term a "black eye" in the sense of black-and-blue to "blue eye" in our sense of blue, but the precise chronology of the change is left unclear. Unlike most eye colors, "blue eye" receives its own entry in the *OED*. The first cited usage of "blue eyes" in the nineteenth- and twentieth-century sense appears to be to 1735 (Alexander Pope's *Moral Essay* 2.284.[18] The *OED* glosses our specific crux – Shakespeare's description of Sycorax – to mean black or blue around the eyes rather than blue-eyed in the more recent sense of the term.

At this point, as Smedley Force would be happy to inform us, our potential case against the standard annotation of "blue-eyed hag" appears lost. If the *OED* and standard editions confirm each other, we are confronted with a powerful array of authority. We need to remind ourselves, however, that the *OED*, however invaluable, is not without its biases: it is a product of the same late nineteenth-century codifying impulse that has given us our standard editions of Shakespeare and many other writers. Some of the same minds who prepared the Shakespearean editions also participated in the monumental cultural enterprise of the *OED*, and a similar cultural agenda is to be expected in both. Indeed, a major purpose of the *OED* entry on "blue eyes" may have been to help solidify the post-Wrightian interpretation of the Shakespearean line, rather than vice versa. We need to go beyond the *OED* itself if we are to determine whether Sycorax's eyes could have been blue.

In English Renaissance literature, there are hordes of golden-tressed women – particularly in blazons *à la* Petrarch of an idealized beloved – but there are precious few blue eyes. As we have already seen, the traditional eye color for the beautiful woman in earlier literature appears to have been gray. This does not necessarily mean, of course, that people in early modern England favored gray eyes over blue eyes; they may simply have perceived the blue-gray that we call blue as gray. In literature of the late sixteenth and seventeenth centuries, however, black eyes come strongly into favor: Philoclea in the *Old Arcadia* is black-eyed, and so, famously, is Sidney's Stella in *Astrophil and Stella*. Shakespeare's dark lady is also described in Sonnet 127 as having eyes of "raven black," and there are numerous other examples from the period.[19] Part of this preference may relate to the eye color of actual women celebrated in the verse, as in the case of Shakespeare's dark lady and Sidney's Stella: other poets also celebrated Penelope Devereux Rich's "black sparkling eyes."[20]

On stage or in verse celebrating a generic mistress, such specificity might have been a drawback, limiting the range of actors who could play a given part, or the range of women who could be wooed with the aid of a given poem. English Petrarchan poetry is strongly fixated on the beautiful woman's eyes, but more for their power than for their color. Most frequently, the woman's eyes are likened to stars, suns, or some other emitter of celestial light, without their color being specified. Often they are crystal, which may or may not connote a color like our blue: it tends to be associated in verse of the period with the heavens and with "crystal streams" (both of which we might be more inclined to think of as blue) but sometimes it seems to suggest a translucent paleness. Often the eyes are diamonds, or other precious stones. Following Petrarch, whose Laura was clearly what we would call blond-haired and blue-eyed, English poets sometimes described their mistress's eyes as "sapphire," as in Spenser's *Amoretti* and the famous blazon from the *Epithalamion*: "Her goodly eyes lyke Saphyres shining bright."[21]

In Spenser, as in the case of Sidney's Stella, we may be dealing with the perceived eye color of an actual woman, except that Spenser's beloved, unlike Sidney's, happens to conform to the Petrarchan ideal. But only rarely in the English Renaissance verse that has survived are the beautiful woman's "sapphire" eyes explicitly associated with the word "blue." One popular and widely anthologized exception is Sidney's *contreblason* of Mopsa the Shepherdess from the *Arcadia*; it mocks the Petrarchan ideal by interchanging the conventionalized colors of Mopsa's physical attributes. She is as fair as Saturn and as chaste as Venus, "Her forhead jacinth like, her cheekes of opall hue, / Her twinkling eies bedeckt with pearle, her lips of Saphir blew:"[22] The pearls that in the usual Petrarchan blazon would represent teeth here suggest a dropping rheum about the eyes; the sapphire blue that should shine from the eyes is instead the color of her lips. The joke depends on a conventionalized expectation that eyes will be blue and teeth pearly white, rather than vice versa. Obviously, at least some members of a cultural elite in the sixteenth century were able to imagine eyes that were "blue" in our sense rather than in the commoner Renaissance meaning.

The evidence I have collected suggests that the Shakespearean taxonomy of eye color accepted by earlier editors may be too simple. In Renaissance culture, "blue eyes" sometimes suggested black-and-blue eyes, or eyes rimmed with black as a result of pregnancy or fatigue, but, *pace* the *OED*, "blue eyes" sometimes meant what we mean by blue eyes today. The phrase "blue eye" seems to have carried then some of the ambiguity that "black eye" carries in our own culture, where the phrase can be used for an eye with a dark brown or black iris, or for an eye that is black and blue. We can speculate that "blue eyes" in the twentieth-century sense may have been a recent import in early modern England, associated with foreign models and with elite culture rather than with the native English tradition of gray-eyed beauty. Within Shakespeare's own corpus, the color blue is at least once associated with the heavens, but the reference appears in one of his last plays: in a famous textual crux, *Cymbeline* describes Imogen's closed eyes and/or eyelids as "White and Azure lac'd / With Blew of Heauens owne tinct" (F TLN 929–30). A little after Shakespeare, blue eyes become more common in poetry, but may still have been regarded as exotic. Charles Cotton wrote a blazon of his sister's beauty in which he praised her black eyes above "English grey, or French blue eyes," seeming to suggest an equivalence between the two colors: what the French (and Italians?) conventionally termed blue or sapphire eyes the English traditionally called gray.[23]

And indeed, if we move outside the realm of lyric poetry, we find a similar equivalence. In the standard modern translations of Homer, Athena's most customary epithet is "gray-eyed." In Chapman's Homer, however, composed about the same time as Shakespeare's *Tempest*, Athena is regularly described as either "blue-eyed" or "gray-eyed." In translating Athena's Homeric epithet γλαυκῶπις, Chapman uses "blue" and "gray" indifferently: there is no clear contextual reason for the choice of one color over the other; Athena in her irenic, as opposed to her martial, demeanor, is repeatedly called "blue eyed," and her eyes are also associated with things we think of as blue, such as the sky. By the time Dryden translated Homer, Virgil, and Ovid toward the end of the century, Athena was regularly described as "blue-eyed" in our sense of the term.[24] We can safely assume that for neither Chapman nor Dryden did calling the virgin goddess "blue-eyed" connote that she had bleary eyes "ringed in blue, as in pregnancy."

We have turned up a number of alternative possibilities for reading Shakespeare's description of Sycorax. Her eyes may have been "blue" in the popular sense of rimmed with blue or black, but there is at least the possibility that Prospero's brief and fragmentary description of the witch can be read in terms of the Petrarchanists' mock blazon: at the time that she was exiled to the island, she had the blue eyes of a Petrarchan heroine but was (monstrously) pregnant. Can we imagine that at the time of her exile, as opposed to the time of her death, she may have been physically attractive rather than repulsive, that she may have radiated an aura of eroticism? Interestingly enough, eighteenth and nineteenth-century adaptations of the play regularly retain the description of Sycorax as "blue-eyed," even though by those periods the phrase had lost the ambiguity of its earlier meaning. In Restoration adaptations of *The Tempest*, one of which survived on stage until the early nineteenth century, Sycorax is regularly brought to life as a character on stage – Caliban's sister, daughter of his blue-eyed mother. The Restoration stage Sycorax is comically loathsome but sexually available – perhaps like her mother?[25] The witch's sexuality seems to have been a more acceptable subject for Restoration and eighteenth-century audiences than for their Victorian descendants. At least one adaptation makes Sycorax the subject of a mock blazon like Sidney's on Mopsa.[26] In such an eroticized conceptualization of the witch, "blue-eyed" might well mean "blue-eyed."

Or, alternatively, the "blue-eyed" Sycorax could be associated through her exotic eye color with the blue-eyed Athena as popularized by Chapman, much in the way that the play appropriates for Prospero's own magic spells some of the incantatory language of the Ovidian witch Medea. As Orgel's edition has recently emphasized, Prospero's magic has not always been envisioned as benign before our own century: on the eighteenth-century stage, in particular, it carried sinister overtones of black magic, and Prospero's spirits were sometimes referred to as "devils."[27] For both Prospero and Sycorax, the play's surface moral valuation of an enchanter is complicated by resonances that contradict the superficial impression. The eyes of Sycorax, like the charms of Prospero, eerily reverberate with their supposed moral opposites, and the play's many Virgilian echoes facilitate a contextualization of "blue eyes" in terms of classical epic tradition rather than in terms of the native English tradition. To associate Sycorax's mysterious eye color with the uncanny power and attributes of a goddess rather than with the debility of pregnancy is to achieve rather a different perspective on her nature and activities, and on those of her inheritor, Caliban. It is also to adopt a reading of the "hag" that is far from the one promulgated by Prospero.

All of Shakespeare's linkings of "blue" with eyes are difficult cruxes, and we will never know certainly what he "meant." Nor, if we wish to operate within a traditional intentionalist scheme of explanation, can we expect that Shakespeare was utterly consistent in his conceptualization of "blue eyes." But even if we were able (by some miracle) to establish that chimerical entity, the meaning of the passage as the author intended it, we would still be left with the strong likelihood that in Shakespeare's culture, the phrase "blue-eyed" was highly ambiguous and likely to be understood differently by different segments of his audience, depending on their social class, education, and life experience. *The Tempest* is a play that dramatizes a series of encounters between Europeans and denizens of a strange island that appears alien to the Europeans. It was written at a time when similar Europeans were embarked on actual voyages of discovery, and beginning to confront racial and cultural difference in an unprecedentedly radical form through their encounters with natives of the New World. What greater likelihood than that the play itself should record a sense of dissonance, even shock, over the difficulty of using physical characteristics to separate the cultural "self" from the "other"?

How, then, should the "blue-eyed hag" be explicated in our modern editions? Our investigation has been inconclusive in that it has not allowed us to settle on any single eye color or condition as properly glossing the phrase, but it has been highly conclusive about the suspect origins of the standard emendation. If the edition's format allows only very brief indications of meaning, I would suggest that the phrase is best left unglossed, rather than glossed in a way that replicates nineteenth-century cultural assumptions and removes too much of its Renaissance range of signification. In an edition permitting more copious annotation, however, the phrase should be annotated with due respect to the broad perspective of meanings "blue-eyed" could have carried in early modern culture; the highly restrictive interpretation of "with dark circles about the eyes as a result of pregnancy" should be offered to readers only as one possibility among others. In thinking about Shakespeare's "blue-eyed hag," we need to remember that the whole rickety twentieth-century superstructure of historical investigation of "blue eyes" was reared on a base of nineteenth-century assumptions about what was acceptably English as opposed to unacceptably alien and threatening. To unedit the phrase "blue-eyed hag" is to cast off a set of strict cultural delimitations by which the witch has been kept under control in modern editions of *The Tempest*. It is to declare a preference for variability over fixity of meaning. It is to open the play once more to an unsettling, polysemous menace that Prospero and modern editors have worked very hard to contain.

THE NEW PHILOLOGY

The "blue-eyed hag" is by no means an exceptional crux in the history of editorial practice. There are dozens, probably hundreds, of similar Shakespearean passages that cry out for new investigation and annotation, and standard editions of other authors of the period are often similarly outdated. As has frequently been noted of late, we are in the midst of a major paradigm shift in the ways that we conceptualize literary texts and their relation to the author and the surrounding culture. Bearing in mind that all such generalizations are rough and oversimplified, we can identify three important models that have guided late nineteenth and twentieth-century textual criticism of Shakespeare. In the late nineteenth century, the dominant model was evolutionary and progressive. Just as human society progressed over the centuries, so an individual author and his work could be said to develop and improve over time. In late nineteenth-century editions, it was common to view Shakespeare, for example, as maturing as an artist, refining his craftsmanship as he gained experience; it was also common to view him as a reviser of his own and others' work. Thanks in part to Heminge and Condell's disparaging reference in the First Folio to "stolne, and surreptitious copies," there have been some scholars and editors in every generation who have viewed early quartos that differ markedly from the folio versions of the plays as mutilated copies, but that was not the dominant opinion in the century before our own. Early printed versions of the plays that would be labelled piracies or memorially constructed "bad quartos" by a later critical consensus were more usually identified until the early twentieth century as Shakespeare's apprentice efforts, or as the source plays he polished and improved to create his own masterpieces. Other cultural phenomena were similarly interpreted in terms of progress or historical layering. As Martin Bernal has pointed out, the dominant way philologists still conceptualized Greek culture well into the nineteenth century was in terms of its evolution from earlier cultural forms, particularly the Egyptian: rather like the nineteenth-century version of Shakespeare, the Greeks were perfecters of earlier, received artifacts.[28]

As we have already noticed, considerable attention went during the dominance of the "evolutionary" model toward codifying and ordering the chaotic mass of early modern manuscripts and printed books scattered in archives, libraries, and old attics so that this embarrassing disarray could be translated into editions that would make the authors uniformly accessible to a wide readership. Monumental endeavors like the *OED*, the reprints of the *Early English Text Society*, and the *DNB* date from that era. Vast labors of historical scholarship were brought to the task of explicating literary texts and arranging them in a way that reflected the author's developing powers. Editors created an elaborate textual stemmatics that allowed them to chart the genealogy of a given text over time and carefully separate various layers of its development so that they could distinguish the more genuine versions of it from those judged corrupt.

It has long been fashionable to disparage the ponderous efforts of the industrious codifiers of the "evolutionary" era, who so singlemindedly consolidated the works of revered authors into collections of "Works." But we should not be too quick to deride them. As McGann has suggested, their emphasis on historical modes of explanation can serve as a useful antidote for more recent, less historically relativist critical and editorial modes.[29] Whether or not we agree with their conceptualization of the literary work, they at least promulgated a model by which the work can be understood as interacting with larger cultural and historical forces. Our own poststructuralist generation has had the luxury of disassembling much of this scholarship because we have received it ready-made, bound up in imposing tomes with massive footnotes. Confronted with the same disorderly plenitude of materials that beset nineteenth and early twentieth-century historicists, many of us might well develop a similar yen for order. We might turn codifiers ourselves.

Nevertheless, as our investigation of the "blue-eyed hag" has suggested, the evolutionary model enshrines a number of assumptions that we may no longer wish to share. Its sprawling, often tendentious historicism gradually gave way toward the end of the nineteenth and beginning of the twentieth century to a second, cleaner model for conceptualizing texts by which the literary artifact is conceived as integral and monolithic, impermeable to history. The second model can be associated (at least in some respects) with literary modernism, especially modernism after the Great War, with the "New Criticism," and with the "New Bibliography." As the adjective chosen to characterize both of these movements suggests, the disciplines of literary criticism and bibliography self-consciously defined themselves away from an older philological criticism and textual studies, in part by claiming greater reliability and professionalism. Nineteenth-century historical scholarship was largely the province of amateurs and scholar-gentlemen; one of the things that was "new" about the New Criticism and Bibliography was the increased identification of both with academic institutions and with academic, as opposed to lay, standards of verifiability and objectivity.

There are, perhaps, profound reasons for the greater receptivity toward history on the part of nineteenth-century textual scholars. Their subject of study was enabled, in large part, by historical upheaval. As recent historians of the book have noted, the great nineteenth-century philological enterprise was made possible by the French Revolution and other similar disruptions, which caused a flood of early books and manuscripts to pass out of the possession of royal and noble households and into public archives where they became available for research.[30] The colonial enterprise, similarly, enabled a vast expansion of the terrain claimed by West European culture and challenged its adherents to give firmer definition and articulation to that culture. Given the nineteenth-century background of dispersal and gradual democratization of scholarly materials, historical change, however cataclysmic, could be perceived as enabling to scholarship.

In the twentieth century, by contrast, history has often seemed inimical to intellectual work of all kinds. The increasing democratization of culture contributed to a sense of profound alienation among intellectuals of the modernist era: after the Great War in particular, there was a widespread feeling among Europeans that a whole civilization had been swept away. During both World Wars, major archives were threatened by bombing and many artifacts were irretrievably lost. The American treasurer for the Malone Society has made the interesting suggestion that the New Bibliography and its antecedents can be understood in part as a reaction to the experiences of wartime, first in Britain, then in America.[31] Immediately after each major war, there was a burst of bibliographical activity which is only partly explicable in terms of a lifting of wartime restraints on scholarly activity. Toward the end of the first war, Alfred Pollard and Gilbert R. Redgrave set in motion the mammoth project of the *Short Title Catalogue*, which was finally published in 1926. As we shall see in later chapters, during the same postwar years there was a major swell of scholarly activity toward reclassifying early printed texts of Shakespeare's plays.

At the end of the second war, similarly, there was a push toward stock taking and codification. In 1945 the Bibliographical Society published its *Studies in Retrospect*, which surveyed the society's first fifty years and set the agenda for the postwar "New Bibliography" that was to dominate the next several decades. That volume, which was delayed three years by the war, is marked by strong anxiety about the war's effect on surviving artifacts and on the continuing health of bibliography as a discipline. It was followed by W. W. Greg's seminal and highly influential essay "The Rationale of Copy-Text," given as an English Institute paper in 1949, and Fredson Bowers' equally important *Principles of Bibliographical Description* (1949), which established a uniform method for bibliographical description based on the construction of an "ideal copy" of any given edition – the text as it was intended by the printers or publishers rather than as it existed in any single copy of the edition. Whatever their other differences may have been, Greg and Bowers shared a common agenda in that they communicated to the discipline new standards for the construction of literary works that transcended the particularities of individual texts rather than preserving their marks of historical specificity. Twentieth-century scholars moved to catalogue, examine, and process surviving materials from the past – fragments shored up against our ruin – in terms of an agreed-upon set of "scientific" or at least methodized operations by which the essence of the artifacts (if not the physical documents themselves) would be protected against the depredations of history.

That bibliographical agenda is closely allied to a dominant strain in literary modernism that sought to insulate the text even in the process of its inception through the disruption of sequential and developmental patterns within it. And, as has been noted with tiresome frequency, the New Criticism developed parallel strategies within the realm of literary interpretation by conceptualizing the literary text as monolithic, invulnerable, existing in its own luminous, uncanny extra-temporal reality. Under the sway of the New Criticism, many of the concerns of an earlier philological scholarship suddenly found themselves relegated to the dustheap as "fallacies," or to the dark kingdom of Smedley Force and his industrious crew of bibliographers. Despite the considerable differences among these twentieth-century movements, all of them have tended to conceptualize historical process as inimical to the pursuit of truth about the products of human creativity.

As the discipline of literary criticism became increasingly professionalized and defined as a distinct field in its own right, there developed an additional reason for keeping historical concerns at the periphery of literary studies. In the words of Herbert J. C. Grierson, "Literary history has for the historian a quite distinct interest from that which it possesses for the student and lover of literature." The historian takes "positive interest" in connecting "Donne's wit with the general disintegration of mediaeval thought" or in recognizing Machiavelli's influence on Elizabethan drama. But for the "lover of literature none of these facts has any positive interest whatsoever. Donne's wit attracts or repels him equally whatever be its source; Tamburlaine and Iago lose none of their interest for us though we know nothing of Machiavelli." For the lover of literature in Grierson's view, "literary history has an indirect value. He studies history that he may discount it."[32] Literary criticism demanded as a condition of its integrity that historical matters be kept clearly subordinate to its own central concerns.

The two textual paradigms identified thus far are not necessarily mutually exclusive, nor did the "evolutionary" give way to the "monolithic" with the dramatic suddenness of a Foucauldian epistemic shift. Throughout much of twentieth-century criticism, the two have continued along parallel and sometimes intersecting tracks, with some editors, bibliographers, and historically-minded critics continuing to refine upon the older philological model at a time when others declared their allegiance to the "new" atemporal monolithic model that was achieving dominance. Nevertheless, E. K. Chambers' influential speech on Shakespeare to the British Academy in 1924 may be regarded as a clear marker of the change. Given his own exhaustive research into the Elizabethan theater and its cultural contexts, we might have expected Chambers, if anyone, to have conceived of Shakespeare as an historical figure bound by the institutions and mores of his times. But that is not the dominant note of Chambers' address. He, like Grierson, advocated the study of history in order to discount it. Decrying textual scholarship that "disintegrated" Shakespeare, Chambers conceptualized England's premier dramatist as a Gibraltar impervious to time and weather, a single "rock" standing "four-square to the winds of Time" and invulnerable, by implication at least, to foreign incursions of any sort. The operative idea here for our purposes is the clarity with which the different elements of the landscape can be distinguished. Just as the Rock of Gibraltar was sharply set off from the heaving seas around it, so the grand figure of Shakespeare loomed impassively above the shifting historical matrix that surrounded the man and his work. As I have noted elsewhere, Chambers' speech was very much a part of a postwar movement to salvage and support major cultural monuments. Even in the thinking of this giant of archival research, historical method could not be allowed to threaten the basic identity and integrity of the artist.[33]

According to the new "monolithic" paradigm, Shakespeare was no longer commonly understood as progressing in quite the sense he had been earlier, nor could he comfortably be envisioned as a reviser. Instead, his plays were imagined as fully realized from the moment of their inception: early works like *The Comedy of Errors* were as perfect in their own terms as the acknowledged masterpiece, *Macbeth*. In an interesting turnabout that we shall examine in greater detail in ensuing chapters, the early quartos of Shakespeare and Marlowe that deviate markedly from later published versions came to be characterized as "bad" quartos that postdated the "good" authorial texts rather than preceding them. Alfred Pollard had identified six early Shakespearean quartos as "bad" in 1909; by 1919 W. W. Greg had written studies of *The Merry Wives of Windsor, Alcazar,* and *Orlando* arguing that the "corrupt" versions of these texts were memorially reconstructed. After the war, Greg's view gradually became orthodoxy as many other scholars brought their erudition and ingenuity to the task of proving the "bad" quartos to be late, corrupt copies rather than Shakespeare's original versions.[34]

As Joseph Loewenstein has recently shown, there was a strong correlation between bibliographers' increasing valuation of the author's "original" as the most fully realized version of a text and a rise in the bookmarket prices for first editions.[35] Under the impact of what has been termed the modernist "scene of writing," by which literary creation was conceptualized as a solitary, intensely individual act achieved through the artist's self-isolation from the culture at large,[36] editors and critics during the 1920s and 1930s developed strong resistance to the idea that Shakespeare might willingly have revised, especially to meet the exigencies of that lowly institution, the Elizabethan playhouse. Had not the editors of the First Folio assured us that Shakespeare never blotted a line? Other Renaissance authors – even John Milton, who was one of the first English authors to publicly conceptualize his own life as an artist in developmental terms – were subjected to a similar reformulation that deemphasized social and historical pressures upon the author's intent and achievement. In Milton's case, it has been the influence of the printing-house that we have most neglected (or even demonized): the idea that an artist of his sublimity would interest himself in the practical details of publishing and printing or willingly suffer his work to be reshaped by those processes is an idea that has been anathema to most twentieth-century Miltonists.

Much of our discussion in ensuing chapters will give a local habitation and a name to these rather sweeping statements about shifting conceptual-izations of the text: as I hope readers will agree, specific cases tend to be more interesting and more credible than a belaboring of generalities. Before moving on to particulars, however, we will note, yet once more, an interesting parallel between the development of the monolithic paradigm in English studies as I will be discussing it further here and the refiguration of the model of Ancient Greece as envisioned by Classical scholars. Bernal has demonstrated how ancient Greece was remodelled in nineteenth- and early twentieth-century philology from a borrower culture, one that perfected the thought and artifacts of earlier non-Hellenic civilizations, to an originator culture that owed little to the pre-Hellenic past and that created its own forms full-blown. In a close parallel to the strange turnabout that demoted the "bad" Shakespearean quartos, Bernal shows how architectural, philosophical, and linguistic forms that earlier philo-logists might have interpreted as survivals of pre-Hellenic culture were systematically reconceptualized as originating with the Greeks only to be borrowed and corrupted by other lesser civilizations. Although scholars have successfully contested many of Bernal's specific arguments, they have not attacked his broad delineation of the shift from what I have been calling an "evolutionary" to a "monolithic" paradigm for interpretation.[37] The noblest cultural monuments had to be *sui generis* and self-generated.

As the heading to the present section suggests, however, there has recently been yet another paradigm shift in the ways editors and literary critics imagine the texts they work with. Building upon McGann, I am terming this movement a "new philology" because it represents a return to the some of the historical concerns of nineteenth-century philologists, although, as I have tried to suggest through our excursus into the color of Sycorax's eyes, the new philology may arrive at very different conclusions than the old. The dominant textual paradigm for the new philology can be characterized as a network, even though there is no convenient adjectival form of the word to parallel "evolutionary" and "monolithic."[38] The idea of the text as network or field of force is common in post-structuralist theory – we may think immediately of Ronald Barthes's famous essay "From Work to Text" and its irreverent rejection of an older philological conceptualization of the literary "Work," along with all of the ponderous nineteenth-century interpretative baggage traditionally carried by the term, for a fresh conceptualization of the "Text" as free of the "Work's" inhibiting ancestry, turgid solidity, and tyrannical domination by the presence of its author. The idea of the text as network was, of course, commonplace within modernism itself: Hugh Kenner has explicated the literary movement in terms of the development around the turn of the century of new urban transportation and communication grids that violated time-honored demarcations of class and neighborhood.[39] What sets the "new philology" apart from New Critical and poststructural conceptualizations of the text is its insistence upon a wider historical and cultural matrix as constitutive, an integral part of its network.

In "From Work to Text," Barthes displayed considerable common ground with an earlier modernist and New Critical rejection of history, and with the New Bibliography's tendency to define the literary text in ways that move it out of the vulnerable arena of historical change. By contrast, in the new textual studies – the "new philology" – and in historically oriented modes of poststructuralist criticism, the text loses its privileged separateness and is conceptualized as part of a much wider vectoring of forces and objects. This reconceptualization is understandably difficult for scholars trained in the earlier modes to accept. It requires an imaginative leap rather like the giving up of the isolate majesty of the traditional image of Gibraltar, which can no longer be perceived as distinct from the shifting seas around it. As one of my Iberian students has kindly pointed out, Gibraltar has beaches on its far side where sea and sand intermingle: for us, it is not quite the majestic and clear-cut monolith that the "rock" stand-ing "four-square" was for Chambers. Similarly, in the new textual work on Shakespeare, Milton, and other demigods in the pantheon of English authorship, we are less inclined to keep the individual artist clearly separate from his contemporaries and their institutions.

In the new work, as befits the paradigm of the network, earlier and later versions of a given work are accorded fairly equal status. They are not typically arranged in a hierarchy to reflect the author's developing powers; nor are the "bad" texts automatically dismissed as corrupt copies of the "good" ones. Instead, the differences among them are investigated inter-textually and rhetorically with a keen eye on other elements in the network that may have impinged upon them. Where different versions of a given work differ markedly, the areas of instability tend to be interpreted in terms of multiple factors rather than single ones: deviant versions of a given text are not the mere by-product of institutional "corruptions" impinging upon some texts but not others; nor are they only a record of the author's developing powers, although writers may indeed change over time. Rather, areas of instability are interpreted in terms of alterations in the text's complex network of contemporaneous events, institutions, and potential audiences – not because more traditional explanations are always entirely mistaken, but because they have been overemphasized to the neglect of other factors.

This characterization of the emerging paradigm is, of course, partly prescriptive. My view of the changes sweeping the field of textual studies is strongly influenced by my own sense of the most fruitful directions for the new work to take, and other scholars who consider themselves part of the new textual studies may strenuously object to my characterization of their labors. Indeed, the new revisionary work on Shakespeare's "bad" quartos tends to remain strongly author-centered; scholars and editors quite cheerfully dismantle Greg's theory of "memorial reconstruction" for the "bad" quartos, but tend to resist theories of textual variability that subordinate the author to other sources of alteration. Taylor and Warren's *The Division of the Kingdoms* in particular has been criticized by post-structuralist critics for its adherence to traditional interpretive standards that demand clarity and consistency of literary texts.[40] As I shall contend in later chapters, however, perceiving a text previously regarded as "corrupt" as fulfilling the desiderata of unity, clarity, and complexity is a necessary stage in its rehabilitation: we need to demonstrate the insufficiency of the "monolithic" paradigm in its own terms before we can move beyond it. As in the previous paradigm shift, in the "new philology" there continues to be considerable interlayering of methodologies, with strongly author-based studies of textual difference being produced alongside more radically destabilizing studies of textual variability. We have only to browse through two or three issues of the new annual *TEXT* along with recent issues of *Studies in Bibliography* and the *Library* to recognize the diversity of the discipline as it is presently being reconceptualized.

Nevertheless, we can identify a marked tendency in the field at present from "Text" in the Barthean sense of a field or network engaged by the reader in the solitary play of reading and interpretation, back to "Work" in Barthes's sense of a predefined piece of writing carrying with it a long history of material and scholarly interventions. The Barthean contempt for the fixity of the Work is not thereby cancelled out; rather, history and culture are reimaged in poststructural terms so that what Barthes would call the "Work" can carry some of the same liberating instability he associates with the "Text." Scholars as methodologically disparate as McGann, Edward Said, Darnton, and Chartier have all called for reinvestigation of what McGann would term the "Work" – the literary artifact as reinvested with the enriching welter of historical circumstances that helped to determine its shape at its inception, and with the shifting material forms in which it was made available to early and later readers.

This emphasis on "The Sociology of Texts" (to use McKenzie's phrase) does not mean that the author and authorial intentionality are entirely bypassed, only that they lose their dominating centrality. In Barthes's witty formulation, the author can still be invited as a guest into his or her own creation.[41] In the new textual work, other traditional areas of scholarly inquiry are also opened up to new investigation, but without the same emphasis on closure and codification. Those may come later on: it would be foolhardy to predict the future direction of the discipline, and as I have already indicated, we will need to go on generating new scholarly and popular editions if only to create new standardized bases for our continuing interchange of ideas. But for the present what is required is closer attention to micro-investigation of literary texts in their local and historically contingent forms. We need to inquire into "blue-eyed," "black-eyed," "gray-eyed," and any other particulars with which we may find ourselves dissatisfied in received editions. The "new philology" is not so neat and streamlined as its forerunner the New Criticism; it has much of the disorderly plenitude of the "old" philology, but without the same drive toward cultural and textual stabilization. Such stability as it finds exists not at the level of the "Work" in McGann's historically cumulative sense of the term, but at the level of the individual, material artifact.

THE MATERIALITY OF THE TEXT

Something quite interesting is happening in graduate programs at present – at the University of Texas and Emory, at Toronto, at Oxford and Cambridge, at the University of California (to mention only the institutions for which I have specific information), and no doubt many other places as well. Graduate students in literature are beginning to display what to an older generation of scholars is an almost heretical interest in physical objects from the past – early printed editions of the "classics," printed histories, chapbooks and popular literature of all kinds, manuscripts, manuscript books, and other artifacts. Unlike most graduate students of my own generation, for whom the discipline of editing and bibliography was still sharply demarcated from the discipline of criticism, these students find the problems of editing and classifying texts as captivating as other forms of interpretation. Bibliographical work with primary materials is no longer "dry as dust" but has become infused with a new intensity. Much of the energy of the "new philology" has developed out of the avid interest of an emerging generation of students.

The new (or renewed) fascination with material texts of the early modern era may have developed in part out of a greater availability of copies: now that most of the *Short Title* and *Wing* catalogues are widely available on microfilm, an increasing number of students can encounter a broad spectrum of Renaissance books in a form that whets their appetites to consult sixteenth and seventeenth-century editions firsthand. By using the printers' index to the new *STC*, they can easily delve into the business of printing as part of their study of printed texts. Then too, the new fascination with material texts may represent a response to the increasing computerization of literary studies: through their strong interest in working with books and manuscripts from the past, students may be seeking to retain contact with a time when written materials had clearer, less fluid boundaries than they do at present, given that literary texts are becoming increasingly available in hypertext or other computerized forms. New global computer networks like SHAKSPER allow scholars to communicate information almost instantly across vast distances; Shakespeare, Milton, and other authors are emerging in new electronic editions that can be used alongside the editions in book form; there is at least one computer, Apple's NeXT, that comes with the plays of Shakespeare already collected on its hard drive, and editions are becoming widely available as part of software packages, albeit usually in versions that are less textually innovative than one might wish. The computerized technology for literary studies is expanding so rapidly that this paragraph will be woefully out of date long before it reaches print.[42]

In Austin, Texas, a computer scientist who specializes in the development of new software recently built himself a medieval-style cob house, citing a need to create something that would, unlike his software, retain its value for more than a year or two. The computerization of literary scholarship has meant that the field moves much faster than it did before: ink and paper are relatively stable media by comparison with the computer screen. Books and manuscripts from the past can be damaged or destroyed, but they, like the medieval house, have relative permanence in a world of typographic instability and lightning change.

I suspect, however, that these explanations carry more cogency for people of my generation who are ambivalent about computerization than for our students, who have grown up with the computer and do not display much regret over its supplanting of books and notepads. The core of the matter for most of today's students expressing a strong interest in working with early printed and manuscript materials is not the recuperation of past stability but enablement in the present. As both computer technology and poststructuralist theory have made inroads into the field of literary studies, most of us have come to think of texts as more malleable, less fixed, than we did before. If texts are generated by computer, the idea of the "original" loses much of its charisma: how can we reliably differentiate "originals" from copies? Printing out our own computer-generated work, we have ourselves become printers and designers on a small scale, and may therefore take more interest in past modes of book production and the ways in which format can influence interpretation. The "new philology" investigates textual instabilities at a grassroots, material level.

For an older generation of scholars and informed lay readers, the idea of textual instability was profoundly disquieting: one of the functions of the standard edition was to calm that unease and convince readers that they were being offered a text that could be counted on. By contrast, students now tend to be awed and charmed by the discovery of textual difference – the realization that early manuscripts and printed editions of a given author may offer them an array of different texts, rather than a single textual "authority." Students in the 1990s – advanced graduate students but often undergraduates as well – are inclined to distrust editions that legislate a single set of meanings when their own sense of textual reality is multiple and protean. For them, instability does not necessarily provoke anxiety, but may be associated *à la* Barthes with feelings of play and release, or even with comfortable familiarity. These students are eager to work with primary materials as a way of claiming and remolding the materials of scholarship for themselves instead of accepting received wisdom, particularly when that wisdom fails to confirm their own sense of the malleability of all discursive forms. Such revisionism often looks sacrilegious to scholars of my generation and earlier but there is nothing new about the generational rivalries involved: the New Criticism in which we were trained appeared equally irresponsible to an older generation of philologists; the New Bibliography on which we depended for our scholarly editions struck many of them as soulless and technocratic.

Then too, the use of primary materials does not carry quite the same political stigma for students now that it did a generation ago. When I was in graduate school in New York City during the politically active late 1960s, many of us considered the investment of large sums of money on old books and documents by universities and other institutions to be a politically retrograde activity: such funds, we felt, would be better spent on soup kitchens for the poor. Now that the great age of collecting by American institutions has passed its peak and most universities at least appear to be more socially conscious than earlier, to posit research libraries and soup kitchens as mutually exclusive alternatives in competition for institutional support is to create a false dilemma. The use of rare books and manuscripts does not necessarily imply assent to the prevailing institutional mentality at the time such materials were acquired. Indeed, as I have tried to suggest through the example of the "blue-eyed hag" (even though that example was not particularly enlightening about early printed versions), going back to primary materials may well accomplish the opposite – help to reverse some of the past century's increasing rigidification in the editing and projected reception of canonical texts. Those scholars who consider themselves Cultural Materialists, Materialist Feminists, or New Historicists should be particularly interested in revisionist archival work, unless they are willing to rely on the textual monuments of historical epochs whose assumptions they seem eager to repudiate on other grounds. Indeed, many of those who are interested in the "new philology" willingly espouse one or more of the above-mentioned labels, so long as the labels are not applied too restrictively. Investigation of the material forms taken by literary texts is an increasingly vital part of materialist scholarship in general; it is at the very heart of the new international project for the history of the book.

Of course, such primary work has to be undertaken with wary attention, particularly in American libraries, where made-up, "sophisticated" copies of old books are as much the rule as the exception. Already by 1800, the Shakespearean editor George Steevens was complaining about the prevalence of First Folio copies eked out with material from later folios. Thomas Dibdin noted a few years later that half the First Folios he saw were sophistications rather than intact originals, and many such copies have made their way into research collections like the Folger Shakespeare Library and the Harry Ransom Humanities Research Center of the University of Texas.[43] It goes without saying that spurious "originals" of other Renaissance authors have been similarly patched together. For research dependent on the integrity of an early printed text, such copies are useless, although they may possess considerable interest on other grounds. We need, in working with early materials, to be as attentive to the labors of the bibliographers as to the work of previous editors, even though we may not accept all of their conclusions: in many instances we may need to turn bibliographer ourselves. For the "new philology," the shape and format of a given book are finally not separable from its contents; literary works are not universal in any useful sense of the term, but local and locally specific, existing in an array of concrete forms that need to be studied as an important part of their meaning.

The "new philology" as I have been defining it is singlemindedly materialist in its way of understanding literature. Indeed, for many in the emerging discipline, literary works only exist insofar as they can be read and consumed. To the extent that there is a rift between the New Bibliography and the "new philology" – and that rift seems to be diminishing, since as the new movement gathers impetus the older scholarship is reconceptualizing itself to meet some of the objections of the new – the rift exists not so much over specific (and invaluable) techniques for the analysis of individual artifacts as over the degree to which materiality is to be accepted as part of the definition of a text or work. The New Bibliography as represented in the work of scholars like Alfred Pollard, W. W. Greg, and Fredson Bowers achieved particular cogency as a method in the field of Renaissance studies because of its remobilization of idealist Renaissance categories of analysis. During the early Renaissance in particular, many scholars and writers thought of literary works in strongly

Platonic or neo-Platonic terms, and resisted the idea that their conceptualization of a work could or should be limited to any single physical embodiment. Writers of the period, particularly those operating within the new "authorial" mode of self-conceptualization as that mode has been defined by Michel Foucault, frequently displayed contempt for the playhouse and printinghouse – indeed for any institution that threatened to contaminate their artistry with the taint of commercialism. We may think of Spenser's monster Error spewing forth printed papers disgusting in their inchoate profusion, or of the regular protests by printed authors of the Elizabethan and early Jacobean era to the effect that they had fought in vain against entrusting the noble purity of their ideas to the indignity of print, printinghouse, and bookstall.

Some of this abhorrence is, of course, mere posturing, and some of it is based on anxiety about the commodification of ideas. But much of it comes out of Christian and neo-Platonic contempt for the physical and material as opposed to the spiritual. The English *locus classicus* for such opinion is Sidney's *Apologie for Poesie*, with its insistence that poetry can deliver a golden world, go beyond the confinements of the author's particular circumstances by communicating not only what exists in our mundane reality, but a realm of "Ideas" beyond it. According to such a formulation, the material is imprisoning, and the ideal, liberating: the ink and paper with which manuscripts and printed books are produced, the physical form in which they are promulgated to readers – these are important only as means to the end of raising readers' attention to a perfection beyond their materiality. And the historical particulars underlying a given work of literature were equally to be transcended. As Ben Jonson described the neo-Platonic world of the Jacobean masques, "though their voice be taught to sound to present occasions, their sense or doth or should always lay hold on more removed mysteries" – the immaterial soul of his creations mattered much more than the material particularities out of which they arose.[44]

Proponents of the New Bibliography have resisted the label "Platonic," but they too have tended to locate the "reality" of a given literary creation outside its extant material embodiments. For W. W. Greg in "The Rationale of Copy-Text," one of the most influential documents within the New Bibliography after the 1940s, the obligation to base a literary edition entirely upon one single physical embodiment of a given work as opposed to other extant versions was unacceptable "tyranny"; his "Rationale," by which the editor could create a composite text in matters of substance while adhering to a base text for "accidentals," was designed to confer some of Sidney's freedom upon the editor, who could then repair the "blushing sins" of the author and produce something approximating an ideal text. While refining upon Greg, subsequent proponents of the New Bibliography have continued to locate the ultimate reality of the literary work outside its material embodiment, usually in the mind of the author. One of Bowers' final essays on Shakespeare and the printinghouse refers repeatedly to the "veil" of print: for Bowers, despite all his erudition about printinghouse practices, it was the editor's business to lift that veil, go beyond particular embodiments of the text to an "ideal" version approximating Shakespeare's intent – we learn about printinghouse practices only to transcend them.[45]

Other recent responses to the "new philology," while conceding ground in some ways, use a similar language of dichotomy between the material form of an individual text and the underlying immaterial "Work" beyond it. Manuscripts and printed books are "simply objects of utility," "vessels" for conveyance of their contents. Pen, letterforms, and paper are "part of the vessel, not its content," which is "abstract." The literary work as it exists in the mind or intent of the author has a "real historical existence" even though that existence is "unrecoverable."[46] Like Renaissance Platonists, New Bibliographers continue to locate the real work outside the realm of the physically visible and palpable, even though many of them are expertly trained in dealing with Renaissance books and manuscripts. Repudiating McGann and others who have insisted on the historical and material nature of the literary "Work," they neatly reverse the degree of historical imbeddedness of the two terms: for G. Thomas Tanselle the "Work" is the ineluctable totality of a literary creation existing outside its individual material embodiments or "Texts" (Tanselle pp. 16–17; see n. 46 below), and located most fully in the author's mind and intentions. We will recognize a strong kinship between this formulation and Grierson's during the early part of the century – for Grierson too, the text's material embodiments were so many veils of "outworn fashions and conventions" that had to be discounted by lovers of literature before a given work could be fully relished in its essential nature (Grierson, 2, p. vi; see n. 32 below).

We all like to think of our own mental activity as possessing some kind of reality. Dante Alighieri described his writing process at the beginning of the *Vita Nuova* as a mere copying down of what was inscribed in the book of his memory. F. Scott Fitzgerald called his writing the noting down of day dreams.[47] But the same F. Scott Fitzgerald did not hesitate to alter his novels in accordance with changing personal and professional circumstances, as the New Bibliography has amply documented. And Dante's "Book of Memory" was a common collective construction of the medieval era.[48] Whether or not writers conceptualize their work as subject to pressures from a world outside their own mental activity, the work has to enter into that world in order to survive, and there is much to be gained by viewing the "worldliness" of the text (to borrow Said's term) as part of its meaning rather than as a series of detractions from, or corruptions of it. For the "new philology," the New Bibliography's insistence on ideal text and ideal copy has become as tyrannical a yoke as precise adherence to copytext was for Greg.

Tanselle is right to insist that human beings are capable of conceptualizing any given "Work" of literature in the absence of actual texts. What he is trying to account for is a classificatory mechanism by which we conceive individual texts as part of a larger "work" that subsumes its various manifestations under a single, definable form. But while Tanselle would resort to a Kantian or Platonic "ideal" of the work to encompass these various manifestations of it, a "new philologist" might point instead to our conceptualization of the work as culturally constructed and altering over time. When we speak of a literary work, what we mean is all the related texts that have been conventionally grouped together under a single title and author's name. Such conventions can (and should) change over time, just as titles and attributions of authorship sometimes change. If we devote our energies to the examination of particular versions rather than to the speedy creation of a composite, it may not be at all clear to us whether a given group of texts is better conceptualized as one work or as several.

The recent controversy over *King Lear* provides a case in point: is the first quarto, with its mad trial scene, its markedly slower pacing, its differing portrayal of Albany, Kent, and Cordelia, to be regarded as the same play as the folio version, or as a different work? We have much to gain by separating variant versions of many such "works" and looking attentively at the patterns of variation between them. As we shall see, in early modern England, printed playtexts were often grouped very differently than they have been in our standard editions. To take but one example to be treated in detail further on, in Jacobean England *The Taming of the Shrew* was apparently regarded, at least for copyright purposes, as the same play as one published much earlier under the title *The Taming of a Shrew*. In modern editions, the two are kept rigidly separate. If we reconceptualize the latter play as a version of the former and grant it at least provisional equality with the more familiar version, then our notion of Shakespeare's "work" may alter dramatically.

Similarly (to take a second example that will not be treated later on), the New Bibliography has insisted on establishing strict boundaries between the 1594 quarto entitled *The First part of the Contention betwixt the two famous Houses of Yorke and Lancaster, with the death of the good Duke Humphrey*, etc., and the 1623 folio version entitled *The second Part of Henry the Sixt, with the death of the Good Duke Hvmfrey*: the former was a memorially reconstructed "corruption" of the latter without any independent authority and certainly no claim to Shakespearean authenticity. Reopening the question of what constitutes the "work," and the relationship between variant texts of the play, enables a fascinating new set of questions to emerge. Even if the contents of the two versions of *Henry VI, Part 2* were identical, in what ways would the marked change in title alter an audience's probable perception of the two plays? A *Contention* between two warring houses, with a title page

31

emphasizing the dynamic of civil war, arouses rather different expectations on the part of a viewer or reader than does a *Henry the Sixt* placed in the folio in dynastic order as part of a series of history plays also named after monarchs and offering a clear locus for authority through their very titles. Given that the contents of the two plays are markedly different, what important correlations might we be able to find between the change in title and an altered political rhetoric within the playtext? What hypotheses beyond the catchall category of "corruption" can we find to account for the differences?[49] And how might the concept of textual corruption in the case of the *Contention* resonate with editorial anxieties about the chaos of civil war as opposed to the orderliness of dynastic succession? We need to investigate the ways in which twentieth-century criticism and bibliography have reengaged Renaissance Platonic theories of the text and work to evade versions of a work that they deem, for one reason or another, unpalatable or to deny outside influences upon it that they prefer not to recognize.

As we have seen, editorial portrayals of the witch Sycorax have controlled and diminished her potential significance for *The Tempest* by presenting her rather as Prospero does – in terms of a vaguely Platonic hierarchy by which the sky and heavenly things are good and earthbound things are evil, and by which inhabitants of the island are judged on the basis of their degree of immersion in the "ignorant fumes" of body as opposed to the higher motions of the spirit. Indeed, Sir John Gilbert's illustration of the gamut from the crouching, earthbound Caliban up to the recoiling Ariel (Figure 1.2) can be fruitfully interpreted as a visualization of the traditional neo-Platonic register which dominated nineteenth and early twentieth-century interpretations of the play. As we shall see, a similar tendency toward valorization on the basis of transcendence of the earthbound has often governed the choice of copytexts in the editing of Renaissance plays and poems.

To "Unedit the Renaissance" is in a very real sense to undo at least temporarily some of that era's own innovative assumptions about the exalted status of literature, its timelessness and transcendence. Renaissance humanists tended to define themselves and their work in terms of a break from the immediate medieval past: they scorned the Middle Ages as a time of monkish darkness when important classical survivals were defaced to meet the need of ecclesiastical and pedagogical institutions rather than being allowed to shine in their "original" purity. The task of the editor was, as it has been in our own recent past, to purge the text of the impurities it has gathered over time and restore it to its original elevation and splendor. The problem with such an image of literature is not that it is necessarily incorrect, but that it is partial, and has in our own times been used to enforce cultural assumptions with which we no longer find ourselves in agreement. To the extent that we investigate textual "impurities" as important constitutive elements of individual texts as they were used and interpreted in specific circumstances, we are declaring a preference for historically specific meanings over more general, transcendent ones. Our goal is not to abolish idealist interpretation, but to resituate it as one interpretive agenda among others, one that should not always receive automatic preference over others. Our emphasis here on literary works in their concrete embodiments is designed not to refute the Renaissance's own intoxication with idealist systems of thought, but to place that current of opinion within a wider network of varying opinion.

In seventeenth-century England, there developed a new emphasis on the materiality of the text – a strong current of opinion that existed in competition with the older Platonic view and gradually supplanted it. As Richard Kroll has documented, under the impact of neo-epicureanism and other materialist modes of philosophy, English writers increasingly engaged with print culture not as a form of shady contamination for their cherished thoughts, but as a form of legitimate embodiment for ideas that would otherwise, for practical purposes, not exist. Rather than professing contempt for the precise form in which their work reached a literary marketplace, John Milton and others became absorbed in the potential of print to shape the consciousness of its readers in precise ways, and in the social negotiability of material signs of all sorts. For materialists like Evelyn, Glanvill, Locke, or Robert Boyle, ideas were not arranged hierarchically and imagined in some cognitive realm beyond materiality; ideas were like coins, circulating as negotiable material forms through a given culture. The neo-epicureans tended to view rhetoric not as mere decoration, but as inextricable from the meaning of the work and exerting material force.

In Kroll's interpretation, neo-materialists like John Evelyn, Jeremy Taylor, and Locke anticipated some of our postmodernist preoccupation with the situatedness and consequent partiality of discourse. They were interested in the pursuit of facts, but were profoundly anti-totalizing in their ways of dealing with systems of knowledge, recognizing that "facts" in any given instance could be only approximate because they were altered by the very social contexts that sustained them. Scholars in a predominantly materialist mode produced the first English *Biblia Polyglotta*, which constituted scriptural authority as multiple rather than single and invited readers to the comparative study of various versions of scripture through an ingenious arrangement of parallel passages on the page (Figure 1.3). Through their insistence on the "reality" of the patterning of concrete verbal artifacts, the neo-materialists of the late Renaissance anticipated many of the concerns of the "new philology."[50]

If we feel the need to find a prototype from within the Renaissance itself to provide historical respectability for our own inquiry here, then the broad late-Renaissance current of materialist thought is available as a model. Just as the New Bibliography's emphasis on ideal text and ideal copy replicated Renaissance Platonist conceptualizations of the text as

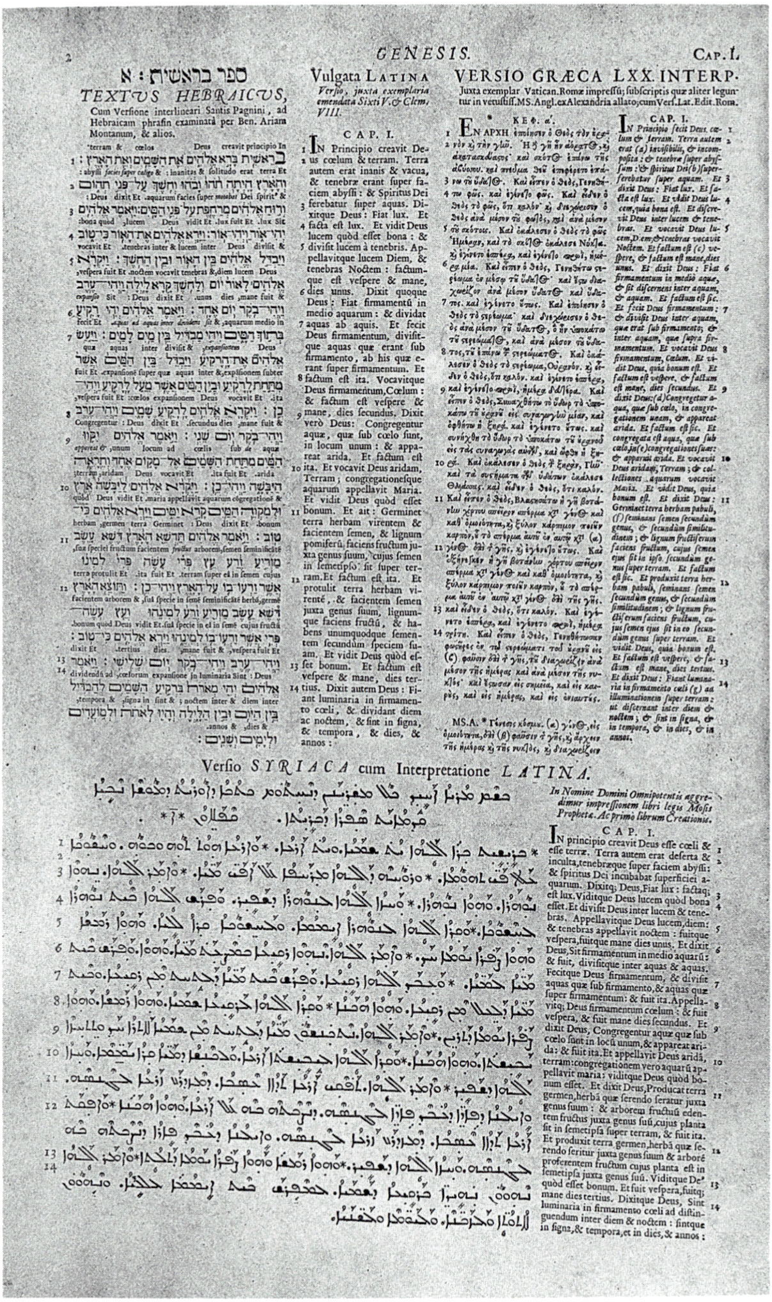
2 GENESIS. CAP. I.

ספר בראשית : א
TEXTUS HEBRAICUS, Cum Versione interlineari Santis Pagnini, ad Hebraicam phrasin examinatâ per Ben. Ariam Montanum, & alios.

Vulgata LATINA
Versio, juxta exemplaria emendata Sixti V. & Clem. VIII.

CAP. I.

1 IN Principio creavit Deus cœlum & terram. Terra autem erat inanis & vacua, & tenebræ erant super faciem abyssi: & Spiritus Dei ferebatur super aquas. Dixitque Deus: Fiat lux. Et facta est lux. Et vidit Deus lucem quòd esset bona: & divisit lucem à tenebris. Appellavitque lucem Diem, & tenebras Noctem: factumque est vespere & mane, dies unus. Dixit quoque Deus: Fiat firmamentũ in medio aquarum: & dividat aquas ab aquis. Et fecit Deus firmamentum, divisitque aquas quæ erant sub firmamento, ab his quæ erant super firmamentum. Et factum est ita. Vocavitque Deus firmamentum, Cœlum: & factum est vespere & mane, dies secundus. Dixit verò Deus: Congregentur aquæ, quæ sub cœlo sunt, in locum unum: & appareat arida. Et factum est ita. Et vocavit Deus aridam, Terram; congregationesque aquarum appellavit Maria. Et vidit Deus quòd esset bonum. Et ait: Germinet terra herbam virentem & facientem semen, & lignum pomiferũ, faciens fructum juxta genus suum, cujus semen in semetipso sit super terram. Et factum est ita. Et protulit terra herbam virentẽ, & facientem semen juxta genus suum, lignumque faciens fructũ, & habens unumquodque sementem secundùm speciem suam. Et vidit Deus quòd esset bonum. Et factum est vespere & mane, dies tertius. Dixit autem Deus: Fiant luminaria in firmamento cœli, & dividant diem ac noctem, & sint in signa, & tempora, & dies, & annos:

VERSIO GRÆCA LXX. INTERP.
Juxta exemplar Vatican. Romæ impressũ; subscriptis quæ aliter leguntur in vetustiss. MS. Angl. ex Alexandria allato, cum Vers. Lat. Edit. Rom.

Versio SYRIACA cum Interpretatione LATINA.

Figure 1.3 Pages from the *Biblia Sacra Polyglotta* (1654–57)
Reproduced by permission of the Harry Ransom Humanities Research Center, University of Texas, Austin

PARAPH. CHALD. Edit. BASIL. cum Verf. LAT.   TEXTUS HEBRÆO-SAMA-   TEXT.ET VER.SAM.
תרגום אונקלוס TARGUM ONKELOS.   RITANUS.   Tranflatio Latina.

CAP. I.

IN principio creavit Deus cœlum et terram. Terra autem erat deferta et vacua: et tenebræ fuper faciê abyffi: et fpiritus à cõpellês Dei inflabat fuper faciem aquarum.
3 quarú d. dixitDe°, Sit lux:
4 & fuit lux. Et vidit De° lucem, quod effet bona: & divifit De° inter lucê, et inter tenebras. Appellavit Deus lucem, Diemq́; tenebras, vocavit Noctê: & fuit vefpere et fuit mane, dies unus.
6 Et dixit De°,Sit firmamêtû in medio aquarú: & dividat inter aquas et aquas.
7 Et fecit De° firmamentú: & divifit inter aquas, quæ erant fubter firmamentû, inter aquas, quæ erant fuper firmamentum: et fuit ita.
8 Et vocavit Deus firmamentum, cœli : Et fuit vefpere & fuit mane,dies fecundus. Et dixit De°,Congregentur aquæ, quæ fub cœlo funt,in locum unú;et appareat arida. Et fuit ita.
10 Et vocavitDeus aridã,terramq́; et collectiones aquarú, appellavit maria:& vidit Deus quod effet
11 bonú. Et dixitDe°,Germinet terra germen, herbam cujus fili° fementis feminatur; arboreq́; fructifera facientê fructú, fecundûm genus fuú,cujus fili° fementis in ipfo fit, fuper terram:Et
12 fuit ita. Et produxit terra germen, herbã cujus filius fementis feminatur, fecundû genus fuum: arboreq́; facientê fructú,cujus filius fementis eft in ipfo, fecundû genus fuum:Et vidit Deus,
13 quod effet bonum. Et fuit vefpere & fuit mane,dies tertius. Et dixit Deus,Sint luminaria in firmamento cœli, ut dividant inter diê et noctem:Et fint in figna et in tempora,et in dies et annos.

VERSIO SAMARITANA.

[Samaritan and Latin parallel text]

per faciem aquæ(*s*) feminatum (*s*) progerminantem germen(*s*)plantam (*s*)cujus fructificatio in feipfá eft,(*s*) orbe conft.

IN Principio creavit De- us cœlum & terram. Terra autem erat inanis & cooperta, obruta mari : & tenebræ fuper faciem abyffi, & ventus Dei fla- bat fuper faciem aquæ. Voluit que Deus ut fieret lux, & fuit lux. Et vidit De- us lucem effe bonam. Et feparavit Deus inter lucem, & inter tenebras. Et vocavit que Deus lucem, & tenebras vocavit noctem. Et fit vefpere, & fit mane, dies unus. Et dixit Deus, fiat firmamentum in medio aquarum : fepa- ret que inter aquas, & aquas. Et fecit Deus firmamentum, feparavit que aquas, quæ funt fub firmamento, ab aquis, quæ funt fuper firmamentum: & fuit ita. Et vocavit Deus firmamentum, cœlum : & fit vefpere, & fit mane, dies fecundus. Et dixit Deus, congregentur aquæ, quæ fub cœlo funt in locum unum, & appareat arida : & fuit ita. Et vocavit Deus aridam, terram, & congregationem aquarum, vocavit maria : Et vidit Deus quod effet bonum. Et dixit Deus, ger- minet terra herbam vi- rentem, (*s*) facientem fe- men, & arborem fru- ctiferam, facientem fru- ctum, fecundum fpecie fuam, cujus femen in fe fit, fuper terram : & fu- it ita. Et produxit terra herbam virentem (*s*) facientem femen fecun- dum fpeciem fuam, & arborem facientem fructum, cujus femen in fe fit, fecundum fpe- ciem fuam : Et vidit De- us quod bonum eft. Et fit vefpere, & fit mane, dies tertius. Et dixit De- us, fiant luminaria in firmamento cœli, ut fe- parent inter diem & no- ctem : fint que in figna, & tempora, & dies, & annos.

VERS.SA.(*s*)erefuere fe- minantem in feipfá orbe conft.

Verfio *ARABICA* cum Interpretatione *LATINA*.

بِسْمِ اللهِ الرَّحْمٰنِ الرَّحِيمِ نَبْتَدِي نَحُمُ التَّوْرٰيةَ المُقَدَّسَةَ السِّفْرَ الأَوَّلِ

وَهُوَ سِفْرُ الخَلِيقَةِ . الفَصْلُ . آ .

In Nomine Dei mifericordis mi- feratoris aggredimur impref- fionem Legis facrofanctæ. Liber primus,viz. Liber Creationis.

CAP. I.

PRimum quod creavit Deus, fuit cœ- lum & terra : Erat que terra apuda, cooperta, obruta mari : & tenebræ fuper faciem aquæ. Voluitque Deus ut fieret lux, & fuit lux. Et cognovit Deus lucem effe bonam & tenebras. Et vocavit Deus tempora lucis, diem, & tempora tenebrarum, Noctem. Cumque præteriiffet nox & dies, dies unus. Voluit Deus ut effet firmamentú 6 inter aquas. Et fecit Deus firmamentum, divifitque inter aquas quæ fub illo funt, & fupra illud : & fuit ita. 7 Voluit Deus ut effet firmamentum, Cœlum. Cum- que præteriiffet nox & dies, dies fecundus. Voluit Deus ut congregarentur 9 aquæ fub cœlo in locum unum, & ap- pareret arida : fuit que ita. Et 10 vocavit Deus aridam terram, & congregationem aquarum, vocavit maria : Et vidit Deus quod bonum effet. Voluit enim ut 11 Deus ut germinaret terra germen, & arbores fru- ctiferas, quarum planta eft fe mentis fuper terram : & fuit ita. Et produxit terra germen, herba-12 feminatum in fe, & arbores producentes fructum, quorum planta eft femen in feipfis : Cum cognovit Deus quod 13 bonum. Et dies tertius. Voluit Deus ut fieret luminaria in firmamento cœli, divide-14 rent inter noctem & diem, & effent in figna, & tempora, & dies, & annos.

transcending its corrupt and transient earthly embodiments, so the "new philology"'s centering upon those very transient embodiments remobilizes an earlier concern with texts as material objects within a broader material setting. Like seventeenth-century materialists, we will, in the chapters that follow, combine a healthy respect for "facts" as we are able to determine them and objects from the past insofar as we are able to consult them, with the recognition that our grasp of these things is at best approximate and liable to be overturned by those who come after us and choose to construct the past differently than we do.

Chapter 2 will open the discussion on more neutral territory than the sacred terrain of Shakespeare by considering the two early quarto texts of *Doctor Faustus* and the ways in which the play as we have it has been reshaped by the New Bibliography's assumptions about what constitutes proper dramatic form and content: what happens to our conception of Marlowe if we insist on the integrity of both early quarto versions of the play? The third chapter will extend the argument into more rugged and controversial territory – the relationship between quarto and folio versions of *The Merry Wives of Windsor*. The first or "bad" quarto of *Doctor Faustus* has from time to time had its defenders, but nearly everyone until recently has followed Greg in regarding the quarto version of *Merry Wives* as a fabricated un-Shakespearean mish-mash. As it happens, however, the quarto version makes more sense than it has been given credit for if we are willing to work within a different set of social assumptions than dominate the folio version and to accept as "genuine" a play affording greater autonomy than the folio to the good wives and middling sort of Windsor. To what extent is the almost reflexive editorial denigration of the quarto version of *Merry Wives* an attempt to keep Shakespeare pure, elevated, and properly skeptical about women's autonomy?

Chapter 4 will consider the two texts of *The Taming of the Shrew* in terms of the incipient feminist argument from the previous chapter. To what extent can the editorial controversy surrounding *The Taming of the Shrew* be explicated in terms of the gender assumptions behind traditional editorial practice? In what ways will our conceptualization of Shakespeare's play alter if we undo some of those assumptions? Chapter 5 will take on an editorial issue that has even broader cultural ramifications than those considered previously, in that it will deal with *the* quintessentially Shakespearean play, *Hamlet*, and with our persistent need in Western culture to distance ourselves from the play in its first quarto version. What unacknowledged collective assumptions about Shakespeare and his place in our culture does the 1603 *Hamlet* violate? What would admitting it as "Shakespeare" do to our strong twentieth-century need to identify the play's protagonist with the playwright's deepest thoughts? In particular, chapter 5 will consider the earliest printed versions of *Hamlet* in terms of recent speculations about residual orality in late Elizabethan and early Jacobean culture. I will argue that the Shakespearean theater was far more predominantly "oral" than "literate" in its functioning, and that Shakespeare and his company only gradually came to conceptualize their plays in terms of readerly assumptions about how and where meaning is constituted.

Finally, chapter 6 will depart from the dramatic textual material of the rest of the book to consider twentieth-century editorial reshaping of published collections of poetry from the 1630s and 1640s – Robert Herrick's *Hesperides* (1648), John Donne's *Poems* (1633), and especially John Milton's *Poems* (1645). This is the chapter in which the consideration of early texts as material artifacts will be the most sustained and steeped in bibliographical considerations. I will argue, following Roger Chartier's speculations about authorial "embodiment" in the seventeenth century, that Milton and other publishing poets of the same decade conceptualized their published verse as authorial *corpus* in a way unprecedented in English poetry. Or was it the printers and publishers who deserve credit for creating the textual body of the poet? As so frequently in the study of early printed editions, the intentions of the author are inextricably intertwined with the process of publication itself. Here again, as in the *Hamlet* chapter, I shall explore elements of residual orality within seventeenth-century culture; I shall interpret Milton not as the first modern man of letters (as he has often been termed of late), but rather as a writer in some ways looking backwards and still profoundly engaged in the oral and aural elements of poetic craft.

There are interesting parallels between the shift in dominance from neo-Platonic to materialist conceptualization of texts in the mid to late seventeenth century and the corresponding paradigm shift in our own late twentieth century that has enabled my inquiry here. Might it be that, in both cases, the shift to materiality is related to unease over the assimilation of a new technology of writing and dissemination of written materials? Just as seventeenth-century authors expressed anxiety over the increased distance from their audience imposed by the medium of print, so we of the computerized era sometimes feel insecure over our impending separation via CD-ROM and hypertext from our old friend, the printed book. I will occasionally speculate in the pages that follow about possible effects of the altered technology. But in the main, I will offer focussed, detailed arguments about specific edited texts and editorial traditions. Textual minutiae, if allowed to accumulate sufficiently, can produce large and startling effects. My goal throughout will be to undo rigidities inherited from the past and free up scholarly energy for reconceptualizations of the field at the most basic possible level – the level of the texts we read, contemplate, and use to influence others.

2

TEXTUAL INSTABILITY AND IDEOLOGICAL DIFFERENCE

The case of *Doctor Faustus*

Here is a wish-fulfillment scenario for Marlovian editors and biographers: in the bricked-off attic of a suburban London cottage, workmen clearing the way for a car park discover a parcel of old manuscripts, among them several letters dating from the 1590s and directed to "Christopher Marley" or "Marlowe." They are partly in code but decipherable, and turn out to contain passages detailing his duties as an intelligencer in Her Majesty's service. In the bundle are also several papers, apparently in the hand of Marlowe himself, elucidating such mysteries as the nature of his religious belief and the reasons for his brush with the Privy Council in 1593. There are also drafts of letters sent by Marlowe; one of them, dated later than the rest, hints at his fears of assassination, thus lending support to time-honored speculation that his violent death was not just the result of private feuding. Also in the packet are fair copies in the same hand of several of Marlowe's known works, among them *Hero and Leander* in the unfinished version of the 1598 printed edition but including a note affirming the author's intent to leave it unfinished; among them also an autograph copy of *The Tragicall Historie of Doctor Faustus* inscribed at the end "as written by me, Christofer Marley, 1592. *Terminat hora diem, Terminat Author opus.*" The *Faustus* manuscript – perhaps the most sensational find of all – allows scholars to settle once and for all the vexing textual problems surrounding the play by establishing a definitive authorial version that is polished and close to flawless, far superior to either the quarto of 1604 or the quarto of 1616 over which modern editors of Marlowe have puzzled and wrangled for over a century.

This imaginary cache of manuscripts fills many blank spaces in Marlowe scholarship and undoes many ambiguities; with one fell stroke, it also sweeps away the scholarly industry devoted to the recovery or reconstruction of a lost Marlovian "original" for *Doctor Faustus*. The present chapter will analyze the shape of the editorial controversy surrounding the play in order to critique some of its guiding assumptions – particularly its futile pursuit of the "lost original." My wish-fulfillment fantasy set aside, the *Faustus* problem is this: we have two early printed versions of the play, each with features lacking in the other, each displaying gaps that the other seems to fill. The first existing quarto version of the play was published in 1604, after which there were several reprintings of that text; in 1616 a second version of the play was printed, with subsequent quartos following it rather than the 1604 version until 1663, when yet a third version of *Doctor Faustus* appeared in quarto.

In twentieth-century editorial practice, the 1604 and 1616 printed versions have become bitter rivals: to choose one text as closer to "Marlowe" has invariably meant devaluing and debasing the other. The A text (the quarto of 1604) is closer in time to Marlowe in terms of publication but (much like a "bad" quarto of Shakespeare) too short and seemingly truncated to appear a satisfactory play – whole episodes that exist in the later 1616 version do not exist in the A text; moreover, the A text includes topical references to the Lopez affair of 1594, which postdated Marlowe's death. The B text (the quarto of 1616) is fuller and longer than A, but filled out for the most part with "low" comic scenes that appear, to some readers at least, insufficiently Marlovian.[1]

For anyone trained in traditional methods of critical analysis, the experience of reading the two versions of the play in W. W. Greg's parallel text edition (1950) induces a sense of textual paradise lost. The edition is valuable in that, like any good parallel text edition, it facilitates comparison of the A and B versions of the play. But this edition in particular, in progress at the time that Greg's important paper on "The Rationale of Copy-Text" was delivered before the English Institute in 1949 and published the same year as the paper was, seems designed to offer graphic evidence of the major point made in Greg's paper – that it is usually necessary to conflate early texts to achieve a satisfactory edition of a work of Elizabethan literature.

Greg's introduction whets the reader's appetite for the reconstruction of Marlowe's "original" version of the play – a version assumed to be unencumbered by infelicities and ambiguities that mar the surviving printed playbooks. The 1604 and 1616 quartos, if approached through a modern conception of authorship, offer extraordinary "evidence" of Marlowe's original control over his materials. Both quartos end with the enigmatic comment "*Terminat hora diem, Terminat Author opus*," which, for twentieth-century readers at least, has evoked a seductive image of the author working intensely and in solitude on his masterwork, which he finished and "signed" with a majestic gesture of authorial finality. But in the absence of the wish-fulfillment evidence offered at the beginning of this chapter, we have no certainty that the line was actually Marlowe's. Some editors have speculated that it could have been added by the printer or someone else close to the publication process. Even more disconcertingly for our modern ideas of authorship, the line appears at the end of both versions of the play, so that both, although different, have the same claim to authenticity.

Greg's parallel text edition of *Doctor Faustus* encourages readers to think in terms of recapturing the single authentic *opus* that we can so vividly imagine Marlowe writing. The edition gives passages that exist in one early text but not in the other "absent presence" in the text from which they are "missing" through blank spaces – even in the middle of lines – that interrupt the flow of reading and make each version appear fragmentary by itself. The editor offers his readers a strong temptation to escape from the anxiety created by the apparent lacunae through a process of selection and consolidation that chooses one reading as "superior" and rejects its rival version across the page, thus actively constructing a composite version that will be better than either flawed quarto. Indeed Greg published his own "Conjectural Reconstruction" of the play in the same year as his parallel text edition.[2] His two editions of *Doctor Faustus*, together with the nearly simultaneous article on "Copy-Text," offered a formidable and influential display of an editorial method that was to freeze into dogma during the next several decades.

For most readers, however, the two texts of *Doctor Faustus* have proven curiously resistant to assimilation, and do not mesh satisfactorily to form a single composite whole. In the case of Shakespeare plays with both good and bad quartos, twentieth-century editions have for the most part settled into comfortable consensus. Readers encounter only minor textual differences in moving from one edition of a given play to another, or at least they did before the publication of the controversial new Oxford Shakespeare. Indeed, it could be argued that the elaborate apparatus of dictionaries, concordances, and even the *OED* itself built up around the text of Shakespeare has required the texts to remain stable so that the apparatus could preserve its accuracy. Not so with Marlowe. Different editors of *Doctor Faustus* have offered us markedly different versions of Marlowe's intended *opus*. The usual editorial practice of creating a composite text from elements of A and B have brought us no closer to a Marlovian original because editors have seldom agreed as to what is Marlowe and what isn't. Greg's efforts notwithstanding, we are left with an array of different reconstructions of *Doctor Faustus* that tell us more about the personal tastes and unspoken value-systems of individual editors than they do about the elusive "original."

Michael Warren has argued persuasively that we need to set aside the passion for textual syncretism and take a harder look at the early quarto texts of *Doctor Faustus* we actually have.[3] There is much to be gained by keeping the two separate and distinct. They are profoundly different – much more unlike than the quarto and folio versions of *King Lear*, for which Warren and others have proposed a similar separation. Merely to read each in its original quarto edition (or a facsimile or modern edited version thereof) is to get a much stronger sense of the textual integrity of each than if they are read in Greg's fragmenting parallel columns. If we read each text of *Doctor Faustus* on the assumption that it is sufficient in itself rather than a deficient simulacrum of the other, we will find that each has its own distinctive atmosphere and dramatic logic. We will not, however, find ourselves moving closer to the absent authorial presence we call Marlowe.

It is time to step back from the fantasy of recovering Marlowe as the mighty, controlling source of textual production and consider other elements of the process, particularly ideological elements that the editorial tradition has, by the very nature of its enterprise, suppressed. I would like to second Warren's call for a separation of the two texts of *Doctor Faustus*, but carry his argument further by contending that for *Faustus*, and for Renaissance drama more generally, a key element of textual instability is ideological difference. Except for minor shifts in wording, the disparities between the 1604 and 1616 versions of *Doctor Faustus* are not random; they form a rough but fairly coherent pattern of "relocation" that alters the site of dramatic conflict. The A text places the magician in "Wertenberg" and within a context of militant Protestantism; the B text situates him instead in "Wittenberg," within a less committedly Calvinist, more theologically conservative and ceremonial milieu. Each placement of Faustus carries different implications in terms of the play's engagement of political and religious controversy. More interesting for us, perhaps, are the implications for modern editorial practice: to a significant degree, twentieth-century editorial opinion has organized itself around a secularized version of the same ideological polarities.

WITTENBERG AND WERTENBERG

The attempt to reconstruct a pristine Marlovian "original" has been, in part, an attempt to separate Marlowe from historical process and from the contingency of meaning that historical interpretation usually implies; it is an attempt to give the Marlovian text a fixity and permanence it certainly did not have in the Elizabethan theater. Interestingly enough, the key New Bibliographical work on the play appeared in the five years after World War II, at a time when traditional philological scholarship was on the wane among leaders of the discipline of English. Greg's editions and Leo Kirschbaum's seminal 1946 article (see n. 1 below) defining the 1604 text as a "bad" quarto of the play can be seen in retrospect as part of the postwar effort to stabilize and preserve important cultural monuments. But the play we call *Doctor Faustus* was malleable and unfixed from the outset, acted in different "local" versions which can be correlated with different historical moments; it was, as I shall argue, dependent upon those moments to achieve its full power in the theater.

I will speculate here about the origins and significance of the A and B quartos of *Doctor Faustus* in order to demonstrate the inevitable historicity of our editorial practice, but also to make a plea for the recovery of "local" differences in Renaissance texts more generally. In the case of *Doctor Faustus*, the differences between early printed versions are more flamboyant than they are for early printed versions of most Shakespearean plays, and lead us farther away from the playwright as authority over the meaning of his work. Most of the discrepancies between quarto and folio versions of Shakespeare that recent textual revisionists have brought to our attention could at least conceivably have been created during the author's lifetime and could therefore have been the product of authorial revision; the different versions of Marlowe I will discuss almost certainly were not.

Doctor Faustus enjoyed a long and colorful theatrical history in the late sixteenth and early seventeenth centuries. Its illicit acts of conjuring were able to "ravish" and terrify audiences, as is witnessed by the numerous tales of demonic interference during performances of the play: at Exeter, an extra devil suddenly appeared among the actors on stage, causing a panic; in London the "old Theater crackt and frighted the audience" during one performance, at others, the "visible apparition" of the devil appeared on stage "to the great amazement both of the Actors and Spectators."[4] The play did not hold its ability to spellbind English audiences for nearly half a century by remaining always the same. For Renaissance audiences of *Doctor Faustus*, to the extent that they took notice of the playwright at all, watching "Marlowe" meant watching a theatrical event balanced on the nervous razor edge between transcendent heroism and dangerous blasphemy – transgression not only against God but also against cherished national goals and institutions.

The "Marlowe effect," as we can perhaps term it, is particularly fully documented in terms of audience response to *Doctor Faustus*, but was probably part of the appeal of other Marlowe plays as well (*Tamburlaine* will be mentioned later on). I would like to contend that the differences between the A and B quartos of *Faustus* functioned to keep the "Marlowe effect" alive – to keep the play, amidst shifting conditions in church and state, on the same "ravishing" razor edge between exaltation and transgression. As I have argued elsewhere, the different early texts of a Shakespeare play often seem to disperse authorial identity, at least to the extent that authorial identity is associated with consistency of method and purpose, in that they alter the ideological message of the play in subtle but significant ways.[5] In the case of Marlowe, or at least of *Doctor Faustus*, just the opposite is true. The different versions of the play carry different ideological freight – the A text could be described as more nationalist and more Calvinist, Puritan, or ultra-Protestant, the B text as more internationalist, imperial, and Anglican, or Anglo-Catholic – but each version places the magician at the extreme edge of transgression in terms of its own implied system of values.

In order to consider the quartos of *Doctor Faustus* in terms of ideological difference, we need first of all to temporarily suspend the almost inevitable tendency to rank one version higher than the other – a judgment usually made in aesthetic terms but masking an array of other concerns. By attempting to winnow out "Marlowe" from the chaff of non-authorial intrusions, editors uphold an elite cultural ideal: the text judged more defective than the other is almost invariably associated with a lowering of social standards. Editors disagree, however, about which version of the play is too "low" to be genuine Marlowe. W. W. Greg opted for the 1616 version (the B text) as closer to Marlowe on grounds that it has a more coherent plot and more "orderly succession of scenes," as well as greater polish and more effective theatricality. The 1604 quarto (the A text), by contrast, is for Greg a jumble of "merely disjointed episodes," the "mutilated remains" of an "original form" which B more nearly reflects. The A text "lacks" many of the comic episodes of the B text, it also "lacks" the episode of Faust's intervention in the struggle between the Emperor and the Pope and many of the visual elements (the final appearance of the Good and Bad Angels, the vision of the heavenly throne, the hell mouth) in the play's closing moments. The A text's "feebleness," "gibberish," and "inapposite rant" are, for Greg, the probable effects of popularization and professional decline. In the course of time, the text of the play was "progressively adapted to the needs of a declining company and the palate of an uncultivated audience" (G pp. 20–39).

This is precisely the style of argument we would expect from the innovative New Bibliographer who argued for memorial reconstruction as the source of Shakespeare's "bad" quartos. It was followed (albeit more temperately) by Fredson Bowers, who in his own edition of the play disagreed with Greg's conviction that the scenes unique to the B text were Marlovian, but nevertheless used B as the copytext on grounds that A was "corrupt" and B "purer," more "textually coherent," and "superior."[6] What makes the case of *Faustus* particularly interesting, however, is that other reader-critics have used similar criteria to reach the opposite judgment about what is "genuine" Marlowe. Constance Brown Kuriyama, for example, has complained that "acceptance of the B text as 'original' or authoritative leaves us with a work that is, to put it plainly, an aesthetic monstrosity and a critical nightmare." A has an "aesthetic integrity" far superior to B. B is full of "infelicitous bungling," it confuses the play's theology, and "because of its authors' fatal attraction to the coarser episodes of the *Faustbook*" it "tends to reduce Faustus' struggle to terms that I find hopelessly lurid and vulgar."[7] Roma Gill uses more cautious language but similarly prefers the A text on grounds that the B "additions" are "trivial" and the serious scenes in A are "clearly superior."[8]

The case of *Doctor Faustus* throws into stark relief the relativity of editorial judgment, the ease with which we construct an "original" that will satisfy our own tastes and assumptions. The critic's chosen version of the play is idealized or at least given the benefit of elaborate explanation of what might otherwise be perceived as its "defects"; the rejected version, like its dark, monstrous double, is perceived as formless, fragmentary, *basse classe* and uncouth, attributable to inferior authorship. And so, we find, Greg goes to considerable lengths to defend the comic scenes and Papal-Imperial episodes of his preferred B text as closer to the play as Marlowe originally wrote it; Kuriyama, like most editors before Greg and a growing number since him, identifies these scenes instead as the non-Marlovian "adicyones in doctor fostes" for which Philip Henslowe paid Samuel Rowley and William Birde or Borne £4 in 1602 (G p. 11, Kuriyama pp. 180–81; see n. 1 below).

Part of the conflict I have sketched out here can be correlated with postwar generational differences. Greg speaks for what we used to call "establishment" opinion, preferring smoothness, polish, a brand of theatricality which relies on spectacle and special effects to communicate widely accepted cultural ideals. The B text, with its imperial hijinx and busy damnation scene, a "huge phantasmagoria of scenic properties, emblematic costumes, allegorical actions on all three levels of the Elizabethan stage," does that far more successfully than the A text. Greg also finds more sympathetic the ceremonial style of Anglicanism in B; to him the more iconoclastic A text registers as jarringly uncouth.[9] The work of somewhat younger critics like Warren, Kuriyama, Michael Keefer, David Bevington, and Stephen Greenblatt (who also prefers A) postdates the heyday of the theatrical avant-garde in the 1960s and early 1970s and the broader critique of "the establishment" with which both the avant-garde theater and an emerging generation of young scholars of the Vietnam era were associated. These scholars display more tolerance, even active preference, for theatrical starkness, iconoclasm, dissonance. They are happier with the A text, which far more often relies on a bare, unadorned stage and casts Faustus's conflict in a more introspective, psychological mode. The A text has recently appeared on its own in three published editions – additional evidence of the rise in its status.[10] Editorial preference for either version of *Doctor Faustus* will continue to alter along with other cultural forms and dominant ideologies.

There are interesting correlations between the generational differences I have identified here and a much earlier controversy surrounding the figure of Faustus which has left its mark on the A and B quartos of the play. The two versions differ as to Faustus's base of operations: as I have noted, he hails from Wittenberg in the B text, from Wertenberg in the A text. All editors of the play (even those who prefer A) have at least tacitly accepted "Wertenberg" as a corruption or, in Greg's phrase, a "nominal perversion" (G p. 39) of the "correct" location, Wittenberg. We all know, or think we know, that the historical Dr Faustus lived in Wittenberg, a prominent university town, a haven for lingering elements of late-medieval scholasticism but also the intellectual center of Lutheranism. In maintaining this knowledge, we are following an editorial line which has so dominated thinking about the play that the A text's locale of "Wertenberg" is, editorially speaking, nowhere. If we look up "Wertenberg" in a standard topographical dictionary to the Elizabethan drama, we will find (in a circularity familiar to us from our earlier discussion of the "blue-eyed hag") that "Wertenberg" is listed only in reference to *Faustus* as the A text's error for "Wittenberg," with the English Faustbook cited as an authority.[11]

And yet in the Renaissance (as today) Wertenberg was not nowhere: "Wertenberg" or "Wirtenberg," in its standard sixteenth-century spellings, was the independent Rhineland Duchy of Württemberg, well known to English Protestants through its associations with the uprisings by radical Zwinglian Protestants during the early sixteenth century which caused Martin Luther and his followers to retreat from the most revolutionary implications of Reformation doctrine. The Duchy of Württemberg took a consistently anti-Imperial stance during the late sixteenth century and was one of the foreign powers with which England was on the most intimate terms. The Duke of Württemberg (or "Wirtemberg," as he himself signed it), was ostensibly a Lutheran, but of a theological school that Wittenberg branded as heretical; he was widely suspected of crypto-Calvinism, and some modern historians call him a Calvinist. He lent his support to the English side in the French wars; he visited England himself and was a familiar enough figure at least in court circles to be satirized (we think) in Shakespeare's *Merry Wives of Windsor*. English actors also visited his court in Württemberg.[12]

Moreover, even in relation to the historical figure of Faustus, Wertenberg was not nowhere. In the late sixteenth century there was an alternate tradition associating Faustus with Württemberg (and its University of Tübingen) rather than with Wittenberg. According to Philipp Melanchton of Wittenberg, who was eager to dissociate such a marginal figure as the magician from the intellectual center of Lutheranism, Faustus perished in Wertenberg, not in Melanchton's own Wittenberg; later Lutheran propagandists followed Melanchton in attempting to undo the abuse and slander of the "school and church of Wittenberg" that placed the magician as a Doctor of Divinity there. A similar association is made in *The Merry Wives of Windsor*: the folio version of the play calls the three "cozen Germans," one of whom appears to be a satirical portrait of the Duke of Württemberg, "three German devils, three Doctor Faustuses."[13] Nor is the Faustbook itself as consistent as editors have claimed; in at least one instance, it gives the magician's place of residence as "Wirtenberg."[14] So the A text, in placing Faustus in "Wertenberg," may not be marred by "nominal perversion" after all. Rather, it draws on an alternate tradition associating Faustus with a German duchy that was a hotbed of left-wing Protestantism rather than a place which had become, by the late sixteenth century at least, the center of a more conservative Lutheran orthodoxy.

The editorial suppression of "Wertenberg" elides a potentially significant historical difference between the two texts; it also obscures an interesting correlation between twentieth-century and Renaissance generational difference. W. W. Greg, who prefers the "Wittenberg" B text, chooses the version of the play that places it in a relatively conservative religious setting, at least by the standards of the 1590s. Kuriyama, Gill, and Warren, who prefer the A or "Wertenberg" version, do not concern themselves with the implications of the name, but nevertheless choose the version of the play which places Faustus in a locale associated with revolt against official Lutheran orthodoxy. Michael Keefer's recent edition of *Faustus* goes considerably further, appropriating Marlowe for the political left and de-crying the B text's "deformation of the originally interrogative thrust of the play."[15] Modern editorial preference thus recasts elements of sixteenth-century religious and political controversy.

Considered in historical terms, "Wertenberg" is not the textual "accidental" Marlowe editors have taken it to be. It is, however, precious little to hang an argument on. We need to look at other elements of the A and B texts which seem to correlate, at least in terms of the implications they would have carried for late sixteenth and early seventeenth-century audiences, with the difference between "Wertenberg" and "Wittenberg." We will be dealing not with the places in themselves but with the ideological resonances they carried in England. We will be dealing in particular with the conflict between left-wing Protestant opinion and conservative Anglican orthodoxy as it was played out in the Marprelate controversy of the 1580s and 1590s, in later outbursts of a similar reforming "frenzy," and also in literary works like Spenser's "May Eclogue." Baldly summarized, it was a conflict that pitted the Anglican establishment – its advocacy of bishops, a set liturgy, ecclesiastical vestments, and ceremonial worship, its tendency (becoming more pronounced over time) to dilute or reject some of the most rigorous theological tenets of Calvinism – against more radical Protestant or "Puritan" opinion characterized by hostility to the established ecclesiastical hierarchy, rejection of all set liturgies and "superstitious" Anglican ceremonies, and insistence upon the full rigor of Calvinist doctrine.[16] That is not to say that either version of *Faustus* focusses directly on the conflict between religious ideologies, only that if we suspend the almost irresistible tendency to view one text as a defective image of the other, we will notice that the two present markedly different versions of what constitutes normative religious experience. In terms of the set of polarities I have suggested, the *Faustus* A text is clearly more "Protestant" and the B text more "Anglican" or Anglo-Catholic.

Both texts, and indeed all of the quartos before 1663, were issued, as the English Faustbook had been before them, in black letter – a type that was still quite common in the early seventeenth century for popular books of all kinds, but became less common for secular materials except for lawbooks as the century wore on. Particularly for readers of the 1620s and 1630s, we can speculate, the black-letter type may have given *Doctor Faustus* a faintly archaic and ecclesiastical air.[17] Both the Bishops' Bible (last edition 1602) and the King James Version (first edition 1611) were published in black letter. Whether fortuitously or by design, the title pages of the 1604 and 1616 versions of *Doctor Faustus* display some of the same differences we have already discussed in terms of the elaboration of visual effects. The 1604 *Faustus* is adorned only by a printer's device, albeit a fairly appropriate one for a play in which psychomachia figures prominently (Figure 2.1); the 1609 and 1611 quartos use a different device and add an ornamental border at the top but are otherwise equally plain. It is only with the publication of the 1616 version of the play that the famous picture of the Doctor, face to face with the devil he has just conjured up and surrounded by mysterious tools of the magician's trade, appears on the title page (Figure 2.2). After 1616, the picture of Faustus becomes a regular feature of seventeenth-century editions of the play, but the icon was associated only with the "ceremonial" B text, not with the more iconoclastic A.[18]

The doctrinal differences between the A and B versions of *Doctor Faustus* are encapsulated nicely in the two contrasting versions of the Old Man's appeal to Faustus.[19] He enters in both versions almost at the end of the play to try to win Faustus back from the devil. Here are both forms of the speech:

A: *Old.* Ah Doctor Faustus, that I might preuaile,
To guide thy steps vnto the way of life,
By which sweete path thou maist attaine the gole
That shall conduct thee to celestial rest.
Breake heart, drop bloud, and mingle it with teares,
Teares falling from repentant heauinesse
Of thy most vilde and loathsome filthinesse,
The stench whereof corrupts the inward soule
With such flagitious crimes of hainous sinnes,
As no commiseration may expel,
But mercie Faustus of thy Sauiour sweete,
Whose bloud alone must wash away thy guilt.
                      (A 1302–13)

B: *Old Man.* O gentle *Faustus* leaue this damned Art,
This Magicke, that will charme thy soule to hell,
And quite bereaue thee of saluation.
Though thou hast now offended like a man,
Doe not perseuer in it like a Diuell;
Yet, yet, thou hast an amiable soule,
If sin by custome grow not into nature:
Then *Faustus*, will repentance come too late,

> Then thou art banisht from the sight of heauen;
> No mortall can expresse the paines of hell.
> It may be this my exhortation
> Seemes harsh, and all vnpleasant; let it not,
> For gentle sonne, I speake it not in wrath,
> Or enuy of thee, but in tender loue,
> And pitty of thy future miserie.
> And so haue hope, that this my kinde rebuke,
> Checking thy body, may amend thy soule.
>
> (B 1813–29)

Editorial opinion has focussed on the "inferior artistry" of the A version – which Greg called Senecan bombast (G p. 384) – but neither version is intrinsically preferable on aesthetic grounds alone. Rather, the two present strikingly different analyses of what Faustus must do to be saved. In A, the Old Man is a spiritual counsellor very much in the bracing Protestant or Puritan vein. He does not quite preach a doctrine of Calvinist predestination in that he describes heaven as a goal Faustus may "attaine" if he follows the "way of life," but his exhortation bears all the usual hallmarks of strenuous Protestant spirituality: the emphasis on sin as a state of "loathsome" inward corruption, the portrayal of spiritual experience as an arduous pilgrimage toward the goal of "celestial rest" and of repentance as a soul-searching individual struggle. The Old Man makes clear that his mere commiseration, though heartfelt, can accomplish nothing – everything depends on Faustus's inner condition and that is a matter between the sinner and God.

The B version is milder and gentler: it has been called semi-Pelagian, but perhaps a less inflammatory term like "Arminian" or "latitudinarian Anglican" would do.[20] In B, Faustus's sin is not an inborn condition, but a bad habit which is gradually becoming engrained. To be saved, he must give up his magic. Even at this perilously late stage in the game, the Old Man in B describes Faustus as having an "amiable soule" if "sin by custome grow not into nature." In contrast to A, the Old Man in B hopes that his words of admonition may have almost sacramental efficacy: "checking thy body," to "amend thy soule." His emphasis throughout is more on love than on punishment; he has the more priestly, confessional function of guiding the erring Christian into paths of right conduct.

There is no need to belabor the arresting contrasts between the speeches in A and B: a number of recent critics have begun to find them of interest.[21] What I would like to emphasize is their correlation with more scattered elements of each version of the play. The two texts of *Doctor Faustus* contain numerous editorial "accidentals" which can be read just as easily as configurations of ideological difference. Elsewhere in the A text, sin is portrayed in the "Genevan" mode as an ingrained condition of

THE TRAGICALL

Hiſtory of D. Fauſtus.

As it hath bene Acted by the Right
Honorable the Earle of Nottingham his ſeruants.

Written by Ch. Marl.

LONDON

Printed by V. S. for Thomas Bushell. 1604.

Figure 2.1 Title page of *Doctor Faustus* (1604)
Reproduced by permission of the Bodleian Library, Oxford, and the Henry
E. Huntington Library, San Marino, California

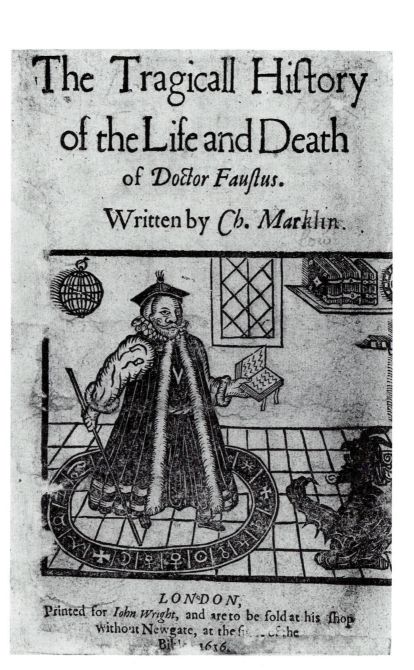

The Tragicall History
of the Life and Death
of *Doctor Fauſtus.*

Written by *Ch. Marklin.*

LONDON,
Printed for *Iohn Wright*, and are to be ſold at his ſhop
without Newgate, at the ſ: ... of the
Bit: 1636.

Figure 2.2 Title page of *Doctor Faustus* (1616)
Reproduced by permission of the British Library, London

infected will. B emphasizes outward forms and "works": sin is incorrect action prompted by enemies outside the self. Early in the play, for example, the good angel in A says "Neuer too late, if Faustus can repent" (A 708). The B version has "if *Faustus* will repent" (B 649). In A, the Old Man leaves the stage "fearing the ruine of thy hopelesse soule"; in B, it is "Fearing the enemy of thy haplesse soule." Faustus's response in A is, "Accursed Faustus, where is mercie now?" In B, it is "Accursed *Faustus*, wretch what hast thou done?" (A 1328–29, B 1842–43). Damnation in A is a matter of inward conviction – a psychic event. Faustus utters his final speech alone on a bare stage and the devils enter only at the end to carry him off. In B, his damnation is sealed through outward ceremonies. The trinity of devils descends to claim him for themselves and Mephistopheles reveals that he maliciously "Damb'd vp" the scriptural passage that would have promised Faustus life (B 1990). The Good and Bad Angels orchestrate a pageant of heavenly throne and hell mouth that shows Faustus his infernal destiny in hideously graphic form. In B also, after the devils carry him off, the scholars return to find Faustus's fragmented body on stage – the outward signs of perdition. In A, there are no visible remnants; the stage is empty.

Even though the spirituality of A appears more strenuous and psychologically demanding throughout, the fate of Faustus is less unequivocally established in that version than in B. The intimate, introspective nature of Faustus's experience in A leaves open, as it sometimes does in Puritan spiritual biography, the (admittedly faint) possibility of salvation even at the very last instant and beyond the power of observers to perceive. Despite the chorus's pious final speech about Faustus's "hellish fate," which closes the play in both A and B, more than one reader has seen in the A text a potential for Faustus's escape even at the moment of his exit to the words "ah *Mephastophilis*" (A 1508).[22] The ways of God remain inscrutable to the end. The B text allows no such hope: damnation is enacted as public ritual, imprinted upon Faustus's very body. Marjorie Garber and C. L. Barber have called attention to the play's insistence on eucharistic imagery, which is particularly prominent in the B version of the papal banquet (B 1085–94).[23] Also in B there is far more emphasis than in A on Faustus's bodily fragmentation as a symptom of spiritual decline: the removable head, the false leg. At the end of B, his fragmented body on stage suggests the state of inner fragmentation associated in conservative eucharistic doctrine with denial of the sacrament. The 1604 text presents a man in the throes of psychic torment; the 1616 text enacts his literal dismemberment and encodes that bodily condition with ritual significance.[24]

I do not mean to suggest that the degree of Faustus's responsibility for his fate is altogether clear in either A or B, or that either text delivers an unequivocal doctrinal message. Interpretation based on comparison and contrast between two texts can easily make each look more coherent in itself than it would if not measured against a massively different version. I would suggest, however, echoing Warren, that if lay readers or literary critics wish to discuss *Faustus*'s handling of doctrinal issues, we would do well to distinguish A from B, inscribed as they are with very different configurations of religious experience. Much critical energy – including Greg's – has been wasted over murky doctrinal issues that would unravel themselves readily if the interpreter were not burdened with a composite text.

Conversely, however, the precise cause of Faustus's damnation becomes much clearer if one conflates A and B. Edited versions of the play have frequently identified Faustus's kiss of Helen of Troy as the single experience that seals his hellish fate, using as evidence the contrasting speeches by the Old Man before and after the kiss: before the kiss, he implies that Faustus may yet be saved; after the kiss, he characterizes him as irrevocably damned. That interpretation cannot be made with any certainty unless A and B are combined. In A the Old Man comes to admonish Faustus about the "loathsome filthinesse" that has led him into sin and to entice him toward repentance. Faustus vacillates and backslides, however, calling up Helen and praising her beauty in some of the most famous lines of the play. During his encounter with Helen in A, the Old Man returns and remarks:

> Accursed *Faustus*, miserable man,
> That from thy soule excludst the grace of heauen,
> And flies the throne of his tribunall seate
>
> (A 1377–79)

Devils enter to torment the Old Man, and after a few more lines he exits, vowing "Hence hel, for hence I flie vnto my God" (A 1386). The Old Man's speech appears to be a judgment upon Faustus's eventual fate, but the Old Man's opinion cannot be definitive in the A text because in his previous speech he has already defined repentance as an internal process of transformation. As we have seen, other elements of the A version also support that definition. In A, conversion is a psychic event, not a set of perceivable behaviors.

The B text offers even less evidence than A that the kiss is Faustus's undoing. In B the Old Man delivers his "semi-Pelagian" speech to Faustus as we have already discussed it above: he emphasizes good works and outward behavior as a reliable gauge of spiritual health. Faustus vacillates, then calls upon Helen as in A. *But in B the Old Man never returns.* Standard editions of the play have adopted the B form of the Old Man's initial speech to Faustus, thus establishing its standard of a "religion of works," in which outward behavior reliably signifies inward condition. But in B, the fact that the Old Man does not reenter to identify Faustus's behavior with Helen as an exclusion of divine grace leaves Faustus's moral status uncertain even at this late stage of the play. Much too uncertain to be tolerable for traditional editors, who conclude that the necessary lines must somehow have become "lost" from the B text. But (to adopt the intentionalist language in which the discussion has usually been carried out) what if Marlowe never intended Helen's effect on Faustus to be absolutely clear? The play offers other signs that even thereafter, Faustus was not completely lost. After Faustus's encounter with Helen, editors have typically tidied up the uncertainty by inserting the Old Man's second speech as it appears in A. In the context of the B version's religion of works, the Old Man's judgment upon Faustus's spiritual condition becomes an unequivocal assertion of his damnation.

That is the pattern of meaning adopted in Greg's reconstruction, which is based on his 1946 article contending that Faustus is damned irrevocably by committing the mortal sin of demoniality with Helen.[25] Even more ingeniously, F. S. Boas' influential earlier edition had given several lines from the Old Man's initial speech in A to Faustus himself, as a response to the Old Man's speech in B. In Boas's version, the Old Man returns, as in A, and Boas comments in a note, "If A is correct, the Old Man in the background overhears the latter part of Faustus's apostrophe to Helen, and is thus convinced of his damnation."[26] This is more tentative than Greg but equally satisfying in its symmetry and clarity. Reading audiences of the 1604 and 1616 versions of the play received no such certainty that the scene with Helen was the precise moment in which Faustus's doom was sealed. Nor, I strongly suspect, did audiences in the late sixteenth and early seventeenth-century theater.

Is Greg necessarily correct in identifying Helen as a devil? In his and most other modern editions, the scene with Helen is editorially shaped to give us the seduction of Eve all over again, except that the temptress is not only inspired by a demon (as Eve was) but has become a demon herself. "Bad" texts, it would seem, can sometimes become acceptable if they confirm ancient wisdom about the danger of the feminine. Marlovian editors like Greg and Boas have willingly adopted elements of the "corrupt" and vilified A text if those elements help to tilt the play's meaning toward a desired clarity about the stages of Faustus's decline. But the clarity thus achieved is, in all likelihood, an artifact of twentieth-century rather than Renaissance sensibilities.

The "forme of *Faustus* fortunes good or bad" is, as I have tried to argue, differently shaped in the A and B texts in part because the two texts place such different valuations upon inward spiritual experience and ecclesiastical "forms." Perhaps because of *Doctor Faustus*'s highly loaded theological subject matter, the idea of original textual unity is particularly hard to resist for this play. In the early scene in which he gave up theology for magic, Faustus's mistake was to trust the literal words of a text as he read them on the page: "*Stipendium peccati, mors est*: ha . . . / The reward of sin is death: that's hard" (A 69–70; cited from B 66–67). He has, of course, cited the first part of Romans 6:23 but neglected the rest; further on in the speech, he similarly overlooks the second half of 1 John 1:8. In the A version of the play, we never know whether this blindness is the result of his own prejudice or of demonic tampering with the text. In the B version, however, he is manifestly the victim of Mephistopheles' textual contamination: the devil confesses that he "damb'd vp" the passages that promised Faustus life eternal (B 1990). Faustus has been betrayed by the material text before his eyes. The perceptible surface pattern of a book is posited as untrustworthy. Within the milieu of the B version of *Doctor Faustus*, the editorial task of filling in gaps to create a more reliable "original" becomes a praiseworthy undoing of demonic influence. God, his scripture, and his creation are unified and self-identical; it is the devil and demonic texts that are legion.

THE MARLOWE EFFECT

How are we to account for the pronounced doctrinal and ceremonial differences between the A and B texts of *Doctor Faustus* in terms of the play's arresting impact upon Renaissance audiences? It is possible to imagine the two versions as existing simultaneously within the repertory of Henslowe's company, in much the same way that contemporary religious engravings were sometimes published in contrasting Protestant and Catholic versions, or that morality plays like Nathaniel Woode's *Conflict of Conscience* existed with two different endings, in one of which the despairing protagonist is saved and in the other of which he is damned.[27] In such cases it is useless to posit an "original" outside the specific rhetorical situation that each variant version was created to address.

Possessing two different versions of a play in repertory would give an acting company tremendous flexibility in terms of its ability to satisfy different audiences, either public or private. If the company were on tour, the capacity to present a more strenuously Protestant or a more conservatively Anglican version of a popular play would allow the actors to match the prevailing belief system in a given locale. What played well in Puritan Banbury (to the extent that plays were tolerated there at all) would not necessarily succeed in ultra-conservative Northumberland. In the seventeenth century, perhaps earlier as well, *Doctor Faustus* was also performed by English companies in Germany; performances there may also have made interesting demands in terms of the play's religious ideology.[28] The effect of adjusting Marlowe to fit different audiences would not be to put a given auditory at its ease: quite the reverse. By situating the magician as the seductive antagonist of the style of belief that a given audience predominantly favored, particularly during a period when issues of doctrine and ceremony were highly inflammatory and at the center of public debate, the theatrical company would be insuring the highest possible pitch of "ravishment" and horror in terms of audience response. The alternative version of the play would, of course, be available as a back-up in case the "Marlowe effect" looked too much like sedition to local authorities.

It is overwhelmingly likely, however, that the relationship between A and B in performance was sequential rather than simultaneous – that the A text more closely resembles the play as it tended to be performed during the 1590s, and the B text, the play as it was revived by Henslowe's company after 1602. That is by far the dominant viewpoint among present-day editors and critics; it is also the view that accords best with the information we have. The first record of the play in performance dates from 1594. *Doctor Faustus* was highly popular on stage during the mid-1590s, but in 1597 or 1598, as Henslowe's diary records, it began to suffer from declining receipts and was withdrawn from the Admiral's Company repertory. At about the same time, Edward Alleyn, who had played Faustus during the 1590s, retired from the stage, to return by popular demand in or shortly after 1600. By 1602, according to Henslowe's diary, a revised version of *Faustus* was paid for and presumably delivered by Rowley and Birde. In 1604, the A quarto appeared in print; a version of *Faustus* had been entered in the Stationer's Register as early as 1601, and given the play's enormous popularity, the 1604 quarto we have may not have been the first to reach the public. Thereafter, it was very frequently reprinted. Copies of *Doctor Faustus* in quarto must have been literally read to death – most surviving early quartos exist as unique copies and the play could conceivably have been performed and/or printed in other early variant forms that have not survived. As we shall note later on, it underwent yet another textual metamorphosis when it was staged after the Restoration.

To return to its earlier history, our evidence suggests that in 1604 or a little earlier, at just about the same time that the A text was printed, *Doctor Faustus* returned to the London stage. If Henslowe followed the usual practice of the theatrical companies, he was willing to see the A version in print because it had lost its marketability on stage.[29] It is hard to imagine Henslowe, hard-headed businessman that he was, paying good money for the renovated *Faustus* and then letting it go to waste. It is also hard to imagine him again launching on stage in 1604 a version of the play that already existed in print or was on the verge of being printed. Almost certainly, Henslowe's "new" *Faustus* was a version resembling the B text much more than it resembled A. That is not to claim that either A or B represents a precise record of any theatrical performance, any more than we can claim the two early printed texts we have are the only important versions of the play that ever existed in print. We need to think ourselves back into a situation in which "revision" or "adycion," as Henslowe's diary terms it, does not so much create a new fixed, authoritative document to replace the old as it brings into play a new set of structural elements that create new possibilities for signification and cause those elements remaining from the old to take on different nuances of meaning.

Beyond the circumstances surrounding the publication of the A text and *Faustus*'s return to the stage, there are other scraps of evidence that contribute to the likelihood that the B text came after A. As Glynne Wickham has pointed out, no London theater before the late 1590s had the technical capacity to produce the final scenes of the play in the B version.[30] Contemporary descriptions of the play in performance after 1604 sound more like B than A in that they emphasize visual effects.[31] Moreover, there are minute signs in the texts themselves that B was performed later than A: A has Faustus refer to the gold that "yearely stuffes olde *Philips treasury*." B acknowledges the death of Philip II of Spain in 1598 by recasting the line in the past tense: "yearely stuff'd old *Phillips* treasury" (A 165, B 154). At least two other topical references which would have given the play currency in the mid-1590s do not exist in B (G pp. 32–33). The Bruno materials, which do not exist in A, would have had enormous topical interest after Giordano Bruno's execution for heresy at the hands of the Roman Inquisition in 1600. Like Giordano Bruno, Saxon Bruno in the B text was held in the strongest tower of Ponte Angelo while he awaited execution; had Faustus not saved him, he would have burned "on a pile of Fagots" as did Giordano Bruno (B 994).[32]

To assume that the B text more closely represents the play as it was staged after the turn of the seventeenth century is much the simplest hypothesis, and the only one that squares with the historical data we have. By the late 1590s, the A version (and versions resembling it closely) had worn out their welcome with London theatrical audiences. The revisions commissioned in 1602 gave the play a new lease on life and it again became successful on stage. We could contend that the play faltered in 1598 solely because of Alleyn's retirement from the role of Faustus, or that the revisions commissioned by Henslowe were a response to rising audience expectations: the theater-going public needed more spectacular visual effects in order to continue to be "ravished" by the play on stage. But neither of these explanations can account for the significant shifts in religious ideology between A and B. The 1602 revisions worked to keep *Doctor Faustus* on the thrilling/unnerving edge of transgression by inscribing the play with a new set of national priorities and anxieties. A theatrical company and its hired "hack" writers transformed what was then extant as "Marlowe" in order to keep the "Marlowe effect" alive, to keep Marlowe sounding like himself even decades after his physical demise. In the curious case of *Doctor Faustus*, non-authorial revision functioned to heighten, not to destroy, an aura of authorial "authenticity" in the theater.

During the early and mid-1590s, issues relating to "Wertenberg," and to other beleagured centers of independent Protestantism on the continent, were at the center of public concern in England. The nation was in the grip of "war fever." English troops were fighting in the Low Countries and France to aid the Protestant cause, but to the rage and frustration of England's "hotter Protestants," the central government was mired in factional strife and balked at a wholehearted commitment of troops and money on the Continent. There was "war fever" on the English stage as well. Numerous dramatic productions of the early and mid-1590s, among them Shakespeare's *Henry VI* trilogy, capitalized on emerging nationalist sentiment by obsessively reenacting events of the Armada year or staging military conflicts which strongly resembled England's ventures in France and the Low Countries.[33] The public passion for interpreting plays and pamphlets in terms of England's embroilment on the Continent was so intense that Thomas Nashe complained he had only to mention bread to be taken as referring to Breden in the Netherlands.[34]

At the same time, there was dearth, unrest, and xenophobia at home. Early in the decade, the name of Marlowe was swept into the ferment of wartime propaganda through the "Dutch Church Libel" of 1593. That document, affixed to the Dutch Church in London, threatened a massacre of resident foreigners on the grounds that they undermined English prosperity through unscrupulous trading practices while allowing the English to fight in their stead on the Continent: "*Per.* Tamberlaine," according to the libel, the English were whetting their swords to "shedd" the blood of such "Machiavellian Marchant" strangers.[35] Marlowe himself was not the author of the libel; rather, another individual or group chose to interpret the warmongering, xenophobic mood of the English in terms of the violence of Tamburlaine the Great – military commander, rapist, virgin murderer, and infidel. Marlowe was briefly questioned by the Privy Council in connection with the libel, then released, only to die mysteriously by violence ten days later.

If contemporaries were so ready to associate Marlowe's exotic *Tamberlaine* with their own time and circumstances, it is easy to see what they could have made of *Faustus*. Both the A and the B quartos of the play make repeated references to the wars in the Low Countries – to pirate raids like Drake's against King Philip of Spain and his well-stuffed treasury, to the Duke of Parma and the "fiery keele at *Antwerpe* bridge" sent against Parma's blockade of Antwerp in 1585. In both texts, Faustus vows to take on the admirably Protestant objective of ejecting the Spaniards from the Low Countries: "chase the Prince of *Parma* from our Land" (A 125–28, cited from B 120–23).[36]

For audiences in the early and mid-1590s Faustus's vow would have placed the play's action in the very recent past: the Duke of Parma died in 1592. But only the "Wertenberg" A text also places Faustus within an environment of "Genevan" Protestantism like that which dominated the English war party during the 1580s and 1590s. Like England, Württemberg during the 1590s was an embattled outpost of Protestantism threatened by the forces of international Catholicism. In political terms, therefore, an English theatrical audience of a *Faustus* resembling the "Wertenberg" A text was invited to identify Faustus's goals with mainstream militarism of the 1590s. But what was such an audience to make of his necromancy, his blasphemy against the very religious ideology by which they defined their alliance with independent Protestant powers like Württemberg? In religious terms, Faustus was the demonic antagonist of all that England was fighting for, undermining the "true Church" from within; the fact that his anti-Spanish sentiment turns out to cover vast ambition for his own political aggrandizement tarnishes by contagion the motives of the English Protestant enterprise.

In the A text (and only in A), Faustus vows to use his magic to destroy a form of religion that would have registered with contemporary audiences as distinctively Protestant. The A text uses "low church" terms like *parson* and *minister* to refer to local clerics; the references do not exist in B. Rafe rebukes Robin, "Our maister Parson says" conjuring is "nothing" (A 975); Faustus promises blasphemously, only in the A text, "neuer to looke to heauen, / Neuer to name God, or to pray to him, / To burne his Scriptures, slay his Ministers, / And make my spirites pull his churches downe." (A 725–28).[37] The A text, by immersing the blaspheming necromancer in a distinctly Protestant environment of "war fever," creates – or exposes – a dangerous fissure in the ideology of the war party itself. Faustus both reflects and hideously violates the militant nationalist sentiment that dominated English audiences during the 1590s.

The "Wittenberg" B text gives Faustus a markedly different political orientation: the doctrine of the Old Man's speech and the added comic episodes at the Papal court combine to transform the magician from a figure identified with the cause of independent Protestantism into a figure whose religious milieu is no longer distinctively Protestant at all, and who makes himself a willing ally of the Hapsburgs. In B, Faustus is still anti-papal, but has become pro-imperial. In both the A and B texts, Faustus attends upon Emperor Charles V, but only in B does his relationship with Charles have an impact on the fortunes of the empire. Editors who prefer the A quarto over B tend to dismiss Faustus's extended activities in Rome in the B text as "low" and meaningless clowning; they overlook the fact that Faustus, by engineering the escape of Bruno, the imperial candidate for pope, foils the Roman pope's attempt to assert his authority over Charles and therefore tips the international balance of power away from the See of Rome and toward the Holy Roman Empire.

In the A text, Faustus's visit to the court of "*Carolus* the fift" is a display of necromancy. At the emperor's request, he conjures up the spirits of Alexander and his paramour, but this feat has no particular political ramifications, and he performs similar feats of magic for Protestant princes like the Duke of Vanholt. In B, by contrast, Faustus's visit to the court of Charles carries with it a distinct political agenda. The visit follows his intervention to free the imperial candidate for the papacy (episodes which do not exist in A). When Faustus comes into Charles V's presence in the B version, the emperor immediately rewards him for having set Bruno free by promising him that he will be ever "belou'd of *Carolus.*" The magician replies with extravagant vows of fealty:

> These gracious words, most royall *Carolus,*
> Shall make poore *Faustus* to his vtmost power,
> Both loue and serue the Germane Emperour,
> And lay his life at holy *Bruno's* feet.
>
> (B 1250–53)

Not to be outdone in the exchange of honors, Faustus offers to present Charles with whatever wonders his magic can perform: the vision of Alexander and his paramour in the B text is no mere feat of necromancy, as it is in A, but acts to seal a significant political alliance. At the end of the scene, Charles invests Faustus with command over all of Germany. In terms both of its political alignment *and* of its more conservative religious doctrine, the B text can be called anti-papal only if the pope in question is assumed to be the Pope of Rome, rather than the Pope favored by the Holy Roman Emperor. B's political agenda brings it very close to imperial Catholicism.

Why the move from "Wertenberg" to "Wittenberg," from a *Faustus* associated with religio-political autonomy and radical Protestantism to a *Faustus* associated with greater religious conservatism and complicity with empire? Our answer will be, of course, highly speculative, and only as convincing as the conclusions about the chronological relationship between A and B upon which this discussion is based. The simplest response would be that audiences had tired of the play in its familiar form, and could, with luck, regain interest if the play took on a new set of targets. Nevertheless, in several important ways, the shift in ideological milieu can be correlated with political and religious developments in England. By the turn of the seventeenth century, particularly after the Earl of Essex's fall from favor in 1598, the Protestant warmongering of the mid-1590s was losing some of its popularity in England, or at least becoming less vocal. England had officially disengaged from her adventures on the Continent and withdrawn government-sponsored troops. In France, Henry IV had converted to Catholicism; he made peace with Spain in 1598. In the Low Countries, there was still an English presence on the battlefield, but only in the form of mercenaries who could be found fighting on either side of the conflict.[38] English withdrawal from the Continent brought with it a blurring of religious allegiances which had earlier seemed relatively clear. The national hope of intervening to save the beleagured remaining outposts of independent Protantism had moved from the center of English political life to the margins.

What is more, the "hotter sort of Protestants" who had pushed hardest for England's involvement on the Continent were more and more abandoning the theaters. As David Bevington and others have noted, around the turn of the century there was a noticeable retreat on the part of ultra-Protestants from the playgoing public (Bevington pp. 25, 294–95; see n. 33 below). They might patronize individual plays satirizing the government's pro-Spanish policy, as in Middleton's *A Game at Chess* later on, but many of them after 1600 were numbered among the enemies of the stage; to attempt a dramatic production that centered on their ideological presuppositions may have become increasingly risky as a commercial venture. And in any case, after 1604, the A version of the play was available in print for the continuing ravishment of the reading public. The B version of *Faustus* eliminates the material that associates Faustus most strongly with zealous Protestantism and moves the arena of transgression from militant Protestantism to empire. In the B version of *Faustus*, the "Marlowe effect" is generated not so much through the play's evocation of the wars in the Low Countries (though references to that conflict remain) as through its unsettling parallels between the activities of the magician and England's growing friendship with the Holy Roman Empire.

In terms of early Tudor political thinking, Faustus's intervention to save the emperor from domination by the pope would have been an admirably "Protestant" gesture. In the *Book of Martyrs*, for example, from which the B text's imperial episodes may have been derived, the triumph of the empire over the papacy is consistently associated with proto-Protestant sentiment and the ideal of national religious self-determination; the figure of Charles V carried much the same significance in other early Elizabethan propaganda.[39] By the end of the 1590s and the beginning of the seventeenth century, however, the idealization of empire had become anathema to most radical Protestants – it was associated instead with a more conservative, conciliatory "Anglican" strain in religious and political opinion that was gaining dominance in England as the war threat subsided.

During the late 1590s, it actually seemed possible to many in England that the nation could revert to Catholicism. Militant Protestants were scattered and demoralized. The queen was aging without having named a successor; Catholics at home and abroad were arguing that the English throne should be claimed by one of the Hapsburgs. In 1596 Irish rebels had invited Archduke Albert of the Austrian Netherlands, the brother of the Holy Roman Emperor, to become their king; during the uprising of 1601, Irish rebels were known to be in contact with Spain and the Hapsburg Archdukes. At the end of Elizabeth's reign, Archduke Albert himself was making repeated overtures of peace. Elizabeth did not sign a treaty but she did offer encouragement, to the discomfiture of many in England who profoundly distrusted the Hapsburgs and regarded their overtures as deeply disingenuous.[40] In 1602, when *Doctor Faustus* was revised in a more imperial mode, peace with the Empire was a more tangible possibility than it had been for decades before.

The revisers of *Doctor Faustus* appear to have had either considerable luck in their imperial reworking of the play, or a canny sense of which way the national winds were blowing. In 1603, only slightly after the play was rewritten in an "imperial" mode, James I ascended the English throne. He was to all appearances a Protestant, but he immediately reversed the Elizabethan policy of hostility toward Spain and the Empire by declaring a cease-fire and showing other signs of cordiality. There was speculation abroad and at home at the beginning of his reign that the king might revert to the Catholicism of his mother, Mary Queen of Scots. Although he made conciliatory gestures toward the Puritans as well, James I openly advocated toleration for the Catholics and declared the Catholic Church to be England's "Mother Church" though defiled.[41] James associated himself far more overtly with Imperial ideology than Elizabeth had. In 1604, he actually signed a formal treaty of peace with the Holy Roman Empire and Spain, despite the furious opposition and visible dismay of much of the English public.[42] In the B text of *Faustus* after 1602, as in the A text during the 1590s, Faustus acts ostensibly in parallel with English policy: he cements an alliance with empire as Elizabeth had showed signs of interest in doing at the very end of her reign, as James I actually did at the beginning of his. But the fact that the goal is pursued by demonic means massively undercuts the "official" ideology of the play.

With the passage of time, the B text's resonances with Jacobean imperial ideology would have increased rather than diminished. England did not turn Catholic, but as the reign of James continued, particularly after the Hampton Court Conference of 1604, the Stuart ideology of empire came to be increasingly associated with controversial domestic policies: with the king's attempts to create his own empire of "Great Britain" by royal fiat, his efforts to impose Roman law on the nation and ceremonial worship on the English Church, eventually also with his assertion of royal prerogative powers to the detriment of common law and parliament.[43] A 1609 reference to *Doctor Faustus* in performance describes the actor Edward "Allen playing Faustus" dressed in a "surplis / With a crosse upon his breast."[44] The reference, if trustworthy, suggests the fascinating possibility that in the early seventeenth century at least, Faustus on stage looked very much like an Anglican priest – attired in the proper canonical vestments and displaying the cross which was anathema to Puritan elements within the church. The title-page illustration on the printed text of the 1616 version does not show Faustus in ecclesiastical garb, but there are good reasons why a printer might not have wanted to recapture that degree of transgression in a woodcut. Interpreted in terms of tensions within England over the growth of Jacobean imperial ideology, the B text of *Doctor Faustus* is not the tame and frivolous thing that those who favor the A text regularly take B to be. Instead, its placement of the magician within a ceremonial context dangerously like England's own official style of worship would have been provocative in the extreme.

In the B text, there is no clear line of distinction between the acts of conjuring performed by the Doctor of Wittenberg and the play's other ritual and doctrinal forms. In B, and only in B, there is a strong potential for contamination between the black arts of the magician, the elaborate "magic" of the stagecraft of the play, the "magic" of outward, ceremonial worship which B presents as normative, and the doctrine of works preached by the Old Man in B. The "Wittenberg" version of *Doctor Faustus* sets in motion a whole series of potential associations between the ritualism and illusionism of the play and similar forms which were gaining favor in the Jacobean world outside it – Anglican liturgical worship, Arminian doctrine, Jacobean state rituals, even, over time, the "magic" of the Jacobean court masque. In the B version of *Faustus*, the demonism of the Doctor of Wittenberg eats away at the authority of all such forms; the fact that the play is cast in the ostensibly Protestant setting of Wittenberg makes its potential for transgression against English orthodoxies of state much stronger than it would have been if the setting had been unequivocally Catholic. In the B text of *Faustus*, the "Marlowe effect" would be every bit as intense as it had been in A, but the locus of its dangerous "ravishment" shifted from the arena of English adventurism abroad to the encroachment of "popery" and empire at home. *Faustus* B replays the eerie theme of heroic/demonic transgression to an imperial tune.

In 1663, yet a third version of *Doctor Faustus* was printed in quarto. Like the 1616 version, this text shows a consistent pattern of alteration designed to retool the play for a new theatrical and reading audience. The title page displayed a recut version of the familiar picture of Faustus from 1616 and later editions, but assured the public that they were being given the play in its most up-to-date form: "Printed with New Additions as it is now Acted. With several New Scenes, Together with the Actors Names."[45] This is the first quarto edition of the play to use Roman type rather than black letter. If, as I have speculated, the use of black letter had, for earlier readers, given the playtext a slight aura of the ecclesiastical, then that association was lost in the 1663 version of the play. In this version, which is obviously and uncontestably non-Marlovian, theological materials are almost totally excised, at least insofar as they refer to the spiritual condition of Faustus. The word "damned" is systematically replaced by "lost." Faustus's "soul" becomes his "spirit." Nearly all the references to divine wrath are removed from the 1663 text, as are some of Faustus's most horrific blasphemies, like his vow to build an altar and sacrifice the blood of new-born babes to Beelzebub (A 450–51, B 400–01). Some of the tavern scenes are also significantly altered, but by far the most spectacular emendation is that the scenes depicting Faustus's visit to the court of Rome are replaced by a visit to the court of Salomaine (evidently Solyman the Magnificent) in Babylon (Bagdad).

In offering the Ottomite scene, the 1663 *Doctor Faustus* ingeniously makes good on a hint in the B text: after his visit to Rome, according to Mephistopheles, Faustus visited "the great Turkes Court," but that visit was not staged in the B version (B 1180). Similarly, in the A text Mephistopheles had promised a visit to "holy *Peters* feast," but the visit was staged only in B (A 819). Historically, the Ottoman emperor had failed to take the island of Malta after a prolonged and bloody siege in 1565. But in the 1663 *Doctor Faustus*, the siege has succeeded. Salomaine calls for a feast of rejoicing in honor of his victory over the Maltese, in which he has been materially aided by Mephistopheles. Salomaine's general Mustapha, who has orchestrated the victory, regales him with an account of how Malta's formidable defenses had been breached. Turkish forces had found a Jew lying insensible near the walls; as a way of revenging himself upon the Maltese for their previous mistreatment of him, the Jew (much like Marlowe's Barabas, Jew of Malta) led the Turkish forces through a vault under the fortifications and into the very center of the town, which then yielded with little resistance. Evidently Mephistopheles aided the Turks against the Christians by working through the Jew. Having heard the gratifying story of his victory over the Maltese, Salomaine calls for his Empress and favorite wife to be brought him from the seraglio so that he can celebrate properly. Faustus, who has been made invisible, kisses her, drinks her wine, and generally confounds those in attendance. When Salomaine calls for his own conjurer to get to the bottom of the tricks, Mephistopheles reassures Faustus that he will take Faustus's part against the Ottomite magician. In one of the most interesting moments of the scene, Faustus responds with astonishment that the devil would act against any man who stood within the protection of a magic circle. Mephistopheles explains that all magic charms are "very fables, forg'd at first / In hell, and thrust on credulous mortals / To deceive'm" ([D3]v).

In this very late version of the play, the "Marlowe effect" has been relocated yet again. Some editors have speculated that the systematic removal of theological matters was an attempt to answer censorship, but it seems to me far more likely that the revisers attenuated elements of Faustus's predicament that might arouse doctrinal disputes like those that had been endemic during the Civil War and Interregnum. After the Restoration, hell was "in decline" among preachers and theologians;[46] moreover, after so many years of religious conflict, there was a concerted effort on the part of government to smooth over past religious differences and reincorporate moderate dissenters within the church. If the tastes represented in Restoration drama are a reliable reflection of the interests of the theater-going public, audiences had tired by then of overtly theological materials, or at least increasingly found them inappropriate for the stage. By attenuating the religious materials and relocating the comic scenes from Rome to Babylon, the revisers of *Faustus* replaced the worn-out subject of strife within Christendom with the more anxiety-fraught topic of strife against a common pagan enemy.

The power of the Ottoman Turks was very much feared in the years after 1660. They had in fact taken over Babylon (Baghdad) only in 1638 (not before the Siege of Malta, as in the 1663 *Faustus*), and had fought the Maltese and Venetians throughout the Mediterranean for several decades. In the minds of the English in the early 1660s, there may well have been renewed fear of a Turkish victory over Malta, which would make the Mediterranean a sea dominated by the Infidel. The 1663 *Faustus* enacts that nightmare of pagan domination. Although England was officially at peace with the Turks, there had been recent skirmishes between Turkish pirates and English merchant vessels and England had been forced to renegotiate its articles of peace.[47] Many in London may have both hungered for and feared the prospect of war with the Turks when the play was staged in 1662.

By evacuating much of the power of the demons and many of the near-blasphemous religious materials, the revisers of the Restoration *Doctor Faustus* lost a large part of the "Marlowe effect" as it had existed in earlier versions of the play. To the extent that they kept the "Marlowe effect" alive, they did so by following the play's time-honored pattern of contamination by association: by suggesting titillating and clandestine parallels between the ideology of an alien power and some aspect of English officialdom, in this case the court of Charles II. The opulence and indolence of the Ottoman Emperor, his sexual infatuation with his Empress and a whole seraglio of other surrogate wives – these traits of Salomaine would have called up uneasy parallels with the dissipations of Charles II, and the perception of likeness could easily have spread into questions about the king's conduct of foreign affairs or his relations with the English Jewish community. But Faustus does not ally himself with Salomaine: by confounding the Turkish court and its magicians, he works in a small way against the Infidel.

The 1663 *Faustus* appears not to have been successful on stage. Samuel Pepys saw a *Doctor Faustus* in 1662 that was probably close to the 1663 quarto version and pronounced it "so wretchedly & poorly done that we were sick of it."[48] Did he object to the acting or to the script? By its publication a year later, the play may already have worn out its welcome with theatrical audiences, despite its title-page promise that it was delivering the text as "now Acted." The form of Faustus's fortunes in the 1663 quarto demonstrates the continuing instability of Marlowe's work over time, and suggests basic similarities between the project of revision as undertaken in 1602 and the less successful Restoration revisions. Nearly seventy years after the death of the "poet and filthy play-maker," there were writers for the stage who were interested in keeping the "Marlowe effect" alive. That they appear not to have succeeded is considerably less interesting than that they made the attempt at all.

MARLOWE AS "AUTHOR"

In arguing that the quartos of *Faustus* offer distinctive patterns of signification that can be correlated with specific phases of English religious and
political history, I may appear by this late point in the discussion to have
made unfair use of the very editorial methods it was my ostensible purpose
to question: I have trusted known "facts" about the performance and printing of the play; I have relied on a holistic style of interpretation that may
appear suspiciously New Critical in its method. Part of my goal has been
to demonstrate that many of the tools of traditional editorial practice still
have great utility, so long as we recognize their limitations. We need to be
able to argue for elements of consistency within given texts for at least
two major reasons: first, in order to rehabilitate them to the point that
scholars will regularly admit them into discussion; and second, in order to
make a convincing case for ideologically significant variations between
them. And, moving to another level of analysis, we need to be able to
identify differences between texts in order to arrive at historically specific
différance – the simultaneous exaltation and undermining of official
ideology that generates the "Marlowe effect." I have collected historical
data in order to demonstrate that both the 1604 and the 1616 texts of
Doctor Faustus have the kind of coherence we usually associate with the
idea of a single "original" and with the positing of authorial intent.
Acting on the assumption that elements of patterning can indeed be
found in seeming "accidentals" and that historical research can help us to
explicate them, I have shown, in a markedly traditionalist manner,
how each of the two early quartos of *Doctor Faustus* can be "redeemed"
from an appearance of textual disfigurement and corruption. But my
argument has not always favored consistency and self-sameness above
difference and variability. To show such a preference without questioning
its implications for interpretation would be to reenter the very labyrinth
of vanishing authorial "originals" I have been at pains to work Marlowe
out of. Instead, I have tried to open up the texts to a process of "unediting"
that will allow for the perception of elements of consistency *and* for a
recognition of difference.

To the extent that it resuscitates notions of authorship and intentionality,
my discussion reintroduces ideas that are usually anathema to post-
structuralist interpretation. But my reading invests the "author function"
with a potential for dynamism and profligacy which it does not have in
the Foucaultian paradigm or in the usual assumptions that guide editorial
practice. To call a play "Marlowe" in the late sixteenth or early seventeenth
century was not at all to associate it with rationality, economy, stability:
indeed, in both the 1604 and the 1616 texts of the play, Faustus's desire
to "Resolue me of all ambiguities" is tinged with the demonic (A 112, B 107).
My argument also reassigns the "author function" from Marlowe to the

dramatic company that owned *Doctor Faustus* and refurbished it – perhaps more times than we are aware of – to keep the play sounding like Marlowe.

Faustus was by no means the only play over which Henslowe and his men assumed "authorship" – another example would be *The Spanish Tragedy*, revised by Ben Jonson in a markedly un-Jonsonian style.[49] No doubt there were other cases as well and in companies besides Henslowe's; in fact, we have reason to suppose that for plays successful enough to warrant the effort and expense, such alteration was less the exception than the rule. Shakespeare scholars are beginning to admit the possibility that Shakespeare, too, could have been successfully revised by other players or dramatists with the ability to sound uncannily like Shakespeare.[50] We shall take up some of those possible instances in subsequent chapters. It is unlikely, however, that for most Renaissance plays, even those billed as Shakespeare, the name of the author carried anything like the sensationalist allure of "Marlowe."

In terms of larger patterns of relationship between textual variability and ideological difference, my focus here on Marlowe has created a deceptive emphasis on dramatic authorship. Unlike most Elizabethan playwrights, Marlowe as a historical figure was relatively well known to the public for his alleged atheism, his reputed contempt for the authority of church and state, the enigmatic strangeness of his violent death. Well into the seventeenth century, we can find frequent printed references to Marlowe's dangerous beliefs: he was "a Poet of scurrilitie, who by giving too large a swinge to his owne wit, and suffering his lust to have the full raines, fell (not without just desert) to that outrage and extremitie, that hee denied God and his sonne Christ."[51] Over time, Marlowe's lurid reputation, which so uncannily replicated the flamboyant excesses of his dramatic heroes, wound itself into the "Marlowe effect" produced by his plays on stage.[52] For readers of the early quartos, a similar association was produced on the printed page. As we have already noted, all of the early quartos end in the mysterious line "*Terminat hora diem, Terminat Author opus*," as though to suggest a connection between Marlowe's authorship of the play, terminated at midnight, and the life of the magician – as though to intimate that the very authoring of such a play might carry with it a penalty like that of Faustus himself. At a time when the authorship of most plays was a matter of considerable indifference to actors, public, and often to the playwrights themselves, there were compelling reasons why an "author function" specifically associated with Marlowe would continue to be institutionally produced long after the death of the "poet and filthy play-maker."

I have argued here that we can learn something about the vagaries of Renaissance authorship and mark out new areas for interpretation if we wean ourselves from the ingrained habit of regarding textual "accidentals" as insignificant. To commit ourselves to such a project, however, we need to reckon with its unsettling implications. In the case of *Doctor Faustus* we are confronted with the likelihood that all extant texts are "impure" composites. We are confronted as well with the perverse, interesting possibility that significant segments of *Doctor Faustus* actually composed by Marlowe may have been cheerfully expunged from the play at various times in order to give it a continuing aura of authorial authenticity.

3

PURITY AND DANGER IN THE MODERN EDITION

The Merry Wives of Windsor

> Was will das Weib?
> Sigmund Freud

The Merry Wives of Windsor has always held a curious status among Shakespeareans. It is Shakespeare's only "English comedy," almost entirely in prose and centering on small-town life as opposed to the more momentous business of marriage or war among aristocrats. Yet it is the Shakespearean comedy most closely associated with a court through the persistent anecdote (first promulgated in the early eighteenth century) that its author wrote it in two weeks or less to satisfy Queen Elizabeth I's desire to see Falstaff in love. Since the early eighteenth century, the anecdote has taken root – witness its concretization in David Scott's striking but historically inaccurate 1840 painting *Queen Elizabeth Viewing the Performance of the 'Merry Wives of Windsor' in the* Globe *Theatre*;[1] witness likewise the fact that most editors of the play have not only accepted the anecdote but embroidered upon it, despite its shaky historical basis.

Within *The Merry Wives of Windsor*, there is additional material linking the play to the court through the elaborate references to Windsor Castle, the Order of the Garter, and a "radiant" Fairy Queen who "hates Sluts, and Sluttery" (F TLN 2528). The dominant editorial view at present is that the play was in some way connected with the Garter ceremonies of 1597, at which Shakespeare's patron Lord Hunsdon was installed in the order; indeed, Shakespeare himself, along with other members of the Lord Chamberlain's Men, may well have served among the spectacular retinue of three hundred gentlemen and men expected to attend Hunsdon at Windsor.[2] If *Merry Wives* was in some way connected with the Garter events of 1597, the most likely date for its performance, editors agree, was St George's Day, April 23, 1597, at the Feast of the Garter before the queen at Westminster.

Not the least part of this play's attraction and vexation for critics is that, like *Doctor Faustus*, it exists in two widely divergent early texts. A quarto version was published in 1602 under the engaging title *A Most pleasaunt and excellent conceited Comedie, of Syr* Iohn Falstaffe, *and the merrie Wiues of* Windsor. *Entermixed with sundrie variable and pleasing humors, of Syr* Hugh *the Welch Knight, Iustice* Shallow, *and his wise Cousin M.* Slender. *With the swaggering vaine of Auncient* Pistoll, *and Corporall* Nym. Could the lively language of this page, with its promise of "variable and pleasing" merriment, have been borrowed from broadside playbills advertising the play in performance? The author is identified just below the title, almost as though he too were part of the amiable gallery of rogues and characters, as *William Shakespeare*. This version of the play was reprinted in 1619, but was thereafter superseded in seventeenth-century printings by the 1623 First Folio version, entitled simply *The Merry Wiues of Windsor*. When a third quarto version was published as "newly corrected" in 1630, it offered the folio rather than the quarto text, although it was the quarto that the publisher had license to print. For copyright purposes, the two quarto versions of the text were regarded as one and the same.[3]

Given the recently improved fortunes of the first quarto version of *Doctor Faustus*, as discussed in the preceding chapter, we might suppose that Q1 *Merry Wives* has undergone a similar revival and rehabilitation in editions of the play. We would be wrong, although there are glimmers that such a movement may be just over the horizon. The transvaluation of "bad" Shakespeare quartos is proceeding more slowly than for the similarly "bad" A text of *Doctor Faustus*: it seems that we as a culture demand far greater perfection of Shakespeare than we do of Marlowe. And, as most Shakespearean editors are still agreed, Q1 *Merry Wives* is one of the worst of the "bad" quartos. Among its perceived shortcomings is the fact that it "lacks" the courtly associations that elevate its folio counterpart above the mundane, small-town concerns that otherwise dominate the play. The 1602 quarto advertises itself on the title page as having been performed "diuers times" both "before her Maiestie, and else-where," but that is one of the very few courtly references in this version of the play – nearly all the mentions of Windsor Castle and the Order of the Garter, as well as the allusions to the "radiant Queene" and her abhorrence of sluttery, are "missing" from the 1602 quarto text. As I shall argue later on, this play, like *Doctor Faustus*, shows evidence that the action has been systematically relocated from one printed version to the next, though the alteration in place is less clear-cut than that from Württemberg to Wittenberg. The degree to which we are able to perceive *Merry Wives* as bearing the impress of a Garter Feast or some other royal occasion will depend to a significant degree on whether we are talking about Q or F.

Like the A text of *Faustus*, the first quarto of *Merry Wives* is much shorter than the alternative text, indeed drastically shorter – 1620 lines in the Bankside parallel-text edition as opposed to 2729 according to the Norton Through Line Numbering of the folio.[4] It "lacks" a few of the folio scenes – like William's Latin lesson (4.1) – and "truncates" many others. The fortunes of the 1602 quarto have closely followed the Shakespearean paradigm shift I outlined in the introduction and that we have seen operating in *Doctor Faustus*. Alexander Pope made use of the 1619 quarto of *Merry Wives* for his edition of Shakespeare and considered it Shakespeare's "first imperfect sketch" of the play. Lewis Theobald was the first to call the public's attention to the 1602 quarto; he and subsequent editors until the late nineteenth century generally agreed that it was Shakespeare's earliest version of the play. Since P. A. Daniel's introduction to an 1888 facsimile edition of the 1602 *Merry Wives* and Greg's influential 1910 edition of the same text, which argued for Q as a "memorial reconstruction" pirated by ignorant and semi-literate actors, scholarly opinion has veered around to the still dominant view that the folio was Shakespeare's "original" or at least very close to it, while the 1602 quarto was a later and corrupt version of the play.[5] There has been disagreement about whether Q is a simple memorial reconstruction, a reconstruction of an abridged stage version, or perhaps even, as Alfred Pollard and John Dover Wilson contended briefly around 1920 before they were won over to Greg's more dominant view, Shakespeare's embroidery upon a lost original by another author.

Pollard and Wilson's conjecture was in some ways a throwback to the nineteenth-century "evolutionary" paradigm of the author. A similar case had been made in a 1917 Shakespeare Association address by the famous (and infamous) "Disintegrator" of Shakespeare, J. M. Robertson.[6] But their view did not gain wide acceptance: it was at odds with the postwar need to consolidate and settle the Shakespearean canon. Indeed, E. K. Chambers' influential 1924 British Academy address on the "Disintegration of Shakespeare" was aimed squarely against Robertson and Wilson's efforts to save Shakespeare from material beneath his genius by attributing inferior patches of his plays to the contaminating hands of others. Since Chambers, a few hardy souls have defended the 1602 *Merry Wives* as an authorized revision rather than a piracy. But the dominant view by far has been Greg's. As a piracy of some kind, the quarto *Merry Wives* has been damned with all the usual terms of opprobrium – "illegitimate," "filched," "wretched," "mere patchwork."[7]

Part of our attention here will be devoted to a rehabilitation of the first quarto *Merry Wives*. I shall argue, in accordance with a very recent surge of critical sentiment in its favor, that this version needs to be considered as distinct from the folio rather than a mere corruption of it, and vastly different in terms of its dramatic patterning and ideological functioning.[8] Indeed, I shall argue for a significant connection between the extraordinary degree of critical contempt for the play in this version and its "lack" of the Windsor and Garter materials that elevate its folio counterpart. A large part of the appeal of *Merry Wives*, at least in the late nineteenth and twentieth centuries, has been its evocation of the "Myth of Merry England": a timeless vision of court and countryside in harmonious alliance, of simple rural folk and their superiors, nay even the queen herself, as working reciprocally for mutual prosperity and betterment. In the quarto *Merry Wives*, the top of Merry England's social pyramid is missing. The court all but vanishes as a source of benevolence; indeed it vanishes almost entirely except insofar as it is evoked in speeches by that fat and larcenous liar, Sir John Falstaff – hardly the best possible ambassador of goodwill from the court to the townspeople. Worse yet, many of the anti-commercial sentiments editors have lauded in the folio are far more visible in the despised quarto version, so that if the quarto is taken seriously, it can be used to expose elements of falsity in the much-touted benevolence of the folio. As we have seen, the quarto's crowded and elaborate title is considerably merrier than the simple heading of the folio version; as we shall observe later on, the conclusion of Q is also merrier than that of F. Small wonder that the quarto *Merry Wives* has caused much editorial unease, and that so much twentieth-century editorial energy has gone toward suppressing it as an independent source of meaning.

In this chapter our attention will be devoted as much to the mechanisms by which the "bad" text has been kept down as to arguments for its rehabilitation. Modern Shakespearean editions vary greatly among themselves, but they tend to impose a strict separation between the discussion of textual problems and matters of "interpretation" so that readers can feel free to undertake the latter activity in tranquil indifference to the turbulence and uncertainty created by the former. The dark shadow of Smedley Force still hangs over modern editions of *The Merry Wives of Windsor* in that the clearing away of bibliographical questions is assumed to be a necessary antiseptic precondition for reading. In John Sutherland's amusing language, "the literary work is [made] ready, like a prepped patient, for the separate operations of the literary critic."[9]

Despite many decades of research and speculation, we do not have strong external evidence (like that provided by Henslowe's record of payment for revisions of *Doctor Faustus*) that allows us to establish the date of revision for either version of *Merry Wives* with any degree of probability. Even the date of the play is up in the air at present – on the basis of slippery topical evidence, some analysts date it as early as 1592 and others as late as 1601.[10] For *The Merry Wives of Windsor*, as for *Doctor Faustus*, we have no reliable "original." We have only two mutually-dependent versions, both obviously revised and transcribed, probably more than once; both displaying obvious flaws and marked elements of haste and incoherence. And yet in modern editions, through the cleansing procedures of the editor, one is made error-free while the other is discarded as refuse. Because of the inconsistencies in both early printed texts, the process by which one is exalted and the other debased is a strenuous procedure indeed. Much, it would seem, is at stake in maintaining the essential probity of the preferred folio text of *The Merry Wives of Windsor*.

71

THE EDITOR AND THE PIRATE

On the average page of the usual multi-volume Shakespearean edition, the playtext is separated from the historical and explanatory notes by what Thomas L. Berger has amusingly termed the "band of terror" and Lewis Mumford and Edmund Wilson had earlier derided as "barbed wire" – a bristling hedge of textual notes that are incomprehensible to the average reader and therefore serve as a forbidding barrier between the "text itself" above the band of terror and culturally variable questions of meaning taken up in the historical notes beneath the barrier.[11] Why aren't the two kinds of notes integrated into a single set of annotations explicating textual differences along with other historical questions? Most editors would contend for clarity and expedience as the motivating force behind the standard format, but there is also a powerful rhetoric attached to it. Over the "band of terror," the text has a seeming serenity and permanence; it is both literally and figuratively above the textual notes and historical materials discussed at the bottom of the page. The illusion thereby created, even if only subtly, is that bibliography and critical interpretation are divided realms – the text as "literature" is essentially separable from the multiform messiness of textual history.

The front matter of the average multi-volume edition is often arranged similarly: the editor's discussion of his or her (but still overwhelmingly his) choice of copytext from among potentially competing early quarto and folio versions is cast in dauntingly technical language, and placed either first or last in the introduction, where it is carefully set apart from the sections taking up interpretation of the play. The effect is, yet once more, to establish strict boundaries between history, text, and interpretation – as though the various components of the editor's task were not profoundly mutually dependent. We who are interested in textual matters routinely (even eagerly) read the textual section of the introduction, but most readers – even our graduate students who should know better – do not. The discussion of copytext serves for most readers as what I shall call a "zone of terror," the editorial equivalent of a fire lane, cutting the text itself off from the potentially damaging inroads of historical investigation that go before it in the (usually elaborate) introduction.

What the traditional arrangement of the modern Shakespearean edition has meant for *The Merry Wives of Windsor* and other plays with "bad" quartos is that the quarto version is brought to life only fleetingly and partially within the "zone of terror," where it is usually barred from inter-pretation. As nearly every editor has readily admitted, the first quarto of *Merry Wives* offers readings that are essential for the interpretation of the folio version of the play. The quarto version is too important to be ignored. But the "poor little debased Quarto" is allowed to enter the edition, in the vivid language of the first Arden editor, only "upon sufferance" and provided that it is carefully "fenced in" from the text it might otherwise contaminate.[12]

The standard format for multi-volume editions can readily be interpreted in terms of the New Bibliography's goal of creating an "ideal" text – a text freed from playhouse and printinghouse accretions that were not part of the author's original intention, a text approximating the "work" in Tanselle's sense of the term. But the yearning for order behind this traditional editorial practice goes much deeper than mere bibliographical convention. It has proven to be a powerful system for handling Shakespeare because, I would contend, it taps into a deep and pervasive human need to define and uphold the boundaries between order and chaos, between the clean and the unclean. The greater the degree to which we perceive the name of Shakespeare as intimately bound up with civilization and civility, however we may wish to define them, the greater will be our need to separate the acceptably Shakespearean text from that which cannot be tolerated as Shakespearean.

In *Purity and Danger: An Analysis of the Concepts of Pollution and Taboo* Mary Douglas has called attention to the pervasiveness of rituals by which not only non-Western cultures, but also our own, generate a sense of order through the banishment of disorder or "dirt."[13] The Bengali Brahmin's food, grown and harvested by people of inferior caste, must be passed through an elaborate series of preparations before it can be consumed. The Dinka put their aged spearmen to death through ritual suffocation rather than allow these particularly valued members of the society to perish in a manner outside the control of the group. In a more muted but essentially similar way, our own culture has rules about the proper placement of things that assert our hierarchical valuation of them: old tennis shoes are not to be placed on the dining table; a back hallway full of garden tools and equipped with a makeshift toilet does not thereby become an acceptable bathroom, but remains unstable and therefore disquieting in terms of definition; food that falls on even the most sparkling floor must be discarded, and so forth. Much of the interest of Douglas's discussion arises from her refusal to see these matters of ritual purification only in terms of hygiene – a modern rubric under which we perform daily activities of cultural classification and subordination that have existed since long before the advent of Lister and Pasteur. Instead, Douglas insists, we need to consider the culture-making function of such rituals. There is no such thing as pure dirt or refuse; the ways in which we define and separate "dirt" from non-dirt are a key to our systems of order and meaning.

We may rebel against the sometimes relentless structuralism of Douglas's mode of analysis, but it offers a useful way of understanding curious features of the discussion of copytext in the modern Shakespearean edition. Although some of the characteristics of danger and dirt-avoidance ritual can be found in editions of plays for which there is only a single early text, the ritual exists in its most exfoliated and interesting form for plays with a "bad" quarto lurking somewhere in their past. Textual discussions of such plays invariably begin on a note of cool objectivity – just what one might expect from an inquiry into scientific bibliography – but that tone is quickly abandoned for a surprisingly vehement language of vilification. It is a pattern encountered by anyone reading the front-matter of a standard edition of one of Shakespeare's multi-text plays, but not, perhaps, quite as strange in our perceptions as it should be. What parallel structural elements can we find between non-Western rituals of aversion and purification and the Shakespearean editor's negotiation of the perilous passage from a hypothesized authorial original, through polluting institutions like the playhouse and printinghouse, to the single, "good" and reliable text generated in most modern editions?

For purposes of illustration, I shall concentrate on the most recent edition of *The Merry Wives of Windsor*, T. W. Craik's 1989 Oxford Clarendon edition, with apologies in advance to Dr Craik for singling out his work as representative of the common pattern. In terms of its treatment of the "bad" quarto, Craik's edition is, in fact, unusual for its irenicism – possibly a sign of changing textual *mores*, but more probably an indication that in his view, Q *Merry Wives* has been too effectively vanquished by past editors to require the same degree of vehemence on his part. Craik's edition represents the culmination of a twentieth-century trend by which the quarto version has gradually been reduced to nonentity and fragmentation and the folio version gradually exalted to the status of an organic, unified work of art. Because my discussion is aimed not *ad hominem* but *ad artem*, I shall hereafter substitute for Craik's name the more representative appellation of Editor.

In the new Oxford *Merry Wives*, the 1602 quarto is dangerous in Mary Douglas's sense because it threatens the purity of the 1623 folio text, the copytext for the edition. As we know, the folio version has impurities of its own. It was highly regarded in the eighteenth century for its adherence to the classical unities, but more recent editors, particularly the Disintegrators, have faulted its construction, its uneven tone and style, its many lacunae (that have to be filled by recourse to the bad quarto), its blatant contradictions, as in the time sequence of the play, the Christian name of Mr Page (is he Thomas as in 1.1.42, or George as in Acts 2 and 5?), and the matter of who is to play the part of the Fairy Queen in the masque (Anne Page or Mistress Quickly?). Given these flaws, we might expect the folio to be regarded by the Oxford Editor as "dangerous" in the same way that the quarto is, since it derogates from an image of Shakespeare's artistic mastery, but it is not so portrayed. Rather, its foibles are exposed only after the alternative text has been subjected to a process of dismemberment by which Q is first conceptualized as a disorderly heap of materials, some of which are salvageable, and then reduced to dirt, rubbish, non-form. As in so-called primitive rituals, one of the most curious features of the process is its seeming illogicality: the categories of pure and impure are not constant, but shift along with the precise goal to be achieved at a given stage in the process.

The interpretive introduction to *Merry Wives* is eclectic and non-dogmatic, for the most part, but does have several recurring features. Like many another Shakespearean editor, the Oxford Editor plunges directly into interpretation of the play on the premise that it is a single entity, even though he has not as yet established in textual terms just what that entity is. Unlike many other editors of *Merry Wives*, however, he rejects topical readings unless they relate directly to the by now traditional linkage of the play to the Garter Feast of 1597 and are non-hostile in intent. He discounts the contention that the luces on Shallow's coat of arms are meant as a dig at the Lucy family near Stratford or at William Gardiner, JP, whose wife was a Lucy. He likewise rejects arguments that the name of Brooke, adopted by Mr Ford when he jealously tries to ferret out the infidelity of his wife, was intended to satirize William Brooke, Lord Cobham or any other members of that prominent family. Even though the Oxford Editor tentatively accepts the standard argument about the Garter occasion for the play, he scornfully rejects the proposition that Queen Elizabeth might have seen an unflattering portrait of herself in Mistress Quickly's acting of the part of the Fairy Queen. The basis for his privileging of the Garter materials over other potential topical meanings is not made clear, but its effect is to elevate the text and its author above the pettiness of late sixteenth-century bickering and controversy.

Similarly, the Editor rejects or de-emphasizes references to commercial and legal matters: "Though it is a citizen comedy, *The Merry Wives of Windsor* does not obtrude the social and economic hostility frequent in this type of drama" (p. 41). He also gives short shrift to interpretations that violate what he perceives as the expansive, merry, easy spirit of the play. He notes that "No director has tried to centre the play upon social conflict" and argues that "Feminist criticism has had little to say, and that little not illuminating, about the women's roles in the play and in the society that the play depicts" (p. 42). He finds mythic approaches to the play, as represented in the work of Northrop Frye and Jeanne Addison Roberts, uncompelling, in part because they seek to link *Merry Wives* with dark forces that could cast a shadow on its mirth.

But ease, in the Oxford Editor's view, does not imply debasement. One of the most valuable features of his edition is his insistence that the play need not probe into the dark depths of human experience in order to have artistic integrity. Repeatedly, he counters imagined objections to Shakespeare's crudity in dealing with base characters and situations by pointing to the playwright's judgment and craftsmanship. Indeed, of all modern editions of the play, this is the one that offers the most sophisticated argument for its unity and cohesion. The Editor repeatedly defends Shakespeare by offering artistic justification for the playwright's decisions. He remarks, for example, of the comic speech in which Caius utters the ungrammatical and highly idiomatic line "By gar, nor I too. There is nobodies" (cited from the Oxford edition, 3.3.201) that "Anyone who thinks it is unworthy of Shakespeare to indulge in this kind of humour should ponder the skill that has gone into Caius's comprehensively incorrect remark" (p. 38). He notes, similarly, that although there are repeated allusions to cuckoldry in the play, all of the women remain chaste.

Nevertheless, in keeping with the genial spirit of the piece, he allows Shakespeare a few foibles and mistakes of the kind that might be expected in the heat of composition. As a summary to the interpretive portions of the introduction, the Editor restates his premise that "*Merry Wives of Windsor* is a merry play, all the merrier for the gravity with which so many of the characters regard themselves" (p. 48). A footnote links his reading of the play to a broader national self-image. He cites Hugh Hunt, who explained the choice of *Merry Wives of Windsor* for the Festival of Britain in 1951: "I would like to justify it by showing the English humour of the play – the merry England which has played so large a part in the building of our institutions and national character" (p. 48, n.).

Immediately after this interpretive climax comes the introduction's "zone of terror" – the Editor's discussion of the quarto and folio texts. It is as though this section were written by a different person. Gone at least temporarily is the amiable spirit of the editorial persona projected during earlier segments of the introduction. The marked difference in tone results, I would suggest, from the fact that we (and the Editor) are in the presence of danger emanating from playhouse, printinghouse, and the quarto version of the play. A fear of textual contamination or fragmentation is palpable despite the fact that it is never quite articulated. Unlike most previous editors, this one does not assume the burden of opening up anew the relationship of the 1602 quarto to the 1623 folio version of the play, but takes as "accepted" the view that the quarto is "corrupt" and "unreliable":

> There is no need to set down all the evidence that has been accumulated to prove that Q is a 'bad Quarto' and prints an imperfectly reconstructed text (a 'reported text') of the play. It is sufficient to illustrate from it three kinds of corruption characteristic of such reported texts.
>
> (pp. 48–49).

In both Q and F, the English language is so stretched and abused by the characters that we may wonder whether the Editor's insistence on the reliability of F is in part an attempt to stave off the play's vertiginous fragmentation of "proper" English. Of all the Shakespearean comedies, it is arguably Shakespeare's "English Comedy" that features the most serious depradations upon the national language – by a French doctor, a Welsh priest, and Mistress Quickly, all of whom "hack" and make "Fritters of English" (F TLN 1226 and 2628; Q p. 564, D3r). More significantly, we will observe a possible alignment in his discussion between a rejection of recent "dark" readings of the play and a refusal to entertain the 1602 version of the play as Shakespearean. As we shall observe later on, this alignment is not fortuitous, but functions to keep alive a traditional editorial mythos about Shakespeare, the play, and England.

While Q is corrupt and unreliable, F has occasional "imperfections," most of them attributable to the transcriber, Ralph Crane, or to the demands of censorship (pp. 53–63). Q is described in a language of transgression markedly different from the careful qualifications surrounding F. Even though the Editor has stated as given that Q is memorially reconstructed, he feels called upon to enumerate some of its flaws, which are determined to be signs of corruption through comparison with the folio version. This is quite a standard procedure in the discussion of bad quartos, but we will note that it is self-contradictory. In the early parts of the introduction, Shakespeare was allowed to nod occasionally in the composition of his play. According to the circular logic of the danger zone, however, inconsistency becomes instead the mark of "faulty reconstruction." Another peril to textual purity is matter out of place: if fragments of dialogue turn up in one part of F and elsewhere in Q, then Q has improperly moved them to a spot where they do not belong. Q is also characterized by inauthenticity – lines like Nym's "there's the humour of it" in Q are corruptions of the "correct" F version, "That's the humour of it," because "there's the humour of it" is also used in the bad quarto of *Henry V.*

Later in the chapter I will suggest other ways of understanding at least some of the "corruptions" of Q. Like the two quartos of Marlowe's *Doctor Faustus*, the quarto and folio versions of *Merry Wives* place the play's action in different ideological milieux; indeed, in some respects Q can easily be seen as a critique of values expressed in F. But what we need to notice for the present is the stern and unyielding ritual process by which one text is cleansed of its pre-acknowledged imperfections, while the other is gradually turned into "dirt," incoherence. In the danger zone of many twentieth-century editions, Shakespeare is conceptualized as pure and perfectly *sui generis*: his scenes are consistent, his matter is never out of place, he does not ignominiously steal phrases from other writers or even echo them. He has, in fact, perfect authorial mastery over his text, by contrast with the wretched compiler of Q, who is not conceptualized as an author at all, but as a pirate, with all of the moral implications that piracy implies.

Even when Q provides alternate readings obviously not derived from F, those readings are, in the language of the Oxford Editor, "the loose paraphrase which is a characteristic of reported texts" (p. 50). The term *loose* is inadequate for the degree of contrast between Q and F and at least fleetingly suggests sexual transgression. The suggestion is not this Editor's alone: bad quartos are regularly gendered as feminine, in part because of their association with errancy and unreliability. The pirates simultaneously reconstructed and deformed the "pure" authorial document for purposes of crass financial gain. In other words, they prostituted the true text. An 1863 *Quarterly Review* article on "Sensation Novels" used the analogy of the book as prostitute, serving "market-law," actively circulating through society by means of libraries and bookstalls, and transmitting disease from one reader to another.[14] That is very much the image of the Renaissance marketplace still promulgated in many twentieth-century editions. Small wonder that the editor's task is a weighty and heroic one. He or she must defend the purity and probity of the true text against any taint of commercialism or pilferage.

In some cases, thematic differences between "bad" quartos and "good" ones or the folio may have contributed to the editor's gendering of the "bad" ones as waywardly female. That is a possibility in the Oxford edition: as we shall see later on, what the woman wants (and succeeds in getting) is different in one version than in the other. The women's triumph in Q is unallayed by larger patriarchal forces, while in F, Windsor, the court, and the Order of the Garter loom over the antics of the townspeople. Whether or not the texts being considered encode significant differences in the degree of authority allowed to women, male editors like to heroicize their perilous task in terms of the conquest of feminine disorder and allure – a matter to be considered at greater length in the next chapter. As Gary Taylor has suggested, textual editing is regularly gendered as a highly masculine activity, and it is particularly so if the author in question has the inspiringly martial and phallic name of Shake-speare.[15]

Within the zone of terror, the Oxford Editor is also, of course, barred from considering textual differences between Q and F that might tell in Q's favor – such as, to anticipate an argument that will be made later, Q's relative lack of emphasis on mercenary values. That trait, if admitted into discussion, might make Q closer than F to the Oxford editor's preferred image of the play as a microcosmic "Merry England" in which monetary matters are erased in favor of charity and brotherhood. Within the zone of terror, Shakespeare has to be kept free of any taint of commercialism, because that taint is reserved for the contaminators – to some extent the printers, who sold his precious creations in cheap popular editions, but more especially those pirates the memorial reconstructers, who perverted his language out of greed and ignorance.

By the end of the textual discussion in the Oxford *Merry Wives*, the quarto version of the play has ceased to exist as an independent source of meaning. After the Editor has successfully established the 1602 text as rubbish, except for those bits he salvages (rather like war trophies) for his own edition, the terms of the ritual shift once more. The folio text, and even Shakespeare himself, are once again allowed to have at least some minor imperfections. The Editor goes on in a milder vein than before to consider the various difficulties with F before his passage through the danger zone is complete. But by then, the worst is past. Curiously, once Q is safely neutralized, its trophies to be imported into the good text carry an almost talismanic energy. Mary Douglas discusses a similar pattern in non-Western rituals, in which we may discover that an ordinarily abominable item is suddenly "singled out and put into a very special kind of ritual frame that marks it off from other experience. The frame ensures that the categories which the normal avoidances sustain are not threatened or affected in any way. Within the ritual frame the abomination is then handled as a source of tremendous power" (Douglas p. 165; see n. 13 below). Such is the editorial apparatus in the introduction and on every edited page of the modern Shakespearean edition – framing and containing the power of potentially dangerous quarto readings by separating them from other historical matters and subduing them to the authority of the editor, who has himself gained tremendous power as a result of his successful negotiation of the zone of terror.

The introduction to the Oxford *Merry Wives* ends curiously – with a fleeting evocation of the Editor's earlier geniality in the final paragraph of his discussion of textual issues. His ostensible subject is an inconsistency between Q and F in terms of Falstaff's disguise for the final scene of the play. After Falstaff's ordeal in Windsor Forest, Q's stage directions call for him to remove his "*bucks head*" or horns before encountering the Fords and the Pages (Q p. 576, G3r), while F leaves the matter undecided. But underlying that issue is the meaning of the horns: is removing them an admission of cuckoldry or a sign of renewed potency? The final sentence of the introduction is curiously abrupt and specific, seemingly an inadequate conclusion for the sixty-three pages of discussion that have gone before. It reads: "But there is nothing in F's text to suggest that Falstaff has pulled off his horns before he is confronted by the Fords and the Pages, and an editor must decide for himself what the appropriate directions are" (p. 63).

This brief and seemingly lame conclusion is, I would suggest, actually a modestly understated assertion of the Editor's power, once he has safely mastered the perils that Q could potentially offer for the authority of F. It is not, I would submit, mere happenstance that the power is being wielded over a matter of sexual definition. What is at issue is, indirectly, the degree of female power and danger to be admitted into the Oxford edition of the play, since it is the women who have cosened the fat knight into donning his horns in the first place. By closing with an evocation of the editor's power to legislate the matter, this particular Editor sets a final seal of closure on the troubling textual issues that he had confronted earlier on. Q has been vanquished, its residual mana is in his hands, and he can move on to the shaping of the playtext itself without fear of further pollution. The power to legislate textual purity now belongs to him. And now that his authority has been affirmed, he is free to return to the genial manner of earlier parts of the introduction. We are ready to move into the irenic "Merry England" of the play itself.

Although some features of the editorial ritual for separating pure from impure are distinctive to this edition, the general pattern is not. Different editions order its parts differently, but nearly all treat the danger zone of potential textual contamination in similarly dogmatic fashion. Indeed, the Oxford edition represents the final stage of a twentieth-century process by which the quarto version of *Merry Wives* has gradually been marginalized almost to the point of extinction. In the 1908 *Old Spelling Shakespeare* edition of *Merry Wives*, the quarto equivalent of each scene appears at the bottom of the page to facilitate reader comparison. In the old Arden edition of 1904 and the New Shakespeare of 1921, the editors wage a tough and extended battle against the quarto version. But William Green's 1962 full-dress topical reading of the play in terms of its putative occasion of a Garter Feast of 1597 helped sound the death-knell of Q. As Green candidly put the matter, the best way of defending the authority of the folio version of the play was "a bold frontal advance on the Quarto."[16]

Green's book, handsomely decorated with crowns to echo his contention about the play's Garter milieu, ushered in an era of new critical and editorial emphasis on the royal dimensions of the play. The 1971 Arden *Merry Wives*, edited by H. J. Oliver, accepted Green's reading and forcibly suppressed the quarto through an elaborate analysis in the introduction but like the cockney's eels in the pan, the wanton text wouldn't stay down. In his interpretive notes, Oliver frequently cites parallels from the quarto to continue his battle against the 1602 text. The Oxford edition relies on Oliver for textual matters, but in this most recent edition of the play, the sense of strain required to combat the pirates is significantly reduced because the quarto has already been silenced by a "consensus" of earlier opinion.

And from one point of view, the silence has much to recommend it. To admit the quarto into substantive interpretation of the play would be to reenter a seemingly endless morass of hypothesis and uncertainty about the status of both Q and F that twentieth-century editors have finally worked themselves out of – only with considerable effort and after many decades. Small wonder that modern readers and critics have been reluctant to interrogate the editorial ritual by which the "good" text is solidified and the "bad" one rendered harmless. In its bare outlines, it repeats for an entity called Shakespeare an age-old elevation and separation of pure from impure that reaffirms some of our basic assumptions about order both within texts and in the world outside them.

In Shakespearean editions of the last several decades, the author is overwhelmingly associated with civilization and civility as opposed to their unsavory opposites. The notion of "civilization" underlying each Shakespearean edition will, of course, be implicitly defined by its editor and by the consensus of opinion with readers that the editor is able to build through introduction, text, and annotations. As we have seen in the case of Marlowe, disparate editors, particularly across different generations, can be expected to carry markedly different visions of the "true" *Doctor Faustus*. The remarkable thing about most late nineteenth and twentieth-century editions of *The Merry Wives of Windsor*, by contrast, is their agreement about what is most valuable in the play. They share the same mythos.

Most of us have seen films or videotapes about the life and times of Shakespeare that feature heartrendingly beautiful shots of the English countryside, along with a warm but authoritative voiceover assuring us of the abiding strength of Shakespeare's ties to the quintessentially English image of tranquility displayed on the screen. Indeed, in some evocations of the connection, Shakespeare becomes inseparable from the landscape – he incarnates "Merry England." Where does this image of Shakespeare come from? His rural origins are surely a factor: the survival of several of his properties in Stratford-upon-Avon makes it easy for us to imagine him in the midst of an idyllic rural scene, provided, of course, that we can mentally excise the more recent signs of a burgeoning tourist industry. A desire to place Shakespeare in a typically English rural landscape surely lies behind the many antiquarian efforts to link the Bard himself with events of the play – his putative deer-stealing and possible punishment at the hands of Sir Thomas Lucy; his possible connections with Windsor. His long reputation as "nature's child" is surely another factor: he is our Anglo-American native genius, almost untutored, demonstrating an indigenous, almost avian talent for "warbling woodnotes wild." I suspect, however, that if Shakespeare had not had rural roots we would have invented them for him. Our foremost poet has to be tied to the Myth of Merry England so that the two idealizations can reinforce one another. He is the presiding Genius of the place in both the modern and in the classical, mythological sense of the term.

As cultural historians have demonstrated, the "Merry England" ideal can be traced at least as far back as Shakespeare's own era, where it was deployed by different groups for various political purposes but most consistently and visibly by early Stuart monarchs intent on forging an alliance between court and countryside in order to shut out urban commercial interests that they perceived as inimical to Stuart rule.[17] The myth is not entirely myth, of course, but it was and is still invoked as a way of deflecting attention away from elements of social and economic conflict within any area of English culture in which such conflict is deemed unnatural or otherwise inappropriate. Even now, it is an ideological construction associated with twentieth-century nostalgia for an earlier, simpler, more communal way of life based on harmony rather than discord among the various levels of society. Anglophone populations outside the British Commonwealth are by no means immune from the power of the construction: indeed, Americans are probably more taken with the mythos than most British subjects are. For those who identify strongly with the "mother country," the greater cultural distance increases the pangs of nostalgia.

Most of Shakespeare's plays are disappointingly un-English, at least insofar as their action is ostensibly set in Padua, Venice, Athens, Illyria, or Vienna. His histories, which are set in England, can scarcely be said to create an image of rural tranquility except in fleeting and vulnerable snatches. No, the one place to go for a Shakespearean "Merry England" is *The Merry Wives of Windsor*, which is chiefly valuable, according to the first Arden editor, for the picture it gives us of "country life, sports, and manners in England, which we have not elsewhere drawn for us with the same fulness by Shakespeare" (Hart p. ix; see n. 12 below). The same editor later states:

> the purpose of the play is merriment – rollicking, riotous mirth. . . . There is nothing serious in the play. But there is a beautiful picture of country life, and a delineation of simple, everyday, unsophisticated people, full-blooded and up to anything in the nature of fun that make this play a treasured possession, for which we could better afford to part with, perhaps, half of the author's other works, admittedly superior though several of those may be.
>
> (pp. lxx–lxxi)

Similar sentiments are common in nineteenth-century editions, which typically praise the play for its wholesome evocation of the virtue of magnanimity in humble rural folk, and feature elaborate attempts to link the play (and Shakespeare) directly with the landscape and personages of Windsor.[18]

More recently, the evocation of harmony has intensified. In the New Shakespeare edition (1921), Sir Arthur Quiller-Couch's introduction moves from the vexing matter of establishing the text of the play as from a "thicket of difficulties" into a playground of rural serenity that he conceptualizes as the play itself, "in which Shakespeare gets back from London to the country, if not so far as to his native midland, and lies and kicks his heels in joy of old liberty recovered." The editor first makes a case for Pollard and Wilson's theory that *Merry Wives* was hastily grafted onto an earlier non-Shakespearean play in order to comply with Queen Elizabeth's command. Then, with a "sign of relief" we emerge into the clear, upon one of the pleasantest brick-and-green open spots in Elizabethan England; upon Windsor by the Thames, with its royal castle crowning the slope high over the river, and, around it and beside, a comfortable well-kept town, all the inhabitants whereof dwell within easy stretch of green fields, stiles, and such simple sports as that on which intent Izaak Walton would start, a few years later, from the City of London, up Tottenham hill, to fish the River Lea for chub and bring back "the herb called heart's ease."[19]

We will notice the harmony and congruence between the top of the picture – the "royal castle crowning the slope" – and the prosperous town and countryside below, a fitting landscape in which to find Shakespeare "in joy of old liberty recovered." Quiller-Couch's reference to Izaak Walton is particularly interesting, given that that avid angler was one of the seventeenth-century Englishmen most interested in continued promulgation of the Stuart "Myth of Merry England" during the Civil War and Interregnum. American editors have been at least as susceptible to the myth as their British counterparts. Fredson Bowers notes in his Pelican edition of the play (1963):

> One of the striking features of the play is its abandonment of the central focus of a popular audience, the narrow streets of London, for the fields and woods of Windsor. The change in atmosphere is a deliberate one, away from the dog-eat-dog cheats of the city that Jonson and Middleton liked to explore, to the proverbial purity of the countryside where, in the best tradition, pastoral virtue triumphs over the city slicker.

Bowers has an active sense of the limitations of the play and surprisingly little interest in its courtly connections, but praises it for its "sturdy middle-class self-respect" and "admiration for unspoiled English virtue," not otherwise found prominently in Shakespeare. His introduction ends on an almost rhapsodic note: "If this is the world as the world should be, the arcadianism has a basis in truth. *The Merry Wives of Windsor* may even be called a patriotic play. Despite its contrivances, it is a very English one. We should be thankful for it."[20]

Oliver's Arden edition is far more reticent, making brief note of the play's charming portrait of "life in an English country town" and its theme of "the natural superiority of plain 'honesty' or virtue to the sophisticated or sophistical arts of the gallant or courtier" (pp. lxvi–vii). But as we have already seen, the most recent Oxford edition of the play participates fully in the "Merry England" tradition of *Merry Wives*, by which dissonant elements and interpretations are magically silenced and the play becomes a celebration of rural harmony and solidarity. It is this idealized image of the play and of Shakespeare that is at stake in the editor's battle with the pirates.

WINDSOR OR ELSEWHERE?

If the quarto version of *The Merry Wives of Windsor* has struck a succession of editors as unauthentic, part of the problem is surely that it happens in the wrong place. It has an urban setting strongly suggesting London or some provincial city, while the 1623 folio version comes close to mapping Windsor and its surrounding villages through many topographical references to the area, its palace, park, river, and environs. Indeed, the more urban milieu of the quarto version was one of the features that prompted Robertson, Pollard, and Wilson to posit that version of *Merry Wives* as hastily grafted upon an earlier play of London life in order to satisfy the Queen's command for a play about Falstaff in love.

Rather than reopen the textual debate at the level of the determination of origins, however, we need to cut through that particular Gordian knot and "unedit" the play: we need to ask ourselves what the two early printed versions are like and in what major ways they diverge. We will readily discover that the pattern of difference between Q and F is quite regular – much too regular to be the product of hazy and haphazard recollection on the part of some inferior memorial reconstructer. The names of surrounding towns are similar in both versions, but in nearly every place where the folio specifies a Windsor locale, the quarto substitutes a more generalized location which could easily be London or a largish provincial town rather than Windsor. Falstaff's great buck basket is carried "among the Whitsters in *Dotchet* Mead" in the folio (F TLN 1363–64), merely "to the Launderers" in the quarto (Q p. 565, [D4]r). In the folio, one set of characters runs madly "through the Towne [of Windsor] to *Frogmore*" while others run "about the fields with mee through *Frogmore*" (F TLN 1134–35, 1144–45). In the quarto, they go "Through the fields to *Frogmore*" (Q p. 563, D2r) – a slight change, but one which makes that line more parallel to the London experience of going "through the fields" to reach the open countryside. Characters in the folio text habitually offer ejaculations and comparisons anchored in their locale: "as any is in *Windsor*" (F TLN 866), "neuer a woman in *Windsor*" (F TLN 514–15), "for ye welth of *Windsor castle*" (F TLN 1543). This trick of language does not exist in the quarto text.

In nearly every case where the folio refers to some feature of rural life in Windsor, enlivened by the presence of the court, the quarto creates a more identifiably urban or at least neutral equivalent, without any mention of the court. The folio version portrays Doctor Caius as a physician who has achieved a certain following among courtiers. In 1.4 he several times mentions that he is on his way to court: in his own fractured French, "*Ie man voi a le Court la grand affaires*" (F TLN 444–45). He needs to fetch "Simples" from his "Closset" (where Simple is hiding) so that he can dispense them at court (F TLN 456). To see passers-by from his house, one looks out the "Casement," as Mistress Quickly orders Rugby to do when Caius is on his way home. In the quarto, Doctor Caius's establishment more resembles the shop of a town apothecary. Simple is hiding not in the "Closset" but in the "Counting-house," where the Doctor keeps his herbal remedies in Q (Q p. 557, [B3]v). His establishment evidently also has a stall in front, since he later orders Rugby to look out "ore de stall" for Pastor Evans (Q p. 563, [D1]v). In this version of the scene, the doctor is in a hurry to be off, but there is no evidence he is going to court (Q p. 557, [B3]v).

There are similar differences between Q and F in the handling of Mistress Quickly. She offers a long and appreciative description of the court's visit to Windsor in 2.2 of the folio. Describing Falstaff's effect on Mistress Ford, she assures her:

> the best Courtier of them all (when the Court lay at *Windsor*) could neuer haue brought her to such a Canarie [as you have]: yet there has beene Knights, and Lords, and Gentlemen, with their Coaches; I warrant you Coach after Coach, letter after letter, gift after gift, smelling so sweetly; all Muske, and so rushling, I warrant you, in silke and golde, and in such alligant termes, and in such wine and suger of the best, and the fairest, that would haue wonne any womans heart:
>
> (F TLN 831-39)

Given that Doctor Caius describes the court as nearby, there is an apparent conflict in F over its location during the action of the play – precisely the kind of conflict that, if found in Q, would be seized upon in the "zone of terror" as clear evidence of the illiteracy of the pirate. But the apparent discrepancy is easily enough resolved. As the Oxford editor suggests, Mistress Quickly may be recollecting a previous period of residence. Evidently courtiers are returning to Windsor, since Doctor Caius is bound for court and Mistress Quickly has recently profited by the largesse of some petitioner of high rank: "I had my selfe twentie Angels giuen me this morning" (F TLN 840–41).

Mistress Quickly's breathless evocation of aristocratic glamor does not exist in the quarto. The equivalent speech there is brief and without the slightest reference to the court. She says of Mistress Ford, "she is not the first / Hath bene led in a fooles paradice" (Q p. 560, C3r). Falstaff's response, "Nay prethy be briefe my good she *Mercury*," has struck editors as sure evidence of piracy, since it is only in F that Quickly's previous speech has been long and elaborate. But, like the discrepancy in F over the location of the court, this apparent contradiction need not be taken as evidence of corruption. In neither version of Falstaff's speech is he referring to Mistress Quickly's remarks just made; he is rather attempting to stave off a predictable attack of volubility on her part, since Quickly's reputation for that trait has been amply established already even in this short version of the play. If F were not postulated as a standard by which to measure other versions, we would find nothing amiss in Q.

At many other points, courtly references are similarly "missing" from the quarto. In F, Fenton is also linked to the court – identified by Mr Page as having "kept companie with the wilde Prince, and *Pointz*" (F TLN 1332–33). In Q he has no such affiliations. F 2.2 has Ford praising Falstaff's "war-like, court-like" preparations (F TLN 986); in the quarto Falstaff is simply "A man of such parts that might win 20. such as she" (Q p. 561, [C4]r). In F 3.2 Mistress Page calls Robin a "little Gallant" and avers, "now I see you'l be a Courtier" (F TLN 1271, 1277); that speech is "absent" from Q. In F 4.3, there is a mysterious duke who will be "tomorrow at Court" though he is not yet heard of "in the Court" (F TLN 2110, 2113) and Doctor Caius later avers, "der is no Duke that the Court is know, to come" (F TLN 2304–05). In Q, there are instead three men come from a mysterious duke who "would haue your horse" (Q p. 572, [F2]v); later on, in one of this version's very few references to court, the Doctor notes there is a German duke come to "Court" (Q p. 574, [F4]v). In F, the court is a felt presence, referred to by a number of characters in a number of contexts. In Q, it is distant, almost absent.

Perhaps the most salient of the quarto's "relocations" of the action appears in the Fairy Queen's instructions to her underlings. Instead of the folio's fairy visits to "Windsor-chimnies" and the castle, which must be kept clean since "Our radiant Queene, hates Sluts, and Sluttery" (F TLN 2525–28), the quarto has Puck sending Peane to "countrie houses" and Pead dispatched to a more recognizably city setting:

> go you & see where Brokers sleep,
> And Foxe-eyed Seriants with their mase,
> Goe laie the Proctors in the street,
> And pinch the lowsie Seriants face;
>   (Q p. 576, [G2]v)

For the first Arden editor, these "very inferior" lines breathed "pure London" – "bring one back to the Poultry and the Counter-Gate" as though "the complete play was adapted expressly for Windsor, and the shortened one for representation elsewhere" (pp. xviii–xix). This view of the relationship of Q and F has much to recommend it, provided that we do not regard shortening as an inevitable sign of piracy. More recent editors have been inclined instead to view the quarto lines as an urban contamination of the "correct" locale, Windsor.[21]

Worst of all for the reputation of Q, the folio's long, elaborate blessing of the castle and St George's Chapel, which caps and recontextualizes that version's long series of references to the court, does not exist in the quarto:

Search Windsor Castle (Elues) within, and out.
Strew good lucke (Ouphes) on euery sacred roome,
That it may stand till the perpetuall doome,
In state as wholsome, as in state 'tis fit,
Worthy the Owner, and the Owner it.
The seuerall Chaires of Order, looke you scowre
With iuyce of Balme; and euery precious flowre,
Each faire Instalment, Coate, and seu'rall Crest,
With loyall Blazon, euermore be blest . . .

(F TLN 2538–46)

These lines of verse stand in marked contrast to the chatty prose of most of the play. They provide the folio version with its putative occasion – a Garter installation or Garter feast – and serve, like a lodestone, to orient the text's other courtly references toward Windsor and the Chapel of St George. In the last act, the folio *Merry Wives* transcends its small-town setting and takes on some of the quality of a court masque – exalting mundane subjects by bringing them into contact with rarer and finer things. If drama can be compared to landscape painting, then what we have is the achievement of a "seigneurial" landscape in Svetlana Alpers' sense of the term: individual elements of Windsor life do not exist in a horizontal network with one another, as they do in Q, but in relation to the seat of authority imagined above them.[22]

As I have already suggested, references to the court in Q that are "absent" from F occur exclusively in the language of Falstaff. As if by contagion from other elements of the play, Falstaff's locutions are some-times more rural in F than in Q. In the folio he says, "I will vse her [Mistress Ford] as the key of the Cuckoldly-rogues Coffer, & ther's my haruest-home" (F TLN 1026–28). For "haruest-home" the quarto has "randeuowes [rendezvous]" (Q p. 562, D[1]r). In F, as part of his attempted seduction of the wives, the corpulent knight compares Mistress Ford favorably to ladies of the "Court of France"; she would, he assures her, "make an absolute Courtier" (F TLN 1397–1405).

Curiously, however, his references to court in the quarto version are confined to the scene of his shaming at the end. There, after the pinching fairies have left him, he comments, "Ile lay my life the mad Prince of *Wales* / Is stealing his fathers Deare" (Q p. 576, G3r); a little further on, once he understands the "merry Iest" that has been played on him, he expresses the fear that when the "fine wits of the Court" hear of his misadventures, "Thayle so whip me with their keene Iests, / That thayle melt me out like tallow, / Drop by drop" (Q p. 577, [G3]v). This second reference exists in F but is placed much earlier, as a response to his beating as the Witch of Brainford. It is significant that in Q Falstaff attempts to associate himself with the court in connection with his final shaming; he is clearly trying to regain his lost dignity by asserting ties with a higher social milieu than that of the townspeople. But Q's association of courtliness with Falstaff is scarcely laudatory toward the court. Again we sense greater distance or simple lack of interest: the culture of the court is far away and alien from the lives of the townspeople.

Finally, Falstaff's punishment as Herne the Hunter is firmly localized to Windsor in F, portrayed more generally in Q. The "*Herne*" of the folio is imagined as a long-dead keeper of Windsor Forest who haunts a giant oak known by all as "Hernes Oake." The mysterious and "ancient" rural "tale" of Herne is apparently Shakespeare's invention, though nineteenth-century antiquarians made quite a point of identifying just which oak of the forest was Herne's and therefore Falstaff's (F TLN 2150–60). In the quarto, Falstaff is not Herne but "Horne the Hunter." Horne is a dead hunter who is the subject of superstition, but not associated with an ancient keeper of Windsor Forest or with a giant oak, or any topographical fable. He haunts "field" and "woods" more generally, and is, through his name and lack of other associations, more directly a figure of cuckoldry than the mighty Herne of the folio. As Horne, Falstaff still calls himself the fattest stag "In all *Windsor* forrest" (Q p. 575, G2r), but that is almost the quarto text's only reference to Windsor aside from the title itself.[23] The folio version of *Merry Wives* is a comedy of small-town and rural life, steeped in rustic customs and topography but also imbued with the "high" presence of the royal court; the quarto version is "lower," more urban, closer to the pattern of city or "citizen" comedy.

Already we can see some of the alarming consequences of accepting Q as an alternative version of the play rather than a debased travesty of it. In F, "Shakespeare" is associated with an affectionate mapping of rural topography and customs. In Q the text is deracinated – "Shakespeare" is loosened from his attachment to a specific, well-known piece of England and from the rural associations that have delighted many readers and theatrical audiences of *Merry Wives* as well as most twentieth-century editors of the play. Q fails to confirm Shakespeare's organic connection as national Genius with a quintessentially English country landscape; indeed, it moves the play to something more closely resembling the City environs so disparaged by editors of the play, but in all probability the *locus* of most of Shakespeare's creative activity as an actor and playwright. The quarto *Merry Wives* dissociates the Merry England myth from its time-honored rural setting.

SCAPEGOATING AND SENTIMENTALISM

Northrop Frye, Jeanne Addison Roberts and others have called attention to the scapegoating pattern of *The Merry Wives of Windsor*: in keeping with ancient seasonal folk ritual, Falstaff is symbolically slain and cast out to restore the community to health. After his punishment in the guise of Herne, he calls himself "Iacke-a-Lent" in the folio text (F TLN 2611), which suggests a Shrovetide context like that C. L. Barber has offered for Falstaff as scapegoat in the *Henry IV* plays. Jeanne Roberts prefers to associate the play with Halloween and All Saints' Day, and in fact, *Merry Wives* was performed in the court of James I on November 4, 1604.[24] Both of these festival contexts are linked to red-letter days in the Anglican Church and both are easily assimilated to the "Myth of Merry England," with its idealized portrayal of the age-old round of seasonal pastimes by which the rural community casts out discord and restores harmony and fertility.

As historians of the early modern era have recently reminded us, however, not all communal village sports were anchored in ecclesiastical observances. Even more suggestive than the play's fleeting links with All Saints' and Shrovetide are its parallels with a very different ritual. Falstaff's various trials, particularly the last, strongly echo the pattern of the early modern "rough music," *charivari*, or Skimmington, which was not a seasonal observance but a rather freeform ritual shaming performed in towns and villages as need arose, and often in defiance of local authorities. The main features of Falstaff's three punishments are similar in both versions of *Merry Wives*, but our reading of the function of this ritual will depend on which text of the play we use.

The Skimmington was a form of communal shaming by which early modern communities ridded themselves of scolds, adulterers, or other prominent defectors from the accepted standards of the group.[25] Many Skimmingtons culminated in the ducking of an adulterer in the local pond or stream, a punishment which resembles Falstaff's first trial in the buck basket. The fat knight is, of course, only a would-be adulterer, much more interested in fleecing the wives than in bedding them. But the buck basket and the idea of "buck-washing" carry overtones of cuckoldry in both texts, particularly F, where Ford obsesses at greater length than in Q: "Buck? I would I could wash my selfe of y*e* Buck: /Bucke, bucke, bucke, I bucke: I warrant you Bucke, / And of the season too; it shall appeare" (F TLN 1488–90). Falstaff's strong sense of shame and outrage at the indignity of his dumping in the Thames "as they would haue drown'de a blinde bitches Puppies, fifteene i'th litter" surely derives in part from the similarity between his ordeal and the dunking imposed through traditional communal shaming (F TLN 1688–89; cf. Q p. 568, E2).

Often, men participating in the Skimmington wore women's clothing. The ritual's targets were usually disorderly females, but if there was a male target, the person representing him was often carried on horseback or carted about dressed as a woman, just as Falstaff is in his second trial when he is forced to don the gown of "My Maids Aunt the fat woman of *Brainford*," (F TLN 1965–66) or, in the more specific language of the quarto, "my maidens Ant, *Gillian of Brainford*" (Q p. 571, F2r). Like the carted adulterer of the Skimmington, Falstaff as the Witch of Brainford is thoroughly beaten before he is allowed to limp off in disgrace. But his punishment implies impotence as well as adultery: his disguise forces him into the passive, non-resisting role of a powerless old hag. The ritual implications of cross-dressing may carry over into the final scene, where Anne's unsuccessful wooers are similarly shamed by marrying boys disguised as Anne. In Q, at the very end of the play, Ford cannot resist a final dig at the losing suitors: "He [Fenton] hath got the maiden, each of you a boy / To waite vpon you, so God giue you ioy" (Q p. 578, [G4]v).

Horns for an adulterer or cuckold were also a common feature of the Skimmington. Often, a pair of horns would be affixed to the house or gatepost of a cuckold, but in more complex versions of the ritual, towns-people dressed a symbolic victim in horns (like Horne or Herne the Hunter) and punished him as a way of shaming sexually deviant neighbors into conformity or departure from the community. Falstaff's third and final ordeal takes place in Windsor Forest, where, dressed in what he takes to be the horns of virility, he expects to consummate his relationship with one if not both of the wives. Instead he is burned, pinched, and thoroughly terrorized by the fairies. As the horned man, Falstaff is both the symbolic victim of the ritual and its real target, since he is the one who has assailed the virtue of the wives. We will note an interesting congruence between the scapegoating of Falstaff within the play and the editorial scapegoating of the quarto text in most modern editions. Could it be that the continuing health of the ritual even in very recent editions of the play is at least partly explicable through the fact that a similar ritual proves efficacious within the play itself?

In terms of our inquiry here, however, the most interesting aspect of the play's various echoes of the early modern Skimmington is how differently we are likely to analyze their function, depending on whether we are considering the quarto or the folio text. In the quarto version, Falstaff and his disreputable hangers-on are the only characters with significant courtly associations. As we have briefly noted, Fenton in Q has no connection with the court and certainly none with Falstaff. Moreover, Falstaff seems to have done a bit more harm in Q than in F. In the folio, Justice Shallow threatens to complain to the king because Falstaff has "beaten my men, kill'd my deere, and broke open my Lodge" (F TLN 107–08). In Q Shallow will complain to the "Councell" because Falstaff has "hurt my keeper, / Kild my dogs, stolne my deere" (Q p. 553, [A3]v). Falstaff's punishment in Q has very much the quality of a ritualized expulsion of the corrupting intrusiveness of the court, its attempted seductions and financial exploita-tion. Indeed, Falstaff personifies the court, at least in the perceptions of the townsfolk.

Falstaff's ordeal as Horne the Hunter is funnier in Q than in F, because unallayed with higher matters, but also more of a piece with the milieu of the rest of the play. Instead of blessing Windsor Castle and its accou-trements, the fairies in this version of the final ritual humorously correct defects in their own community. Sir Hugh in the guise of a Satyr sends the fairies off to pinch sluttish housewives in the countryside and similarly punish representatives of commerce ("Brokers") and law ("Proctors" and "Foxe-eyed Seriants") in the town. The corrupt "man of middle earth" interrupts their rites just as he has previously disrupted the community itself through his deer stealing, dog-killing, and cony-catching (Q p. 576, [G2]v). The fairies' punishment of the buck-headed knight is the citizenry's collective expulsion of an unwelcome debauchery associated with a social world beyond their own.

In the quarto version and that version only, courtiers and would-be courtiers are mocked by name. *Brooke* (*Broome* in the folio version) has been taken by editors as a thrust against one of the Lords Cobham, whose surname was Brooke; the thieving "cosen garmombles" of the quarto (changed to "Cozen-Iermans" in the folio) almost certainly glances at our old friend from the *Faustus* chapter, the German Count Mompelgard (later Duke of Württemberg), who had toured England in the early 1590s and made himself a laughingstock at court through his eagerness to be made a Knight of the Garter. He was expected to be installed in the 1597 Garter ceremonies with which the folio version of *Merry Wives* has been associated by many editors and critics, but did not attend, and indeed in the folio version an unnamed German Duke connected with the cosin-Germans is expected at court but has not arrived (F TLN 2109–19).[26]

The folio version is much kinder than the quarto to figures associated with the court. The references to actual personages are disguised: *Brooke* becomes *Broome* at the sacrifice of several aqueous puns; Garmombles, a probable reference to Count Mompelgard, is "replaced" by vaguer refer-ences to a "Duke *de Iamanie*" (F TLN 2303). The Oxford editor and a few others have denied that the quarto references could have been deliberate digs at actual personages about court, but in the highly charged environ-ment of the late 1590s, topical interpretation was endemic, and both figures were well known. Audiences of both versions of *Merry Wives* would readily have interpreted both references as *ad hominem* whether or not they were so intended. The fact that they appear undisguised in the less court-centered version of the play is of a piece with Q's general lack of interest toward the court – except as a subject for jest.

In F, by contrast, the population of Windsor is for the most part deferential toward the court. The "masque" at the end of the play is performed by Windsorites, with Mistress Quickly taking on the unlikely role of the Fairy Queen and local boys serving as her minions. The townspeople thus mimic the pattern of a court for the purpose of casting blessings upon Windsor Castle, its special knights and its queen. The Fairy Queen orders the elves to spread good luck in all the rooms, annointing the Chairs of

Order and installations in the Garter Chapel with special balm and blessing. The meadow fairies take on a more complex task: they are mimetically to configure the central symbol of the Order of the Garter by singing in a ring "Like to the *Garters*-Compasse"; they are also to write its motto "*Hony Soit Qui Mal-y-Pence*" with flowers upon the rural landscape in a "characterie" that echoes the pattern of "Saphire-pearle, and rich embroiderie, / Buckled below faire Knight-hoods bending knee" (F TLN 2547–54). What the townspeople accomplish through this fairly elaborate ritual is to assert (or reaffirm) an organic connection among the countryside, the town of Windsor, and the castle. The same "characterie" of order is written upon each. Within this mimetic universe, Falstaff cannot personify an innate courtly corruption, since the court is imagined as worthy, albeit in need of periodic renewal. He is rather the debased imitator of courtly ideals articulated within the play itself. If the Fairy Queen's ritual in F constitutes a rudimentary masque, the previous antics of Falstaff are its anti-masque.

In the folio the image of the court and the Windsorites work together against Falstaff. The ritual function of the Skimmington is more strongly emphasized in F: in that version, as they devise their trap for Herne the Hunter, the wives repeatedly aver that Falstaff must be "publikely sham'd" (F TLN 2102–04). But in the folio, the Skimmington, which was historically a ritual under village or town control, has been colonized by the court. Given the garter context of the folio version, Falstaff's punishment there, which follows directly upon the blessing of Windsor Castle and the Garter Knights, is subsumed within the masque and takes on the quality of the ritual expulsion of an unworthy desecrator of the rite as a way of cleansing the Order itself. He is a "corrupted hart" deserving the shame of *Hony Soit Qui Mal-y-Pence* and therefore by definition outside the purified ranks of initiates.[27]

Moreover, in the folio version, Anne's successful wooer, Fenton, is also of the court. While one courtier loses, another snatches the prize. As we have noted, Page distrusts Fenton because "hee kept companie with the wilde Prince, and *Pointz*: he is of too high a Region, he knows too much" (F TLN 1332–34). In this version of the play, however, both the audience and the characters on stage are invited to discriminate between "good" and "bad" versions of courtliness rather than generalizing from a single corrupt instance. Page finally learns by the end that things "high" and courtly do not necessarily merit distrust. One of the things that happens in the denouement of this text, at least by comparison with the quarto, is that the court and Windsor citizenry are brought into closer proximity through the marriage of Anne Page and Fenton.

Indeed, in F the court has colonized the Windsorites on a much subtler level. As we have seen, editors of the play have liked to portray *The Merry Wives of Windsor* as a bucolic refuge from the corrupt values of the city. But paradoxically, it is the "city" version of *Merry Wives* that more successfully evades the demons of money and status. In the quarto, the relationship between Anne and Fenton is presented in a sentimental and romantic vein. Theirs is a love match predating the play: Fenton appears to be a local boy, albeit of higher station than most of the other characters. He reminds Anne at one point that he has long loved her. In Q we never find out how much Anne is "worth" in money, and it is clear that Fenton, although initially attracted to her, as he admits, for her wealth, remains attached to her out of love. In the folio, by contrast, the match is only being negotiated as the play itself unfolds. Anne is declared to have "good gifts" – namely, £700 from her grandfather plus the inheritance expected from her father. Fenton is distinctly more mercenary throughout, less convincingly in love with Anne as opposed to her money. In Q he tells Anne:

> Thy father thinks I loue thee for his wealth,
> Tho I must needs confesse at first that drew me,
> But since thy vertues wiped that trash away,
> *I* loue thee *Nan* . . .

> (Q p. 569, [E4]r)

In the parallel speech from F, he has greater difficulty separating the woman from her fortune:

> Albeit I will confesse, thy Fathers wealth
> Was the first motiue that I woo'd thee (*Anne:*)
> Yet wooing thee, I found thee of more valew
> Then stampes in Gold, or summes in sealed bagges:
> And 'tis the very riches of thy selfe,
> That now I ayme at.

> (F TLN 1582–87)

The second speech is more polished, but also more centered on "riches" which Q dismisses as "trash." Fenton's thanks to the Host for arranging his clandestine marriage is a telling indication of the slight but significant difference in his character. In F Fenton assures the Host, "So shall I euermore be bound to thee; / Besides, Ile make a present recompence" – that is, offer a monetary reward once he is in possession of the dowry (F TLN 2398–99). In Q Fenton's lines are "So shall *I* euermore be bound vnto thee. / Besides Ile alwaies be thy faithfull friend" (Q p. 575, [G1]v).

At the end of the play in F, when it is clear that the lovers have triumphed over both parents' efforts to enforce Anne's marriage, Ford sums up with the wry comment,

> Stand not amaz'd, here is no remedie:
> In Loue, the heauens themselues do guide the state,
> Money buyes Lands, and wiues are sold by fate.

> (F TLN 2713–15)

Andrew Gurr has argued that this message is particularly characteristic of Shakespeare and the Lord Chamberlain's Men during the 1590s in its rejection of arranged marriage as opposed to marriage for love.[28] But F is still imagining the transaction in mercenary terms – wives are still "sold" even if only by fate. Ford's equivalent speech in Q instead places sentimental emphasis on the heart's desire of the lovers:

> Ifaith M. *Page* neuer chafe your selfe,
> She hath made her choise wheras her hart was fixt,
> Then tis in vaine for you to storme or fret.
>
> (Q p. 578, [G4]v)

This speech is less smooth metrically than the folio equivalent – like much of the quarto and occasional patches in the folio, it is set as blank verse but is actually closer to prose. Against editors who would damn the quarto in particular as non-Shakespearean, we can respond that neither version of Ford's speech is particularly distinguished as poetry; indeed, Pollard and Wilson flatly rejected Fenton's speech in F as Shakespeare. More noteworthy than the stylistic difference between the two versions is their different perspective on marriage.

As we might expect, in Q there is also a stronger feeling of family and community solidarity in acceptance of the love match. In Q, Page formally embraces both renegade lovers with a half-rueful speech of reconciliation:

> Come hither F*enton*, and come hither daughter,
> Go too you might haue stai'd for my good will,
> But since your choice is made of one you loue,
> Here take her F*enton*, & both happie proue.
>
> (Q p. 578, [G4]v)

Sir Hugh vows to "dance & eat plums" at their wedding feast, which Ford invites all present to go in forthwith and enjoy. In F, the play's conclusion is less celebratory, more uncertain in tone. Page briefly wishes Fenton well, but not his daughter.[29] The rest of his speech as quoted above is "absent" and the degree of his reconciliation with Anne is therefore less clearly established in the text. Nor does F end in feasting and merriment for the wedding. Mistress Page proposes: "Good husband, let vs euery one go home, / And laugh this sport ore by a Countrie fire" (F TLN 2724–25).

The quarto's sentimental benevolence extends to other characters like Ford and even to Falstaff himself: in that text, once properly reformed, the fat knight is forgiven his debt of £20 to Ford; in the folio he is expected to pay up. Similarly, Mistress Ford shows more sympathy toward her husband in Q, where, confronted with his insanely irrational jealousy, she exclaims, "Alas poore soule it grieues me at the hart" (Q p. 567, [E1]v). The difference is largely a matter of emphasis, but in Q Mistress Ford seems at least as interested in curing her husband as she is in diverting herself through the manipulation of Falstaff. In the equivalent passage of F, neither wife expresses much sympathy for Ford; they enjoy their elaborate and dangerous game much more for its own sake and as revenge against Falstaff for his arrogant surmise that either of them could be successfully wooed by a form letter (F TLN 1500–65).

It is not only the court itself that is "missing" in Q. The folio version exudes a subtle aura of gentrification that is inseparable from the presence of the court. In Q, the Pages and Fords perceive themselves as people of the middling sort (except that Ford in his disguise as Brooke presents himself as a gentleman, as he does in F). In F (and only in F) the two couples accord themselves higher social status. Both Mr and Mrs Ford include Mr Page within the collective "Gentlemen" (see especially F TLN 2063, 2078); similarly, in F Broome calls Mrs Ford a "Gentlewoman"; in Q she is "one *Ford's* wife" (F TLN 951; Q p. 561, [C4]r). In Q, Slender can offer Anne a jointure of £300 to "make you a Gentlewoman" (Q p. 570, F[1]r). In F, a subtle change in the language suggests she may already be perceived as one: Slender can offer a jointure of £150 to "maintaine you like a Gentlewoman" (F TLN 1612–16).

Given the size of Anne Page's inheritance as specified in the folio version and that version only, Mr Page might well claim the status of gentleman. At the Folger Shakespeare Library there is a manuscript copy of the folio *Merry Wives*, probably dating from the 1650s, that includes an informative cast list on which Falstaff is described as "A Fat old decayed lecherous Court Officer" (we will note how closely this description ties the knight to the court), and Mr Page as "A rich Country Gentleman in or neer Windsor."[30] At least this early folio reader saw the Pages as gentry – rather than simple tradingfolk. Another intriguing feature of the Folger manuscript is that pointing fists in the margin call attention to places where the text champions marriage for love rather than for money. For its transcriber, the matter was obviously of particular interest.

Some of Ford and Page's fellow townspeople also assign themselves higher status, or at least signs of higher status, in F than they do in Q. In Q Doctor Caius orders his servant to bring him his rapier so that he can go out. In F, he commands, "Come, take-a-your Rapier, and come after my heele to the Court" – in order to claim the status he desires, he needs not only a sword himself but a sword-bearing servant (F TLN 452-53). Similarly, in F Slender has been reading Tottel's Miscellany to school himself to love in the language of court Petrarchanism (F TLN 184). He can safely boast gentry status, but feels the need to take on the aura of a courtier in order to succeed with Anne.

Other characters in F are also "contaminated" by the proximity of the court. I use the term *contamination* not out of agreement with the moral judgment it implies, but as a way of turning standard editoral value judgments back upon themselves. The heavily laden editorial opposites of "pure" and "impure," or of rural innocence for F and urban contamination for Q, can easily be reversed if we attend to divergent textual meanings as opposed to the more traditional questions of provenance and authenticity. As we have seen, in the folio *Merry Wives*, love and devotion tend to be semi-playfully equated to, or expressed through, money. Mistress Quickly and Doctor Caius are both affected by the lure of affluence and status created by the close proximity of the court. Mistress Page is likewise susceptible: one of the main reasons she offers for preferring Caius as a spouse for Anne is that he is "well monied, and his friends / Potent at Court" (F TLN 2214-15). Other characters like the Host and Bardolph keep an ear out for the latest gossip at court and, as we have seen, in F, Falstaff attempts to woo the wives with visions of the visibility at court they will attain through affiliation with him. If innocence of commercialism is to be taken as a prime value for the play, as it has been by the "Merry England" school of editors and critics, then Q is clearly preferable to F, in which there is scarcely a personal transaction free of the lure of money. Once allowed out of its shadowy limbo, the quarto can expose fissures in the sentimental benevolence of the preferred folio text.

The sexual politics of the quarto version is also subtly different from the folio. In the quarto, the wives and Mistress Quickly win an unequivocal victory against the court and the jealous husband; in the folio, they defeat Falstaff, but to the extent that their actions further Fenton's match, they are cementing an alliance with the court or, in a less charitable interpretation, helping a young courtier cash in on the market for affluent town wives even as they thwart the old courtier's rather similar ambitions. In an important recent reading, Peter Erickson has called attention to the play's participation in patriarchal structures even while it invokes subtle parallels between the wives of Windsor and Queen Elizabeth I as successful manipulators of men. The wives, like Elizabeth I, hate "Sluts, and Sluttery" and serve as enforcers of chastity, but insofar as they exert their power only through the control of sexuality and in tandem with the code of the Order of the Garter, they are reenforcing patriarchal definitions of the sphere of the feminine rather than subverting them.[31] Erickson's reading of gender tensions of the play in terms of the anomalous reign of Elizabeth I works well for the folio version, in which the wives' castigation of the "corrupted hart" is over-shadowed by the ritualized chastity of the court, and in which some of their apparent power is appropriated by a courtier. But Erickson's analysis is less applicable to the quarto version, in which the wives' activities are not at all linked to a courtly or Petrarchan ethos of chastity, but register instead as a bustling effort on the part of women of the "middling sort" (who were proverbially more autonomous than their sisters higher up on the social scale) to protect and enhance their own marriages and community. In its printed form, of course, Q registers the presence of the queen on its title page: the reference to "her Maiestie" serves as an imprimatur and brings the play in its 1602 printed form under the aegis of royal authority. But Q in performance would have had no such limits. There, the merry wives not only display considerable autonomy within their marriages, but act to protect the autonomy of their community against outside intrusion.

Like most other recent Shakespearean critics working in a cultural materialist or new historicist vein, Erickson fails to consider the striking class/gender differences between Q and F. Indeed, he cannot, for he has already acceded, as he himself makes clear, to the current editorial doctrine by which Q is too contaminated to be admissable into discussion of the play (p. 135, n. 3). If he allows textual authority only to F, he will, of course, articulate the ideology of *The Merry Wives of Windsor* only in terms of F's courtly ethos and thereby replicate for his own interpretive agenda the circularity of the "zone of terror." Indeed, there may be a more than accidental congruence between the editorial preference for the "court" version of *Merry Wives* over the past several decades and a much-remarked tendency, particularly among American New Historicists, to privilege the court as a locus of meaning and power in their interpretation of early modern literature. Despite the divide that has traditionally separated editors and literary critics, both groups seem attracted to the same modernist image of Shakespeare as spokesman for a cultural elite. By teasing out the differences between Q and F rather than suppressing them, we can break out of that overworked interpretive mode and discover a broader spectrum of localized class/gender functions operating under the rubric of "Shakespeare."

SHORT SHAKESPEARE

Why are there two versions of *The Merry Wives of Windsor*? It is tempting but hazardous to explain the differences between Q and F in terms of differences in audience like those we hypothesized for the two versions of *Doctor Faustus*. Following such a line of speculation, the "short" quarto version, even though it may, as its title page asserts, have been performed before the queen, would probably have been geared for performance before a "middling sort" of public. We would expect the more sentimental version of Anne and Fenton's relationship to appeal more strongly to a such an audience, and the folio's more skeptical and mercenary portrayal of marriage to appeal more strongly to a "higher" audience more closely identified with the court. If we accept the contention of some recent cultural historians that the early modern valorization of wedded love was more prominently associated during the period with the middle orders than with the aristocracy, to which it was only gradually beginning to spread, the quarto version of the play can be seen as articulating a "lower" pattern of class expectations about family life than does the folio.

Then there is the matter of educational level, which may or may not operate in tandem with other patterns of social difference. F has frequently been characterized as more intellectually sophisticated than Q. As numerous editors have pointed out, little William's Latin lesson, which exists only in F, offers a hilarious travesty of the standard grammar-school drill that would have been funnier for an educated public than for an audience not exposed to that particular regimen. The language and syntax of Q are usually, but not always, less "literate" than the equivalent passages in F, but, as I shall argue in chapter 5 in connection with a similar problem in the texts of *Hamlet*, the greater "literacy" of F may have more to do with its appearance in the First Folio, which was particularly geared for readers in numerous ways foreign to the quarto text, than with the projected educational level of its theatrical audiences.

Generalizations about audience based on issues of class difference are hazardous for the early modern period, if only because they are usually based on the same circular logic as are hierarchically structured arguments for textual difference. If one version of a play employs simpler language than the other and offers fewer complexities of plot, we are likely to posit the audience of one as "lower" than the other. But as revisionist social historians have been pointing out for at least the last decade, the period's own thinking about social groupings was far more complex than our modern speculation usually is. By establishing correlations between the "lower" and "higher" versions of *Merry Wives* and a "lower" and "higher" public, we risk replicating the overreductive editorial assumption that the "low" form of a text could have been produced by "illiterates" for consumption by a public as uncultured as they. In many instances, audiences may have preferred to see what they were not: the "middling sort" could participate vicariously in the glorious exploits of the nobility as reflected on stage in a court-centered play; the aristocracy could savor a rough and "uncouth" glimpse of everyday town and village life that was otherwise inaccessible to them by watching the "middling sort" on stage. The strict demarcation between elite and popular literature under which we labor yet today was only in process of formulation in the early modern era itself. And most Shakespearean audiences were, in any case, decidedly mixed in terms of social grouping and expectations.

The quarto title page indicates that that version of *Merry Wives* was taken on tour, and several astute textual analysts have considered its specific function a key to Q's brevity and relative simplicity. We know that Shakespeare's company toured regularly, perhaps to stave off insolvency or perhaps, as has been suggested more recently, to enjoy a welcome break from urban life. If the quarto *Merry Wives* is defined as a travelling version of the play for a reduced cast and shortened performance time, then many of the characteristics for which it has been condemned as a piracy can be regarded instead as sensible, deliberate – even "authorized" – alterations to meet the demands of staging in the provinces.[32] Its less gentrified, court-centered milieu would also make sense in terms of provincial performance. One advocate of that theory has suggested that Q could have been cut during the summer of 1597 to be taken on tour: the Lord Chamberlain's Men performed that summer and fall in Rye, Dover, Marlborough, Bristol, and Bath.[33]

Even recent textual revisionists often balk at the idea that Shakespeare might willingly have adapted his own work for some special purpose, particularly for the low commercial purpose of performance in a town hall or market square. A Shakespeare play has to have a certain amplitude and elevation to properly incarnate the cultural ideals that we have traditionally linked with the author's name. In the late Elizabethan and early Jacobean era, by contrast, the name of Shakespeare may have been as closely associated in the public mind with short, rapid performances as with the full-dress productions we hypothesize at the Globe Theater itself. In just such a way, "*William Shakespeare*" is associated with "variable and pleasing" merriment and swaggering humors on the title page of the "short" Q version of *Merry Wives*. Despite numerous and weighty editorial efforts, we still have no definitive proof that Shakespeare was not at least one of the people involved in the creation of Q, just as we have no proof that he wrote the whole of F. As I have already suggested, it is strongly possible that both are composite texts, part "Shakespeare" and part something else.

Another possibility is that the quarto *Merry Wives* could have been shortened for some special performance in London itself – perhaps in the public theaters, but more likely in a private house. Although we have no record of such an event beyond the quarto title page itself, the evidence linking F to a Garter Feast of 1597 is equally speculative. I can easily imagine Queen Elizabeth attending a performance of the quarto version, either in the London area or elsewhere while she was on progress. To suppose that she would only have been captivated by the more elevated, "garter" version of the play is to adopt a cripplingly limited view of her tastes. Indeed, insofar as she reputedly "liked to see her people merry," she might have had reason to prefer Q over F. Very possibly she saw both.

It is, however, much too soon to attempt some new editorial closure about the relationship of Q to F. There is strong evidence of deliberate shortening in Q: the very few references to court and to Windsor there tend to occur toward the end of the play and appear vestigial, as though overlooked by a reviser. Similarly, the stage directions in Q regularly include characters who lack speaking parts within the scene in question, as though they were deliberately written out and the stage directions preserved in their fuller form, perhaps as a way of identifying the scenes for actors or a prompter accustomed to the longer version. But if Q shows symptoms of deletion, F shows signs of augmentation: the Garter materials at the end may well have been patched onto an earlier text because the masque in its folio form creates a number of loose ends that do not exist in Q. The stage history of the play suggests that the Garter material has had limited appeal for audiences. Usually it is cut, the loose ends are tidied up, and the play as staged resembles the short Q version of the play almost as much as it does F.[34]

But what are loose ends? And how do we decide that they are loose? These aesthetic judgments are variable over time because they depend on how we, or readers and theater audiences of any given era, conceptualize unity. The quarto title page, with its advertizement of "*conceited Comedie . . . Entermixed with sundrie variable and pleasing humors*" can scarcely be said to promise a tightly constructed play. We have, as yet, no reliable way of distinguishing revision from adaptation. It could still be the case, as Pope suggested long ago, that Q antedates F and that at least some of its apparent "loose ends" are instead the bare beginnings of ideas developed later. As I have tried to suggest, our sense of the priority of either text is likely to arise out of our preestablished paradigmatic image of the Shakespeare rather than out of a "scientific" study of the data. The same caveat applies, of course, to the present discussion, which can be described (somewhat bombastically) as the adaption of a holistic, New Critical insistence on the interpretive importance of small textual details to a fundamentally historocist methodology in order to combat traditional editorial practice, for the purpose of advancing a poststructuralist sense of the undecidability of the works we like to call "Shakespeare." I have tried for sharpness of contrast in my differentiation between Q and F because I hope to demonstrate that, even in terms of the editors' own preferred interpretive strategies, a "bad" text can readily be shown to be "good" if we suspend our need to sacrifice one version to uphold the honor of the other. We need to imagine both Q and F *Merry Wives* as fixed evidence of unfixity. The play's identity over time was mobile rather than static; it makes fritters of our need to pin it down to a single, stable entity, just as some of its more colorful characters make "fritters of English."

4

THE EDITOR AS TAMER
A Shrew and *The Shrew*

In *Let Your Mind Alone! And Other More or Less Inspirational Pieces* James Thurber tells the story of a small-town Ohio high-school teacher who "for years had read to his classes a line that actually went 'She was playing coquette in the garden below' as if it were 'She was playing croquet in the garden below.' " Finally one day, "a bright young scholar raised his hand and pointed out the mistake" but the teacher grimly replied, "I have read that line my way for seventeen years and I intend to go on reading it my way." Thurber's response is, "I am all for this point of view."[1] The anecdote is interesting as an illustration of textual conservatism – the deep-seated need on the part of scholar and public alike to have our literary works in the form we have grown comfortable with, even if that form can be shown to be inaccurate by any reasonable standard of perception. But it is also, perhaps, an illustration of textual avoidance. To what extent might the schoolteacher's truculent unwillingness to read "coquette" rather than "croquet" relate to the subtle allure emanating from "coquette" by comparison with the safety of "croquet"? The received meaning of a given work can alter markedly in accordance with gender-based expectations we bring to it, some of which can be predicted in terms of broad cultural norms and some of which (like the schoolteacher's response) may appear more idiosyncratic.

As psychoanalytically inclined critics have long contended and many of the rest of us have also observed, reader anxiety about the subject matter of a text can be projected onto the text so that the text, not the reader, is perceived as disturbed and full of perturbation. In the nineteenth and twentieth centuries, strong women in Shakespeare have tended to arouse in editors just such anxiety, which translates into the judgment that scenes (or even whole plays) containing such figures are corrupt, probably not genuine Shakespeare. In the late nineteenth century, F. J. Furnivall expressed a fervent hope that Shakespeare was not responsible for "all the women's rant" in *Titus Andronicus*, the *Henry VI* trilogy, and *Richard III*. The portions of *Henry VI, Part I* that featured the appearance of Joan la Pucelle took longer to be accepted as "Shakespeare" than did the scenes featuring battles and

101

negotiation among men. Among twentieth-century editors, John Dover Wilson has perhaps been the most sensitive to emanations of feminine danger from the Shakespearean text: he not only suspected Joan to be non-Shakespearean, but found Act 1, scene 2 of *The Tempest*, with its repeated references to the "blew-ey'd hag" Sycorax, to be highly corrupt – marred by fissures and deformities.[2] The scene in question does indeed contain a number of irregular lines, but is not, in the dominant opinion of more recent readers, markedly more corrupt than the rest of the play. In this instance, Wilson's perception of contamination appears to have displaced onto the folio text a discomfort arising out of its subject matter.

All readers are, of course, subject to similar distortions of one kind or another. Nor, in our poststructuralist universe, can we hope to achieve the chimera of unmediated access to any literary work through the process of "unediting" it. We can, however, interrogate outmoded gender expectations as they have shaped our standard editions, recognizing all the while that our own more "enlightened" preferences may themselves appear dated as gender roles continue to alter over time. I have already noted several examples of such shaping in our standard editions: Sycorax's eyes cannot be blue in any positive sense of the term; Faustus is unequivocally lost only through his contact with Helen of Troy; the wives of *The Merry Wives of Windsor* must remain bound within the folio version's court-centered expectations about appropriate female activity. And, at a higher level of generality, the "bad" quartos are gendered as feminine – they are lax and chatty rather than rigorously formed and poetic, reminding "us of the vulgar gossiping of the immortal Sairey Gamp or the chattering irrelevancy of the inane Mrs. Nickleby."[3] Worse yet, they are sexually suspect – a prostitution of the "true" text.

This language of transgression was not born out of nineteenth and early twentieth-century prudery; it has carried considerable explanatory power for editors because it echoes a common Renaissance habit of mind by which the translation from mental idea to writing on a page is imagined in Platonic fashion as a descent from spirit to flesh, and by which the feminine as opposed to the masculine is envisioned in Aristotelian fashion as inevitably mixed and secondary. Stephanie Jed has shown how, in the consciousness of Renaissance humanists, textual errors register as seduction or spoliation.[4] The idea of the "bad" text as sexually contaminated is frequently to be encountered in Elizabethan and Jacobean printed books, perhaps in part because authors and printers felt uneasy about their own commodification of manuscript material and liked to fix the blame elsewhere. A good example of such discourse is the printer John Day's extraordinary introduction to the second edition of *Gorboduc*, which damns the first as what twentieth-century editors would call a "bad quarto" version of the play. According to Day, the first printed version was a stolen copy brought into print excedingly corrupted: euen as if by meanes of a broker for hire, he should haue entised into his house a faire maide and done her villanie, and after all to bescratched her face, torne her apparell, berayed and disfigured her, and then thrust her out of dores dishonested.

The ravished text "caught her shame, as many wantons do," by running "abroad without leaue" – circulating too widely in manuscript to be properly controlled by the authors.

In Day's formulation, all printing potentially resembles pandering, because it makes available to a promiscuous rout of readers what might better have been left private at home. But Day extends the allegory to provide for the text's rehabilitation. Not for him is the common Renaissance dictum that the ravished maiden can only salvage her honor through death. Since there is no remedy for her altered condition, the authors have "for common honestie and shamefastnesse new apparelled, trimmed, and attired her in such forme as she was before" so that the printer can dress her in a new "blacke gowne lined with white" and send her "among you good readers, so it be in honest companie." If she is not now made welcome among such, "she, poore gentlewoman wil surely play Lucreces part, & of her self die for shame."[5] So long as she is acknowledged by her parents, the authors, and taken for a decent gentlewoman by readers, she can safely claim that status; but if she is rejected, she will be thrown back into the role of wanton or forced to the desperate remedy of Lucrece. Her moral and sexual status will be defined through the response of select readers, very much as the moral worth of "good" and "bad" Shakespearean quartos has been adjudicated in the late nineteenth and twentieth centuries. And she will be perceived as properly genteel only if she is kept among "good" company, not allowed to gad about after anyone she wishes. Insofar as the text is gendered as feminine, elite status is a function of proper comportment and containment.

ONE SHREW, TWO SHREWS

The Taming of the Shrew, like *Gorboduc* in John Day's allegory, exists in both a "wanton" and a "decent" version, a "bad" quarto of 1594 and the "good" folio text of 1623. We all know how the play ends in modern Shakespearean editions. Katherine, the shrew, makes a long and eloquent speech of submission to Petruchio in which she argues for the subordination of wives on legal, biological, and ethical grounds, finally offering to place her hand beneath her husband's foot if that will "do him ease." Petruchio responds with gusto, "Why there's a wench" (F TLN 2737–38),[6] and after a bit more repartee the company scatters, commenting on the miracle of Kate's taming, even though, at least as we like to read and teach the play nowadays, it is by no means clear that Katherine is thoroughly converted to the system of patriarchal hegemony she advocates. Whether she is or not, there is a strong illusion of reality surrounding her speech at the end of the play: we are invited to forget that the taming of Katherine by Petruchio started out as a mere play within a play performed for the delectation of one Christopher Sly, drunken tinker turned temporary aristocrat.

In actual productions of the play within the last fifteen years in London or New York, Stratford or New Haven, however, Christopher Sly is harder to forget. As often as not in recent performances, he remains on stage and alert until almost the end of the taming plot, calling for the clown figure to come back on stage, commenting on the action, and even intervening to stop it when some of the characters appear about to be hauled off to prison.[7] When he finally does drift into sleep around the beginning of Act 5, the Lord orders him carried back to his original place and he becomes once more a drunken tinker lying in a stupor before an alehouse. After the conclusion of the main action, Sly awakens, somewhat dazed, and concludes that the taming play he has watched has been a vivid dream, the bravest and best he has ever had.

The reality of the taming plot in this version is severely undercut: it has remained "only" a play – or even a dream – throughout. Moreover, Sly's final lines compromise Kate's message even further. He lurches off, vowing to tame his own termagant wife at home now that his dream has taught him how to do it. He is unlikely to succeed, we can confidently predict, given his staggering condition and his obvious characterological distance from the charismatic stage figure Petruchio. Instead of convincing us that the inner play's wife-taming scenario is a possible one in reality, Sly's vow turns it into the wish-fulfillment fantasy of a habitual drunkard who is as likely to be punished by his wife for this night out as he has been for past transgressions. Shrew-taming becomes the compensatory fantasy of a socially underprivileged male.

It is not difficult to imagine why the Christopher Sly ending is gaining increasing popularity in theatrical productions of *The Taming of the Shrew*: it softens some of the brutality of the taming scenes, which can then be viewed as tailored to the uncultivated tastes of Sly; it distances late twentieth-century audiences from some of the most unacceptable implications of Kate's pronouncements on male sovereignty. But on what authority do directors tack the Sly episodes onto the written text as we all know it from our standard editions? By examining the textual and performance history of *The Taming of the Shrew* we will gain a fresh sense of the provisionality, even the fragility, of our standard text.

The easy and traditional answer to the question "On what authority?" is "On no authority whatsoever." The scenes of Sly's intervention in the action and eventual return to the alehouse are, as most recent editors of the play agree, "not Shakespeare," and therefore inadmissable into the canonical text of the play and usually relegated to an appendix. These Sly episodes come from *The Taming of a Shrew*, a play generally regarded by editors as artistically inferior to *The Taming of the Shrew* but apparently viewed in its own time, for copyright purposes at least, as the same play as *The Shrew. A Pleasant Conceited Historie, called The taming of a Shrew* (or *A Shrew*, as it is termed to differentiate it from *The Shrew*) is now quite rare, its 1594 quarto existing in a single known copy now at the Huntington Library in San Marino, California. *A Shrew* was reprinted in 1596 and again in 1607. *The Shrew*, by contrast, appeared in print for the first time in the 1623 First Folio of Shakespeare's works without having been entered separately in the Stationers' Register. It was reprinted in quarto form in 1631 by the printer who owned the copyright to *A Shrew*.[8]

Although, so far as we know, the earlier printed version of *A Shrew* was not republished after 1607, it was closely associated with early quarto versions of Shakespeare plays during its early history. It was, according to its 1594 title page, "sundry times acted by the *Right honorable the Earle of* Pembrook his seruants," a company with which Shakespeare may have been briefly associated; it was sent to the printer around the same time as the quarto versions of *Henry VI, Parts 2 and 3* and *Titus Andronicus*, very likely because by 1594 the Earl of Pembroke's Men had become indigent and dissolved. A play called by Henslowe "the tamynge of A shrowe" was performed at Newington Butts in 1594 by the Lord Chamberlain's Men, a company with which Shakespeare was probably already associated by the end of that year if not earlier; other plays performed alongside it included *Titus Andronicus* and some version of *Hamlet*.[9] At the very least, *The Taming of a Shrew* was closely connected with other early plays now accepted by textual revisionists as Shakespearean.

Nevertheless, beginning with Edmund Malone in the late eighteenth century, an enormous amount of editorial energy has gone into proving – over and over again and by various ingenious strategies – that no part of *The Taming of a Shrew* can be accepted as reliably Shakespearean. Whether consciously or not, recent editors have suppressed the degree of visibility *A Shrew* has had in the textual history of *The Shrew*. Modern editors, when they consider *A Shrew* at all, tend to state that of all Shakespeare's previous editors, only Alexander Pope admitted the Christopher Sly episodes and conclusion into his text of *The Taming of the Shrew*. That significantly understates the matter: not only Pope, but, following him, Thomas Hanmer, Lewis Theobald, Samuel Johnson, William Warburton, and Edward Capell all included some or all of the Sly materials in their editions as "Shakespeare."

The eighteenth-century pattern was broken by Edmund Malone, who argued that *A Shrew* was not Shakespeare, but Shakespeare's source play for *The Shrew*.[10] Since Malone's edition of Shakespeare in the late eighteenth century, *The Taming of the Shrew* in printed versions has looked much as we know it in our standard editions today – with Sly dropping out early on and the taming plot opening out into "reality" at the end. In every generation, there have been a few hardy souls who have argued that *A Shrew* is indeed Shakespeare – an early apprentice version of the play that later became *The Shrew*. From time to time there have also been hardy souls who have argued that their preferred text, *The Shrew*, or at least most of it, was also not written by Shakespeare.[11] But the dominant view of the relationship between quarto and folio *Shrews* has altered in accordance with the paradigm shift discussed in previous chapters, albeit slightly later and with less unanimity than has been the case for most of the "bad" quartos.

The first extended case for *A Shrew* as a corrupted copy of *The Shrew* was made as early as the mid-nineteenth century, but that view did not dominate until many decades later. F. S. Boas's 1908 edition of *A Shrew* could still be titled *The Original of Shakespeare's 'Taming of the Shrew'*, and Alfred Pollard did not include *A Shrew* among the "bad quartos" in his groundbreaking 1909 study of *Shakespeare's Folios and Quartos*. Indeed, in that book and in his later *Shakespeare's Fight with the Pirates*, *A Shrew* goes unmentioned. But after Peter Alexander's highly influential 1926 *TLS* study of *A Shrew* branded it as yet another "bad quarto," editorial opinion shifted around to the usual twentieth-century configuration: *A Shrew* post-dates the genuine taming play and is either a rewriting of it by an inferior hack dramatist or a pirated copy. Recent editions of *The Shrew* characteristically scapegoat *A Shrew* through danger-avoidance rituals familiar to us from our study of *Merry Wives*. The "bad" version is treated not as an artistic structure with its own patterns of meaning and its own dramatic logic, but as a heap of shards thrown together by ignorant actors with no capacity for coherence.[12]

Yet even by comparison with other "bad" quartos, *A Shrew* represents an unusual case. As we have noted in our discussion of *Doctor Faustus* and *Merry Wives*, editors characteristically mine the "bad" version of their play to patch up defective passages and infelicities of language in the "good" version, although the degree to which such materials are admitted into the authoritative text varies greatly from edition to edition. But passages from *A Shrew* are not used to supplement *The Shrew*. In none of the standard editions is Christopher Sly allowed to return at the end of the play as he does in *A Shrew*, even though editors commonly express confidence that Shakespeare must have created a similar ending that was lost or cancelled. Nor is *A Shrew* included among the other "bad quartos" in Michael J. B. Allen and Kenneth Muir's handsome facsimile edition of *Shakespeare's Plays in Quarto*, on grounds that its text is anomalous, "longer and more coherent than the texts of the other bad quartos."[13] *A Shrew* is indeed anomalous – so radically different from *The Shrew* that a vocal minority of critics have preferred to regard it as a separate play altogether, despite its many historical ties to the more familiar version of the play. The case of the two *Shrews* is a healthy reminder that the authorial category of "Shakespeare" is quite malleable, shifting over the years along with literary fashions, along with social mores, and most significantly for our concerns in the present chapter, along with changing views of male violence and female subordination.

In *The Taming of the Shrew* we are dealing with a particularly tricky area for speculation – what might Shakespeare have written or helped to write when he was not yet sounding like "Shakespeare"? Given the howl of outrage over Stanley Wells' and Gary Taylor's inclusion of what most readers regard as the wooden and uninteresting "Shall I Die" as canonical in the new Oxford Shakespeare, there is reason for considerable trepidation in suggesting that any inferior work might possibly have been authored by Shakespeare. Many of us are sure that we know what genuine Shakespeare sounds like. We need to remind ourselves that past readers and editors have held the same conviction and yet come to different conclusions than we. With the passing of a generation or two, "bad" piracies can become "good" Shakespeare, or at least profoundly interesting Shakespeare. Even though the early history of *A Shrew* so closely parallels that of *Titus Andronicus*, which now has a secure place in the canon, and that of the quarto versions of *Henry VI, Parts 2 and 3*, which are now accepted as Shakespeare by revisionist critics, *A Shrew* remains in a curious limbo. It is too regular and original to be a "bad quarto," yet somehow too derivative and uncouth to be acceptable Shakespeare.

The differences between *Shrews* are numerous and arresting. *A Shrew* is shorter and often simpler; the verse has many borrowings from Marlowe and is often metrically irregular, though that is occasionally true of *The Shrew* as well. More strikingly, *A Shrew* has a different setting (Athens) and different names for all the main characters except Katherine. Petruchio is named Ferando. In *A Shrew*, the subplot to the taming play is quite different – Kate has two sisters instead of one and each of the three sisters has her own suitor, so that the rivalry of *The Shrew* for the hand of Bianca is absent. One of these suitors (Aurelius) is a noblemen and the other (Polidor) is not, while in *The Shrew*, the wooers of Bianca are all on much the same social footing, although differing in the degree of their wealth. What would happen if, instead of regarding *A Shrew* as *ipso facto* a foul corruption of the "true" play, we were to regard it as a text in its own right, a text in which difference does not have to be read as debasement?

There are signs at present that *A Shrew* may be emerging from its limbo. Since I first published on the *Shrew* plays, one very useful new edition of *A Shrew* has appeared in print and another is reaching print.[14] But the Sly ending that is "missing" from *The Shrew* has yet to appear as part of the play in any standard edition. There are reasons beyond the shift in textual paradigms why twentieth-century editors and critics have been particularly

107

reluctant to associate *The Taming of a Shrew* with Shakespeare – as source play, as Shakespeare's early version of the standard text, or even as a repository for scattered passages and phrases that somehow survived the maurauding ignorance of the pirate and are therefore available for repairing defects in the folio text. In *A Shrew*, as I shall argue, the women are not as satisfactorily tamed as they are in *The Shrew*. The former text is therefore less "manly" than the latter. More to the point, perhaps, it has been perceived as an affront to the editors' own manhood. For traditional editors, *A Shrew* has been kept strictly separate from *The Shrew* at least in part because of an affinity between shrew-taming as valorized in *The Taming of the Shrew* and the regularizing activities editors have traditionally performed upon aberrant, individual texts. Good texts are not supposed to be wild and unruly, but *A Shrew* is too anomalous to be "tamed" by normal editorial procedures. It must therefore be suppressed. Twentieth-century editors tame texts into culturally acceptable meaning, ironing out uncouthness and grotesqueries just as the sixteenth-century printer John Day, aided by the authors of *Gorboduc*, turned a wayward "wanton" into a modest gentlewoman fit for sober company.

In *The Shrew*, shrew-taming is explicitly associated with humanist pedagogy: Petruchio's subduing and refinement of Kate operates parallel to the purported efforts of Bianca's tutors to teach the two sisters Virgil and the art of the lute. By learning to speak the pedagogue's language of social and familial order, Kate shows herself to be a better student of standard humanist doctrine than her sister.[15] She also earns the right to be treated like a gentlewoman rather than a hoyden. In *A Shrew*, as we shall see, the taming process is considerably less efficacious and less clearly linked to social status than it is in *The Shrew*. To accept *A Shrew* as Shakespeare would be, from the standpoint of traditional editorial practice, to leave the shrew (and the text) in disorder. It would also be to lose a convenient mechanism by which the forcible suppression of female insurgency is naturalized as reality and truth.

THE ACTOR AND THE WIFE

In a compelling recent argument, Lynda Boose has contended that *The Taming of the Shrew* uses the promise of wife-taming to dispell the deeper threat of male insurgency. Like Sly, if Sly had watched the "play within a play" to the end, male members of the audience would learn how to be as much the ruler of their households as Petruchio is of his. Their envy of their betters would be transmuted into identification and the danger posed to public order thereby defused.[16] Sly's final vow to tame his wife in *A Shrew* nicely complements this reading, whether or not we accept the likelihood of his success. But in the world of *A Shrew*, mastery in all of its forms is less attainable. If we consider the cultural dynamics of the two versions separately, as we did for *Merry Wives*, we will find, yet once more, that the name of Shakespeare is closely associated with a subtle process of gentrification that simultaneously narrows the autonomy of the women in the play. Unlike the subplots, the taming plots in *A Shrew* and *The Shrew* are close enough to be comparable, but there are subtle ideological shifts from one to the other. The incidents in *A Shrew* are arranged somewhat differently, the characters are less vividly and fully drawn, Katherine's motivation in accepting Petruchio is clearer, and Petruchio's in taming her is less clear.

Editors have traditionally disparaged *A Shrew* on the grounds that its portrayal of motivation is murky, failing to notice that their generalization applies only to the male characters, not to Kate herself.[17] In *A Shrew* Kate tells the audience in an aside that she will play along with her tamer:

> But yet I will consent and marrie him,
> For I methinkes haue liude too long a maid,
> And match him to, or else his manhoods good.[18]

That aside does not exist in *The Shrew*; indeed, in the more canonical text of the play Katherine has no asides at all.

Moreover, Petruchio's habitual language of patriarchal appropriation is not present in *A Shrew*. Petruchio/Ferando never states that his only motive in wiving is financial, nor does he refer to Kate as one of his possessions – goods, chattels, household stuff, "My horse, my oxe, my asse, my any thing" (F TLN 1618). Indeed, *A Shrew* is remarkable for the absence of such language – none of Petruchio's most demeaning speeches in regard to female weakness and impotence exists in *A Shrew*. In *A Shrew*, as he carries Kate off after the wedding, Petruchio/Ferando even suggests that if she humors him for the present, he will do her recompense later on:

> Come *Kate* stand not on termes we will awaie,
> This is my day, to morrow thou shalt rule,
> And I will doo what euer thou commandes.
>   (D2r, S p. 65)

In *A Shrew*, Petruchio/Ferando's method of taming by opposites is less elaborate and cleverly psychological than in *The Shrew*, or at least less clearly articulated as such by him; on the other hand, in *A Shrew*, Kate has less far down to go in order to appear properly tame – a proper "household Kate" – and Petruchio/Ferando clearly considers some of her most flamboyant gestures of subservience to be excessive.

Kate's speech of submission in *A Shrew* is very different from the parallel passage in *The Shrew*. The very few recent editors who have discussed it have, following the traditional pattern of debasing the "bad" text in order to exalt the "good" one, found *A Shrew*'s version of the speech *more* irredeemably sexist than the authorized Shakespearean version. I would characterize it instead as offering a different and more traditional mode of patriarchal argument. Whether we regard it as more or less misogynist will depend on our evaluation of different modes of patriarchy. Kate's speech in *A Shrew* can be described as a restatement of traditional misogyny on religious grounds. Much of it is taken up with platitudes about the creation: God made the world out of chaos, a "gulfe of gulfes, a body bodiles" before it was shaped by his framing hand. After the six days' work, he fashioned Adam, and out of his rib created woman:

> Then to his image he did make a man.
> Olde *Adam* and from his side a sleepe,
> A rib was taken, of which the Lord did make,
> The woe of man so termd by *Adam* then,
> Woman for that by her came sinne to vs
> And for her sin was *Adam* doomd to die
> (G[1]v, S p. 87)

This interestingly inaccurate view of the fall blames woman, as usual, for the plight of humankind – she is named a "woe" by Adam before she has even had a chance to act, and he is doomed by her sin, not his own. But, as we shall see, the misogyny of the speech is not echoed by other elements of the play, nor does Kate's speech limit the woman's sphere of action as the alternative speech in *The Shrew* does.

By contrast, Kate's rationale for obedience in *The Shrew* has a political rather than a religious base. She advocates wifely obedience in terms of a theory of sovereignty by which the household is modelled on the kingdom and wifely disobedience becomes a form of "petty treason" against her "King" and husband. "Thy husband is thy Lord, thy life, thy keeper, / Thy head, thy soueraigne," (F TLN 2704–05) "thy Lord, thy King, thy Gouernour" (F TLN 2696) – an authority against whom disobedience or even peevishness is (according to the doctrine of petty treason) the same crime as that of a rebellious subject against a monarch:

> Such dutie as the subiect owes the Prince,
> Euen such a woman oweth to her husband:
> And when she is froward, peeeuish, sullen, sowre,
> And not obedient to his honest will,
> What is she but a foule contending Rebell,
> And gracelesse Traitor to her louing Lord?
> (F TLN 2713–18)

The machinery of state lying behind this appeal for submission is rather more awesome and immediate than the diffuse and generalized appeal for order in *A Shrew*.

In the two speeches, the behaviors included within wifely obedience are also startlingly different. In *A Shrew*, Kate appeals to wives to obey because their husbands need their assistance: "Obey them, loue them, keepe, and nourish them, / If they by any meanes doo want our helpes" (G[1]v, S p. 87). The husband is not all-powerful, and wifely obedience is an active virtue. In *The Shrew*, the rationale is precisely reversed: wives are to obey because they need their husbands to take care of them. Their active contribution to the marital unit is elided: women are presented as helpless, passive, creatures of the household, who lie "warme at home, secure and safe" while their hardy lords and masters venture out into the maelstrom for their benefit (F TLN 2709). Katherine's vision of a housewife lying safe and protected at home sounds so familiar to those of us who remember the 1950s and 1960s that we may fail to recognize its relative newness as a social model in the early modern era. *The Shrew*'s image of the household as an intensely private space in which the wife, like other possessions of the husband, is to be tucked out of sight was, in England at least, only beginning to emerge as the most desirable family model. Earlier depictions of normative female behavior had, like *A Shrew*, afforded wives a greater range of territory and action.[19]

To be sure, Kate's final gesture of submission is more extreme in *A Shrew* than in the version we are accustomed to. In *The Shrew*, she commands the wives:

> Then vale your stomackes, for it is no boote,
> And place your hands below your husbands foote:
> In token of which dutie, if he please,
> My hand is readie, may it do him ease.
>
> (F TLN 2734–37)

Petruchio's response "Why there's a wench" registers his approval of her extravagant gesture of submission and also, perhaps, an element of condescension. In *A Shrew*, Kate makes the same gesture, but its symbolic rationale is not articulated (and this is one of the things to which editors have traditionally pointed as an indication that *A Shrew* is a borrowed and derivative text). In *A Shrew*, Kate's act becomes a piece of deliberate excess, which her husband stops instead of approving:

> Laying our handes vnder theire feete to tread,
> If that by that we, might procure there ease,
> And for a president [precedent] Ile first begin,
> And lay my hand vnder my husbands feete.
>
> ([G1]v, S p. 87)

The stage direction calls for her to actually lay her hand beneath his foot, and her language invites her husband to tread on it. Petruchio/Ferando responds, "Inough sweet, the wager thou hast won, / And they I am sure cannot denie the same" ([G1]v, S p. 88). Rather than being a pleasing emblem of submission, in this version her masochistic gesture is acknowledged as excessive – performed to help her husband win the bet. It is possible, of course, to make the same interpretation of her meaning in *The Shrew*, but we have to create it ourselves by reading between the lines. In *A Shrew* it is unequivocally articulated in the text.

The reaction of the other characters is also strongly contrasted in the two versions of the play. In *The Shrew*, Kate's speech silences the other women; only the men speak thereafter. In *A Shrew*, by contrast, Emelia (Bianca) makes it clear that she finds Kate's speech ridiculous. After Kate and Petruchio/Ferando exit at the end, Bianca/Emelia asks Polidor (Lucentio): "How now *Polidor* in a dump, what sayst thou man?" He retorts, "I say thou art a shrew," to which she replies, "*That*s better then a sheepe." He responds, as though with a shrug, "Well since tis don let it go, come lets in" and they exit ([G2]r, S p. 88). It is perhaps significant that Aurelius, the noble suitor who has disguised himself as a merchant in order to win her, does not suffer a similar insurrection on the part of his mate, Phylema. But the playtext specifies no language or action to check Emelia's intractability. In this version, Katherine's sister is not only not silenced, it looks very much as though she has won. When she and her new spouse exit, Sly returns, and Katherine's message of submission is compromised even further – contained within a series of dramatic events, rather like a nest of boxes, that narrows down its applicability and ideological impact to almost nothing.

Perhaps the most fascinating differences between *A Shrew* and *The Shrew* are metadramatic: a play is a much more limited entity in *A Shrew*, much more exalted and powerful in *The Shrew*. To imagine Shakespeare in connection with *A Shrew* is to associate the Bard of Avon with a very lowly profession. The actors in *A Shrew* are humble, ill-educated itinerants. They enter bearing packs on their backs, and one of them is so ignorant that he has not mastered the classical generic terms of his trade. When the Lord asks them what they can perform for him, Sander, the actor-clown, answers, "Marrie my lord you maie haue a Tragicall / Or a comoditie, or what you will," and the other actor fiercely corrects him, "A Comedie thou shouldst say, souns / thout [zounds, thou'lt] shame vs all" (A3r, S p. 45). In *A Shrew*, the actors are also hungry. They craftily ask the lord for "a shoulder of mutton for a propertie, / And a little vinegre to make our Diuell rore" ([A3]v, S p. 46). But there is no devil in the play: the properties are intended for a more mundane purpose. Later on during the dinner scene at Ferando's house, when he prevents the famished Katherine from eating the meat he has offered her, the two of them exit and the stage directions read "*Manent* seruingmen and eate vp all the meate" ([D3]r, S p. 68) – the shoulder of mutton is eagerly consumed, no doubt sauced with the vinegar the actors have craftily finagled out of the lord. In *A Shrew*, the actors and Sly inhabit the same world of hardship, and they are able to give him the entertainment he wants: he remains awake enjoying the taming play almost to the end. Moreover, by their hunger, the actors are also at least temporarily identified with Katherine herself.

In the Induction to *The Shrew*, by contrast, the actors are allied with the Lord and his household against Sly. They are urbane and well educated, at home in the world of humanist discourse rather than alien from it. In this version, unlike the other one, Sly has never seen a play. The butt of the "commodity" joke is not an actor, but Christopher Sly himself, who queries, when offered a "pleasant Comedie": "is not a Comontie, a Christmas gambold, or a tumbling tricke?" (F TLN 291–92). And of course, the play itself is far above him. He wearies of it by the end of the first scene: "'Tis a verie excellent peece of worke, Madame Ladie: would 'twere done" (F TLN 563–64). After that he is never heard from again.

In *The Shrew*'s Induction, the alliance between the Lord and the actors is emphasized through his contemptuous treatment of his huntsman, whom he scorns as a "Foole" when the man fails to confirm his opinion as to which is the best of his hounds. This is a markedly different response than his respectful attention to the actors, whose opinions he appears to share and value. The Induction to the folio version also subtly tips the balance against Katherine's rebelliousness in advance by portraying a considerable degree of wifely deference as normative through the page's extravagant submission to his "husband," Sly, whom he/she addresses, "My husband and my Lord, my Lord and husband / I am your wife in all obedience" (TLN 260–61). The page's only speech to Sly in *A Shrew* is much less gratuitously deferential. It reads in full:

> Oh that my louelie Lord would once vouchsafe
> To looke on me, and leaue these frantike fits,
> Or were I now but halfe so eloquent,
> To paint in words what ile performe in deedes,
> I know your honour then would pittie me.
>
> ([A4]r, S p. 47)

Between the two versions of the Induction, in short, we can observe the same kind of gentrification as between Q and F *Merry Wives*. The general tone of conversation is more elevated in *The Shrew* than in *A Shrew*. Class and gender-based distinctions are accentuated, except, of course, for the striking case of the actors, who can boast a distinctly higher status in *The Shrew* than in *A Shrew*.

In *The Shrew* and in that version only, dramatic and pictorial art are valued for their verisimilitude, as figured through images of rape and male dominance: Sly is presented with sexually explicit pictures of Adonis, Cytherea, and Io "beguiled" and ravished by Jove, "As liuelie painted, as the deede was done" (F TLN 208). The Lord praises one of the actors for a similar verisimilitude in a previous role as wooer of a gentlewoman: "that part / Was aptly fitted, and naturally perform'd" (F TLN 96–97). The same claim is made at least implicitly by the taming play itself, with its ethos of male hegemony and female deference. Instead of being bounded by the reappearance of Sly, it has become independent of his narrow vision and attained, at the end, the status of "nature" rather than performance.

In *The Shrew*, the Induction is also more clearly localized than its counterpart in *A Shrew* through evocations of actual sites from Shakespeare's own early neighborhood in Warwickshire. Sly pronounces himself "old Sies sonne of Burton-heath" and suggests that his identity can be confirmed by "*Marrian Hacket* the fat Alewife of Wincot," whom he owes the precise sum of ninepence (F TLN 171–75). Given our earlier discussion of the tradition by which the Shakespeare of *Merry Wives* has been imagined as organically one with the English countryside, we can posit that the concrete depiction of place has contributed to editorial assessments of *The Shrew*'s superior authenticity. In that version, the verisimilitude called for in the Lord's approach to art is mirrored in the Induction's portrayal of Sly's neighborhood. During the nineteenth century, Bardolators liked to search out historical figures named Sly in the Stratford area as a way of pointing to the wonderful realism of Shakespeare's art – drawn to the very life.[20]

The Shrew's more compelling aura of reality is one of the salient characteristics for which that version has been preferred over the cruder and more farcical *A Shrew*. We will note, however, that in *The Shrew* the rising status of the actors in terms of their ability to claim a kind of truth for their art is bought at the price of woman's power and autonomy, since there is nothing to qualify the "truth" of female subordination they offer up at the end. If we imagine the play as a relatively bounded economy, then the actors triumph by putting women down, "realizing" womanly weakness in both senses of the term through their staging of Kate's submission. In *A Shrew*, the actors are lower and stay low; the women are brought less low. John Harington's *The Metamorphosis of Ajax* (1596) referred to *A Shrew* in a way that suggests he (and other readers of the quarto) found the play's message of shrew-taming in that version to be fatally and ruefully compromised by Sly's fantasy at the end: "For the shrewd wife, read the booke of taming a shrew, which hath made a number of us so perfect, that now every one can rule a shrew in our countrey, save he that hath her."[21]

Given the significant ideological difference between the two versions of the play, it is relatively easy to see why modern editors and critics have been at such pains to distance the two texts from each other, or at least to go along with earlier editorial decisions to keep them apart. As I have tried to suggest, a prime, if unarticulated, impetus behind the separation in twentieth-century editions has been simple misogyny – an unwillingness to accept as partly Shakespearean or even as pre-Shakespearean a play in which the woman (and therefore the text) is less thoroughly tamed and reformed than in the standard version. Positing *A Shrew* as a corrupt copy of the "genuine" play at once disposes of the specter of women as un-regulated and neatly salvages Shakespeare's artistic autonomy. If *A Shrew* is a pre-Shakespearean play, then Shakespeare's originality is compromised, since so much of *A Shrew* reappears in *The Shrew*. If *A Shrew* is a crude, early production by Shakespeare or by Shakespeare in collaboration with one or more other playwrights, then Shakespeare's authenticity is threatened: he is no longer the spontaneous, self-generated monolith that twentieth-century opinion has taught us to value, and the "genuine" folio version of the play loses its status as pure and unadulterated Shakespeare.

Even among recent reader-critics for whom the misogyny of a previous generation of editors would be abhorrent, *A Shrew* has usually been kept at arm's length from the "genuine" play, perhaps because if allowed to come into close proximity with the "correct" text, it would undermine yet another version of "gentle Shakespeare" – his time-honored reputation for unusual benignity, at least by the standards of his day, in his understanding of and sympathy for women. Second-wave feminists sometimes got around the misogyny of the play by claiming that Shakespeare had handled the case of the shrew as positively as the culture and literary tradition would let him. *A Shrew* exposes that argument as fallacious.

To the extent that they have considered *A Shrew* at all, even recent feminist critics, who are in theory committed to reversing the long tradition of misogynist interpretation of Shakespeare, have regularly fragmented the play according to the traditional rituals of avoidance, citing it piecemeal in order to demonstrate the superior artistry and humanity of the "authentic" version. They regularly excerpt parts of Kate's speech of submission from *A Shrew*, which argues for wifely obedience on the basis of Eve's responsi-bility for the Fall, in order to demonstrate the vastly decreased misogyny of Kate's arguments in Shakespeare's "authentic" version; but they ignore elements of the 1594 play that can, by the same criteria, be interpreted as less misogynist than the version of 1623. Just as regularly, they identify as defects features of *A Shrew* which, if analyzed instead as alternate versions of the text, might make the canonical *Shrew* sound less than humane by comparison.[22]

So long as it is assumed that *A Shrew* postdates *The Shrew*, Shakespeare's chief source for the taming plot can be safely postulated to have been folk materials like the horrific ballad *A Merry Iest of a Shrewd and Curst Wife Lapped in Morel's Skin for Her Good Behaviour* (circa 1550), in which a wayward wife is reduced to submission by being immobilized in the salted dermis of a dead horse. Shakespeare can therefore be shown to have altered the sexual politics of his antecedents for the better. The assumption behind such arguments is often that medieval and Renaissance farce are by their nature misogynist, and that Shakespeare is to be excused for the elements of farce that survive in his version of the play. But *A Shrew* is both more solidly within the category of farce than *The Shrew*, and considerably less misogynist.

To accept *A Shrew* as earlier than the preferred version of the play raises the unpalatable specter of a Shakespeare who may have increased rather than decreased the patriarchal violence of his materials, a Shakespeare not always already of "gentle" and gentlemanly status, but perhaps associating early in his career with mean, indigent actors like those of *A Shrew* and not at all disconcerted by the prospect of raising the status of his own profession by debasing that of some other group. If *A Shrew* is allowed out of its editorial and critical limbo, it can serve, like Q *Merry Wives*, as a critique of values operating in the received text of the play. Interpreters who accept the canonical text of the play without question are accepting a structure through which class aspiration and female submission operate as coordinate concepts, much as John Day's preface to *Gorboduc* conferred gentility upon the wanton text by restricting her range of mobility.

TRANSVALUING *A SHREW*

With the passage of the centuries, the gulf between the two *Shrews* has widened. In the Renaissance, as we have noted, the two texts were treated as one in terms of copyright; in the early eighteenth century, they were considered an earlier and later draft by Shakespeare. Beginning with Malone, *A Shrew* was less frequently considered early Shakespeare, more frequently identified as Shakespeare's source for *The Shrew*. In all of these hypotheses, *A Shrew* comes out as the earlier play, and I have made a case for that view as well. The shifts from *A Shrew* to *The Shrew* can be seen as the articulation of "modern" ideas (for the Renaissance at least) about women's place within the household and within the absolutist state; the name of Shakespeare thus becomes identified with the development of a more private, intimate model of family life. Similarly, the rising status of the actors from *A Shrew* to *The Shrew* runs parallel to the rising status and prosperity that theatrical historians associate with the profession during Shakespeare's time and with Shakespeare's own career in particular.[23] But the historical paradigms behind both of these postulated patterns of change are themselves subject to interrogation – a matter to which we will return in the next chapter as we consider "bad" *Hamlet*. Rather than prematurely fix a revised chronology between the two texts, we need to address at least some of the specific aesthetic judgments by which *A Shrew* has been long defined as "bad" and *The Shrew* as "good."

The textual arguments by which editors have convinced themselves (and others) that *A Shrew* is a contaminated version of *The Shrew*, or of an earlier play that was genuine Shakespeare, rest (as is usually the case in such discussions) on an implicit prior ranking by which *The Shrew* is assumed to be "what Shakespeare meant," so that deviations from it are invariably read as corruptions. In the subplot, the two plays are for the most part too divergent to be compared line for line. But, as we have already noted, the scenes involving shrew and tamer often correspond very closely. To the extent that they exhibit even minute differences, editors have seized upon these as telltale marks of corruption.

In the two versions we have already noted of the climactic moment in which Kate offers to place her hand beneath her husband's foot, for example, the standard editorial argument against the quarto version is that

> the imitator, as usual, has caught something of the words of the original, which he has laboured to reproduce at a most unusual sacrifice of grammar and sense . . . he has by omitting the words "in token of which duty" omitted the whole point of the passage.[24]

I have argued earlier that the "imitator," instead, is making a different point: Katherine is not placing her hand beneath her husband's foot as a symbolic affirmation of her status "beneath" him, but as a flamboyantly masochistic assertion the basic purpose of which is to win the bet for her husband. Both passages are violently patriarchal on the surface, but in *A Shrew* the surface message is undercut by the tamer himself and is thus less "genuine" as an articulation of patriarchal values.

The scene involving Petruchio/Ferando, Kate, and the tailor has also been fertile ground for editors intent on proving that *A Shrew* is a tainted text. In the "authorized" version, Grumio protests to the tailor, "Master, if euer I said loose-bodied gowne, sow me in the skirts of it, and beate me to death with a bottome of browne thred" (F TLN 2118–20). The equivalent speech in *A Shrew* is, "Maister if euer I sayd loose bodies gowne, / Sew me in a seame and beate me to death, / With a bottome of browne thred" ([E2]v, S p. 74). The criticism of *A Shrew* here is that "the reporter is very close but the difference is enough to show his hand. 'Sew me in the skirts of it' has meaning, whereas the variation has none."[25] The talk during the scene has been of facings, and facings quite commonly require the type of seam (though admittedly not quite the amplitude) in which a person could be sewn. Why does the idea of being sewn in a seam have no meaning? The speech in *A Shrew* is more ludicrous than its counterpart in *The Shrew*, and also more deviously ribald if one takes the idea of being sewn in a lady's seam as relating to her person, not her clothes. But in what way is the passage clearly derivative? Only if one has already decided what constitutes "good sense" in the text of the play, with variations representing nothing more than "rant" or "nonsense."

Slightly later in the same scene, *A Shrew* has the following exchange:

San. Doost thou heare *Taylor*, thou hast braued
Many men; braue not me.
Thou'st faste [faced] many men:
Taylor. Well sir.

San. Face not me Ile nether be faste nor braued
At thy handes I can tell thee.

([E2]v, S p 74)

The equivalent passage in *The Shrew* reads:

Gru. Thou hast fac'd many things.
Tail. I haue.
Gru. Face not mee: thou hast brau'd manie men, braue not me:
I will neither bee fac'd nor brau'd.

(F TLN 2108–11)

In this case, editors argue, *A Shrew* misses the puns on "fac'd" and "brau'd" and therefore declares itself as the derivative version. But all that would be required for *A Shrew* to make as much "sense" as *The Shrew* would be for the actor to indicate through gesture that the braving and facing he has in mind are punningly linked to the tailor's trade. *A Shrew*'s version of the passage is less explicit, but would hardly be regarded as corrupt if it were allowed to stand on its own: it is editorially suspect only because it does not replicate every nuance of *The Shrew*.

More clearly "contaminated" than either of these is a passage occurring earlier in the scene in the folio version, when Petruchio denies Katherine the cap she fancies. Kate protests, "Ile haue no bigger, this doth fit the time, / And Gentlewomen weare such caps as these." Petruchio retorts, "When you are gentle, you shall haue one too, / And not till then" (F TLN 2053–56). *A Shrew* has a similar interchange shortly before the scene with the tailor, when, denied her dinner, Kate threatens, "I will home againe vnto my fathers house" and Ferando answers her, "I [Aye], when you'r meeke and gentell but not / Before" ([D4]v, S p. 71). As editors have pointed out, the clever wordplay of the authorized version is missing from the "debased" version, but so, we will note, is the implied connection between social status and behavior. In *The Shrew*, as in an emerging set of late-Renaissance cultural norms by which it is the lady's behavior rather than her birth that determine her status and reputation, Katherine has to be "gentle" to be taken as a "gentlewoman."[26] In the equivalent passage from *A Shrew*, it is less than axiomatic that a woman must be submissive in order to claim "gentle" status.

Another passage which, according to editors, appears in corrupted form in *A Shrew* is Petruchio's speech likening Katherine to a falcon in training. In *The Shrew*, he utters a soliloquy that lets the audience in on his method of achieving sovereignty

> Thus haue I politickely begun my reigne,
> And 'tis my hope to end successefully:
> My Faulcon now is sharpe, and passing emptie,
> And til she stoope, she must not be full gorg'd,

> For then she neuer lookes vpon her lure.
> Another way I haue to man my Haggard,
> To make her come, and know her Keepers call:
> That is, to watch her, as we watch these Kites,
> That baite, and beate, and will not be obedient: . . .
>
> (F TLN 1822–30)

Petruchio's comparison is apt because the falcons and hawks used in hunting were more often females than male, and because training them to hunt on command was called "manning" them. He is describing an early stage of the taming process, when the bird is kept hungry until she finally "stoops" to a lure on the ground and learns to return at her master's call.

The equivalent passage in *A Shrew* is considerably briefer and lacks, as we might expect from our previous experience of the play, the initial emphasis on the husband as ruler. Instead of informing the audience as to the progress of his reign, Ferando acknowledges that he is adopting a temporary "humor":

> This humor must I holde me to a while,
> To bridle and hold backe my headstrong wife,
> With curbes of hunger: ease: and want of sleepe,
> Nor sleepe nor meate shall she inioie to night,
> Ile mew her vp as men do mew their hawkes,
> And make her gentlie come vnto the lure,
> Were she as stuborne or as full of strength
> As were the *Thracian* horse *Alcides* tamde,
> That King *Egeus* fed with flesh of men,
> Yet would I pull her downe and make her come
> As hungry hawkes do flie vnto there lure.
>
> ([D3], S p. 68)

This speech is admittedly more prosaic and labored than its folio counterpart, but has suffered a comical excess of attention on the part of disapproving editors. It has been damned for mixing metaphors of hawk taming and horse taming, for its repetitiveness, for its illogicality (how can "ease" be a "curb"?), and for its failure to understand the sport of falconry.[27] The accusation that Ferando mixes his metaphors is easily enough answered – so does Shakespeare, with what some eighteenth and nineteenth-century editors regarded as lamentable regularity. The accusation of infidelity to the sport of falconry is more interesting. *A Shrew* is not less accurate than the authorized version, but it is different. By promising to mew Katherine up, Ferando describes the practice of contemporary falconers who kept newly caught birds "mewed" until they were tame enough to be flown to the lure. In such a situation, "ease" would indeed be a "curb." We may wish to note parenthetically that here, as in Katherine's final speech, the quarto version implicitly rejects the folio argument that women should enjoy the soft ease of being kept pent up at home.

If we wished to adopt the hairsplitting editorial logic of many attacks on the textual integrity of *A Shrew*, we could contend that Petruchio's language drawn from falconry may well be less "correct" than Ferando's, since Petruchio seems to advocate watching a "bating" falcon – that is, one who flaps its wings violently and risks injury during its confinement. The best authorities of the period held that such birds, if unhooded, should not be approached at all.[28] But the issue could be argued either way, and is scarcely worth further attention. If we attempt to answer editorial arguments point by point, a law of diminishing returns quickly sets in by which a full enough argument to satisfy doubting experts would put off a wider readership. Suffice it to say that advocates of the memorial reconstruction theory of *A Shrew*'s origins have severely distorted that version in order to demonstrate its impurity.

Yet another telltale sign of *A Shrew*'s contaminated nature has been identified as Sly's reaction, during one of his interruptions of the taming plot, to the entrance of Valeria and Kate. The stage directions read "Enter *Valeria* [Aurelius's servant, disguised as a singing master] with a Lute and *Kate* with him"; Sly remarks, "O braue, heers two fine gentlewomen" ([C1]v, S pp. 57–58). It has been assumed that the disjunction between Sly's comment and the actual sex of the characters who enter is a result of textual disturbance of some kind. But is Sly's admittedly curious perception an unequivocal sign of corruption or a clue to early staging of the scene? Valeria in disguise, if the singing master was imagined as being in minor orders, might have worn a soutane or similarly skirted garment, in which case Christopher Sly's telltale gaffe might point toward the singing master's effeminacy: he waxes eloquent on the subject of music's power but finds it inefficacious against Katherine. Sly's "error" also points toward *A Shrew*'s more fluid gender boundaries. Appropriately for a comedy about a "woman on top," *A Shrew* likes to play with the exchange of gender roles. Just as the music master becomes a woman in Sly's perception, Kate becomes a man: she and other characters refer to her "manliness" and "manhood." The play exhibits considerably less anxiety about male prerogative than the authorized version, and creates considerably less polarity between masculine and feminine gender expectations.

Perhaps the most damning flaw of *A Shrew* in the minds of those who have argued for its derivative status is its frequent Marlovian echoes, of which the lines about the "Thracian horse" in the falcon-taming passage quoted above are typical examples. The argument here is that the ignorant actors who patched together the pirated version of the play threw in snatches of Marlowe whenever their memories failed them, creating a pastiche with no claim to independent literary integrity. Peter Alexander characterizes the putative compiler(s) as having "a mentality very like that of ancient Pistol, and a head no more proof against the intoxication of tragic diction."[29] That *A Shrew* contains numerous passages echoing *Tamburlaine the Great* and *Doctor Faustus* is undeniable, though some of the alleged parallels are too faint to be convincing. If we grant that text the same privilege of putative intentionality that is routinely granted to *The Shrew*, however, we can regard the Marlovian passages not as mere unassimilated bombast, but as deliberate stage quotations of tragedies well known to audiences in the early 1590s – quotations designed to create a ludicrous effect of mock heroic in their new and incongruous setting.

In the Induction to *A Shrew*, for example, when the Lord and his men first enter, his grand language echoes the famous speech with which Faustus first conjures up his devils:

> Now that the gloomie shaddow of the night,
> Longing to view Orions drisling lookes,
> Leapes from th'antarticke World vnto the skie
> And dims the Welkin with her pitchie breath,
> And darkesome night oershades the christall heauens . . .
>
> (A2r, S p. 43)

What the Lord conjures up, however, is not demons from hell but the drunken, sleeping Sly. The humor can scarcely be said to be subtle, but the scene might have been quite funny on stage, and adds a vague aura of otherworldly menace to the person of the drunken tinker. In the corresponding scene at the end of the play, when Sly is once again lying before the alehouse, the Tapster utters a parallel passage just before stumbling upon him:

> Now that the darkesome night is ouerpast,
> And dawning day apeares in cristall sky,
> Now must I hast abroad: but soft whose this?
> What *Slie* . . .
>
> ([G2]r, S p. 88)

The device is doubly ludicrous the second time, and helps to underline the return of Sly, whose discovery once again takes center stage.

Similarly, the love-stricken suitors of Katherine's sisters in *A Shrew* can scarcely articulate their passion without plunging into Marlovian bathos. The sisters' answers are frequently simple and matter-of-fact, deliberately and comically deflating the suitors' eloquence. *A Shrew* does not so much plagiarize Marlowe as borrow Marlovian language to undercut the heroic pretensions of the speakers. There are more limited examples of the same technique in canonical Shakespeare: ancient Pistol himself, or the Prince of Morocco, whose Marlovian style of utterance in the *The Merchant of Venice* contributes to the derision in which he is held by Portia and Nerissa.

Sometimes *A Shrew*'s Marlovian echoes take the form of stage business. In the scene at Petruchio's house, *A Shrew*, unlike *The Shrew*, specifies that Petruchio/Ferando enters "with a peece of meate vppon his daggers point" ([D4]v, S p. 70), echoing the hideously powerful moment in the First Part of *Tamburlaine the Great* 4.4 in which Tamburlaine offers food at his sword's end to the conquered Bajazeth. Published in 1594, *A Shrew* was staged at a time when the fashion for Marlowe ran high and numerous playwrights made deliberate use of his diction, not necessarily out of an impoverished ability to imagine any other kind of language, but out of a canny sense of how a dominant stage discourse could be turned to their own dramatic ends. The many Marlovian echoes of *A Shrew* help to keep the play firmly within the realm of farce, overturning any faint whisper of the heroic about Ferando's bombastic campaign against the shrew, undercutting any incipient claim to realism (of the kind so prominently made in *The Shrew*) before it has a chance to develop.

Barring the discovery of new evidence, we are unlikely ever to settle the question of which play came first, or how much of either is genuine Shakespeare. We may settle such matters to our own satisfactions, but if past editorial opinion is any guide, what pleases us as explanation may not equally please those who come after us. To my own ear, *A Shrew* sounds distinctly earlier, sounds as though it could perhaps contain bits of early Shakespeare and be designed to capitalize on the public passion for Marlowe during the early 1590s. *The Shrew*'s rejection of a ranting, overblown acting style for one "aptly fitted and naturally perform'd" could then be interpreted as not only a general artistic credo, but also as a generic critique of its uncouth, farcical precursor.

Advocates of the theory of memorial reconstruction have spent ample energy on the parallel scenes, but never adequately accounted for the difference between the subplots of the quarto and folio *Shrew*s. There is no way that the Bianca subplot, with its rivalry among the suitors, could have been "remembered" as the Emelia-Phylema subplot. Indeed, the latter is far too coherent in its own right to be the work of a thief whose abilities were as low as those posited for the average memorial reconstructor. Advocates of the theory of memorial reconstruction who confront the problem of *A Shrew*'s subplot are usually forced to posit an intermediate version of the play between the "original" *The Shrew* and its debased copy, or to contend that both the quarto *A Shrew* and the folio *The Shrew* are derived from Shakespeare's original version, albeit the former more corruptly than the latter. Both of these alternative explanations relocate the problem of the subplot without solving it.

Then too, some advocates of the theory of memorial reconstruction have been distinctly uneasy about dating *The Shrew* to the early 1590s, a dating that is necessary if *A Shrew* was to be pirated and published by 1594. John Dover Wilson, for example, ends his textual introduction to the 1928

New Shakespeare edition with the caveat, "If the reader be prepared to accept this conclusion [as to the chronological priority of *The Shrew*], let him not shut his eyes to the consequences." One of these is that "Shakespeare at this early date was already capable of the verse we find, for instance, in Petruchio's speech at the end of 4.1. or Katharina's at the end of 5.2." This is "not a remarkable feat for the greatest of all poets at the age of 27 to 30, and yet one that orthodox Shakespearian criticism will, unless we are mistaken, find it very difficult to credit."[30] Wilson's caveat beautifully illustrates the clash between paradigms of the Shakespearean text in the early decades of our century. For the older, "evolutionary" model, Shakespeare started out imperfect and improved at his craft with age and experience; for the newer "monolithic" model, Shakespeare was a master of his craft from the beginning. Wilson's allegiances were not entirely won over to the latter.

There are, on the other hand, several indicators that *The Shrew* may have been revised from *A Shrew*. The patriarchal theory featured in *The Shrew* – by which the family is a microcosm of the state and its patriarch a figure of the monarch – was widely promulgated during the early 1590s, when *The Shrew* is presumed to have been written. But the theory as it appears in the folio version of the play, with its more strikingly absolutist language and its emphasis on the prerogatives of the husband's reign, is closer to Jacobean than to Elizabethan rhetoric on the subject. Elizabeth I had occasionally taken on a distinctly male language of royal prerogatives, but her use of the rhetoric was, because of her biological sex, more limited than that of either James or Charles I. As other scholars have noted, Jacobean and Caroline love poetry, like *The Shrew*, often described the male lover in a male-gendered language of royal prerogative powers that was foreign to poetry written under Elizabeth.[31] It has been credibly argued, moreover, that the Bianca subplot, borrowed from George Gascoigne's *Supposes*, was grafted onto an earlier version of the play rather than being part of the "original." The interface between subplot and main plot in *The Shrew* shows minor inconsistencies and "loose ends" of a kind similar to those we briefly noted earlier in Windsor castle portions of *Merry Wives*.[32] And, as Eric Sams has suggested, the echoes of other plays in *The Shrew* would have been timely during the early seventeenth century, just as the Marlovian echoes of *A Shrew* were timely during the early 1590s.

If *The Shrew* was revised from the 1594 text of *A Shrew* or from some other text closely resembling it, then Shakespeare's contribution to the play may well have been the amplification and polishing of the Induction and the Petruchio/Katherine materials, the substitution of the more interesting and witty Bianca subplot for the earlier one, and – quite possibly – the deliberate dropping of the earlier play's epilogue. The burnished, eloquent language of capitalist commodification that is one of the distinguishing features of *The Shrew* by comparison with *A Shrew* would then be a salient element of Shakespeare's revision of the play. Indeed, it may have undergone continuing revision even after his death, and could well have been touched up by other hands for its publishing debut in the First Folio.

Whether or not we label *A Shrew* as Shakespeare, we need to recognize it as a more intriguing play than its long history of suppression would suggest. But what would be the point just now of insisting on the priority of one or another version? To do so would be reverting to the old editorial mode of creating textual hierarchies that are invariably value laden. I would suggest instead that we start thinking of the different versions of *The Taming of the Shrew* intertextually – as a cluster or network of related texts that can be fruitfully read together and against each other as "Shakespeare." To do so is to carry Shakespearean textual studies out of the filiative search for a single "authentic" point of origin and into a new discursive world in which the authority of the author loses its élan and the work is recognized as unstable, existing as an array of concrete, physical documents rather than as that elusive disembodied entity, the work as the author intended it.

THEATRICAL *SHREW*S AND TEXTUAL TRANSMUTATIONS

The theatrical history of shrew texts has altered along with shifting gender stereotypes, but not always in the ways we might expect. As noted above, *The Taming of the Shrew* we have seen on stage during the last decade or two has increasingly resembled *A Shrew* in its ending. Directors employ the return of Christopher Sly as a device for denying or at least mitigating the "reality" of the taming plot, which carries overtones of oppressive brutality toward women that are difficult for modern audiences to tolerate. Meanwhile, our standard editions continue to label the Sly epilogue as non-Shakespearean. There is nothing new about this disjunction. During the long performance history of the play, there has frequently been a wide gap between what passes as genuine Shakespeare in the printed text and what is accepted as Shakespeare in performance.

During the eighteenth century, it was the stage rather than the page that banished Christopher Sly. Eighteenth-century editions of *The Taming of the Shrew* regularly include the Sly epilogue, perhaps because the idea of a prologue without the balancing epilogue was uncomfortable to neoclassical tastes. But at the same period, Sly was excised from the shrew play as staged and given his own separate venue. During the late seventeenth and eighteenth century, the cultural need to naturalize the story of the play was so intense that in Garrick's highly popular afterpiece *Catharine and Petruchio* (printed 1756), *The Taming of the Shrew* was whittled down to the taming story *tout seul*. In Garrick's rewriting, Petruchio's rough edges are rounded off somewhat, Sly and the subplots are banished, and the conclusion is softened: Petruchio and Kate share in the delivery of the final speech, which loses some of its didactic impact through frequent interruptions by the other characters. John Lacy's *Sauny the Scot, or The Taming of the Shrew* (1667), similarly omitted the frame entirely. The Sly material did not fall by the wayside, however; it formed the basis of two farces both called *The Cobler of Preston* by Charles Johnson and Christopher Bullock respectively and both published in 1716.

On the eighteenth-century stage, it would seem, the Sly plot and the taming plot were kept strictly separate so that neither could compromise the credibility of the other. As Samuel Johnson noted scoffingly in his edition of Shakespeare, the story of the shrew and her tamer was printed as fact in the *Tatler*, passed off as a notable "transaction in Lincolnshire."[33] During the same century, Kate's speech was split off from the play and published separately (with a few added lines) as a wholesome sermon on wifely duty. Eighteenth-century readers and playgoers seemingly wanted the taming story to be true, though some women readers even then found Kate's submission excessive. However, they didn't much care whether or not the story was labelled "Shakespeare."[34]

Garrick's *Catharine and Petruchio* continued popular on stage until almost the end of the nineteenth century. But during the same period, there was a growing thirst for "authentic" Shakespeare on the part of both editors and theater-goers. The name of the Bard had to be reattached to the taming story. *The Shrew* in its folio version had been absent from the stage for two hundred years. It was revived, with the Induction but without the Sly interruptions and conclusion, in England in the 1840s, in America in the 1880s. Thereafter the "authentic" text of *The Shrew* gradually won the stage from *Catharine and Petruchio*. In Victorian productions, most directors took great care to keep Christopher Sly and the Induction from undercutting the taming story. Some prominent productions also followed *Catharine and Petruchio* in omitting lines from *The Shrew* that provide motivation for Katherine's ill humor by showing Baptista's preference for Bianca.[35]

Critics and audiences of the Victorian productions of *The Shrew* seem generally to have liked Kate's speech of submission, applauding it wildly and calling it the "choicest gem of the play." H. N. Hudson asserted that *The Shrew* was worth "All the volumes on household virtues that I know of." Even the most successful and fiery of nineteenth-century actresses to play the part of the Shrew, Ada Rehan, saw the taming of Kate as bringing her "to the saving grace of woman." In the first British production of the "authentic" *Shrew*, one of the actors in the Induction was made up to resemble Shakespeare, then proceeded to take the role of Petruchio, brandishing the traditional whip, so that wife-taming became a Shakespearean virtue indeed.[36] "Authentic" Shakespeare for the Victorians showed the beauties of wifely acquiescence. We probably do not need to remind ourselves that the same century, through the theories of Sigmund Freud, gave us the concept of normal female masochism, by which Katherine's rebelliousness becomes comprehensible as reaction-formation against her own deepest desires.

In the course of the nineteenth century, the play as edited and the play as staged gradually drew closer together. One of the mechanisms by which this was accomplished was the marginalization of *A Shrew*. Sly dropped out of the play's ending on stage as he had since Malone in Shakespearean editions. *The Shrew* and its message of wifely submission became the "original"; *A Shrew*, with its freer relationship between Petruchio/Ferando and Katherine, its many undercuttings of the shrew-taming moral, was increasingly perceived, in a subtly sexualized language of transgression, as a debased and brazen travesty of the "manly" Shakespearean version.

In the early twentieth century, a new fissure developed between the play as staged and the play as edited. Widespread editorial agreement with the textual theory by which *The Shrew* was original Shakespeare, or close to it, and *A Shrew* a "vamped up" copy, came in the 1920s, along with the rise of the "vamp" and the triumph of women's suffrage. The term *vamped* or *vamped up*, as used in editorial discussions to describe a text that was cobbled or patched together, predated the arrival of the "new woman" in the aftermath of World War I and the 1920s. But the term *vamp* occurs with special frequency in textual discussions of the 1920s and early 1930s, which were, as D. C. Greetham has noted, decades of particularly strong misogyny in textual studies.[37] James Thurber, from whom this chapter's opening anecdote was cited, also penned an essay entitled "Why I Hate Women" and numerous other misogynistic bits originally designed to amuse the mixed audience of the *New Yorker* during the 1920s and 1930s. Before and during World War I, the scold's bridle had been revived as a recommended regimen on postcards linking Peace on the Home Front to the curbing of women's tongues.[38] Small wonder that the editorial "vamp" aroused some of the same anxieties as the "new woman." The twentieth century's "vamp" was the younger sister of the Elizabethan John Day's wanton: we can identify, yet once more, a fascinating cultural seepage by which a vocabulary of sexual transgression filters into discussions of the "bad" quartos. Given the many differences between the two plays, *A Shrew* might never have been identified as a memorial construction at all if the times had been different. Its freer treatment of gender issues made its danger to *The Shrew* far greater than would have been the case in a period when such issues were less volatile.

Meanwhile, the late nineteenth and early twentieth-century struggle for women's rights made "authentic Shakespeare" on stage in *The Taming of the Shrew* increasingly uncomfortable for audiences. Directors often tried either to engage the play's topical potential directly – at least one production cast Kate as the "new woman" – or to mitigate the tensions by staging the play as farce. Reviewers commented regularly on Kate's submission as unlikely to commend itself, as one of them put it, "to the out-and-out feminists of the Women's Federation League or the generality of the shingled and Eton-cropped sisterhood."[39] In 1926, two years before Women's Suffrage in Britain, Peter Alexander wrote his influential article in the *Times Literary Supplement* contending that *A Shrew* was a "later and degraded version" of Shakespeare's play and relying heavily on arguments first broached a half century before. Other editors during the 1920s and later put Shakespeare at even greater distance, arguing that his original play was lost, and that both *A Shrew* and *The Shrew* were derivative, though the latter more strongly Shakespearean than the former.[40] At the same time that "new women" were agitating for the vote in England, editors were burying the "vamped up" version of *A Shrew* deeper and deeper – like a shameful madwoman in the Shakespearean attic that had to be kept out of sight. Even editors who remained skeptical about Alexander's view of the relationship between the two plays displayed a nostalgia for past simplicities, as in Quiller-Couch's comment in the New Shakespeare (1928):

> avoiding the present times and recalling Dickens, most fertile of inventors since Shakespeare, with Dickens's long gallery of middle-aged wives who make household life intolerable by various and odious methods, one cannot help thinking a little wistfully that the Petruchian discipline had something to say for itself.[41]

In twentieth-century productions of *The Shrew*, the patriarchial violence of the piece has been evaded or at least attenuated by many ingenious methods: Katherine may wink at the audience even as she hoodwinks Petruchio, as in Mary Pickford's film version, or the shrew may be portrayed as a loveless neurotic who is cured by Petruchio through a psychodrama that shows her her own excess. Quite often she abases herself out of love and a desire for offspring, as in the Burton/Taylor Zeffirelli film. Or the whole production can be reduced to farce, as in Joseph Papp's Wild West version of the play in Central Park. At present, however, all of these methods seem to have played themselves out on stage (and film) and there are signs that the equivalent critical readings are playing themselves out as well – not only among modern feminists, who find the text too alienating to be "set right" by such strategies, but also among our students, who are increasingly unhappy with our usual readings emphasizing the mutuality of the taming and other such palliatives designed to smooth over the reality of Petruchio's domination. We can choose, of course, to quietly remove the play from the list of those we teach and discuss, as a number of perceptive readers have recently suggested we do.[42] Or we can bring back *The Shrew*'s long suppressed intertext *A Shrew*, the tactic resorted to on the modern stage.

In the eighteenth century, readers of Shakespeare got the Sly ending to the play, while theater-goers saw the play cleansed of Sly and rechristened *Catharine and Petruchio*. Now, the opposite pattern prevails: theatrical productions vary among themselves, but often depend on the Sly framework to cast the patriarchal argument of the taming plot into doubt and unreality, while reading texts continue to banish Sly at the end and conclude with the "reality" of Katherine's capitulation. Amidst all of the experimentation with the Sly materials on stage, our texts of *The Shrew* have remained stubbornly, disappointingly stable and uniform.

If *A Shrew* comes to be accepted by editors and readers as an acceptable intertext of *The Shrew* (whether as a first draft, source, or early derivative), then *The Taming of the Shrew* will again be subject to the shapeshifting that has characterized its past textual history. In editions of Shakespeare that offer composite texts of other plays, *The Shrew* could also become composite, as it was in eighteenth-century editions from Pope to Capell. In the same way that modern editors have regularly inserted the mock trial scene and other brief segments from the 1608 quarto of *King Lear* into the folio text, even though that quarto has been branded by some as "bad," so they could insert the Sly episodes and other material from the 1594 quarto *A Shrew* into *The Taming of the Shrew*. It is not as though editors have been altogether fastidious in barring other questionable material from our standard editions: witness the parallel case of *Macbeth*, in which the witches and Hecate in 3.5 and 4.1.38–43 are, by strong editorial consensus, a non-Shakespearean interpolation, yet almost always kept in the playtext, despite the vast stylistic difference between their free, airy diction and the clotted imprecations of the witches elsewhere in the play. Perhaps we need to coin an adjective for the Sly materials and other such matter that is too close to Shakespeare to be discarded but not quite established as canonical. The return of Christopher Sly is "Shakespearish" even if it is not quite Shakespeare.

A composite edition amalgamating the two *Shrew* plays would, of course, violate the author's intent, if Shakespeare himself was responsible for the deletion of the Sly ending. Moreover, if the publication history of the play is any guide, early modern readers preferred *The Shrew* over *A Shrew*. *The Shrew* appeared in quarto after its publication in the 1623 First Folio, while *A Shrew* quietly dropped into oblivion. There are many possible explanations for this preference by contemporaries: *The Shrew* is wittier and would have appeared more refined and up to date than the farcical, Marlovian *A Shrew*, which was very old fashioned by the time of *The Shrew*'s publication in 1623. But the more "absolutist" patriarchy of *The Shrew* may also have been perceived as more up to date. Even some of my strongly feminist students have contended that we need to keep the play's traditional ending intact on the grounds that *The Shrew* draws the battle lines in unequivocal terms while *A Shrew* evades the unsavory truth.

To take such a position is to reify and solidify a set of gender relations that were unstable during the period. I am not so sure that the play's patriarchal logic aroused anything approaching universal assent during the period of the play's earliest reception. We have already noted John Harington's comment with reference to *A Shrew* that wife-taming was an impossible dream. If Shakespeare (or someone else) did deliberately drop the Sly ending, that move may well have been taken to make the play more nakedly controversial – a deliberately provocative contribution to the *hic mulier* debate that raged on and off from the 1580s until the 1630s. Patriarchy in early modern English culture was not a single, palpable thing, but rather an array of disparate processes, some powerful and negative, others more benign. As some recent feminist theorists have insisted, we need to replace the singular with a plural – posit for any complex culture not a single patriarchy, but an array of more dispersed patriarchal ideologies.[43] It makes good cultural sense that there was more than one *Shrew* generated during our period. To insist on preserving any single form of patriarchal discourse at the expense of others operative within the same culture would be to mime the activity of *The Shrew*'s indefatigable and autocratic tamer, Petruchio.

I have pointed to a process of naturalization by which, in the theatrical and textual history of the play, the ideology of *The Shrew* gradually became "reality" in terms of public expectations in the theater and reader expectations of Shakespeare. But that process was not without its glitches, temporary reversals, and ambivalences in any period – certainly not in the Renaissance itself. The same culture that preferred *The Shrew* to *A Shrew* also made space for an antidote. In the early seventeenth century, John Fletcher continued the story of Petruchio in *The Woman's Prize, or, The Tamer Tamed*, in which Katherine has died and Petruchio marries a second wife, Maria, who subjugates him as effectively as he had earlier tamed Kate, except that Maria's methods are Draconian to the point of paramilitarism. When Shakespeare's *The Shrew* and Fletcher's *The Woman's Prize* were performed within a few days of each other at the court of Charles I in 1633, Shakespeare's *The Shrew* was "liked" but Fletcher's play was "very well liked."[44] Patriarchy as a system has regularly been more consistent and orderly in the minds of historically inclined editors and readers than it has been in society at large.

Throughout the present book, I have been arguing against composite editions of plays that exist in markedly variant early texts on the grounds that the troublesome doubles of the standard texts can provide us with an array of culturally available choices that cast the received texts in an interesting new light. The argument applies with particular strength to *A Shrew* and *The Shrew*. A much more satisfying format than the composite text for future editions of the play would follow the pattern of the newest editions of *King Lear* or the Bevington–Rasmussen *Doctor Faustus* and print both

A Shrew and *The Shrew* in their entirety, one after the other.[45] Such a format, particularly if it keyed scenes in one version to close parallels in the other, would preserve the integrity of each early version while offering readers the ability to work back and forth between the two with ease. Those who continue to prefer the canonical ending of the play would have it before them, but would be forced to deal with the implications of *A Shrew*'s vastly different configuration of patriarchal ideology instead of fragmenting that version in order to shore up and justify *The Shrew*.

If present trends toward the computerization of Shakespeare continue, both texts will soon be available as well in a computerized hypertext format, which will offer a dazzling, unsettling new form of empowerment. With only a slight stretching of the traditional rationale of copytext by which the best possible text is arrived at through the combination of variant early versions, electronic readers will be freed, if the task appeals to them, to become their own editors, to create onscreen combinations of the two texts that follow the editorial procedure used for composite texts but yield, perhaps, a very different play. To many scholars and more general readers, such an arrangement raises the dread specter of textual chaos: if all readers become their own editors, then myriad texts will be generated and we will no longer be able to talk about *The Shrew* as a single, determinate thing. Even before the arrival of computerized hypertext as a dominant technology in Shakespeare studies, however, the old sense of textual stability we have enjoyed and suffered in past decades is already fatally compromised by our recognition of the constructed nature of all editorial practice. As they have for some time, scholars may feel the need to agree on a standard text of Shakespeare for use in communicating with each other, for use in the classroom, and perhaps also for general readers who prefer their Bard in the form they are accustomed to. But electronic classrooms based on Shakespeare in hypertext are not far in the future; they already exist at some institutions. Soon those of us who choose to will – for better or worse – be able to construct our own editions of this and other plays on the computer screen and bring them almost instantly into the more stable medium of print via desktop publication.

The seemingly inevitable computerization of Shakespeare studies is helping to increase the authority of the early quarto and folio texts. As consensus about the "correct" text of *The Taming of the Shrew* gradually weakens, the concrete artifacts will, so long as they can be kept intact, remain available as a relatively stable reference point for the definition of Shakespeare. Indeed, as I argued in the introduction, the present revolution in writing technology has helped to generate new interest in the materiality of Renaissance printed materials. The early texts can, of course, be scanned onto the computer, where they too can become subject to revision. But by their alien typography, they will remain a little less open than modern versions of the plays to the intruding hand of the corrector/defiler. And so, in our fearful speculations about a future we cannot control, we come full circle to the humanist anxiety discussed at the beginning of the chapter: if the "wanton" text is "free" to all comers, who is to save it from spoliation? Our unknown computerized future eerily replicates sixteenth-century fears about the promiscuity and uncontrollability of print, except that sixteenth and seventeenth-century writers were beginning to recognize the power of print to preserve literary works even as it made them vulnerable to appropriation.

For us, however, the chief danger is not so much a sexualized defilement of Shakespeare as a disintegration of the standardization by which we are able to imagine that, in talking about Shakespeare, we are all talking about the same thing. No doubt the fears are unjustified. No doubt future scholars and editors will continue to be able to distinguish *A Shrew* and *The Shrew*, and develop mechanisms to control the proliferation of all variant texts just as they have in the past – most notably for us through the development of the New Bibliography in the early and mid-twentieth century. As we heap scorn upon past editors, their unthinking misogyny, and their seemingly desperate devices for containing and solidifying the Shakespearean canon, it will do us no harm to recognize that the degree of anxiety some of us experience in the face of an unknown electronic future is much the same as – and certainly not greater than – theirs as they faced a different set of unknowns.

5

BAD TASTE AND BAD *HAMLET*

We are apt to call *barbarous* whatever departs widely from our own taste and apprehension, but soon find the epithet of reproach retorted on us.

David Hume

The centuries-old ritual is about to begin anew. In a small theater, Hamlet nears his most famous soliloquy, the immortal language of which has remained relatively stable over time, even as other elements of the play have altered. The audience shift in their seats and become still with concentration. The house lights seem to dim and the stage lights, to brighten. How will this actor's delivery measure up to that of the thousands who have preceded him in the role? What new nuances, new emphases, will he (or occasionally she, as in the case of Sarah Bernhardt's Hamlet and more recent female Hamlets) bring to the performance? In what way will this Hamlet mark the soliloquy as his own? He begins traditionally enough, but then something goes radically wrong:

> To be or not to be – aye, there's the point.
> To die, to sleep – is that all? Aye, all.
> No!
> To sleep, to dream – aye, marry, there it goes.
> For in that dream of death, when we awake –
> And borne before an everlasting judge –
> From whence no passanger ever returned –
> The undiscovered country, at whose sight
> The happy smile, and the accursed, damned –
> But for this, the joyful hope of this,
> Who'd bear the scorns and flattery of the world:
> Scorned by the right rich, the rich cursed of the poor,
> The widow being oppressed, the orphan wronged,
> The taste of hunger, or a tyrant's reign,
> And thousand more calamities besides,
> To grunt and sweat under this weary life,

When that he may his full quietus make
With a bare bodkin? Who would this endure,
But for a hope of something after death,
Which puzzles the brain and doth confound the sense,
Which makes us rather bear those evils we have
Than fly to others that we know not of?
Aye, that!
O this consciènce makes cowards of us all.[1]

The Hamlet uttering these lines will, needless to say, forfeit his opportunity to measure up to the long tradition of great Hamlets, since his lines will not be perceived as *Hamlet*. So deeply engrained in our cultural expectations is the established text of "To be or not to be" that any deviation from it is likely to be greeted as parody, and the audience on this theatrical occasion is no exception. Hamlet's first wrong turn of language meets with polite titters, but as the mistakes multiply, the titters quickly expand into guffaws. While some laugh at the apparent burlesque, others sit in uneasy silence, not sure how to react. Still others quicken to intellectual alertness: this is not the usual soliloquy, but something strange and heterodox, too close to the received version to be effective parody, yet too distant to communicate the same message. What is the meaning of this speech, the message of this strangely altered *Hamlet*?

The scene being described is a hypothetical reconstruction of events that have actually occurred in recent productions of the first quarto of *Hamlet*, yet another of our "bad" quartos, but one that has aroused extraordinarily strong interest during the past decade, particularly in theatrical circles.[2] My reconstruction is in one major way fallacious: during performances of Q1 *Hamlet*, it would be an uneducated audience indeed that would fail to recognize before the moment of "To be or not to be" that they were watching a radically different *Hamlet* than the usual one – different not only in terms of its brevity, since many productions prune the play down almost to bare bones, but in terms of its choice of words and altered syntax – its consistent debasement, bastardization, or (to adopt a more neutral term) simplification of the refined, poetic language of the play as we expect to find it.

The textual situation of *Hamlet* is more complex than any treated so far in the present study in that, since 1823, when the first of two extant copies of Q1 *Hamlet* was discovered, the play has existed for us not in two, but in three early versions: the first and second quartos (1603 and 1604–05 respectively), and the First Folio (1623). All three texts are interrelated: the folio version resembles Q1 more closely in some respects, Q2 more closely in others. Each has significant pieces of dialogue that exist in no other version. As Philip Edwards has acutely noted, our sense of the deep ambiguity of the play is closely connected with its lack of a clear text: "Both the prince and his play come down to us in more shapes than one. If the prince were not so mercurial the text would be more stable."[3]

Of the three early *Hamlet* texts, the second quarto has most often served as the copytext for modern editions, although G. R. Hibbard, Stanley Wells, and Gary Taylor adopt the folio for substantives in their recent Oxford editions on the grounds that the folio version represents Shakespeare's own revision of the play.[4] But in their attempts to establish a stable text for *Hamlet*, those who have constructed the major twentieth-century editions have ransacked all three early versions and related plays (the German *Der bestrafte Brudermord*, *The Spanish Tragedy*, *Antonio's Revenge*) for recurring configurations that would lead them to Shakespeare's intent. *Hamlet* as we usually read it is an elaborate mosaic of readings culled from early quartos, folios, and a long tradition of editorial emendation whereby the irregularities and grotesqueries of the early printed texts are smoothed over. Having made use of Q1 and other contemporary plays, however, most recent editors have gone on to suppress them as possible influences on Shakespeare, according to elaborate versions of the "Purity and Danger" ritual analyzed above in chapter 3. Indeed, in Harold Jenkins' Arden edition, the ritual is enacted twice: first to protect the editor's preferred *Hamlet* against John Marston's *Antonio's Revenge*, which includes many similar incidents and which older editors had regarded as the earlier play and therefore an influence on Shakespeare, and second to protect Q2 against the marauding energies of Q1. To the extent that they adopt readings from Q1 or confirmed by Q1, editors tend to avoid mentioning that text in their notes.[5] Q1 is an embarrassment, a potential blot on the reputation of Shakespeare.

In general, the fortunes of Q1 *Hamlet* have altered along with that of the other "bad" quartos considered in previous chapters. After its discovery in the 1820s, most scholars regarded it as Shakespeare's earliest sketch for the play, albeit probably marred by corruptions. Charles Knight described it as a "vigorous sapling" that grew luxuriantly over time to become the "monarch of the forest."[6] After 1900, more and more editors regarded it as a corrupt adaptation or memorial reconstruction of the "real" *Hamlet*, even though they conceded that Shakespeare's *Hamlet* could not have been the first play of that name. For A. C. Bradley in 1904, Q1 *Hamlet* was still the "original form" of Shakespeare's play; in textual matters, as in many others, Bradley was heir and culmination of a long nineteenth-century tradition. By the time of John Dover Wilson's *What Happens in Hamlet* (1935), Q2 was the obvious choice for copytext and Q1 could be confidently dismissed even by Wilson, who had earlier posited it as Shakespeare's source play somewhat touched up by Shakespeare. For the later Wilson, Q1 was a "garbled text based upon notes got together by someone, whether actor or spectator, present at original performances of the play, as all critics are now agreed."[7] Editors after Wilson still acknowledged that there must have been some sort of "Ur-*Hamlet*," a pre-Shakespearean play of the same name. But they posited the Ur-*Hamlet* as unrecoverable and thereby created an unbridgeable gulf between it and Shakespeare's version of the play: the Ur-*Hamlet* receded into a mythic past and Shakespeare's *Hamlet* magically achieved the status of a charismatic original independent of any forebears.

The modernist consensus still holds firm in terms of editorial practice in mainstream editions of *Hamlet* despite a strong movement recently afoot in other circles to rehabilitate Q1.[8] Most recent editors continue to assert that Q1 is a memorial reconstruction – even Gary Taylor and Stanley Wells, who have done so much to rehabilitate Q *King Lear*.[9] But in their attempts to sort out the echoes and transformations from one early printed text to another, modern editors have been driven almost to a version of Hamlet's madness: which textual ghost speaks the truth of Shakespeare's meaning? Or do all of them bear treacherous false witness to the author's intent?

In the present chapter, I will not reenter the vast, disorienting labyrinth of conflicting evidence that has had to be negotiated by every modern editor of the play, but will confine myself for the most part to a small corner of it – to a reexamination of the early quarto versions of the play, the first of which is "bad" and the second of which is "good." Q1 *Hamlet* is indeed "bad" *Hamlet*, and will continue to be bad so long as we rank the early texts of the play on the basis of their adherence to culturally predetermined standards of literary excellence. Given that "To be or not to be" in its traditional form is itself generally regarded as a touchstone for rarefied, discriminating taste – a pinnacle of literary artistry – any attempt to assert the value of an alternative version of the immortal lines is automatically defined as evidence of a tin ear, an inability to appreciate the sublimity of Shakespeare. The matter is therefore unarguable within the established limits of the inquiry: "To be or not to be" in its traditional form is quintessential Shakespeare. Either you grasp its inexpressible excellence or you don't, and if you don't, God help you. As Samuel Taylor Coleridge put the matter long since, "O heaven! words are wasted to those that feel and to those who do not feel the exquisite judgement of Shakespeare."[10]

But the soliloquy has served as a powerful cultural shibboleth in part because it is uttered by an attractive, strongly-drawn, noble character who himself posits a hierarchy of taste by which the "judicious" are sequestered off from the "general" on the basis of their ability to see the world – and human artifacts – with the same discriminating taste that Hamlet himself does. We need to remind ourselves of the almost overpowering degree to which literate culture in general and professors of literature in particular are invested in an appreciation of literary excellence as a guarantor of their membership in an intellectual elite. *Hamlet* in its high cultural form is "caviary to the general," and we who have the ability to savor it earn inclusion in a select circle that Hamlet himself – and through him, Shakespeare – has defined.

As Barbara Herrnstein Smith and others have argued, literary value is contingent: the degree and kind of artistry we attribute to a given play or poem will depend not only on the particular era we inhabit, but also on our specific situation within that era – the cultural group we come from, belong to, aspire towards.[11] Indeed, as we have already noted earlier, much of the power of traditional editorial practice has derived from the editor's ability to call upon and reinforce seemingly unquestionable standards of taste shared with the more enlightened members of his or her readership. These standards, and the editions that both reflect and promulgate them, can alter markedly over time. For I. A. Richards, anyone who liked a sonnet by Ellen Wheeler Wilcox was "incapable of surviving in a complex environment and therefore biologically unfit" (cited in Smith, p. 37). Feminist scholars operating successfully in the yet more complex environment of the 1990s may question the critical assumptions behind Richards' assessment. Alexander Pope's Shakespeare would scarcely serve the present age, any more than our Shakespeare would serve his.

Moreover, the existence of shared standards of taste is much easier to document in broad matters than in instances of textual detail: literary scholars and other informed readers may agree in general about the authors to be included in an established canon, and about the basic shape of the works attributed to those authors, but when it comes to minute discriminations of language, the apparent consensus breaks down into wrangling and petty difference. *Hamlet* itself supplies an excellent case in point: for much of our century, at least before the new Oxford Shakespeares, editors were in substantial agreement about the broad shape of the play, thereby cementing an elite community with each other and with their discriminating readers. But when it comes to choosing or amending the precise wording of individual passages, the consensus falls into fragments and the text remains in flux, with no two editors precisely in accord. One famous example is the array of suggested language for the famous crux in 4.2 – Hamlet's sarcastic reference to Claudius and his creatures in terms of (variously) apes, apples, nuts and jaws, depending on the edition that we happen to consult.

The proliferation of readings here and elsewhere in *Hamlet* derives in part from each editor's need to document that she or he has perused the early materials independently of previous editors. But that need is itself driven by a strong urge to make "progress" against the insidious and intractable textual problems of the play. "Advancement in perfectness" has been one of the chief goals of *Hamlet* editors at least since that goal was articulated by Edward Capell in the late eighteenth century.[12] "To be or not to be" in its traditional form has been important for nineteenth and twentieth-century culture in part because it is, unlike much of the rest of the play, a passage upon which (with the exception of two or three words) there has long been strong unanimity. Here, at least, is immortal language that exists precisely as Shakespeare intended it. And here, at last, is Shakespeare disclosing his deepest thoughts about the human condition. The soliloquy is difficult and subject to a variety of interpretations, but the words themselves can be relied on. They are woven deeply into the fabric of our culture and their static, monolithic power serves the useful function of helping to keep the community of good taste intact and deflecting attention away from textual variations elsewhere in the play that might destabilize the apparent consensus.

It will not be the business of this chapter to attack the hierarchy of taste by which "To be or not to be, that is the question" is defined as high, refined, and Shakespearean, and "To be or not to be, aye, there's the point," as low, vulgar, and fraudulent. The theoretical bases for such an argument have been clearly set out by others already cited in my notes, and the argument itself, although easily made, will not convince anyone who is not already willing to admit the fallibility of his or her own judgment. Rather, I will seek to recast the discussion about Q1 *Hamlet* entirely by considering that text and its "betters" in terms of the differing expectations created by orality and writing as competing forms of communication within the Renaissance playhouse. Was Shakespeare's theater as literate as modern editorial practice, with its insistence on the sovereign authority of Shakespeare's manuscripts and acts of writing, assumes it was? How did actors in the Elizabethan and early Jacobean playhouses learn their lines? How did they conceptualize the plays they worked on – as written "text," as oral discourse, or as a complicated mixture of both? And finally, how might recent studies of memory and mnemonics in early modern and earlier culture alter our received notions about the role of memory in the early modern theater?

For advocates of the theory of memorial reconstruction, memory is inherently contaminated and texts generated by that means, by definition untrustworthy. According to W. W. Greg, memorial reconstruction denotes "any process of transmission which involves the memory no matter at what stage or in what manner."[13] By such a definition, as I shall argue later, nearly all Renaissance playtexts are culpable in one degree or another. Over and over again within Shakespeare's plays, but particularly in *Hamlet*, bad taste is associated with an outmoded oral theatrical culture. Similarly, for twentieth-century adherents of the theory of memorial reconstruction, "bad" Shakespeare is the product of defective memory and insufficient literacy. Modern readers and critics have, quite understandably, recapitulated Shakespeare's own apparent assumptions about the relative value of oral and literate culture: good taste is associated with writing as opposed to orality; and "good" Shakespeare, with the creation of a theater that is specifically literary.

These matters are obviously highly speculative, but as we shall see, the cultural authority that defines the first quarto as "bad" *Hamlet* derives in large part from Hamlet himself, and from the new, more self-contained literary theater that he favors. When the ghost commands Hamlet to "Remember me" the prince does not trust to his memory, but writes the words down, except that he doesn't record them quite accurately: in both Q1 and Q2, the ghost thrice cries "adiew" before the command "remember." Hamlet writes down only two adieus. Modern editors follow the folio in having the ghost utter only two adieus, so that Hamlet's writing has the precision we expect of a "copy." Just as in this instance the folio version is more "literate" in its reproduction of language than either quarto version, Q2 is regularly more literary and literate than Q1 in terms of formalized criteria of difference between primarily oral and primarily literate cultures.[14] Insofar as Q2 participates more fully in our own profoundly literate assumptions about the proper shaping and complexity of art, Q2 and F (which resembles Q2 much more closely than it does Q1 in terms of language) will remain a standard against which Q1 is found wanting. But Q1 will remain like a beckoning ghost who does not write but intones, urging us to remember that the theatrical culture of the Elizabethan playhouse may have been profoundly different from the literary cultures within which *Hamlet* has been edited.

HAMLET, Q1 AND Q2

The textual mystery of *Hamlet* begins with the peculiar circumstances of its early publication. The first quarto appeared in 1603 with a title page that reads in full:

> THE / Tragicall Historie of / HAMLET / *Prince of Denmarke* / By William Shake-speare. / As it hath beene diuerse times acted by his Highnesse ser- / uants in the Cittie of London: as also in the two V- / niuersities of Cambridge and Oxford, and else-where / At London printed for N.L. and Iohn Trundell. / 1603.

The printer of this edition has been identified as Valentine Simmes. As has frequently been noted, there was an irregularity in the publication, in that "A booke called the Revenge of Hamlett Prince [of] Denmarke as yt was latelie Acted by the Lord Chamberleyne his servantes" had already been registered in 1602 to another printer, James Roberts.[15]

The plot thickens with the appearance of the second quarto in late 1604 and early 1605. Its title page reads:

> *THE* / Tragicall Historie of / HAMLET, / *Prince of Denmarke.* / By William Shakespeare. / Newly imprinted and enlarged to almost as much / againe as it was, according to the true and perfect / Coppie.

/ AT LONDON. / Printed by I.R. for N. L. and are to be sold at his / shoppe vnder Saint Dunstons Church in / Fleetstreet. 1604 [or 1605].

This time, James Roberts, to whom *Hamlet* was registered, was the printer. For many twentieth-century editors, the second title page has seemed actively to supplant the first, so that a narration of the publication history of the play might read rather like this: some low character, probably John Trundell (who was mentioned as co-publisher on the Q1 title page, and who was known for his sponsorship of base, popular printed materials – ballads, marvellous narratives, and the like) illegally acquired a corrupt copy of the play. Rather than suffer such a debased text to be promulgated under his name, Shakespeare hastened to put the "true" play in print the very next year with the printer whom he had previously authorized to publish *Hamlet*, so that Q2 would be based on the author's genuine papers and not on a pirated copy.[16]

Recent research has somewhat diminished the cloak-and-dagger drama of this narrative: Roberts regularly printed for the publisher Nicholas Ling, whose device appears on both title pages, and Ling made a practice of acquiring texts from others in the trade. Since Roberts and Ling worked together uninterruptedly both before and after the first quarto was published in 1603, it is likely that the two reached some understanding about Q1 and that it was published with Roberts' consent.[17] Nevertheless, the two title pages, with their double and conflicting guarantees of authenticity to performance (in the case of Q1) and to the written copy (in the case of Q2), have helped to generate a strict dualism in our understanding of the two texts: Q1 was a performance text of some kind, or a debased copy thereof, with all of the corruption that such a suspect origin suggests; Q2, on the other hand, was a literary text based on the author's own manuscript "Coppie," with the promise of genuineness that such provenance implies. I am less interested in disputing this differentiation of the two quartos for descriptive purposes than in probing into the subtle moral and evidentiary valuation that causes one text to rank very high and the other, very low. Why such privilege for the literary over the theatrical?

Before delving further into the matter of provenance, however, we need to look more closely at differences between the two quarto versions. As usual with the bad quartos, the specific scapegoat function to which Q1 has been put has caused it to appear a disjointed heap of fragments rather than a respectable work of literature possessing its own claim to unity. In fact, Wilson characterized it as a thing "of shreds and patches," adapting Hamlet's closet scene description of Claudius as a way of rendering it both morally bad and uninterpretable.[18] To prefer Q1 over Q2 would be to demonstrate the same base perversity of taste that has caused Gertrude to prefer loathsome Claudius over fidelity to the memory of King Hamlet.

Ironically, however, it is only in Q1 that the ragtag language is unequivocally applied to Claudius. In that version, Hamlet demands to know how
his mother could "leaue him that bare a Monarkes minde, / For a king of
clowts, of very shreds" (H 168 [G2]v),[19] and the ghost enters only after
twelve more lines of dialogue. In both Q2 and F, however, the equivalent
phrase does not occur until after the entrance of the ghost – a timing that
makes Hamlet's meaning more problematic:

> *Ger.* No more.
>
> ### Enter Ghost
>
> *Ham.* A King of shreds and patches,
> Saue me and houer ore me with your wings
> You heauenly gards: what would your gracious figure?
>
> (H 170 [I3]v)

In both Q2 and F (but not in Q1) it is possible that the "King of shreds
and patches" Hamlet describes is the ghost whose entrance has been
recorded immediately before. In Q1 the stage directions call for the ghost
to enter "*in his night gowne*" but his attire is unspecified in the alternative
texts: might he be wearing a cerecloth or some other strange and irregular
apparel?

Only by reference to Q1 can editors achieve certainty as to Hamlet's
meaning and thereby keep intact the hierarchy of taste by which Hamlet
Sr is associated with the "good" quarto and Claudius, with the "bad."
Indeed, one of the defining marks of Q1 is that it is usually clearer and
more straightforward than the other early texts – not only in terms of
language, but also, preeminently, in terms of action. It is not a "thing
of shreds and patches" if considered in its own terms, but shows the same
pattern of consistent difference that we have already observed in the other
"bad" quartos.

In Q1, Polonius is named Corambis, and some other names vary slightly:
Ophelia is spelled Ofelia, Laertes becomes Leartes, Q2's *Gertrard* is Gertred
in Q1, and *Guyldersterne* and *Rosencraus* (Q2) have the more sinister names
of Gilderstone and Rossencraft. Their behavior in Q1 matches the more
foreboding nomenclature. In Q2, Hamlet greets them as "good friends,"
refers to them later as "deare friends," and several times alludes to his love
for them and theirs for him; moreover, his mother confirms that he has
"much talkt" of them. In Q1, she makes no such claim and the relationship is more distant: he greets them only as "kinde Schoole-fellowes" (H
96, 98) and engages in none of the affectionate badinage with them that
he does at least initially in Q2. Indeed, in Q1 their primary allegiance
appears to be to Claudius – he, not Hamlet, calls them "friends" and
protests his "great loue" for them (H 76). Fittingly, in Q1, unlike Q2,
Horatio expresses not the slightest regret over their death: they were
Claudius's creatures from the start.

Other characters' roles are also subtly but significantly altered in the first quarto so that the line between good and evil is sharper. In Q1 Claudius is a more thoroughly villainous character than he is in Q2: he lacks the unctuous surface geniality he often displays in Q2, and works less in concord with the queen. In Q1, it is he, not Leartes [Laertes], who suggests the stratagem of the poisoned sword to ensure Hamlet's death. If Claudius is more clearly nefarious in Q1, however, Gertred is more clearly innocent of at least the worst crimes of which she stands accused.[20] She acts less in concord with Claudius, and swears to her son in the closet scene that she was unaware Claudius had dispatched her first husband: "But as I haue a soule, I sweare by heauen, / I neuer knew of this most horride murder" (H 172 G3r). Moreover, in Q1 only, at the end of the scene she hastens to promise her help in Hamlet's revenge:

> I vow by that maiesty,
> That knowes our thoughts, and lookes into our hearts,
> I will conceale, consent, and doe my best,
> What stratagem soe're thou shalt deuise.
>
> (H 176 G3)

Later on, in a scene unique to Q1, Horatio reveals to Gertred Hamlet's successful evasion of Claudius's plot for his execution in England and she responds by renewing her allegiance to her son, remarking of Claudius, "I perceiue there's treason in his lookes / That seem'd to sugar o're his villanie" and assuring Horatio that she will cover up her true feelings, "soothe and please" Claudius "for a time" only to allay his suspicions, "For murderous mindes are alwayes jealous" (H 208 [H2]v).

Hamlet, too, is less unfathomable in Q1 than in Q2, but also more "healthy minded" in the conventional meaning of the phrase. Nearly all of his language of sexual loathing is absent from Q1. To be sure, in the soliloquy parallel to Q2's more famous "O that this too too sallied flesh would melt," he exclaims in Q1, "O that this too much grieu'd and sallied flesh / Would melt to nothing," and later on in the same speech he notes (as in Q2) his mother's sexual hunger for Claudius: "Why she would hang on him, as if increase / Of appetite had growne by what it looked on" (H 32 [B4]r). But that speech is almost the only point in the first quarto version at which Hamlet seems to dwell on his mother's sexual frailty and his own "sallied flesh," and even there, the idea of his mother's gaining appetite by "looking" on Claudius lacks some of the grotesqueness of Q2's conflation of the sexual and the alimentary: "As if increase of appetite had growne / By what it fed on" (H 32).

Similarly, in the stage direction describing the dumbshow, Q1 is empty of most of the sexualization that is so prominent in Q2 and F. The Q1 stage directions read:

Enter in a Dumbe Shew, the King and the Queene, he sits downe in an Arbor, she leaues him: Then enters Lucianus with poyson in a Viall, and powres it

in his eares, and goes away: Then the Queene commeth and findes him dead:
and goes away with the other.

(H 140 F3r)

In this version from Q1, it is never stated on what terms she "*goes away with*
the other." In Q2, by contrast, her behavior with both men is explicitly
sexualized by the stage directions – the queen embraces the king and he,
her; he "*declines his head vpon her necke*"; finding him dead she "*makes*
passionate action" and allows herself to be wooed by the poisoner: "*shee*
seemes harsh awhile, but in the end accepts loue" (H 140 [H1]v). In the Q1
version of the actual play, the murder takes place in "*guyana*" rather than
"*Vienna*" and the Duke's name is *Albertus* rather than *Gonzago*. But a more
crucial difference is that in the Q1 "Mouse trap" the pair has been married
for "Full fortie yeares" rather than thirty, as in Q2; appropriately, the
husband in Q1 is more seriously burdened with age and loss of sexual
potency: the "blood" that filled his "youthfull veines" now "Runnes weakely
in their pipes" (H 142). In Q2 the parallel passage is, for once, less graphic
than Q1: "My operant powers their functions leaue to do" (H 142).

There is a similar contrast in the two closet scenes: the Hamlet of Q2
dwells yet again on his mother's appetites: the "ranck sweat of an inseemed
bed / Stewed in corruption, honying, and making loue / Ouer the nasty
stie" (H 168 I3r). In Q1, his language is far less voyeuristically graphic:
"Who'le chide hote blood within a Virgins heart, / When lust shall dwell
within a matrons breast?" (H 168 [G2]v). For a broad stream of Freudian
critics beginning with Freud himself and his disciple Ernest Jones, Hamlet
is the English Oedipus – unable to kill Claudius because of his own
repressed desire for his mother and covert identification with Claudius as
the man who has won her away from his father.[21] That interpretation is far
less available in Q1, in which most of Hamlet's "diseased" language is not
present and in which most of his sexual anguish seems to relate to the
breach with Ofelia rather than repressed desire for his mother. Indeed, in
the speech cited above, he seems to regard "hote blood" as (relatively
speaking) appropriate for a "Virgin" – perhaps for a virgin like Ofelia?

Q1 also "lacks" Hamlet's wonderfully ambiguous lines from the final
soliloquy that exists only in the second quarto " . . . how stand I then /
That haue a father kild, a mother staind, / Excytements of my reason,
and my blood, / And let all sleepe" (H 190 [K3]v). A Freudian reading
of the passage would take its lack of clarity over agency as an unwitting
confession of Hamlet's unconscious desire to possess his mother and
dispose of his father – is it he who, in the labyrinthine world of his own
repressed fantasies, has killed his father and stained his mother? By failing
to include most of Hamlet's incestuous preoccupation with his mother's
sexuality, Q1 fails to confirm one of the master discourses of the twentieth
century. Given that the Freudian reading of Hamlet's relationship to

Gertrude has been prominent in screen and stage versions of the play since Laurence Olivier's classic film version a half century ago, it is understandable that Q1 *Hamlet* has seemed during the same period to lack authenticity in terms of its psychodynamics.

Q1 is also more "healthy minded" than Q2 in terms of the philosophical and religious attitudes it articulates, at least to the extent that adherence to mainstream opinion can be defined as healthier than deviance. Q1 is a short, strangely powerful revenge play in which Hamlet almost entirely "lacks" the crippling melancholy or weakness or depression that many critics have found central to his character. In his conversation with Rossencraft and Gilderstone, for example, the Hamlet of Q1 is decidedly less melancholy than in the Q2 version of the speech, which confesses a pervasive heaviness of disposition that has caused Hamlet's world to lose light, color, and meaning to the point that it appears but a "pestilent congregation of vapoures" (H 100). In Q1, he complains merely "No nor the spangled heauens, nor earth nor sea, / No nor Man that is so glorious a creature, / Contents not me" (H 100 [E2]v).

Similarly, at the end of the encounter with Polonius/Corambis in which Hamlet taunts him as a "Fishmonger," Q2 has Hamlet respond to Polonius's announcement that he will take his leave with the arresting speech, "You cannot take from mee any thing that I will not more willingly part withall: except my life, except my life, except my life" (H 94 [F1]v). Q1 omits the world-weary repetition and Hamlet offers only insult: "You can take nothing from me sir, / I will more willingly part with all, / Olde doating foole" (H 94 [E2]v). In Q1's version of "O what a rogue and pesant slaue am I," by contrast, Hamlet's opening appears to display a more vehement self-contempt than in the standard version. The first line of the soliloquy in Q1 reads "Why what a dunghill idiote slaue am I?" Further on in the same soliloquy, moreover, Hamlet refers, as in Q2, to "my weakenesse and my melancholy." But in Q1 those passions have a clearer "objective correlative" in that, as part of the same speech, he articulates (in Q1 only) his bitterness at his loss of the throne: "His father murdred, and a Crowne bereft him" (H 114–18 [E4]v–F[1]r).

"To be or not to be" is also vastly different in the two quarto versions. Whatever we may think of the nervous, staccato, almost catechetical questions and answers, interspersed with disjointed speculations, that constitute the soliloquy in its Q1 form (Figure 5.1), we will note that its argument is considerably altered. To put the matter in the baldest possible terms, in Q2, Hamlet contemplates suicide, but rejects it on account of some unknown terror in the afterlife: ills "we know not of." In Q1, he contemplates suicide but rejects it on more conventional religious grounds: not out of dread of something after death, but "for a hope of something after death" – the hope of being numbered among the "happy" rather than the "accursed." In Q2, the "vndiscouer'd country" of the afterlife is totally

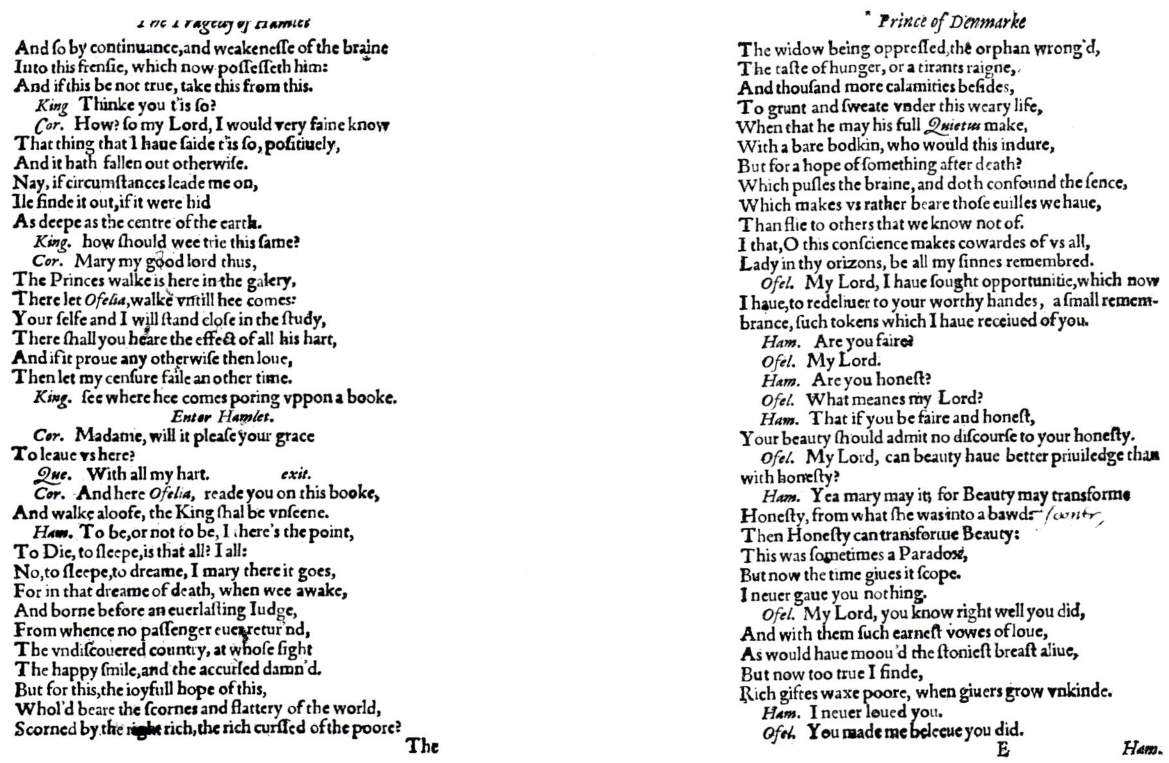

And so by continuance, and weakenesse of the braine
Into this frensie, which now possesseth him:
And if this be not true, take this from this.

King. Thinke you t'is so?

Cor. How? so my Lord, I would very faine know
That thing that I haue saide t'is so, positiuely,
And it hath fallen out otherwise.
Nay, if circumstances leade me on,
Ile finde it out, if it were hid
As deepe as the centre of the earth.

King. how should wee trie this same?

Cor. Mary my good lord thus,
The Princes walke is here in the galery,
There let *Ofelia*, walke vntill hee comes:
Your selfe and I will stand close in the study,
There shall you heare the effect of all his hart,
And if it proue any otherwise then loue,
Then let my censure faile an other time.

King. see where hee comes poring vppon a booke.

Enter Hamlet.

Cor. Madame, will it please your grace
To leaue vs here?

Que. With all my hart.   exit.

Cor. And here *Ofelia*, reade you on this booke,
And walke aloofe, the King shal be vnseene.

Ham. To be, or not to be, I there's the point,
To Die, to sleepe, is that all? I all:
No, to sleepe, to dreame, I mary there it goes,
For in that dreame of death, when wee awake,
And borne before an euerlasting Iudge,
From whence no passenger euer retur'nd,
The vndiscouered country, at whose sight
The happy smile, and the accursed damn'd.
But for this, the ioyfull hope of this,
Whol'd beare the scornes and flattery of the world,
Scorned by the right rich, the rich curssd of the poore?

The

The widow being opprest, the orphan wrong'd,
The taste of hunger, or a tirants raigne,
And thousand more calamities besides,
To grunt and sweate vnder this weary life,
When that he may his full *Quietus* make,
With a bare bodkin, who would this indure,
But for a hope of something after death?
Which puzels the braine, and doth confound the sence,
Which makes vs rather beare those euilles we haue,
Than flie to others that we know not of.
I that, O this conscience makes cowardes of vs all,
Lady in thy orizons, be all my sinnes remembred.

Ofel. My Lord, I haue sought opportunitie, which now
I haue, to redeliuer to your worthy handes, a small remembrance, such tokens which I haue receiued of you.

Ham. Are you faire?

Ofel. My Lord.

Ham. Are you honest?

Ofel. What meanes my Lord?

Ham. That if you be faire and honest,
Your beauty should admit no discourse to your honesty.

Ofel. My Lord, can beauty haue better priuiledge than
with honesty?

Ham. Yea mary may it, for Beauty may transforme
Honesty, from what she was into a bawd—/conty
Then Honesty can transforme Beauty:
This was sometimes a Paradox,
But now the time giues it scope.
I neuer gaue you nothing.

Ofel. My Lord, you know right well you did,
And with them such earnest vowes of loue,
As would haue moou'd the stoniest breast aliue,
But now too true I finde,
Rich giftes waxe poore, when giuers grow vnkinde.

Ham. I neuer loued you.

Ofel. You made me beleeue you did.

       E   *Ham.*

Figure 5.1 Q1 "To be or not to be" (1603)
Reproduced by permission of the Henry E. Huntington Library,
San Marino, California

144

mysterious and unknown, despite the earlier testimony of the ghost (perhaps a sign, as W. W. Greg suggested long since, that the ghost is not to be trusted?). In Q1, the afterlife bears a familiar, more comforting shape: conscience makes men cowards in the very direct sense that he who takes revenge risks damnation. Conversely, however, he who does not take revenge can console himself with hope for the life to come. Hamlet's reservations about the revenge in Q1 are rationally arrived at, for all of the seeming dislocation of his language. Q2 is much darker and more paralyzing, in that he cannot perceive any of his alternatives as clearly preferable to the others: indeed, they all seem to converge upon the same stalemating uncertainty about an afterlife that, if he adhered to standard Christian teaching, would have a much more definable shape. Q1 Hamlet's questioning takes place against a ground of basic epistemological stability. Q2 Hamlet, at least as the play is usually interpreted, inhabits a more inhospitable, unfathomable universe – one more closely in tune with the deep skepticism of twentieth-century modernism.

In Q2, similarly, Hamlet dies uttering the enigmatic line, "the rest is silence." It is left to Horatio to provide the hope of "flights of Angels" that may (or may not) sing the dead prince to his "rest." In Q1, it is Hamlet himself who clothes his death in orthodoxy: his last words are "heauen receiue my soule" (H 266). Yet once more, good and evil are more easily distinguished than in Q2. Despite the blood he has shed, the prince dies in the hope that he has not irrevocably jeopardized his place among the righteous. Much is obviously lost in the first quarto of *Hamlet* through the absence of the moral stalemating and wide-ranging interrogation that is such an important part of most twentieth-century audiences' experience of *Hamlet* in performance and of *Hamlet* in the standard editions. Q1 Hamlet carries little of the existential angst that has endeared the play to modernists; indeed, the young prince in Q1 is scarce recognizable as the "melancholy Dane." But what is lost in terms of Hamlet's relentless, nearly manic probing of the dark borders of human existence is partly gained back by his increased capacity for action.

Q1 *Hamlet*, if recent testimony by actors, directors, and audiences is any guide, can work wonderfully well in the theater. Its rhythms are entirely different from those of Q2: what it lacks in terms of philosophic range and refinement of language, it compensates for through an abundance of theatrical energy. Q1 is "*Hamlet* with the brakes off."[22] While Q2 frequently doubles back upon itself and slows down the action with long meditative speeches, Q1 *Hamlet* has no time for prolonged meditation and very little time for soliloquies. The play moves relentlessly and powerfully from the first, horrifying encounter with the ghost to Hamlet's bloody end. The differing language of "To be or not to be" correlates with larger structure: in Q2 the ontological alternatives constitute a "question" with no obvious answer; in Q1, Hamlet's posing the alternatives instead constitutes a

"point," a step along the way to a decisive conclusion: "To be or not to be
– aye there's the point!"

As has frequently been noted, Q1 "straightens out" the action of the
play so that Hamlet's actions follow logically one from another.[23] The two
main soliloquies in the middle of the play are reversed, as they often are
in modern productions: Corambis [Polonius] reads Claudius the letter in
which Hamlet professes his love to Ofelia, and they decide to eavesdrop
on a conversation between the two. That plan is put immediately into
effect. Hamlet enters upon the lines "To be or not to be" and then
launches into the Nunnery scene with Ofelia. Shortly after, the players
enter and, at Hamlet's request, offer the Priam and Hecuba speech (much
curtailed); Hamlet asks them to perform the "murder of *Gonsago*" with
a few added lines, they exit, he launches into the soliloquy ending "The
play's the thing, / Wherein I'le catch the conscience of the King" (H 118
F[1]r) and, after a brief scene between Claudius, Gertred, Rossencraft
and Gilderstone, the "play within a play" commences. Hamlet moves
effectively from thought to action, his every decision ironically pushing
him closer to his doom. His final major soliloquy, "How all occasions
doe informe against me," is "missing" from Q1, as it is from the folio
version of the play.

In Q2 and modern edited versions, by contrast, Hamlet's every action is
blocked or its energies "turned awry." He draws the seemingly decisive
conclusion, "the play's the thing / Wherein Ile catch the conscience of the
King," early on, before the encounter with Ophelia. But then his resolve is
deflected: we find him brooding on suicide in "To be, or not to be," which
had appeared much earlier in Q1. Well after *The Mousetrap* was supposed
to settle the matter of Claudius's guilt, in Q2 (and that version only) we
find Hamlet reengaging the same knotty questions as earlier, albeit from
a new perspective, in his final soliloquy, "How all occasions doe informe
against me." Only in Q2 is he, at this late point in the action, continuing
to castigate himself for delaying the revenge.

The switchback pattern of Q2 has its own considerable fascination –
Bradley thought it a Shakespearean revision that was one of the most
brilliant coups of the play in terms of revelation of character.[24] But
Q2 Hamlet's self-reversals do slow the play down in the theater – a major
reason why directors frequently adopt the somewhat streamlined pattern
of F or even the greatly increased pace of Q1 for performance. If the two
quarto versions of *Hamlet* are considered intertextually, Q2 can safely be
described as slow, meditative, and introspective. Q1, rather like the *Faustus*
A text, is fast, powerful, and iconoclastic and offers some of the pleasures
of iconoclasm: it brutally excises "idle" verbiage and strips away impedi-
ments to action. That is not to say that Q1 is to be preferred over Q2: in
the absence of the icon, the power of iconoclasm is lost. And Q2, in any
case, offers at the thematic level its own pleasures for the iconoclast – its

restless philosophical searching can be seen as undercutting the relative orthodoxy of Q1.

Moreover, there is a fascinating correlation in the two quartos between the pacing of the action and the putative age of the prince, at least if we are willing to accept the data by which Hamlet's age has traditionally been calculated. In Q1, he is a young man of about twenty: Yorick's skull has lain in the ground "this dozen yeare," and Hamlet's memories of him are those of a child: "A fellow of infinite mirth, he hath caried mee twenty times vpon his backe, here hung those lippes that I haue Kissed a hundred times . . . " (H 234 I[1]r). In Q2, he has the same memories of Yorick, but the jester's skull "hath lyen you i'th earth 23. yeeres" (H 234 [M3]v). Q2 Hamlet has to be thirty because the sexton, who has kept his trade "man and boy thirty yeeres," began it in the year of young Hamlet's birth. (Interestingly enough, Hamlet Sr's victory over Fortinbras is also more recent in Q1: it happened a mere dozen years before, not thirty, as in Q2, which means that Hamlet is considerably younger at the time of the play than his father was at the time he conquered Fortinbras.) Q1's Hamlet has some of the breakneck impetuosity associated elsewhere in Shakespeare, as in the Renaissance generally, with youth: like the young lovers of *Romeo and Juliet*, he hastens to meet his end. By comparison, Q2 Hamlet, although capable of precipitate action, is more cautious and deliberative, perhaps even jaded, as is appropriate for a somewhat older man. Indeed, in Renaissance terms, a man of thirty was on the threshold of middle age. We would not wish to push the contrast too far: there are slow youths in Shakespeare (like Slender in *The Merry Wives of Windsor*) and plenty of rash men a decade or so older. But in both quartos of *Hamlet*, the hero's age is curiously apt in terms of the structure and language of the play.

To what are we to attribute the profound differences between Q1 and Q2? We can easily generate narratives of origin to place in competition with the theory of memorial reconstruction and its wholesale rejection of Q1.

Narrative A

In which Shakespeare, newly arrived in London,
tries his inexperienced hand at a play

We know that there was a *Hamlet* play extant as early as 1589, as referred to in Nashe's preface to Greene's *Menaphon* (1589). Nashe describes a new and uneducated type of playwright, "shifting companions" who can scarcely claim literacy but "will affoord you whole Hamlets, I should say handfuls of Tragicall speeches." As noted in the previous chapter, a *Hamlet* was played at Newington Butts on June 9, 1594, as part of the same run as *Titus Andronicus* and some version of *The Taming of the/a Shrew*. Thomas Lodge saw a *Hamlet* performed at the Theatre by the Lord Chamberlain's

Men in or shortly before 1596: he refers in his *Wit's Misery and the World's Madness* to the pale "Visard of the ghost which cried so miserably at the Theatre, like an oister-wife, Hamlet, revenge."[25] All of these *Hamlet*s but the first were specifically associated with Shakespeare's company, but none was specifically attributed to Shakespeare. Indeed, *Hamlet* was not included in Francis Meres' list of Shakespeare's plays as of 1598, although we have no reason to suppose that his list was meant to be exhaustive.

Eric Sams has recently made a spirited case for Q1 *Hamlet* as the "Ur-*Hamlet*," written by Shakespeare in 1589 or earlier. Shakespeare *could* have been in London early enough for such a feat: we have no sure evidence as to the year of his arrival. As Sams suggestively notes, the specific name Hamlet derives from none of the earlier tales of Amleth, but is closely associated with Shakespeare, who remembered "Hamlett Sadler" in his will along with Heminge and Condell and named his own son Hamlet or Hamnet Shakespeare. Another Hamlett – Katherine Hamlett – drowned in the Avon near Stratford in 1579 and was, like Ophelia, the object of a "coroner's quest."[26] Sams' theory should have elements of attractiveness for Shakespeareans in that it gives over the whole field of *Hamlet* to Shakespearean authorship. There is no longer a mysterious, lost Ur-*Hamlet* to muddy the waters of Shakespeare's dramatic creativity.

On the other hand, Sams' theory puts the Bard in rather disreputable company – among the rough and ready, semi-literate dramatists ridiculed by Nashe, and (worse yet) among oyster wives. Given the persistent tradition that Shakespeare himself played the part of the ghost, we are offered the unsavory spectacle of the Bard managing his part so "miserably" that he can be likened to a fishwife bawling her wares. Most nineteenth-century editors were able to imagine Shakespeare in his early days as part of just such a rough and tumble world, but in the mainstream twentieth-century editorial tradition, he cannot be associated with the *Hamlet* of the 1590s, either as actor or author, because the play is described by contemporaries in such low and contemptuous terms. Hence the editorial energy that has gone into separating Q2 *Hamlet* altogether from the mysterious, vanished Ur-text. However, Robert Greene himself disparaged Shakespeare by name in or before 1592 as

> an vpstart Crow, beautified with our feathers, that with his *Tygers heart wrapt in a Players hide*, supposes he is as well able to bumbast out a blanke verse as the best of you: and being an absolute *Iohannes factotum*, is in his owne conceit the onely Shake-scene in a countrie.[27]

Despite the best efforts of editors and others, there appears to be no way around the uncomfortable fact that Shakespeare, in the early years of his career, was considered by some as *arriviste* and even, if Greene means what he appears to mean, a plagiarist, or at least a habitual borrower of more learned people's work.

My own main difficulty with Sams' argument lies in his assertion of a perfect homology between Q1 and the Ur-*Hamlet*. As editors have noted, there is no point in Q1 at which the ghost utters the precise words, "Hamlet, revenge." He addresses his son as "Hamlet" and cries for "revenge" a few lines later, but the two words are not quite juxtaposed. If the phrase in question became well enough known in the theater to inspire ridicule (we find it again in *Satiro-mastix* (1601) "my name's Hamlet reuenge: thou hast been at Paris garden hast not?"),[28] then that notoriety is perhaps sufficient reason for it to have been excised (if it was) from the play as published in 1603. But given what we know about the instability of Elizabethan playtexts in general and the marked differences among printed *Hamlet*s in particular, is it likely that *Hamlet* would have remained the same play on stage from 1589 to 1599 or even later? Q1 may well have derived from the same "corrupt" line of descent as one or more other *Hamlet*s from the 1590s. Those involved in recent productions of Q1 have sometimes noted that it seems to have the raw, inchoate energy of a work in progress.[29] But we are unlikely ever to know at what stage Shakespeare entered the process. Was he the originator of *Hamlet*, a joint originator working with other dramatists, or the reviser of an earlier play of the same name, to which he was drawn, perhaps, by the many reverberations between its title and his own earlier life in Stratford?

Narrative B

In which Shakespeare becomes dissatisfied
with his first *Hamlet* and revises it
(May be used along with Narrative A, above)

Since nearly everyone prefers Q2 over Q1 in terms of polish and poetic refinement, it is easy to generate narratives to explain Shakespeare's hypothesized revision of Q1 into Q2. We have reached the late 1590s, possibly as late as 1603. As Shakespeare matures as an artist and his company becomes increasingly prosperous, the old *Hamlet* begins to look shabby. The players call upon him to create a fuller, more polished version in much the same way that the King's Company was later to call upon Thomas Middleton to expand *A Game at Chess* from the short and inferior version he initially offered them.[30] Moreover, Richard Burbage, who has long played the title role with great success, is becoming too senior to be happy in the part of a twenty-year-old. Then too, the temper of the nation is changing: stage melancholy is becoming increasingly fashionable and the optimism of an earlier era is giving way to Jacobean gloom. Revenge plays in the ranting old Senecan mode are becoming passé and the old, relatively upbeat *Hamlet* too closely resembles the traditional pattern. It is too conventional in its ideas to suit the emerging mood of the new century.

To these public, institutional considerations may be added a host of speculations about Shakespeare's private sentiments. It is 1601 and Shakespeare has fallen into a depression, possibly brought on by the double blow of his only son Hamnet's death in 1596 and his father's death in 1601, which has reawakened all the pain of the earlier loss. As James Joyce's Stephen Daedalus suggested in his *Hamlet* lecture (*Ulysses*, chap. [9]), Shakespeare maps his own experience of loss onto the play, reviving both of the departed. He is simultaneously father and son: the ghost, father of Hamlet, come back as from the grave to tell of horrors; the son, who of all of Shakespeare's tragic heroes, is the one most immersed in the theater, the one most like Shakespeare himself. He now finds his earlier *Hamlet* to be utterly inadequate to the mystery of the human condition, in which good and evil are so inextricably mixed as to be inseparable.

To this hypothetical narrative may be added still others. In 1601 or thereabouts, possibly as late as 1603, Shakespeare becomes despondent over the recurrence of the plague, or over the unsettled state of the nation and the obvious decline of the reigning monarch, who was to die in 1603. And indeed, as Eric Mallin has suggested, Q2 *Hamlet*, by comparison with Q1, suffers from a pall of disease like that affecting London in 1603 and other plague years: it is sicklied over not only with the pale cast of thought, but also with physical contagion.[31] The list of plausible reasons why Shakespeare should have wanted to portray the world of *Hamlet* more darkly than before is long, intriguing, and also, alas, almost entirely speculative. But there is yet another possibility.

Narrative C

In which Shakespeare,
Having written the true and perfect Copy later published as Q2,
cuts down *Hamlet* for performance.
(Can be used as a substitute for A and B above)

According to this scenario, Q2 precedes Q1, as in the theory of memorial reconstruction, but Q1's origins are more respectable. Shakespeare brings his new play in for reading to the company; all acknowledge that he has produced a masterpiece, but suggest that the stage version needs to be much shorter, simpler, and less philosophically complex to be accessible to the usual audience. Shakespeare, possibly with the assistance of other members of the company, obligingly constructs Q1, which, as its defenders regularly note, skillfully manages to include every significant plot element of the play in its long form, but honed into an effective piece of theater in its own right.

This narrative can be modified in a number of ways. Perhaps Shakespeare and/or the company decide that the play is too long and/or daring for a particular audience, and modify the text for a specific performance or series of performances, possibly for production on tour during one of the London plague times or earlier. Modern companies have performed Q1 *Hamlet* with as few as nine actors by using clever doubling. For Shakespeare's company, the same number would have been possible if a man (rather than a boy) played the role of the Player Queen. Although boys regularly played young women in the Elizabethan theater, men frequently played older women, and the Q1 player queen, having been married a full forty years, scarcely qualifies as young.[32]

To suppose that Shakespeare did the cutting is, of course, to attribute the monstrous brutalization of the major soliloquies to the Bard himself. It goes against the grain for us to imagine an artist deliberately lowering the level of his work's refinement; indeed, most twentieth-century advocates of the theory of authorial or authorized abridgement for Q1 have still felt the need to posit some form of playhouse corruption to account for "To be or not to be" in its Q1 form. The most noteworthy of these advocates has been Hardin Craig: although he was highly respected as a critic, his defense of the "bad" quartos fell on deaf ears in the heyday of the New Bibliography during the 1960s.[33] The sad fact is that we don't know that Shakespeare was at all committed to having his dramatic art appear only in its most polished possible form (he appears to have cared considerably more about the long lyric poems). The Q2 title page has seemed to most twentieth-century readers and editors to fall clearly into the familiar Renaissance category of a published author's lament for the theft and mutilation of his work as a result of unsupervised printing. But as we have already seen in the case of John Day and *Gorboduc*, printers and publishers could make similar laments about previous and "corrupt" printings, perhaps in part to convince the public that the new edition was an essential purchase even for buyers who already possessed the old. Nicholas Ling, the publisher of both quarto *Hamlet*s, was a canny enterpreneur, and certainly capable of such a marketing gesture, as were Heminge and Condell later on in their preface to the First Folio, which similarly dismissed earlier editions of the plays as "stolne and surreptitious."

Then too, we have concrete evidence that at least one other Renaissance playwright – and one who appears to have taken more care over the publication of his dramatic work than Shakespeare did – was inclined to lengthen, shorten, and otherwise "mutilate" his own copy. Trevor Howard-Hill has demonstrated, to his own considerable dismay, that the authorial manuscripts of Thomas Middleton's *A Game at Chess* show the playwright altering his own play seemingly at will.[34] As I shall theorize later on, we may have misconceived the way in which playwrights of the period went about the business of making plays even in cases when they worked alone rather than collaboratively – they may have conceptualized them more in terms of malleable rhetorical "places" (*topoi*) than in terms of fixed language.

Given the parallel case of Middleton, it would be hazardous to rule out the possibility that Shakespeare himself created the "short" *Hamlet* out of a longer version resembling Q2, quite possibly for performance before provincial audiences who might have been put off by the intellectual adventurousness of Q2.

Indeed, in Q1 the ending of the play can be interpreted as alluding meta-dramatically to just such performance conditions. Rather than ordering the bodies to be placed "high on a stage," according to Horatio's petition in the Q2 version, Q1 Fortinbrass orders the captains to carry "*Hamlet* like a souldier to his graue." Horatio is the one who will occupy the scaffold:

> Content your selues, Ile shew to all, the ground,
> The first beginning of this Tragedy:
> Let there a scaffold be rearde vp in the market place,
> And let the State of the world be there:
> Where you shall heare such a sad story tolde,
> That neuer mortall man could more vnfolde.
>
> (H 268 [14]r)

Horatio's public, theatrical telling of the tale in the marketplace mimetically recapitulates some of the actual performance conditions of *Hamlet* on tour, so that the "sad story" he will "vnfolde" becomes the very production of *Hamlet* in which he is performing. By 1603 the staging of a play on a scaffold erected in the marketplace would have appeared, perhaps, anachronistic, since even on tour the actors usually performed indoors or in inn yards. But the ending of Q1 *Hamlet* strongly evokes the conditions of popular performance in the absence of a fixed theater.

Our evidence, yet once more, is far from conclusive as to the chronological order of the two quarto *Hamlet*s: the Q1 ending that puts Horatio on a scaffold-stage can just as easily be interpreted as confirmation of Narrative A above, in which Shakespeare, in his "lost" early years in London during the 1580s, a time of flux and confusion for English dramatic companies generally, finds himself writing for a company as yet without a reliable permanent abode. And there are other possible scenarios: at least one scholar has argued that Q2 postdates both Q1 and F.[35] The mystery generated by the 1603 and 1604–05 title pages remains a mystery. Our admittedly hasty survey of possible narratives as to the origins and chronology of Q1 in relation to Q2 has left us with too many plausible answers, too little conclusive evidence.

ORALITY AND WRITING IN THE PLAYHOUSE

Actors and directors of Q1 *Hamlet* have noticed a curious quality that the play in that version does not share with its more respectable intertexts. As Peter Guinness, who performed the role of Q1 Hamlet in 1985 at the

Orange Tree Theatre in Richmond, England, expresses it, the language of that *Hamlet* was like the language overheard when one is sitting "on the top of a bus" and listening to someone else's conversation. To those involved in the conversation, it made perfect sense, but to the eavesdropper, "it's punctuated with non sequiturs, with the most curious jumps in thinking. People don't always make sense of what they're saying: but nevertheless what they are saying is what they are feeling at the time." Guinness's word for Q1 *Hamlet* was "immediate." He described it as

> unrefined, it hasn't been tidied up (as perhaps the Folio has been tidied up); and for an actor, a play that falls on occasions into that rather stumbling language can provide a great challenge, and indeed a gift, because a lot of the thinking that one has to invent when one is working with a crafted script doesn't come into the play of the First Quarto: all those stumbling thoughts, those half-thoughts, those unfinished sentences, those uncompleted ideas, are actually there: it really is a *working* text.[36]

Guinness's remarks about overheard conversation apply with particular force to Q1 "To be or not to be," in which the language is far more disjointed than in the Q2 version. This time I cite the quarto version itself rather than an edited text: "For in that dreame of death, when wee awake, / And borne before an euerlasting Iudge, / From whence no passanger euer retur'nd, / The vndiscouered country . . . " (H 86, 88 [D4]v). A conversation overheard? That description would appear to be grist for the mill of the advocates of memorial reconstruction. But there is, perhaps, another way of conceptualizing this oddly disjunctive language.

Another Q1 Hamlet, Christopher McCullough, who appeared in a 1982 production of the play by staff and students of the University College of Swansea, makes a similar comment about the Q1 version of "To be or not to be" but sees the form of the soliloquy and others in the play as "important clues to Elizabethan theater practice." For McCullough, as for Guinness, Q1 *Hamlet* was, in some insistent way, immediate. The soliloquies in performance demanded a high degree of audience contact:

> The general understanding of the Shakespearean soliloquy is a very post-Romantic notion, of something very introspective. We think of Redgrave and Gielgud and Olivier – Olivier in this film actually disembodied his soliloquies into voice-overs, and that perhaps is as far as you can go in the direction of introspection. But those lines, "To be, or not to be, I there's the point" perhaps give us a clue as to how the soliloquies were worked, how that particular convention was used in the Elizabethan theater.

McCullough found it impossible to play "I there's the point" by "turning in on myself and pretending there wasn't an audience there." Rather,

"To be, or not to be, I there's the *point*" actually only made sense if I said it *to the audience*. In fact I was using the soliloquy as a way of putting an argument to the audience as to what was going on in the narrative; and I think in that sense the First Quarto is giving us clues about the much more open-ended nature of Elizabethan theater.

For both of these actors, there was something indefinable about Q1 that made it appear more faithful to Elizabethan theatrical practice than either of the more polished texts – something having to do with the creation of a sense of immediate community with the audience, and with the stronger rhetorical impact of the lines under those conditions. As McCullough goes on to note,

> It's interesting that all the activity that followed the Elizabethan theatrical form, the process of turning the play into a literary object, and refining the poetry, has been one of removing it from that open-ended theater practice in which it must have had dangerous potentialities – the danger implicit in the practice of genuinely putting ideas to an audience, rather than showing them a man playing with ideas.[37]

There is more at work in this set of discriminations than the traditional antagonism between academic and theatrical Shakespeareans. The difference between Q1 and Q2 or F *Hamlet* that Guinness and McCullough are struggling to articulate relates to the profoundly "oral" quality of the former text by comparison with the latter two. The disparity in language between Q1 and Q2 can be explicated in terms of the contrast between predominantly oral and predominantly literate cultures as articulated by Walter J. Ong and refined and modified by Jack Goody, Ruth Finnegan, and other recent investigators.

Amidst the flurry of interest in the orality/literacy binary among medievalists and students of modernism and postmodernism, it is odd that the binary has not attracted more attention among Shakespeareans. To be sure, the distinction between orality and writing as modes of communication has often been overworked. Recent conceptualizations of the differences have sometimes pushed the contrast to unreasonable extremes. Moreover, some recent literary scholars have used the appeal to a lost "oral culture" as a retreat from deconstruction and other distasteful recent critical "isms": under orality in medieval society, we are told, signs did not "decay into *signifiant* and *signifié*": a stable "presence" between interlocutor and listener could be assumed.[38] But even if we do not accept the postulate that oral culture had the almost mystical wholeness and integrity of communication that is sometimes claimed for it, we will discover that recent descriptions of orality crystallize some of the aesthetic issues at stake in the editorial controversy over Q1 *Hamlet* and over "bad" Shakespeare more generally.

Here I will be less interested in creating a new master narrative about the chronology of the early texts than in generating new ways of conceptualizing the traits of language that have caused the bad quartos to be so generally perceived as "bad." For civilized Westerners schooled in a long tradition of letters, oral literature can't be regarded as literature: it dies on the page – appears thin and inchoate once it is written down and separated from the immediate milieu of its performance. Insofar as it is associated with illiteracy or with insufficient literacy, it is doubly stigmatized in a society for which literacy is required for success or even competence. Q1 *Hamlet* in particular and the bad quartos in general cannot count as literature because they do not come across to a reading audience as highly literate.

In considering the London playhouse, we will encounter neither orality nor literacy in anything like their "pure" forms. (Indeed a purely literate culture has not thus far existed.) English theatrical culture was a milieu in which oral and written forms jostled up against each other and competed for the allegiance of audiences, and in which literate expectations were slowly winning ground away from earlier oral modes of operation. Since as long ago as Chambers' monumental studies of the medieval and Elizabethan stage, we have at least in theory accepted the postulate that the literate, urbane late-Elizabethan theater did not spring, like Athena, out of the forehead of humanist scholarship; it was grafted onto, and still partly immersed in, an earlier, predominately oral and popular theatrical culture. What was that culture like? How do dramatic texts originating within a predominately oral setting differ from those coming out of a more familiar (to us) literate and literary environment?

According to the standard works on orality and literacy, the use of language in predominately oral cultures tends to be interactional and contextual: like the conversation overheard on top of the double-decker bus, it demands participation in the group in order to be comprehensible. Even highly literate people use language differently in oral situations than they do in writing. They tend to employ less elaborate syntactic and semantic structures (hence the usually disparaging expression, "He talks like a book"). They tend to prefer coordinate as opposed to subordinate constructions, and to prefer imperatives, interrogatives, and exclamations over declaratives and subjunctives. They use fewer abstract terms and a narrower choice of words. Indeed, most people's speech is characterized by generality and vagueness, at least by comparison with written discourse. In oral situations, a speaker can rely on an environment shared with his or her audience to help communicate meaning. For a writer the audience is less immediately present, although it may be quite vivid in his or her mind. The writer must therefore shape discourse with much greater precision in order to achieve the same degree of intelligibility.[39]

I recently had the experience of reading over the transcript of a model class I had given (partly, as it happens, on the subject of Q1 *Hamlet*). Since the transcript was to be published as part of a volume on the teaching of Shakespeare, I expected to furnish my editors with an unaltered record of the model class – would it not be falsification to polish up the transcript for publication? But I quickly discovered that the transcript, albeit accurate in recording the words we used, failed to communicate much of what was going on during the session. It had to be edited – the language had to be made more precise in order to communicate to readers the same ideas that those who spoke in class had communicated. No doubt professional interviewers regularly experience the same phenomenon: even the liveliest and most successful interview needs substantial editing if it is to succeed with readers.

This difference in terms of precision of language, I would submit, is very like the difference in language between a "bad" and a "good" Shakespearean quarto, and between "bad" and "good" versions of "To be or not to be." The aesthetic preferences by which oral literature in cross-cultural context has until recently been neglected in favor of written literature are much the same as the preferences by which "good" quartos have been favored over "bad": the "bad" quarto is a record of oral performance, as nearly every one of them declares itself to be on its title page; the more polished text, with its (usually) more vivid, precise, and amplified language, its more regular meter, its greater lucidity and complexity in terms of syntax, is a version of the play more specifically geared toward readers. In a "bad" quarto, the personality of a character on stage might well be projected quite dynamically through performance, but the character may appear colorless on the page: it lacks the telling precision and "realism" for which Western literate culture has traditionally valued Shakespearean characterization particularly highly. Similarly, a "bad" quarto's defective versification leaps out at us from the printed page, but on stage during an actor's impassioned delivery of the speech, it would be "invisible" and probably unnoticed, offering a welcome jaggedness and muscularity of effect. Moreover, those critics who have faulted the versification of the "bad" quartos have usually overestimated the degree of regularity in the "good."[40]

That is not to suggest that no "good" quarto or folio version was ever performed: one great measure of Shakespeare's success as a playwright, I would argue, was that in the course of his career, he became increasingly adroit at creating performance texts that already carried the polish and precision coming to be expected of reading texts – dramatic texts that played powerfully on stage but also could be read as great poetry, though not necessarily metrically regular poetry. Curiously enough, all of the quartos most often designated as "bad" quartos – 1594 *Contention* (*Henry VI*, Part 2), 1595 *True Tragedy* (*Henry VI*, Part 3), 1597 *Romeo and Juliet*, 1600 *Henry V*, 1602 *Merry Wives*, and 1603 *Hamlet* – date from the earlier years of

Shakespeare's career. The usual explanation has been that his dramatic company gradually became more protective of its playbooks, more efficient in fending off pirates. More recently, however, this cloak and dagger mode of explanation has fallen by the wayside along with the assumption that playtexts were regularly pirated. If the "bad" quartos are indeed earlier versions of the plays, then they may have the peculiarly oral quality recent actors have found in them because the playhouse in the 1590s was still a predominately oral institution, and because Shakespeare (like other dramatists who got their start within the dramatic companies rather than in the universities) only gradually came to conceptualize his playtexts as potential reading texts.

Following this line of conjecture, the early plays that appear highly polished and "literate" to us might well have been subjected to revision after their original composition by Shakespeare or by Shakespeare in combination with others. Elizabethan actors had precious little time for rehearsals. As Andrew Gurr has speculated, plays in their first staging may have been fairly rough, becoming more polished in production if they were successful enough to be retained in the repertory.[41] Q1 *Hamlet*, then, would be roughed-out, theatrical *Hamlet*, before it had been refined and amplified into "literature." Most of the vagueness, tangled syntax, and strange immediacy for which editors have found it wanting and performers have found it compelling can be explicated as signs of a fundamental orality, as opposed to the more sophisticated and reticent "literate" version of the play in Q2.

What evidence do we have of this hypothesized oral culture of the playhouse? Only bits and pieces: I cannot claim to have made a thorough study of the matter, and all of my arguments are to be regarded as highly conjectural. A useful starting point, however, might be the "illiterate actors." It is not only late nineteenth and twentieth-century editors who have (assuming a predictable connection between level of education and moral development) railed against the low and unlettered players who maimed what they performed. Similar complaints were frequently made in the Elizabethan era, albeit usually by university men who were enemies of the stage. At the beginning of our period, some performers (particularly those unfortunates who lived out their lives as itinerants) may well have been semi-literate at best. We have already noticed the insufficiently educated actor in *The Taming of a Shrew* who, to the acute discomfort of his fellow, cannot get his tongue around the latinate word *comedy*, which if applied to the play they are about to present, would elevate it above the status of a mere "commodity." Similarly, the base players in *Histrio-Mastix* admit they are close to illiterate: they "can read nothing but riddles."[42] As the acting companies settled into permanent London theaters and organized themselves according to the apprentice system, the phenomenon of the illiterate actor would gradually have died out, since apprentices

were required to be able to read and write English as a condition of employ-
ment. But the hired men brought in as need arose would not necessarily
have been subject to the same restrictions. The change from an orally based
to a more strongly "literate" theater may have come more gradually than we
have recognized.

How would an illiterate or semi-literate actor function in a Elizabethan
theatrical company? Perhaps more effectively than we think. Such actors
may have possessed "oral literacy," in Rita Copeland's helpful phrase: the
ability to operate within a book or manuscript-based culture without
direct dependence on written texts.[43] When a new play was brought in for
consideration, it was "read" to or by members of the company, but that
reading was oral, as the many examples collected by G. E. Bentley suggest.
That is how the new play is introduced to the company in *Histrio-Mastix*:
the players sit to "heare" the play; the author reads it to them, but cannot
perform without the lubrication of plentiful wine. He is so affected by the
pathos of his own creation that he asks the players to read the rest themselves, whereupon they are forced to declare their inability to do so (sig.
C[1]). In Henslowe's company as late as 1613, new plays were read aloud
to the assembled company. Even when an author wished to acquaint
Henslowe or Edward Alleyn with part of it, he did not simply loan them a
copy, but called upon them to "appoint any hour to read" to them. Such
collective "readings" were regularly accompanied by the consumption of
wine and sometimes took place in taverns, as recorded in Henslowe's
accounts for 1602. The company would decide on the basis of oral rather
than written evidence whether or not a play would make successful theater.
Although records from Shakespeare's company are lacking, we have no
reason to suppose that the Lord Chamberlain or King's Men proceeded
any differently.[44]

Moreover, in the course of their initial collective "reading," at least some
of the actors may well have begun the process of memorizing the plays.[45]
We know that the "plan" of the play would regularly be written out and
displayed on the tiringhouse wall for the actors to consult, and that
individual parts or "sides" including cues and perhaps also stage business
were copied out for the actors of specific roles. Only one side is extant
for the professional theater: that of Edward Alleyn for Orlando in Greene's
Orlando Furioso. But there are other extant examples from university plays.[46]
The rustic actors in Shakespeare's *A Midsummer Night's Dream* must have
been provided with something similar, since Flute speaks all of his part at
once, cues and all (3.1.96). Much of the fun of the Mechanicals' struggles
with their playtext derives from the fact that their grasp of elevated diction
and classical civilization is unequal to the highly literate humanist mode
which their playtext unwittingly burlesques. Dramatic literature of the
period is full of mocking references to marginal actors who are studying
their parts at the last minute or have failed to learn them at all.

But there were other ways in which inexperienced actors could learn their roles – perhaps by imitation, as "Dick" Burbage and Will Kemp train the university men Studioso and Philomusus in the academic play, *The Return from Parnassus*, part 2 (published 1606). Burbage calls upon Studioso to act the part of Hieronimo; he is to read a role in the book of the play: "obserue how I act it and then imitate mee." When Burbage recites the speech beginning "Who call *Hieronimo* from his naked bed?" Studioso repeats it after him. Then Kemp takes Philomusus in hand and gives him an elaborate eighteen-line speech to repeat back to him, which Philomusus is miraculously able to do.[47] The technique in this second instance is somewhat different for there is no book: Kemp's speech is presented as impromptu. Philomusus clearly has a phenomenal memory, as, presumably, did Will Kemp and the other professional actors: he repeats Kemp's elaborate compendium of fooleries after hearing it recited only once rather than through the use of playbook or sides.

After Burbage and Kemp leave, the two university scholars bemoan the baseness of their incipient career in the theater, where they must be "practis'd" to "leaden spouts, / That nought downe vent but what they do receiue" (sig. [G3]v). Theirs is the contempt of the superliterate scholar for the orally oriented and therefore "leaden" player. That is not to suggest that university culture, with its emphasis on academic disputation, was not also profoundly oral; only that among the educated elite, literacy was essential, while it was only becoming so among the players. Both the portrayal of actors in *Histrio-Mastix* and Greene's opinion of Shakespeare and his fellows in *Groats-worth of witte* are startlingly similar to that of Studioso and Philomusus: Greene scorns actors as "those Puppits (I meane) that speake from our mouths, those Anticks garnisht in our colours" (sig. [E3]v). Very much like more recent scholars studying oral forms from a strongly literate perspective, these university men underestimate the degree of artistry that goes into the predominately oral medium.

Interestingly, although the roles of scholar and player are reversed in *Hamlet*, Hamlet adopts a similar pedagogical technique with *his* players. He has evidently just recited one of the speeches he wishes them to add to the "Murder of Gonsago" since he commands them in Q2, "Speake the speech I pray you as I pronoun'd it to you, trippingly on the tongue" (H 130 G3v). In Q1, his language more clearly suggests a pedagogical situation: "Pronounce me this speech trippingly a the tongue as I *taught* thee" (my emphasis; H 130 F2r). In both quarto versions of the passage, the words have been written down previously, but the transmission is primarily oral, as in the Burbage example from *The Return from Parnassus*.

Of course actual plays must be used with caution as evidence of playhouse practice, but there is no particular reason why the oral pattern should be repeated in two plays that are otherwise so different unless it conformed to at least one of the ways in which actors could learn their parts. Hamlet's own conceptualization of the performance is more aural than visual: not "We'll see a play" but "weele *heare* a play to morrowe" (my emphasis, cited from Q2 H114 [F4]r), and this locution is standard for the period.[48] What we appear to be observing as we survey the scanty evidence is a mixed situation in which written language supplemented oral learning to a greater or lesser degree: some actors were "harder of study" than others, some may have memorized their roles by using sides, while others learned theirs through oral repetition. For neither method was the written text as important as it is for us as readers of Shakespeare.

Advocates of the theory of memorial reconstruction have given scant credit to the mnemonic powers of an Elizabethan or early Jacobean actor: they have assumed that a player would (like modern actors) learn only his own role and have a hazy notion of what transpired while he was offstage; they have likewise assumed that the actor (like modern Shakespearean actors) would to have to have his part letter perfect in order to have memorized it adequately in terms of the standards of the company. If the London playhouse functioned as a largely oral institution, in some ways like the more recent oral institutions that have been studied firsthand by anthropologists and students of communications theory, then neither assumption is justified. Considering the number of plays a company would have in repertory at any given time, not to mention other set speeches that could be recited on command, successful Elizabethan actors had to have prodigious and highly trained memories, combined with great flexibility. Given the London deathrate and the high incidence of disease, they were well advised to "know" whole plays – not only a single part – but neither they nor Shakespeare appear to have worried about whether or not they were letter perfect. Nor, according to recent research based on extant playbooks of the early seventeenth century, were the actors as reliant on prompters as most editors have assumed. The so-called prompter – more properly termed bookkeeper – in the late Elizabethan and early Jacobean playhouse was probably less a prompter in the more recent sense of the term than a "production coordinator" concerned far less with the minutiae of language than with the orchestration of large props and special effects (a bed onstage, thunder offstage, a sennet) required at specific points in the action.[49]

As students of the orality/literacy interface have frequently noted, the possession of a written record makes exact repetition of a given document practical and convenient, whereas within oral culture it is more difficult, albeit not impossible or necessarily unknown. Medieval literate culture had recognized two forms of memory: *memoria ad res* and *memoria ad verba*, with a memory for the gist of a speech or written passage frequently valued more highly than word-for-word memory since an ability to paraphrase more clearly demonstrated that the material had been internalized.[50] Our own preference is, of course, for the opposite, at least in the transmission of literary materials and in the performance of a classic like Shakespeare: we have tended to assume that Hamlet speaks for Shakespeare himself when he calls upon the clowns to speak no more than is set down for them lest they neglect "some necessary question of the play." But Hamlet has all the prejudices of the university man; Shakespeare, by contrast, was an actor. Elizabethan and early Jacobean acting was probably closer to modern film acting than to modern Shakespearean stage acting in its tolerance for occasional improvisation, which they termed "extempore shifts" and "fribbling."[51]

That improvisation, insofar as it was assimilated into the fabric of the play, could easily have been recorded as "Shakespeare" in succeeding versions of a given playtext. One likely example is Hamlet's nervous doubling of words and phrases in F as opposed to Q2 *Hamlet* (for example, Q2 "Fie on't, ah fie" in the first soliloquy versus F "Fie on't? Oh fie, fie", or, in the "Fishmonger" speech to Polonius, Q2 "Excellent well" versus F "Excellent, excellent well").[52] Many modern critics regard this stylistic quirk as quintessentially Shakespearean, but it is probably at least partly Burbage – based on the oral "authority" of the playhouse rather than the written authority of the author's text. The consistent patterns of variation among early printed texts of plays discussed thus far in the present study could have originated through purposeful ensemble work accomplished by the acting company collectively rather than through a single writer's labored reshaping of a manuscript. The highly communal, highly oral environment of the Elizabethan playhouse did not make for clear-cut differentiation between author and performer.

In Hamlet's highly literate and authoritarian view, of course, to compromise the integrity of the playtext as "set down" would be "villainous" – acceptable, perhaps, to the more free-form, improvisatory oral style of the Kemps and Tarltons, but insufficiently precise and controlled for the higher form of theater he advocates. And indeed, after Q1 *Hamlet* there are no new Shakespearean bad quartos in most people's definition of the term, although some that were already extant continued to be reprinted.[53] We need to think of Prince Hamlet, and of his play, particularly in its more canonical second quarto and folio forms, as helping to generate a more literate theatrical taste rather than merely reflecting an alteration in audience expectations. At least in theory, Hamlet advocates a drama that is more textually precise, more reticent and less open-ended than the older, more highly "oral" theater had been – a drama that gains its power from the unfolding of its own design and "necessary questions" rather than from its quicksilver ability to transform itself in response to the reactions of a specific audience.

As Leeds Barroll has argued (see n. 31), during plaguetimes when the theatres were closed, Shakespeare was inactive in the writing of plays: he apparently needed, or at least desired, the functioning community of the playhouse to stimulate his creativity as a playwright. He may even have composed orally. In their preface to readers of the First Folio, Heminge and Condell describe the writer thus:

> Who, as he was a happie imitator of Nature, was a most gentle expresser of it. His mind and hand went together: And what he thought, he vttered with that easinesse, that wee haue scarse receiued from him a blot in his papers.
>
> (F *A*3r)

What he thought he *uttered*: did he speak the speeches aloud to himself or to others as he wrote them down? Most of the non-verbal uses of the verb *utter* recorded by the *OED* relate to the sphere of commerce – merchants "utter" commodities by putting goods forth upon the market, putting currency into circulation, and the like. It is possible, of course, that Heminge and Condell had just such a usage in mind. To think of the theater as a market was an early modern commonplace: at an earlier point in the preface, they had themselves urged potential readers, like peddlars hawking their wares, to buy, buy the book. Or the compilers of the *OED* may simply have missed this specific usage.[54] They regularly ignore prefatory material from the First Folio as less authoritative than the plays themselves in documenting vocabulary for the period. But it is just possible that Heminge and Condell were recording a writing practice that was still strongly immersed in the orality of the playhouse. If a speech was sounding vividly in the playwright's mind as he set it down, he might well have "uttered" it before or during the writing of it, as Shakespeare's fellows suggest he did. In his preface to *The Malcontent,* John Marston seems to record a similar process in his own writing of plays: "'tis my custome to speake as I think, and write as I speake."[55]

As we have already noted in the case of Thomas Middleton, at least some playwrights of the period could work alterations upon their own compositions with slapdash efficiency and ease. Rather than working laboriously from written copy, I would suggest, in copying out *A Game at Chess* Middleton may have been writing from memory: trained in the ways of the theater, he kept his texts carefully fixed in his mind, *ad res* but not necessarily *ad verba*. An author writing from memory might well create the small, "indifferent" variations between one textual version and another that have so bedevilled editors.[56] He or the company, working from memory, might also reconstruct a play with ease to meet new pressures in terms of audience or occasion. Schooled in the rhetorical *topoi* as both a scheme for memory and a device for insuring amplitude of discourse, Middleton may well have composed the play afresh each time he penned it out. Actors who supplied written copies to oblige friends or patrons may also have written from memory.[57] The grammar schools regularly taught rudimentary memory systems whereby the rhetorical "places" were to be imagined as actual *loci* vividly fixed in the mind and used associatively for organizing and retrieving large amounts of material.[58] Might Shakespeare, too, have written from memory? Might he have been, as Middleton appears to have been, a memorial constructor?

In medieval culture, it had been relatively common to envision writing as the copying of preexisting mental images. As we noted much earlier, Dante conceptualized his writing of the *Vita nuova* as a copying out of words written in the "book of my memory." Mary Carruthers has called attention to the parallel functions of our conceptions of spontaneous genius and the medieval construction of memory: she gives a vivid picture of Saint Thomas Aquinas "writing" his works by dictating them in seemingly perfected form to several scribes writing simultaneously. "Nor did he seem to be searching for things as yet unknown to him; he seemed simply to let his memory pour out its treasures." Queen Elizabeth I apparently had the same skill. Sir John Harington's papers include evidence that she could write one letter herself while simultaneously dictating a second and listening to and commenting on the reading of a "tale."[59] She accomplished this feat, we can speculate, by possessing a highly trained memory: having composed the substance of the letters in her mind, she was able, as the memory manuals claim one should, to associate each necessary idea with a specific mental "place" and thus move forward with the epistles nearly simultaneously by moving from one place to the next.

These feats of memory are strikingly like Heminge and Condell's description of Shakespeare in the act of composition, except that Shakespeare does his own transcription and is described as writing out of nature rather than (in medieval fashion) out of a physical book:

> Who, as he was a happie imitator of Nature, was a most gentle expresser of it. His mind and hand went together: And what he thought, he vttered with that easinesse, that wee haue scarse receiued from him a blot in his papers.
>
> (F A3r)

John Fletcher, who succeeded Shakespeare as in-house playwright for the King's Men, is said (in the Beaumont and Fletcher folio) to have had the same talent for mental composition. If Shakespeare wrote from memory, setting down vivid images and basic arguments as they already existed in the storehouse of his mind, but free, in accordance with the practice of *memoria ad res* and standard grammar-school rhetorical training, to augment, diminish, embellish, and alter them at will, then the restless expansion, contraction, and transmutation of playtexts that has seemed until recently to be a monstrous deformation of Shakespearean authorship might instead be of its essence. Harold Love's suggested term for the phenomenon is "serial composition," which, in the playhouse, might involve continuous memorial construction and reconstruction on the part of both Shakespeare and other members of the company, and might involve the extensive use of oral sources that modern editors have discounted. It is not, perhaps, mere happenstance that Ben Jonson, in a discussion of Shakespeare's fluency, compared him to the classical orator Haterius.[60] To reconceptualize Shakespearean authorship thus is to lose the hard distinction between text and orality on which the time-honored disparagement of "memorial reconstruction" is based. Perhaps, as Frances Yates long ago suggested, the physical features of the Globe Theatre itself were used by the actors as *loci* for memorization, just as, in the far more elaborated and philosophically charged memory systems of Renaissance neo-Platonists, human memory was imagined as a theater.[61]

THE SKULL AND THE SCRIVENER

When the ghost asks Hamlet to "remember," the prince responds in extreme fashion by vowing to do violence to his own internalized system of nmemonic "places." In both quarto texts, he, like Dante in the *Vita nuova*, imagines memory as a book or "table" in which he has copied out his reading and experience. All of this he will obliterate:

> Yea, from the table of my memory
> Ile wipe away all triuiall fond records,
> All sawes of bookes, all formes, all pressures past
> That youth and obseruation coppied there,
> And thy commandement all alone shall liue,
> Within the booke and volume of my braine
> Vnmixt with baser matter . . .
>
> (cited from Q2; H 60, 62, [D3]v)

Having razed his internal *loci*, he is forced to turn to writing for the preservation of important material: "My tables, meet it is I set it downe." In Q1, however, he imagines the memory of his father not in terms of a written "commandement" in a "booke and volume," but in terms of a mental image – perhaps an image of King Hamlet seated on the throne? "And thy *remembrance*, all alone shall *sit*" (my emphasis, H 62 [C4]v). Is Hamlet's violent eradication of all other mnemonically systematized wisdom commendable under the circumstances, or horrifyingly rash? In Q1, the havoc seems to be minimal because the prince does not subsequently lose his capacity for efficacious action, but in Q2, arguably, Hamlet's ability to function effectively in the world is effaced along with the "copied" wisdom and experience that defined his memory and selfhood.

D. F. McKenzie has noted significant ways in which late sixteenth and early seventeenth-century culture displays unease over the loss of immediate contact created by the replacement of oral situations with printed books. In medieval manuscripts, the image of the author or patron is sometimes positioned at the beginning of a textblock in a way that suggests that the ensuing words on the page are to be imagined as his utterance – the well-known portrait of Chaucer at the beginning of the Tale of Melibee in the Ellesmere manuscript of the *Canterbury Tales* is an example.[62] But with the multiplication of near-identical copies, the replication of oral setting became more difficult to communicate to readers. In their introductions to collections of printed sermon literature, late sixteenth and seventeenth-century preachers frequently felt compelled to assure their invisible reading public that despite the lessened immediacy of the medium of communication, their readers should still imagine them as physically present – just as if they stood in the pulpit before their congregation and interacted with them directly. In printed quarto playbooks, the common title-page assurance that the printed text within represents the play just as it had been performed served a similar function, bringing the milieu of the playhouse and what John Marston called its "*soule of lively action*" to vivid life for readers. Similarly, Robert Armin offered an introductory apology for the fact that his printed version of *The History of the two Maids of More-clacke* (1609) could offer only "dumb show" instead of his own presence to "put life into this picture," that is, the full-length picture of Armin adorning the title page of the printed volume (Figure 5.2).[63] In such a formulation, printed texts are dead bodies that have to be reanimated. The frontispiece or title page portraits so common in late sixteenth and seventeenth-century books, many of which show the author gesturing toward the book itself as a continuation of his identity, serve in part, as Armin states directly, to reassure readers of an actual physical presence behind the printed page. Even the Shakespeare First Folio observes this convention through its arrestingly large title-page engraving of the author.[64]

By contrast, in our own culture, the picture of the author tends to appear, if at all, on the back jacket of the book: apparently, we do not need or even want to think of our contact with the book in terms of oral communication with the author, although some of us do give the picture a surreptitious glance before beginning to read. The presentation of the author in third-world printed books is more analogous to the late Elizabethan and early Jacobean pattern, perhaps because in cultures for which stories or poems are still thought of as primarily oral forms, the same need for the author's picture has existed more recently. In a 1956 Oriya-language edition of T. S. Eliot's *The Waste Land and Other Poems* printed by arrangement with Faber & Faber in India, for example, unlike Western editions of the poem, the author's picture is curiously placed on the upper left corner of the page facing the author's preface, so that Eliot, who looks across toward the preface with his lips slightly open as though pronouncing the words, can be imagined – exactly as he might have been in a late medieval manuscript – as uttering the words of the preface even as the reader reads them.[65]

THE

Hiſtory of the two Maids of More-clacke,

VVith the life and ſimple maner of IOHN
in the Hoſpitall.

Played by the Children of the Kings
Maieſties Reuels.

VVritten by ROBERT ARMIN, ſeruant to the Kings
moſt excellent Maieſtie.

LONDON,
Printed by *N.O.* for *Thomas Archer,* and is to be ſold at his
ſhop in Popes-head Pallace, 1 6 0 9.

Figure 5.2 Title page of Robert Armin's *History of the two Maids of More-clacke* (1609)
Reproduced by permission of the Folger Shakespeare Library,
Washington, D.C.

166

Despite Hamlet's strong preference for the "literate" over the "oral," Shakespeare's prince appears caught in precisely the same dilemma of an emerging literate culture, for whom books were replacing many instances of oral community without necessarily affording the same assurance of human contact and the same visual cues to interpretation. His personality offers almost a textbook case in the transformations wrought, according to Ong and Goody, by the assimilation of literacy: an increased tendency to work through abstraction, interiority, and solitary thought as opposed to communal interaction.[66] The soliloquies in Q1 are brief and demand to be addressed directly to the audience; the soliloquies in Q2 are more readily interpretable as Hamlet's long and elaborate musings to himself. And yet, in the prince's own perception, the more highly literate forms are somehow empty, inert – lacking the "*soule of lively action.*"

Students of orality have suggested that the difference between author and performer tends to be less clearly drawn in oral cultures than in highly literate ones, if only because in oral cultures one does not encounter an author's work without the simultaneous presence of a performer. In *Hamlet*, the distance has become problematic and requires constant negotiation. On the one hand, in calling for an end to improvisation at the expense of preexisting dramatic design, Hamlet seeks to effect a clear separation between composition and performance. On the other hand, his own behavior as author–performer suggests strong ambivalence about the separation he seeks to legislate. If he calls for a high standard of exactitude in terms of the performance's fidelity to the playtext, he also shows distinct signs of nostalgia for an older, improvisatory oral culture. During the performance of *The Mousetrap*, he proves incapable of retaining in practice the separation between author and player he earlier advocated in theory: he repeatedly interrupts the performance, as though insisting on being numbered among the actors. And afterward, he takes the fool's part by performing an impromptu jig, pronouncing himself a "paiocke" – a "patched or motley fool" in one recent gloss of the term – and playfully asserting his right to a "share" in the dramatic company.[67] Has he earned his percentage as author, player, or both?

Later on, in his conversation with the gravediggers, he encounters the ghost of a vanished orality in the form of Yorick's skull. The mouth of the court fool that once vented forth endless quips and sallies is now empty, a monstrous grimacing void. On the one hand, Hamlet complains to Horatio about the Clowns' impertinent, carnivalesque disregard for properly respectful language toward their betters: "the age is growne so picked, that the toe of the pesant coms so neere the heele of the Courtier he galls his kybe" (cited from Q2, H 232). On the other hand, in contemplating the gaping, empty jaws of the jester, Hamlet seems to regret the passing of Yorick's saucy improvised wit: "where be your gibes now? your gamboles, your songs, your flashes of merriment, that were wont to set the table on a roare?" (H 234, 236). Indeed, in some of his own impromptu sallies earlier, the prince had gone a fair way toward replacing the departed jester. The historical Will Kemp actually performed at Elsinore sometime around 1586 or 1587; by 1599 he had left Shakespeare's company, and was probably dead of plague by 1603, by which time the company appears to have outgrown his improvisatory style.[68] The theater as Hamlet prefers to conceptualize it is regularized, but also somehow impoverished, by the imposition of literate standards of fidelity to the written text and the silencing of its orally based Kemps and Yoricks. In Hamlet's mental world, as for his father's physical body poisoned through the ear, oral/aural modes have atrophied, become tainted with corruption and decay.

With these extended speculations about orality – the play as it existed outside the printed text – we may appear to have strayed far afield from our declared interest in the materiality of the printed playbooks. Indeed, by conceptualizing a playwright like Shakespeare as working primarily from memory rather than from written notes or records, we may appear to have gone a fair way toward conceding Bowers' and Tanselle's point that the literary work needs to be located, finally, in the mind and intent of the author. But the material playtexts, if examined in their order of publication rather than in some hypothesized order of composition, reveal precisely the development from an oral to a more "literate" aesthetic that we have postulated for the Shakespearean theater in general. Despite its supposed theatrical origins, F is a more "literary" text than Q2 in terms of grammar and usage: it regularizes language, smooths out colloquialisms, and creates verb–subject agreement. As John Dover Wilson noted in 1918, punctuation in the first quarto tends to record theatrical emphasis, while by the folio it has become more syntactical. Parentheses are a particularly interesting case: in the first and second quartos, they often register an actor's special emphasis in the delivery of a line as in Q1's "(My tables) meet it is I set it downe," while in the folio, as for us, they are used for parenthetical matters.[69] In the titles and headings of early published versions from Q1 through F, *Hamlet* gradually migrates from the lower status of "Tragicall Historie" to the higher one of "Tragedie."[70] Even though the folio version of *Hamlet* is thought by many editors to be closer than Q2 to Shakespeare's *Hamlet* as performed on the early Jacobean stage, F is also more "literate" than Q2 in terms of its treatment of written texts that arise within the play, just as Q2 is more "literate" than Q1. By looking at the three versions in order of publication, we can document an increased "literate" interest in fidelity toward an original, an increased concern for the aesthetic value of the written text being documented.

As noted earlier, only the Hamlet of F writes down the Ghost's message with the same number of adieus that the Ghost pronounces. But it is the handling of materials of written origin that surface within the play – like Hamlet's letter to Horatio detailing his escape from the pirates – that

differs most markedly in the three versions. In Q1, Horatio tells Gertred
that he has "euen now" received a letter from Hamlet, but rather than read
it aloud to her, Horatio delivers the gist of it orally (*memoria ad res*):

> . . . he writes how he escap't the danger,
> And subtle treason that the king had plotted,
> Being crossed by the contention of the windes,
> He found the Packet sent to the king of *England*,
> Wherein he saw himselfe betray'd to death,
> As at his next conuersion with your grace,
> He will relate the circumstance at full.
>
> (H 208 [H2]v)

In Q2, by contrast, Gertradt is not present. The letter is delivered to
Horatio onstage and he reads it aloud privately to himself: the situation has
become more recognizably "literate" according to the standard criteria. As
we might expect, this version is considerably more detailed and concrete
in its narration of the events that resulted in Hamlet's escape since it is
presented as a word-for-word rendering of the text:

> *Hor. Horatio*, when thou shalt haue ouer-lookt this, giue these
> fellowes some meanes to the King, they haue Letters for him: Ere wee
> were two daies old at Sea, a Pyrat of very warlike appointment gaue
> vs chase, finding our selues too slow of saile, wee put on a compelled
> valour, and in the grapple I boorded them, on the instant they got
> cleere of our shyp, so I alone became theyr prisoner, they haue dealt
> with me like thieues of mercie, but they knew what they did, I am to
> doe a turne for them, let the King haue the Letters I haue sent, and
> repayre thou to me with as much speede as thou wouldest flie death,
> I haue wordes to speake in thine eare will make thee dumbe, yet are
> they much too light for the bord of the matter, these good fellowes
> will bring thee where I am, *Rosencraus* and *Guyldensterne* hold theyr
> course for *England*, of them I haue much to tell thee, farewell.
> *So that thou knowest thine Hamlet.*
>
> (H 210 [L2]v–L3r)

The Q2 version of Horatio's reading, in its series of run-on sentences
separated only by commas, has very much the quality of a quick, hurried
perusal, although the loose punctuation can easily be imagined as reflecting the precipitate conditions under which the letter was penned.

By the time of the First Folio, in marked contrast, the communication
has been made more accessible for readers – divided into proper sentences
and clearly separated from its oral context by the use of italics. Indeed, it
is printed on the page in a way that precisely resembles the format of an
actual royal letter or warrant, complete with initial large capital (Figure
5.3). But who is reading the letter in its folio form? The last indication of

I do not know from what part of the world
I should be greeted, if not from Lord *Hamlet.*
              Enter Saylor.
    Say. God blesse you Sir.
    Hor. Let him blesse thee too.
    Say. Hee shall Sir, and't please him. There's a Letter
for you Sir : It comes from th'Ambassadours that was
bound for England, if your name be *Horatio,* as I am let
to know it is.

              Reads the Letter.
HOratio, *When thou shalt haue ouerlook'd this, giue these*
Fellowes some meanes to the King: They haue Letters
for him. Ere we were two dayes old at Sea, a Pyrate of very
Warlicke appointment gaue vs Chace. Finding our selues too
slow of Saile, we put on a compelled Valour. In the Grapple, I
boorded them: On the instant they got cleare of our Shippe, so
I alone became their Prisoner. They haue dealt with mee, like
Theeues of Mercy, but they knew what they did. I am to doe
a good turne for them. Let the King haue the Letters I haue
sent, and repaire thou to me with as much hast as thou wouldest
flye death. I haue words to speake in your eare, will make thee
dumbe, yet are they much too light for the bore of the Matter.
These good Fellowes will bring thee where I am. Rosincrance
and Guildensterne, *hold their course for England. Of them*
I haue much to tell thee, Farewell.
              He that thou knowest thine,
                          Hamlet.
Come, I will giue you way for these your Letters,
And do't the speedier, that you may direct me
To him from whom you brought them.   *Exit.*

              Enter King and Laertes.
    King. Now must your conscience my acquittance seal,
And you must put me in your heart for Friend,
Sith you haue heard, and with a knowing eare,
That he which hath your Noble Father slaine,
Pursued my life.
    Laer. It well appeares. But tell me,
Why you proceeded not against these feates,
So crimefull, and so Capitall in Nature,
As by your Safety, Wisedome, all things else,

I hat we are made of stutte, so flat
That we can let our Beard be sho
And thinke it pastime. You shor
I lou'd your Father, and we loue c
And that I hope will teach you to
              Enter a Messen
How now? What Newes?
    Mes. Letters my Lord from I
Maiesty: this to the Queene.
    King. From *Hamlet?* Who br
    Mes. Saylors my Lord they
They were giuen me by *Claudio,* I
    King. Laertes you shall heare t
Leaue vs.   Ex
    High and Mighty, you shall kno
Kingdome. To morrow shall I begg
Eyes. When I shall (first asking you
count th'Occasions of my sodaine, and

What should this meane? Are all
Or is it some abuse? Or no such th
    Laer. Know you the hand?
    Kin. 'Tis *Hamlets* Character'
script here he sayes alone: Can y
    Laer. I'm lost in it my Lord; b
It warmes the very sicknesse in m
That I shall liue and tell him to hi:
Thus diddest thou.
    Kin. If it be so *Laertes,* as how
How otherwise will you be rul'd I
    Laer. If so you'l not o'rerule n
    Kin. To thine owne peace: if
As checking at his Voyage, and th
No more to vndertake it; I will w
To an exployt now ripe in my De
Vnder the which he shall not cho
And for his death no winde of bla
But euen his Mother shall vncharg
And call it accident: Some two N
Here was a Gentleman of *Norman*
I'ue seene my selfe, and seru'd agai
And they ran well on Horseback

Figure 5.3 Folio version of Hamlet's letter (1623)
Reproduced by permission of the Harry Ransom Humanities Research Center,
University of Texas, Austin

a speaker was *Say*, for the sailor who delivered it. The letter is presumably being read by Horatio since he addresses the sailor at the end of his reading without any textual indication of a change in speaker. The necessary prefix *Hor.* is omitted after the stage direction "*Reads the Letter*" – possibly by mistake in the printinghouse. But if so, it is a highly interesting mistake, for its effect is to make the folio reader rather than Horatio the actual reader of the letter: the communication has moved from an imagined dramatic setting to the printed page, where we, as readers, are invited into the drama to read over the shoulder of Horatio. As we move from Q I to Q2 to F, the presentation of Hamlet's letter becomes increasingly "literate" as opposed to oral, increasingly private and oriented toward visual rather than aural reception. Later on, in Q2 and F but not in Q1, Hamlet presents himself as a master of the technology of writing, though he shows the contempt of his class for the scrivener's menial craft. He reports to Horatio how he managed to produce a credible forgery of Claudius's commission for his execution, having failed in his attempt to forget how to write "faire" in a good court hand (H 244, 245).

There is a similar progression in the handling of Hamlet's letter to Ophelia/Ofelia, except that in this instance the major issue is Hamlet's increased interest in aesthetic critique as we move from one version to the next. In Q1, Corambis produces the letter and, commanded by the king, reads it to those assembled:

> Doubt that in earth is fire,
> Doubt that the starres doe moue,
> Doubt trueth to be a liar,
> But doe not doubt I loue.
> To the beautifull *Ofelia*:
> Thine euer the most vnhappy Prince *Hamlet*
> (H 82, 84 [D4]r)

It is credible that the Hamlet of Q1, with his habitual neglect for felicity of expression, might have composed such a poem, but by Q2, in which the prince's normal mode of speech is more erudite and polished, the crudeness of his verse has to be accounted for. In Q2, both Hamlet and Polonius/Corambus have turned literary critic. Polonius reads, "*To the Celestiall and my soules Idoll, the most beautified* Ophelia," and continues, "*that's an ill phrase, a vile phrase, beautified is a vile phrase, but you shall heare : thus in her excellent white bosome, these &c.*." He is presumably reading and commenting on the salutation, but the typography does not make clear whose language is whose. Then, after a question from the queen, he proceeds to the body of the letter:

> *Doubt thou the starres are fire,*   *Letter.*
> *Doubt that the Sunne doth moue,*

171

Doubt truth to be a lyer,
But neuer doubt I loue.
O deere *Ophelia*, I am ill at these numbers, I haue not art to recken
my grones, but that I loue thee best, ô most best belieue it, adew.
Thine euermore most deere Lady, whilst this machine is to him.
Hamlet.

(H 82, 84 [E4]r)

The poem in this version is arguably more ambiguous than in Q1 since its
question whether "the Sunne doth moue" was, at the turn of the seventeenth century, a nicer problem than whether "the starres do moue," as in
Q1. But the most important point about the poem is that in Q2 Hamlet
feels obliged to apologize for it: it is beneath his habitual artistry, a sign of
the degree to which his "grones" of passion have interfered with his more
customary verbal sophistication.

The F version is similar to Q2. There too, Hamlet is in the business
of setting up aesthetic hierarchies, but there, as in the case of the later
missive to Horatio, the text of the letter is set on the printed page with the
reader in mind and correctly demarcated off from Polonius's interjected
comments through the use of italics (H 83–85). Q2 and F are more
aesthetically sophisticated than Q1 in that the poem is not merely communication, but has become an instance of the deformity of communication
on the part of a suffering lover. Indeed, the second quarto and folio texts
have a much broader stylistic register than does Q1, in which, to the dismay
of its critics, the style is too uniformly low to register social distinctions
among speakers. As Alfred Hart complained of the "bad" quartos more
generally in *Stolne and Surreptitious Copies*, "King, queen, cardinal, duchess,
peer, soldier, lover, courtier, artisan, peasant, servant, and child all speak
alike."[71]

Who is responsible for these interesting differences among the three
early *Hamlets* in terms of the presentation of written materials? Shakespeare? the players? some other early reviser? the printers or publishers?
However we attempt to account for the gradually increasing "literacy" with
which the three *Hamlets* handle written matter within the play, we need
to recognize a correlation between this pattern and another noticed in
earlier chapters by which, as we move from "bad" quartos to better folios,
the plays are subtly gentrified, particularly in their depiction of the milieu
of dramatic activity. F *Merry Wives* offers characters of slightly higher social
standing and culminates in a masque evoking the courtly milieu of Windsor
Castle and the garter chapel; F *Taming of the Shrew* presents the play's
actors as genteel allies of the lord instead of semi-literate louts on the level
of Christopher Sly, and ends with Sly and his frame having vanished
altogether. Similarly in *Hamlet*, if we consider the three versions of the play
in terms of their portrayal of theatrical culture, we will find a pattern of

gradual elevation of the actors, a gradual separation of them and Hamlet from "low" elements of theatrical life. The exclusionary rituals by which Robert Greene and other learned poets of the 1590s had sought to distance themselves from "illiterate" players like Shakespeare are appropriated by Shakespeare himself.

In all three versions of the play, the Prince of Denmark is on terms of intimacy with a troupe referred to as the "Tragedians of the City." We will note the classical epithet – they are not players but "Tragedians" – strong propaganda, that, for the elevation of the actor's profession! But the content of Hamlet's advice differs significantly from one version to the next. In all three texts he condemns strutting and stage bellowing that tears a "Passion to tatters, to verie ragges, to split the eares of the Groundlings: who (for the most part) are capeable of nothing, but inexplicable dumbe shewes, & noise," (cited from F; H 131 TLN 1857–60), but the rest of the speech differs widely between Q1 and Q2/F. In Q1 he condemns the clowns for speaking more than is set down for them, as he does in Q2 and F, but then continues in lines unique to the first quarto to describe another fault committed by stage fools:

> And then you haue some agen, that keepes one sute
> Of ieasts, as a man is knowne by one sute of
> Apparrell, and Gentlemen quotes his ieasts downe
> In their tables, before they come to the play, as thus:
> Cannot you stay till I eate my porrige? and, you owe me
> A quarters wages : and, my coate wants a cullison:
> And, your beere is sowre : and, blabbering with his lips,
> And thus keeping in his cinkapase of ieasts,
> When, God knows, the warme Clowne cannot make a iest
> Vnlesse by chance, as the blinde man catcheth a hare:
>
> (H 132, 134 F2)

In this version (which is prose written as blank verse, as commonly in Shakespearean quartos), Hamlet lingers over the poorly endowed clown's repeated stock lines and gags – no doubt entirely unscripted – that draw a laugh whatever the theatrical occasion because they have been anticipated by the audience. Gentlemen actually write the stuff down! – perhaps the first time the words have seen paper. Part of the joke is that literate gentlemen are willing to treat an uncouth, orally based theater with such respect. Such gags did indeed circulate in manuscript: two resembling the "ieasts" to which Hamlet refers were eventually published in *Tarlton's jests. Drawne into these three parts* (1613). The quip about sour beer was probably based on a jest in which Tarlton played drunkard before the queen, and the line about the coat wanting a cullison appears in a jest the same clown played on a red-faced gentleman in an alehouse to make the company merry.[72] Successful delivery of Hamlet's speech in Q1 would require the prince to mimic the improvisatory, "oral" theater he despises and perhaps stimulate an audience response quite similar to that clowns like Tarlton had aimed for. The speech is an interesting and highly concrete glimpse of actor–audience relations in the late Elizabethan popular theater, in which there is a strong element of direct, spontaneous interaction between the stage and assembled auditors and a high degree of interpenetration between onstage action and the clown's exploits offstage. But this speech is absent in the second quarto version of the play, which offers instead a sophisticated rationale for playing that does not exist in Q1.

In Q2 and F, Hamlet prefaces his critique of the bellowing actors and clowns who speak more than is set down for them by offering his famous advice about suiting the action to the word, the word to the action, about not overstepping the modesty of nature, and holding the mirror up to nature.

> to shew vertue her feature; scorne her own Image, and the very age and body of the time his forme and pressure: Now, this ouer-done, or come tardie off, though it makes the vnskilfull laugh, cannot but make the iudicious greeue, the censure of which one, must in your allowance ore-weigh a whole Theater of others.
>
> (cited from Q2; H 132 [G4]r)

We will note that in this version, Hamlet has divided the audience between the "low" and the judicious – one of the latter is to be preferred over a whole house of the former. Whatever Hamlet may mean by the "forme and pressure" of the "age and body of the time," the play as he envisions it has assumed a greater distance from its audience: it does not so much interact with its spectators as require sufficient distance for interpretation – a sophisticated "reading" of the "age and body" it mirrors. The first quarto's vignette immersing us (and the Prince of Denmark himself) in the slapstick ethos of the popular stage is absent here, as the elevated talk about holding the mirror up to nature is absent from Q1. The image Hamlet projects of the theatre is noticeably more refined in the "good" than in the "bad" quarto. And he has more strongly disavowed that segment of the audience incapable of the "virtue" and judgment that the theater can teach.

The folio version of Hamlet's speeches is close to the second quarto version, except for a highly interesting addition. The three texts differ markedly in their account of the reasons why the "Tragedians of the City" have been compelled to go on tour. In the first quarto, before the players arrive, Hamlet asks Gilderstone, "How comes it that they trauell? Do they grow restie?" The word *restie* could be either *restive* in the now obsolete sense of "inactive" or *rusty*, meaning out of practice, but in either case implies a diminution of previous powers. Gilderstone advises Hamlet that their reputation holds, but the "principall publike audience that / Came

to them, are turned to priuate playes, / And to the humour of children"
(H 102 E3r). In the second quarto, Hamlet's question is similar, but shows
the players more respect: "Doe they hold the same estimation they
did when I was in the Citty; are they so followed." Rosencraus answers
simply, "No indeede are they not" (H 102 [F2]v). There is no mention of
a possible falling off in artistry, or of the children's companies who have
demeaningly eclipsed the adult players.

The folio version (the one to which we are accustomed in standard texts
of the play) is greatly expanded, and forges, through its topical specificity,
an explicit linkage between Shakespeare's company performing the play
of *Hamlet* and the players of Elsinore. We get much more information
about the children's companies, as well as much fuller analysis of the basis
for their appeal. Hamlet's queries combine the Q1 and Q2 versions, but
the rest of the conversation is unique to this version:

> *Ham.* Doe they hold the same estimation they did when I was in the
>   City? Are they so follow'd?
> *Rosin.* No indeed, they are not.
> *Ham.* How comes it? doe they grow rusty?
> *Rosin.* Nay, their indeauour keepes in the wonted pace; But there is
>   Sir an ayrie of Children, little Yases, that crye out on the top of
>   question; and are most tyrannically clap't for't: these are now the
>   fashion, and so be-ratled the common Stages (so they call them)
>   that many wearing Rapiers, are affraide of Goose-quils, and dare
>   scarse come thither.

To which, Hamlet:

> What are they Children? Who maintains 'em? How are they escoted?
> Will they pursue the Quality no longer then they can sing? Will they
> not say afterwards if they should grow themselues to common Players
> (as it is like most if their meanes are not better) their Writers do
> them wrong, to make them exclaim against their owne Succession.
>
>   (H 103 TLN 1381–98)

In this version, there is an overlay of anxiety about status in the portrayal
of the misfortunes suffered by the "common Stages" and their players.
Given that the plague closed London theaters for extended periods in
1603 and subsequent years, requiring the King's Men at times to resume
their role of itinerants, the company's continuance as "Tragedians of the
City" was indeed a matter for anxiety, quite apart from the inroads made
by the boy companies. Prince Hamlet is incredulous that the children have
achieved the degree of prominence they have, and becomes indirectly a
spokesman for the adult companies. His speeches – particularly when this
segment of the action is combined with his analysis of the purpose of playing later on – subtly define the so-called "common" players away from the

status of menials or children and confer upon them the much higher function of moral teachers who mirror humanity to itself in all of its vices and virtues.

As has frequently been suggested, a similar speech about the "little Yases" may at one point have existed in Q2 as well, and been dropped as the rivalry between companies subsided or for some other reason. But if we take the three texts in order of publication in the material form in which we have them, each version of Hamlet's encounter with the players elevates the status of the theater as an institution by a notch or two, and also elevates the actual company performing the play. Hamlet's comments about the players move them increasingly further from a "low" popular, orally based image of the theater, and toward a more refined, cultivated, and literate vision of it. By the time of the First Folio, the Shakespearean theater presents itself as proudly authorial and claims a capacity for artistic unity and self-containment. As Shakespeare's plays assumed the status of literature and became increasingly distanced for readers from the institution that had given them their "soule of lively action," the name and image of Shakespeare himself became increasingly important as a guarantor of a continuing human presence behind the printed page. *Pace* Foucault, the concept of authorship may have developed at least in part as an antidote to the increased distance created by literacy between the originator of a work of art and its consumers.

Given the profoundly different aesthetic assumptions encoded in the three texts, it is small wonder that our standard editions, despite their general preference for Q2 as copytext, adopt the folio version of Hamlet's pronouncements about theater. That version is the one that brings us closest to Shakespeare as we have traditionally liked to imagine him, and to a Shakespearean theater elegant and sophisticated enough to accord with our image of the author. Similarly, in other cases we have discussed in which the folio offers the most "literate" version of a given passage, most editors have followed the folio. We don't have one single *Hamlet*, we have the pleasure of three interrelated *Hamlet*s, each occupying a different position on the register between orality and literacy. To observe how poorly the rough, highly interactive *Hamlet* of Q1 has fared in editorial and critical discussion by comparison with its betters is to recognize the extent to which our received image of "gentle Shakespeare" has been constructed along the lines of Hamlet's own taste. When it comes to aesthetic judgment, the elite is unquestionably to be preferred over the popular, and the highly literate over the low and suspiciously oral. But there is a lingering aura of the seemingly effaced. Alas, poor Yorick!

6

JOHN MILTON'S VOICE

Charles Lamb has left an amusing reaction to his discovery that John Milton had, like most other authors in our twentieth-century understanding of the term, revised his work in the process of composition:

> There is something to me repugnant, at any time, in written hand. The text never seems determinate. Print settles it. I had thought of the 'Lycidas' as of a full-grown beauty – as springing up with all its parts absolute – till, in an evil hour, I was shown the original written copy of it, together with the other minor poems of its author, in the Library of Trinity, kept like some treasure to be proud of. I wish they had thrown them in the Cam, or sent them, after the latter cantos of Spenser, into the Irish Channel. How it staggered me to see the fine things in their ore! interlined, corrected! as if their words were mortal, alterable, displaceable at pleasure! as if they might have been otherwise, and just as good! as if inspirations were made up of parts, and those fluctuating, successive, indifferent! I will never go into the workshop of any great artist again, nor desire a sight of his picture, till it is fairly off the easel; no, not if Raphael were to be alive again, and painting another Galatea.[1]

The very textual instability that has fascinated scholars of our own era and impelled us back into archival research was, for Lamb in Trinity College Library, "repugnant," even menacing. It is not that he failed to recognize the alteration and displacement of words as a usual element of the creative process, but that, at least on that occasion, he wished to be shielded from it. Great art had to be *as if* born full-blown and perfect in order to be itself, retain its aura of invulnerable unity and strength.

For Lamb at Trinity, "Print settles it" – fixes the art as though in amber so that it can be admired through many ages. But he could preserve his illusion of the immortality of poetic language only insofar as he confined his reading of *Lycidas* to the 1645 and 1673 printed versions of the poem, which are indeed remarkably similar, although by no means identical. If instead he had consulted *Lycidas* as it was first published in the 1638 volume of verse *Obsequies* commemorating the death of Edward King, Lamb would have found several unnerving differences between that version of the poem and the printed *Lycidas* of 1645, and also a markedly different context that altered the expectations readers were likely to bring to their perusal of it.[2] Similarly, the three seventeenth-century printed versions of *A Maske* are far more textually uniform than the extant manuscript copies, yet even the printed texts show small alterations from the first anonymous printing in 1637 to Milton's printings under his own name in 1645 and 1673. Perhaps more significantly, the three early printed versions of the Maske at Ludlow gradually reassign the masque's "author function" from the Earl of Bridgewater, for whose investiture as President of the Council of Wales it was originally written, to Milton himself. In the course of its printing history, *A Maske* gradually metamorphoses from a public document of state into a more private expression of its author's own convictions.[3]

Another case of the unfixity of print is *Paradise Lost*, which was issued first in ten books, then in twelve with several added lines. In addition, it gradually took on apparatus designed to make the work more accessible for readers. The early publication history of Milton's major epic is sufficiently anomalous that it still has not been definitively sorted out.[4] There are a handful of important variants in language between the first and second editions, but editors usually choose eclectically from both in assembling their own versions. And even if most of the words of Milton's great epic continued the same from the first edition to the second, spelling and punctuation certainly did not. Helen Darbishire's Clarendon edition of *Paradise Lost* (1958) sought to stabilize the text by normalizing its spellings on what she considered to be distinctly Miltonic principles of pronunciation, but her work has lost credence with most Miltonists. We have no evidence that Milton concerned himself overly with small variants in the different printed versions of the epic, despite heroic editorial efforts to demonstrate otherwise.[5] So much for Lamb's faith in the determinacy of print!

Nevertheless, it has been the business of most modern editors to satisfy the Charles Lambs of our own era – to present the Miltonic oeuvre with a grand solidity in keeping with twentieth-century estimations of the sublimity of the poet. The present chapter will argue implicitly for the separability of the two: why should sublimity require textual rigidity and closure? But we shall also probe some of the devices by which Milton himself has appeared, at least to us, to demand the stability our editions have by and large sought to create. Unlike earlier and contemporary poets, who typically portrayed themselves as either betrayed or forced into print, Milton embraced print culture and willingly exploited it for its ability to "embody" his thought and being. Thoroughgoing materialist that he was, although he recognized print's limitations, he valued it for its ability to transmit ideas rapidly and broadly. By no means did he share Charles

Lamb's later view of the poetic masterpiece as necessarily springing full grown from the mind of its creator. Rather, Milton valued print for its ability to record and transmit his life and voice, to give him an almost god-like "presence" among like-minded friends across seemingly insuperable physical boundaries.

The desire to portray Milton's text as stable and "full grown" from the outset has led editors into strange lapses of attention. As Stephen B. Dobranski has recently argued, for instance, they have silently incorporated the "*Omissa*" printed at the end of the first edition of *Samson Agonistes* into their texts of the poem without so much as noting the anomalous status of the lines in the first edition, where their odd positioning might represent a valuable clue to what editors have traditionally claimed to offer – the work as the author intended it. In context, the "*Omissa*" register the hope of a divinely inspired political regeneration and cleansing of the people of Israel, a hope so readily applicable to Restoration England in 1670 and 1671 that Milton, the printer, or someone else involved in the process may have suppressed the lines, then reconsidered and tacked them on at the end, where they were at least separated from their potentially inflammatory context within the body of the poem. Was Milton himself the suppressor, or the one who insisted on the reinsertion of the lines, or was he both? Were the "*Omissa*" in fact suppressed or only left out by accident? If the omission was accidental, as the printer's note suggests, there may have been an interesting reason for the occurrence. Were the lines in question physically separate from the body of the manuscript used by the compositors, either written on a detached leaf or in a margin? Were they perhaps a cancelled passage in the manuscript that had been restored, but was still mistakenly read as cancelled by the compositors?[6] To probe into the origin of the "*Omissa*" might lead us closer to that high desideratum of modern editions, the determination of the author's intent. But it would also, perhaps, unleash a process of questioning that would undo the welcome illusion of editorial infallibility and fragment the text.

In recent years, seventeenth-century poetry has been the focus of much work in a "new philological" vein. Most notably, scholars like Arthur Marotti and Harold Love have insisted on the textual variability of manuscript culture as a way of undercutting some of the false certainties promulgated in modern editions.[7] But relatively little of this revisionist work has been applied to the writings of John Milton. The poet's voice is so seemingly authoritative and individualized – so *authentic* – that those of us who read and teach him can easily assume he had full control over his materials, as though they were written in stone like the two tablets of the law. To admit the process of printing, the vicissitudes of occasion, or other variables into our construction of Milton would be to lose the solacing vision of the artist's supreme mastery.

Modern Miltonists have been ferociously protective of the identity of the poet, in part because Milton himself appears to have had strong fears about the loss of identity and self-integrity. The dreadful image of the dismembered Orpheus recurs again and again in his work, and has come to the forefront of recent critical attention.[8] To many Miltonists, fragmenting the seemingly unitary image of the artist would be particularly difficult – even painful – because of their strong identification with him. Surrendering Milton to the probing hand of historical and textual revisionism would at least symbolically enact the poet's own nightmare – a dismemberment and dispersal of intact selfhood like that suffered by Orpheus. The fear of fragmentation haunts even the best revisionist volume of essays, titled not *Dismembering* but *Re-membering Milton*. The volume's deconstruction of received views of the poet is immediately reinscribed as restitution, lest its editors (both women) reenact the crime of the Maenads.[9] I will argue here that Milton's seeming fixation on images of self-dispersal is in part a by-product of his self-relinquishment to print culture, which had the potential to spread his work and through it himself far beyond his control or even knowledge.

But print culture also helped Milton consolidate a new form of integrated and unified authorial body. As Mary Nyquist and Margaret Ferguson remark in their preface to *Re-membering Milton*, the Miltonic body and his textual corpus are usually envisioned as one: he "continues to enjoy the status of the most monumentally unified author in the canon" (p. xii). We characteristically identify canonical writers with a name that stands for the sum of their work and of their authorial identity imagined as a clearly delimited body, as in "Shakespeare" and "Marlowe" as well as "Milton." But Milton represents an extreme case, in part because his life is plentifully documented by comparison with the lives of Shakespeare or Marlowe, in part because his writings repeatedly insist on the inseparability of the author from his work and from the image of the poet constructed through the work. Very few writers of the period – and certainly not the dramatists Marlowe and Shakespeare of several decades earlier – interweave their textual productions with anything approaching Milton's artistic self-consciousness and reiterated self-definition.

In the present chapter I will reverse the argumentative pattern of my previous discussions of early printed versions of Shakespeare. There I considered strategies by which modern editors have sought to establish authorial identity in ways unwarranted by the early texts that we have; here I will consider ways in which modern editions *undermine* configurations of authorial identity offered in early modern printed materials. Other scholars are "unediting" seventeenth-century poets by positing their identities in manuscript culture as collective and fluid rather than properly authorial in the Foucauldian sense of the term.[10] I will focus instead on printed collections, primarily Milton's 1645 *Poems* and that volume's innovative strategies for producing authorial presence.

THE BLUE-BOUND BOOKS

They stand almost identical on our shelves, dark blue and gilt, with the name of the author neatly stamped on the spine of each. The Clarendon editions of seventeenth-century poets have in some cases been supplanted by more recent editions, but still represent important and authoritative milestones of twentieth-century scholarship. Part of their appeal comes from the fact that many of them closely mimic the typefonts and layout of Renaissance books, so that readers are afforded a sense of contact with an earlier world of printed matter. These handsome volumes seldom induce in readers a desire to consult the manuscript and printed materials on which they are based, however. Rather, the Clarendon editions are offered as a replacement for the defective originals, replicating some of the attractive "period" features of the seventeenth-century printed editions while at the same time promising greater correctness and reliability. The attribution of authorship is notoriously unreliable in early modern manuscript culture and in many early printed miscellanies, but the blue-bound books set up careful and well-demarcated categories of undisputed writings, dubia, and spuria, so that readers wishing to experience the essence of the poet's authorship can (and usually do) avoid the latter two suspect categories to concentrate on the first. The matched exteriors of these volumes serve (like controls in a laboratory experiment) to insure that readers will encounter all of the authors on precisely the same terms so that the essential originality of each will shine through.

Few Clarendon editors have had the fond illusion that their work was infallible. Nevertheless, the editions themselves were designed to fix the canon of their authors so that the ordinary reader and literary critic would not have to bother about matters of provenance and authority. Indeed, in the bad old days of my own graduate training, not using the standard edition of a writer was a scholarly *faux pas* of the first magnitude. Not all of the Clarendon editions were produced according to the methods promulgated by the New Bibliography, but they nevertheless bear witness to the New Bibliography's insistence on authorial intent as the final and best measure of authenticity – the precious kernel to be winnowed from the chaff of "accidentals" and disfigurement produced by early modern manuscript culture and the printshop. As in Grierson's and Bowers' formulations discussed above in my introduction, the material elements of the Renaissance printed book are so many veils that obscure the author's intent until they are sufficiently defined in their functioning to be cast aside. Indeed, modern editors have often so distrusted Renaissance print culture that they have (as with the *Samson "Omissa"*) overlooked printed evidence that might signal authorial intent.

In the case of George Herbert's posthumous 1633 *The Temple*, for example, as recent scholars have noted, the small duodecimo volume in which the collection reached early readers is mobilized as a material aid to the devotional processes enacted within. The volume's minute size, customary for personal prayerbooks and devotional literature, in itself helps to create a mood of spiritual intimacy between the reader and the departed poet-priest. But the poem also depends heavily on visual language to achieve its many interesting effects. The material fixity of print is frequently presented in the volume as an obstacle to spiritual awareness: yet the printed volume itself is mimetically enlisted as part of the devotional process enacted within its pages. Herbert's shape-poem (or poems) "Easter wings," for example, is printed vertically on the two sides of a single opening as two sets of wings, each set metonymically figuring the book itself and aligned with it to emphasize the resemblance. But the words on the page and the symbolic shape they figure appear to work at cross-purposes. As they appear on the page when the book is held normally, the words are obscured and the wings are oriented upward. Like wings, the book itself can be opened to good effect; indeed, the very pattern that creates the wings within the book is made up of fixed printed words. Once the symbolic equivalence between book and wings is established, the reader's turning of the leaves of the book becomes parallel to the motion of the wings in flight as they lead the soul to God.[11] The shaped poem and the duodecimo volume it microcosmically recapitulates are both "fall" and means of recovery, "most thin" and "most poor" in their materiality, yet a means for spiritual flight. Some of the strenuous interplay between matter and spirit in Herbert's *Temple* is lost once we excise the tiny volume itself, held like a prayerbook in the reader's hand, as an active element in the pattern of repeated lapse and recovery.

As Randall McLeod has noted, however, twentieth-century editions of Herbert – most notably the authoritative Clarendon edition of F. E. Hutchinson (1941) – often sever the material connection between wing and book by printing the shape-poems sideways, so that on the printed page held upright, they look more like hourglasses than wings. Modern editions, by their very format, also sacrifice much of the intimacy of the 1633 volume: they are often largish and unwieldy, with many notes and other editorial intrusions, while it was tiny and portable enough to be a spiritual *vade mecum*. And yet – oh fatal flaw – we cannot link the 1633 *Temple*'s interesting exploitations of the visual potential of print to the poet Herbert himself. The choice to print the wings vertically rather than horizontally, as in the surviving manuscript copies, one of which shows corrections in Herbert's own hand, may have been Nicholas Ferrar's rather than the poet's, since it was Ferrar who saw the volume through the press. Nor is it likely that the dead poet played any part in determining the volume's highly effective format and title page. As we consider the subtle rhetoric of the printed remains of George Herbert, we find ourself within the suspect terrain of corporate authorship, in which the poet's intent loses its clarity and becomes melded with other intentionalities mobilized during the process of printing and publication.

But even if the 1633 *Temple* bears treacherous false witness to the author's intent, it offers valuable clues to the volume's reception, particularly by the many poets who were to become Herbert's imitators. If we wish to capture the idiosyncratic "essence" of single-author volumes of Renaissance poems, we would do well to consider their subtle but often highly distinctive visual rhetoric as an inseparable element of their meaning. Instead of appearing as a matched set almost indistinguishable on the outside save for the gold-stamped name of the author, our standard modern editions would need to be mismatched and heterogeneous in format in order to communicate the visual rhetoric that strikingly distinguished one verse collection from another for early readers. In our thirst for completeness and authenticity, we have lost sight of the material book.

Even when an early edition offers clear signs that its author guided it through the press, twentieth-century editors still feel entitled to overrule the author's judgment and reject elements that detract from their sense of the poet's artistry. Modern editions of Robert Herrick's *Hesperides* (1648), with which the author was obviously still tinkering during the process of publication, offer a striking example, although they do display considerable fidelity to the collection's 1648 format. The authoritative Clarendon or Norton editions are close to the size and heft of the original octavo volume and reproduce the amusing frontispiece and some of the varied font sizes that make the seventeenth-century book so lively on the page.[12] Indeed, the frontispiece is highly innovative in its portrayal of a living, rather than a dead, poet. But the substitute *Hesperides* presented through modern editions violates important features of the 1648 volume as a book. Modern editions separate off from the rest a large body of verses that Herrick considered essential to the volume.

Although Herrick was, like Herbert, a churchman, most of his volume successfully suppresses that fact. The most obvious unifying internal feature of the collection is its establishment of an authorial self. On nearly every page we are made emphatically aware that it belongs to Herrick, the poet, its author. Unlike Herbert's *Temple*, which was not issued with a portrait frontispiece until its tenth edition in 1674, Herrick's volume features a frontispiece portrait presumably of the author, resplendent in curls and Roman nose. Herrick is presented as prematurely defunct, and given a semi-parodic monumentalization like that of some classical *vates*. His bust is poised upon an urn and surrounded by nymphs, garlands, and other accoutrements of the artist. The bust is in profile, so that the author appears to gaze beneficently at his own facing title page, a demigod approving of his creation (Figure 6.1). The witty effect is lost in the standard modern editions, which typically reproduce the portrait but not the interplay between portrait and title page.

Figure 6.1 Portrait frontispiece and title page to Herrick's *Hesperides* (1648)
Reproduced by permission of the Harry Ransom Humanities Research Center,
University of Texas, Austin

184

HESPERIDES:

OR,

THE WORKS

BOTH

HUMANE & DIVINE

OF

ROBERT HERRICK *Esq.*

OVID.

Effugient avidos Carmina noftra Rogos.

LONDON,
Printed for *John Williams,* and *Francis Eglesfield,*
and are to be fold at the Crown and Marygold
in Saint *Pauls* Church-yard. 1648.

Within the volume, Herrick entitles numerous poems "*His*," beginning with the very first, "*The Argument of his Book*," and continuing through "*To his Muse*," several poems "*To his Booke*," "*When he would have his verses read*," "*His Poetrie his Pillar*," "*To Musique, to becalme his Fever*," "*Upon the death of his Sparrow. An Elegie*," and so forth throughout the volume. Numerous poems from *Hesperides* are at least quasi-autobiographical, recording his various (imagined?) amours, his discontents in Devonshire, where he held an ecclesiastical living until he was ousted by Puritan forces in 1647, and his joyous return to the London of his birth. These poems help to create identity between writer and book – interfuse his creation with a sense of personal possession, the felt presence of his life. The "divine" poems at the end are similarly marked by his ownership – they are "*His Noble Numbers: or, His Pious Pieces, Wherein (amongst other things) he sings the Birth of his Christ: and sighes for his* Saviours *suffering on the* Crosse."

Even the volume's errata list gives evidence, in a way that is uncommon for the first half of the seventeenth century, to the poet's insistent surveillance over the book and the image of him it communicates. He protests, in a rueful ditty prefacing the list of faults escaped, that he gave the printer "*good Grain*"; if that careless individual sowed "*Tares*" throughout the volume, then they must be fastidiously sought out and eradicated (M p. [4]). And eradicate *Tares* he did. Another feature of Herrick's authorship that can be observed through comparison of the early printed states of *Hesperides* is the poet's willingness, also fairly unusual for the time, to fine-tune his text even during the process of printing. There are several cancels that are almost certainly authorial, since some of them do not correct misprints but refine the poetic language.[13] In *Hesperides*, we encounter not only authorship, but a hypercathexis of authorship: for all its squibs of frivolity and its interpolation of seemingly heterogeneous materials, *Hesperides* is unified by the poet's pathbreaking insistence on its intimate relationship to himself.

Such, at least, is the impression of *Hesperides* we are likely to receive if we leave out the last 270-odd poems, those comprising *Noble Numbers*. In modern editions of Herrick, the editors regularly take care to separate Herrick's "Pious Pieces" from *Hesperides* proper. L. C. Martin's Clarendon edition inserts a page and a half of white space between the end of *Hesperides* proper and the beginning of *Noble Numbers*. In J. Max Patrick's edition, still more strikingly, two nearly empty leaves intervene, with the second bearing a half title of the kind one would expect at the beginning of a separate work. Modern editors have worked to distance *Noble Numbers* from *Hesperides* in large part because they find the "Pious Pieces" a woeful falling off from the aesthetic standards of Herrick's secular verse. As some editors have speculated, *Noble Numbers* may at one point have been intended by the poet as a separate publication. But if we peruse the 1648 *Hesperides* with the care that its author seems to demand of his readers, the two parts of the collection as we have it are inextricably linked – part of a single whole. The title page for the *Hesperides* announces that it is to include "The Works Both Humane & Divine" of its author, so that the name *Hesperides* encompasses both; "*The Argument of his Book*" ends, "I write of *Hell*; I sing (and ever shall) / Of *Heaven*, and hope to have it after all" (M p. 5), placing the divine subjects at the end of his introductory poem, just as *Noble Numbers* appears at the end of the volume. *Noble Numbers* has a separate title page in the 1648 edition, but one lacking the full publication information offered on the title page for the volume as a whole in the six or eight copies I have consulted. Moreover, its numbering begins with sig. Aa, not sig. A, as we would expect if author and printers treated it as a separate work. The list of errata at the beginning of *Hesperides* includes faults escaped from *Noble Numbers*. Beyond that, the last two pages of *Hesperides* proper feature a number of poems that mark the closing of the first part of the collection while simultaneously advising the reader that the voyage is far from over – more verses are to come. At the bottom recto of the last full leaf of *Hesperides* proper (p. 397 sig. Cc7r), a poem entitled "*The end of his worke*" appears to be moving the volume toward closure, but promises that the closure will be temporary, not final: "Part of the worke remaines; one part is past: / And here my ship rides having Anchor cast." (Figure 6.2).

In this instance, as in Herbert's *Temple* of a decade and a half earlier, the operation of the book is made part of the process of poetic discovery. It is, I would submit, no accident that "*The end of his worke*" appears in the pivotal position it holds. If we turn the leaf whose recto ends with the promise of a second "part," we encounter the last poems of *Hesperides* proper on the verso and, without any blank space whatsoever, the title page of *Noble Numbers* on the right hand side of the same opening (Figure 6.3). Indeed, as Herrick bibliographers appear not to have noticed despite their careful collation of the volume and their professed interest in physical evidence that might signal authorial intent, the title page of *Noble Numbers* is the final leaf of the same eight-leaf octavo gathering as the last pages of *Hesperides* proper – they were printed off as a single sheet. With the end of the first part, the poet may have reached a *terminus* and set anchor temporarily, but he is poised to reembark, to offer the other "part of the worke."

Despite the difference in literary genre, we find ourself, in examining this strange editorial *lacuna*, back in the territory of the "bad" quarto. In modern editions, *Noble Numbers* has been cordoned off from *Hesperides* proper by a "danger zone" of white paper – given the place frequently occupied in modern editions by "dubia" and "spuria." Like a "bad" quarto, it offers poetry that is somehow less highly literate, less lyrical, less vividly personal, less obviously "Robert Herrick" than earlier portions of the volume. Most of the poems of *Noble Numbers* use a narrower range of mythological reference, vocabulary and syntax than their counterparts among the secular lyrics, and several, like "*To his Saviour, a Child; a Present, by a child*" and "*Graces for Children*," are explicitly designed for children. Indeed, in *Noble Numbers*, the poet himself assumes the persona of a dutiful child of the church: the poems announced as "*His*" are strikingly similar in tone and language to the poems expressly for children. By happy accident, we know that these poems (along with a few from the first part of the collection) were preserved by oral transmission among the illiterate villagers of Dean Prior. A visitor to the village in 1809 found that several of Herrick's *Noble Numbers* were still being used as prayers by local people.[14] Despite the obvious elitism of many features of *Hesperides*, Robert Herrick was capable of writing in a markedly popular vein: *Noble Numbers*, with its humbler and more uniform lyrics than earlier parts of the collection, can be regarded as a retreat into oral Anglican community amidst the uncertainties of war and ecclesiastical upheaval as the nation slid into civil war.

Noble Numbers is Herrick's final line of defense against the ravages of "*Times trans-shifting.*" The final couplet of *Hesperides* proper reads, with an apparent air of finality, "To his Book's end this last line he'd have plac't, / *Jocond his Muse was; but his Life was chast*" and is followed by "Finis" in Roman capitals. But at the bottom of the previous page, readers have already been promised another "part." Within the book's immediate material context, the Ovidian palinode, which divides *Hesperides* from *Noble Numbers* and separates the jocundity of the poet's muse from the chastity of his life, takes back the exuberant "authorial" selfhood asserted through much of the first part of the collection in favor of a stiller, quieter voice lacking much of the individuality of Herrick's projected identity and sounding (to the discomfort of those who prize the poet's authorial voice as asserted elsewhere in the collection) as part of a broader murmur of nearly anonymous voices.

That is not to suggest that the first part of the collection is necessarily less orally based than the second. As we have seen, in *Hamlet* and elsewhere in Shakespeare, orality is often handled with ambivalence, linked with dramatic power but also with the shame of undistinguished origin and illiteracy. The distrust of orality within Shakespeare's plays relates, I have argued, to the playwright's desire to dissociate himself and his company from an earlier, despised, illiterate or semi-literate dramatic culture. But Robert Herrick was a university man, an erstwhile "Son of Ben," for whom orality was associated with a long tradition of humanist discourse by which sound is accorded a higher and less equivocal status than sight. As Father Ben himself remarked in praise of the aural over the visual, "*Language* most shewes a man: speake that I may see thee."[15] Herrick, too, conceptualized his verses at least in part as an oral/aural rather than a visual event: he characterizes himself in "*The Argument of his Book*" as one who sings, and

At which the hounds fall a bounding ;
While th' Moone in her fphere
Peepes trembling for feare,
And night's afraid of the founding.

The mount of the Mufes.

AFter thy labour take thine eafe,
Here with the fweet *Pierides*.
But if fo be that men will not
Give thee the Laurell Crowne for lot;
Be yet affur'd, thou fhalt have one
Not fubject to corruption.

On Himfelfe.

ILe write no more of Love ; but now repent
Of all thofe times that I in it have fpent.
Ile write no more of life; but wifh twas ended,
And that my duft was to the earth commended.

To his Booke.

Goe thou forth my booke, though late ;
Yet be timely fortunate.
It may chance good-luck may fend
Thee a kinfman, or a friend,
That may harbour thee, when I,
With my fates neglected lye.
If thou know'ft not where to dwell,
See, the fier's by :   *Farewell*.

The end of his worke.

PArt of the worke remaines ; one part is paft :
And here my fhip rides having Anchor caft.

To

Figure 6.2 Penultimate page of the first part of *Hesperides* showing verse couplet at
the bottom
Reproduced by permission of the Harry Ransom Humanities Research Center,
University of Texas, Austin

189

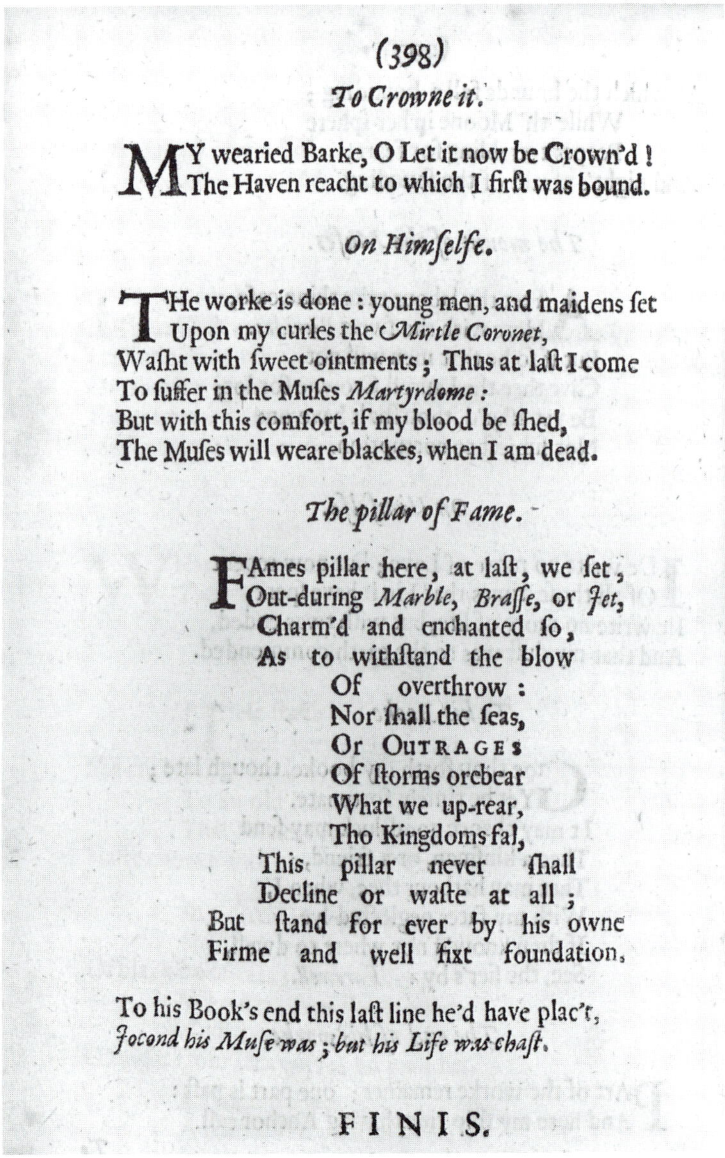

To Crowne it.

MY wearied Barke, O Let it now be Crown'd !
The Haven reacht to which I firſt was bound.

On Himſelfe.

THe worke is done : young men, and maidens ſet
Upon my curles the *Mirtle Coronet,*
Waſht with ſweet ointments ; Thus at laſt I come
To ſuffer in the Muſes *Martyrdome :*
But with this comfort, if my blood be ſhed,
The Muſes will weare blackes, when I am dead.

The pillar of Fame.

FAmes pillar here, at laſt, we ſet,
Out-during *Marble, Braſſe,* or *Jet,*
Charm'd and enchanted ſo,
As to withſtand the blow
Of   overthrow :
Nor ſhall the ſeas,
Or OUTRAGES
Of ſtorms orebear
What we up-rear,
Tho Kingdoms fal,
This   pillar   never   ſhall
Decline or waſte at all ;
But   ſtand for ever by his owne
Firme   and   well   fixt   foundation.

To his Book's end this laſt line he'd have plac't,
Jocond his Muſe was ; but his Life was chaſt.

FINIS.

Figure 6.3 Final page of the first part of *Hesperides* and title page of *Noble Numbers*
Reproduced by permission of the Harry Ransom Humanities Research Center,
University of Texas, Austin

HIS
NOBLE NUMBERS:

O R,

HIS PIOUS PIECES,

VVherein (amongſt other things)
he ſings the Birth of his C H R I S T:
and ſighes for his *Saviours* ſuffe-
ring on the *Croſſe.*

H E S I O D.

Ἴδμεν ψεύδεα πολλὰ λέγᾳν ἐτύμοισιν ὁμοῖα.
Ἴδμεν δ᾽ εὖτ᾽ ἐθέλωμεν, ἀληθέα μυθήσαωχ.

L O N D O N.
Printed for *John Williams,* and *Francis Eglesfield.*
1 6 4 7.

several of the poems from *Hesperides* were circulated and published elsewhere as song lyrics. In fact, the *Hesperides* versions of songs previously published elsewhere sometimes demonstrate precisely the reworking and refinement we would expect as part of the transition from an "oral" to a reading text.[16] But the second part of Herrick's published collection, like the Shakespearean "bad" quartos, is "oral" without being lyrical; with the exception of a few more elaborate poems, it fails to demonstrate the same degree of attention *Hesperides* does to the needs and tastes of highly literate, classically educated readers. The contrasts in tone and projected readership between the two parts of Herrick's book are unquestionably elements of the poet's "intended" effect. To read Herrick's collection in its 1648 form rather than in the modern edited versions is to forfeit the authorial stability they promise in favor of a subtle interplay between exuberant revelry in the newly discovered pleasures of printed authorship and retreat into willed anonymity. The blue-bound books of the twentieth century present authorship as a reliable constant. In poetry collections of the sixteenth and seventeenth centuries, by contrast, it was fitful and unstable, by turns bold, reticent, strident, and mute.

THE BOOK AS AUTHORIAL BODY

In *The Order of Books*, Roger Chartier has called attention to a process by which the author as a historical entity gradually became identified with the body of his printed works: "Controlled and stabilized in this manner, the text was to institute a direct and authentic relation between the author and the reader."[17] The *desire* for such control of course predates the invention of movable type: we can find precursors in Petrarch's attempts to control the manuscript circulation of his materials, or even in the more equivocal and evanescent stabs at authorial presence made by Geoffrey Chaucer. But in England, the prime decades for the installation of the poet's "authentic" presence in the body of the book were the 1630s and 1640s, and its prime agents were, quixotically, not so much the poets themselves as those involved in the process of printing and publication, who exploited the visual and tactile potential of the physical book and its pages to give "presence" to the absent author.

As we noted earlier, the sixteenth-century printer John Day characterized his second edition of *Gorboduc* through the trope of the human body. *Gorboduc* was a previously despoiled and mutilated textual body that had been refurbished and decked out by Day in a fresh garment of black and white. But Day's textual body was feminized, a passive recipient of reader attention and not yet conceptualized as the body of the author. The identification of corpse and *corpus* appears, in England at least, to have been a seventeenth-century invention but not, before the publication of Milton's 1645 poems, an invention that we can attribute with any certainty to the author.[18] And even in the case of Milton's groundbreaking collection, as we shall see, the degree of Milton's agency is unclear. The construction and maintenance of authorial "presence" in seventeenth-century volumes of published poetry was often a non-authorial activity.

The most important English precursors of Milton's 1645 *Poems* in terms of their identification of corpse and *corpus* were undoubtedly the early posthumous editions of John Donne's verses. Between the 1633 and 1635 editions, we can see the poetic body of the book in process of formation and elaboration. Donne's 1633 *Poems* is, as Marotti (see n. 7) has observed, a reflection of the manuscript culture within which the poet's lyrics and verse epistles had circulated (pp. 250–55). Within it, the sacred and secular verses are intermingled. First come "The Progresse of the Soule," Holy Sonnets, epigrams, Elegies, and Epistles to specific authors that establish the verse community within which Donne functioned as a poet. Love poems enter the volume only late and intermingled with other material, like the First and Second Anniversaries. The effect is a striking melange of sacred and secular that refuses to separate John Donne from Jack. Verse epistles to the Countess of Bedford jostle up against scurrilous amatory verses and evocations of human decay in a rough gallimaufry of mingled passions that projects a John Donne very like the Donne most of us value, a Donne for whom the sacred and the secular are so closely intertwined as to be finally inseparable.

The 1633 quarto edition of Donne's poems does not have the frontispiece portrait that was to lend such an air of intimacy to the 1635 octavo edition. Nevertheless, it contrives to communicate a strong aura of authorial presence through its front matter. Most copies of the 1633 *Poems* begin, uncannily, with Donne's own voice as though echoing from the grave – the introductory epistle to *Metempsycosis*, titled "Infinitati Sacrum" and dated 16 August, 1601. This epistle offers a verbal "portrait of the artist" in his own rhetorical "colours": "Others at the Porches and entries of their Buildings set their Armes; I, my picture, if any colours can deliver a minde so plaine, and flat, and through light as mine" (sig. A3r). It is possible that Donne devised the epistle for a manuscript copy of *Metempsycosis* to be sent to a friend along with a portrait miniature.[19] The epistle is a fitting introit to the printed volume of poems because it establishes the poet's "authentic" voice.

Next in many copies of the 1633 *Poems* come two inserted leaves headed "The Printer to The Understanders" (quite likely an afterthought since they do not occur in all copies), which usually interrupt the introductory sequence through their placement between Donne's Epistle to *Metempsycosis* and the poem ("The Progresse of the Soule") itself.[20] The added leaves greatly intensify the effect of "presence" created by Donne's epistle. In "The Printer to The Understanders," the printer (either Miles Fletcher or someone speaking for him) apologizes for offering not

Donne's whole works but only "a scattered limbe of this Author," which nevertheless "hath more amiablenesse in it, in the eye of a discerner, then a whole body of some other . . . " (The whole body of Donne's works would presumably have included the prose pamphlets and sermons as well.) Similarly, on the verso of the second leaf (sig. [A2]v) there appears a poem "*Hexastichon Bibliopolae*" by "Jo. Mar." (identified by Sir Geoffrey Keynes as the bookseller and publisher John Marriot, whose full name appears on the title page as publisher of the volume), in which the edition itself is offered as the best and most enduring possible portrait of the author:

> I See in his last preach'd, and printed booke,
> His Picture in a sheete; in *Pauls* I looke,
> And see his Statue in a sheete of stone,
> And sure his body in the grave hath one:
> Those sheetes present him dead, these if you buy,
> You have him living to Eternity.

The "Picture in a sheete" is the famous frontispiece to *Deaths Dvell* (1632), which depicts Donne in his winding sheet; the "sheete of stone" is his equally famous funerary monument in St Paul's. But the printed volume offers more than either of these – sheets of paper preserving the poet's living soul. What an appealing incentive for acquiring the volume: to possess reliable, intimate contact with the living soul of the beloved Dean of St Paul's! The aura of authorial presence that has for much of the twentieth century been considered an essential, inescapable element of a volume of "authored" poems may have originated at least in part as a marketing device.

Many copies of the 1633 *Poems* intensify the effect of reliquary embodiment through further gestures of personalization. In the Pforzheimer copy at the University of Texas, given by Donne's executor Bishop Henry King to his nephew John King, the title page has a Donne signature – in all likelihood genuine and cut from one of the author's letters – affixed to it, possibly as a memorial gesture for a select circle of recipients (Figure 6.4). At least one other copy – the Harvard Library copy – has the same feature.[21] Later alterations of the 1633 volume of *Poems* go further – many of them adding the frontispiece portrait from the second edition, and at least one also including engraved images of Donne's monument at St Paul's at the end of the poems. This last is not a seventeenth-century, but a ninteenth or early twentieth-century marketing gesture: the copy (University of Texas HRC Wh D719 C633p) is part of the Wrenn Collection, assembled for the collector by the notorious bibliographer and master forger Thomas J. Wise.

Fittingly for a volume designed to embody the life of the poet, the expected commendatory poems in the 1633 edition appear not where we would expect them at the beginning of the volume, but at the end, where

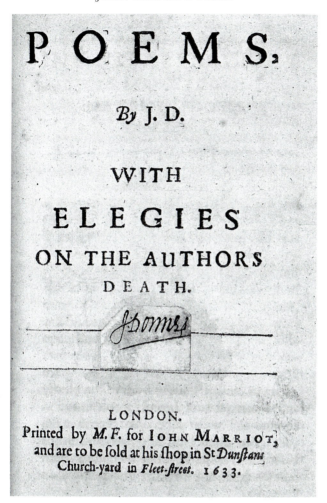

Figure 6.4 Title page of Pforzheimer copy of Donne's *Poems* (1633) showing
affixed signature
Reproduced by permission of the Harry Ransom Humanities Research Center,
University of Texas, Austin

they function as funerary elegies. At least one early reader of the volume –
a Thomas Browne identified by Keynes not as the author of *Religio Medici*
but as a more senior Browne who attended Christ Church College in the
1620s and resurfaces in the records as domestic chaplain to Archbishop
Laud in 1637 – was put off by the volume's intermingling of sacred
and secular materials. Browne's poem "To the deceased Author, Upon
the *Promiscuous* printing of his Poems, the *Looser sort*, with the *Religious*"

195

objected to the fact that the "*Strange Fire*" of sexual raptures and wantonness should be "*mingled with thy Sacrifice*" (sig. [Bbb 4]v).

Laud's future family chaplain was not the only early reader who desired a more decorous arrangement of Donne's poetic remains. The 1635 octavo edition of Donne's *Poems*, brought out by the same printer and publisher as the 1633 edition, offers a very different construction of the authorial body in which the objections of readers like Browne are attended to and the volume becomes a more accurate embodiment of Donne – or at least Donne as they wished to remember him. Unlike the 1633 edition, the 1635 *Poems* has a frontispiece portrait of the author (Figure 6.5). It is shaded to resemble an oval portrait miniature placed on a flat ground and labelled in Roman capitals "Anno Dni. 1591 Aetatis Svae 18." The portrait resembles miniatures of the type that were frequently sent during the period to an intimate friend along with a sheaf of manuscript verses.[22] On the upper right is the Spanish motto "Antes mverto que mudado," which Donne's biographer Izaak Walton interpreted as a reference to death, "How shall I be changed before I change," but which echoes the amatory verse of Jorge de Montemayor and can more credibly be understood as a dashing lover's promise of undying passion: "Better dead than changed."[23] The potential titillation of the erotic message is quickly curbed by Izaak Walton's verses below that interpret the poet's life as an exemplary pattern of Christian conversion, a pattern that has remained canonical until very recently in editions and critical studies:

> *This was for youth, Strength, Mirth, and wit that Time*
> *Most count their golden Age; but t'was not thine.*
> *Thine was thy later yeares, so much refind*
> *From youths Drosse, Mirth, & wit; as thy pure mind*
> *Thought (like the Angels) nothing but the Praise*
> *Of thy Creator, in those last, best Dayes.*
> > *Witnes this Booke, (thy Embleme) which begins*
> > *With Love; but endes, with Sighes, & Teares for sins.*

And, in keeping with Walton's decorous separation of the sacred from the profane, this volume redeems the life of the poet from its earlier manuscript promiscuity in the intermingling of sacred and secular. After "The Printer to The Understanders," carried over from the first edition, we encounter Marriot's "*Hexastichon Bibliopolae*" as before, but below it on the same page (sig. [A4]v) another brief poem expressing the wish that Donne's sermons would also be printed, to the end that not only the poet but "*Hee, We, and Thou shall live t'Eternity.*" Next, as in 1633, we are offered Donne's "Epistle" to *Metempsycosis*, but without "The Progresse of the Soule" itself following the prefatory epistle. In 1635, the poems constituting the body of the edition have been radically rearranged in parallel with Walton's decorous separation of the sacred "John Donne" from the

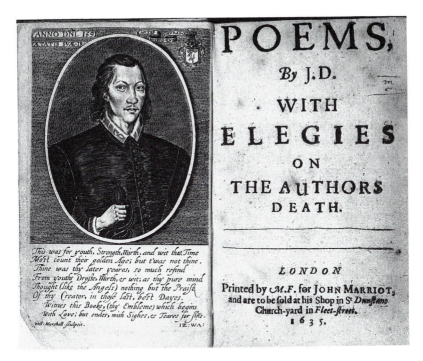

ANNO DNI. 1591
ÆTATIS SVÆ 18

This was for youth, Strength, Mirth, and wit that Time
Most count their golden Age; but t'was not thine.
Thine was thy later yeares, so much refind
From youths Drosse, Mirth, & wit; as thy pure mind
Thought (like the Angels) nothing but the Praise
Of thy Creator, in those last, best Dayes.
Witnes this Booke, (thy Embleme) which begins
With Love; but endes, with Sighes, & Teares for sins.
Will: Marshall sculpsit.   IZ: WA:

POEMS,
By J.D.
WITH
ELEGIES
ON
THE AUTHORS
DEATH.

LONDON
Printed by M.F. for JOHN MARRIOT,
and are to be sold at his Shop in Sᵗ Dunstans
Church-yard in Fleet-street.
1635.

Figure 6.5 Portrait frontispiece and title page to Donne's *Poems* (1635)
Reproduced by permission of the Henry E. Huntington Library,
San Marino, California

profane "Jack." *Metempsycosis*, as a "sacred" poem, is moved back to the second half of the volume, with the Holy Sonnets and other religious verse. The first generic category in the 1635 *Poems* is the Songs and Sonets, beginning with "The Flea" and other pleasantly outrageous erotica.

The wide 1635 separation between Donne's epistle to *Metempsycosis* and the poem itself is puzzling. Could it be that the printer kept Donne's epistle "Infinitati Sacrum" at the beginning of the volume even after he had moved the poem to which it was intended as preface because of the epistle's powerful evocation of authorial presence? In an errata notice on the final printed page of the edition, Marriot apologizes for having separated the "Epistle" from the poem it was meant to accompany, which begins on page 301. But the apology may be partly disingenuous. Donne's epistle is particularly fitting as an introit to the 1635 volume, not only because its quips about portraiture serve as appropriate commentary on the frontispiece portrait of the author, but also because the "Epistle" dwells on the subject of the transmigration of souls, so that "you must not grudge to finde the same soule in an Emperour, in a Post-horse, and in a Maceron" or a "Melon" or a "Spider." Or in a printed book? The

"Epistle"'s speculation about diverse embodiments of spirit offers a splendidly apt introduction for a volume in which the soul of the author is claimed to have transmigrated to the printed page.

In the 1635 edition, the physical space between the covers becomes a measure of temporal duration. The reader's experience of perusing the poems *seriatim* simultaneously recapitulates the poet's life as interpreted by Walton, with the poet's "*Wanton Story*" at the beginning, and his "*Sacrifice and Glory*" as communicated through the sacred verses, at the end. The poems, which were promiscuously scattered "limbs" in manuscript circulation and in the 1633 volume, are here carefully arranged in a generic and chronological order akin to Laudian liturgical order, by which the altar must be carefully dressed and railed off from the profane space given over to the congregation so that one "kind" does not contaminate the other. The poem by Laud's household chaplain is absent from this volume because it is no longer needed. John Donne's life has been appropriated and ordered by the church in whose priesthood he died.

In both of these early editions, the printer and publisher play a striking part in establishing the equivalence of book and body, corpse and *corpus*. It was not John Donne the author who crafted this striking icon of authorship by which the book becomes a "real and authentic" communication of Donne's essence as man and poet. It was at least in part those despised figures the printer and the bookseller. The irony is that, as most bibliographers and editors are agreed, the 1635 *Poems* offers no more accurate a guide to the Donne *corpus* than the 1633 edition, at least in terms of its establishment of the poet's canon, since the 1635 volume adds several poems not now attributed to Donne. As examination of the early editions makes painfully obvious, there is no necessary connection between authorial "presence" and historically verifiable authorship. For that reason alone, these volumes have been haunting and bothersome for modern editors who hope to present authorial presence as unmediated.

THE INVISIBLE AUDIENCE

In publishing his lectures on Jonah in 1597, John King expressed regret for changing his "tongue into a pen, and whereas I spake before with the gesture and countenance of a living man, have now buried myself in a dead letter of less effectual persuasion."[24] As we have already noted in the previous chapter, early modern culture often associated the materiality and fixity of print with the immobility of death: in the language of 2 Corinthians 3:6, "The letter killeth, but the spirit giveth life."[25] Unlike a conversation, the printed page does not alter itself in reaction to even the most vehement expostulation on the part of readers. In its serene indifference to living language, its seemingly demonic (or angelic) capacity to create rapid simulacra of words and images, print carried elements of the uncanny in early modern culture. There appears, in England at least, to have been considerable resistance until fairly late to the use of printed images of living poets – in part, no doubt, because print was still in the process of becoming an acceptable medium for those who wished to claim gentry status; in part, on a more primitive level, because use of the image seemed nebulously akin to idolatry or even body-snatching. Theatrical texts were less reticent: as we have noted, Robert Armin's full-length portrait on the title page of one of his plays shows the author in his professional role of fool (Figure 5.2). But the language with which Armin describes the volume still hints at a connection with nullity: it is mere "dumb show" – dead and inadequate without the immediate resonance of spoken language and action.

Recent scholars have cited Ben Jonson's 1616 *Workes* as an early example of a portrait frontispiece on the published writings of a living poet, but the copies they have consulted in order to make their assertion are spurious later "sophistications" to which the portrait frontispiece has been added rather than intact versions of the 1616 edition.[26] In non-poetic printed materials of the era, such as, preeminently, James I's *Works* (1616), portrait frontispieces of living authors can occasionally be found. The earliest portrait frontispiece I have found affixed to a folio volume of poems is the engraved oval portrait of Drayton crowned with laurel in his 1619 *Poems* and identified as a likeness of the poet at fifty years old in 1613. But "honest Drayton" was notoriously brash in his disregard for accepted rituals of authorial decorum.[27] Generally speaking, before the 1630s and 1640s, if a reader encountered a frontispiece portrait attached to a volume of poetry, he or she could be reasonably certain that its author was defunct. Frontispiece portraits were usually memorial in function rather than aggrandizing – linked with a desire to preserve the illusion of human presence within a medium that was vastly expanding the physical distance between writers and prospective readers. In much the same way, centuries later, the new medium of photography would have as one of its early focal points the portrait, which called lost faces to remembrance with a startlingly poignant fidelity to the originals.[28]

Although the printed book created the possibility of a physical gulf between preachers or performers and their immediate public, it could also be perceived as bridging a vaster space between the living and the dead – offering tangible contact with the "lively presence" of writers far distant in the past. Peter Burke has recently made a cogent case for the Renaissance dialogue as a favorite form of printed discourse during the period because of its replication of oral setting for readers who had not yet adjusted to the seeming anonymity and silence of print; early modern writers often discuss their reading as though it were a similar conversation with the dead. The locus classicus is the exiled Machiavelli's touching description of his nightly perusal of the ancients:

On the threshold I slip off my day's clothes with their mud and dirt, put on my royal and curial robes, and enter, decently accoutred, the ancient courts of men of old, where I am welcomed kindly and fed on that fare which is mine alone, and for which I was born: where I am not ashamed to address them and ask them the reasons for their action, and they reply considerately; and for two hours I forget all my cares, I know no more trouble, death loses its terrors: I am utterly translated in their company.[29]

This elegant "company" consisted, no doubt, of printed Renaissance editions of classical authors. For Machiavelli, reading was not the silent visual analysis that it tends to be for us, but possessed the solacing intimacy of a personal visit during which he was dined, informed, and shown the respect due from one learned statesman to another. If books diminished the living, they could, like necromancy, reanimate the dead. In the less poignant language of the seventeenth-century Englishman John Ramsey, the authors he reads are "Personages to converse with," whether alive or dead in their physical bodies.[30] Books did not have to be printed in order to confer this familiarity: manuscript copies would have served as well or better, provided that they were available. The distinguishing concepts for our purposes here are reliable repetition from one copy to another and ease of repeated consultation by a wide spectrum of readers. Our modern age of pervasive secondary orality has dulled us to some of the early shock value of print's ability to facilitate ready conversation with deceased authorities. That miraculous capacity must, for readers not yet grown accustomed to it, have carried some of the cognitive dissonance we would experience if we could suddenly contact Plato by telephone.

Single-author volumes of published poetry from the early 1630s onward often display ingenious and varied devices for communicating through printed language the "lively presence" of deceased authors. Often there is deliberate disjunction between the age of the poet in the frontispiece image and his actual age at the time of death, as we have already seen in the 1635 Donne volume. Similarly, the second posthumous edition of the *Poems* of Thomas Randolph (Oxford: for Francis Bowman, 1640), who had died young in 1635, undermines the pictorial in favor of the typographic as a record of the writer's "true" identity by displaying the poet in its engraved title-page portrait as though he were a precocious lad of fourteen. Randolph's bust tops a seemingly funerary monument; the effigy is labelled "Obiit Anno 1634 Aetatis suae 27" although Randolph actually died at the age of twenty-nine or thirty. Shakespeare's First Folio adopts a different method. Ben Jonson's frontispiece poem "To the Reader" is placed oppo-site the very large and compelling title-page image of the author, but argues that the "real" presence of Shakespeare is to be found not in the picture but in the language within. However, the 1623 folio was a repository of dramatic materials rather than lyric poems. The commanding, unframed image of Shakespeare on the First Folio title page seems designed (following Robert Armin's example discussed in the previous chapter) to communicate stage presence rather than the intimacy of a portrait miniature.

By contrast, the little-known 1640 octavo edition of *Poems: Written by Wil. Shake-speare. Gent.* reinterprets the First Folio portrait to bring it closer to the usual pattern of printed collections of poetry. The frontispiece portrait by William Marshall (Figure 6.6) reverses the Droeshout engraving from the First Folio, places it within an oval designed to resemble a miniature mounted in a case, and adds visual elements that elevate and canonize the author almost in the religious sense of the term. Shakespeare sports a rich cloak and grasps a sprig of laurel; behind his head is a brightly illuminated area that looks suspiciously like a *gloria*. The accompanying poem (most of which is borrowed from Jonson's poem in the First Folio) calls attention both to St Shakespeare's celebrity as "Soule of th'age" and to his absence in body: the miniature perused by the reader is only "Shadowe." Unlike the other volumes of poetry considered thus far, however, the 1640 Shakespeare *Poems* participate in none of the internal devices by which the body of the book was coming to be made coterminous with the life of the poet. Rather, the volume offers a latter-day miscellany and poetic advice book – the scriptures of St Shakespeare – in which poems by that author and others are captioned with cues to their subject matter for the edification and delight of the reader. Most peculiarly, sonnets are grafted together into 28-line poems on various educational subjects like "The benefit of Friendship" and "A Lovers excuse for his long absence." In these transmogrified sonnets, masculine pronouns referring to the object of the writer's love are sometimes altered to feminines to bring the experience of the poems safely within the norms of heterosexual courtship.[31] Many of the verses included in the volume are, in fact, non-Shakespearean, but thematically akin to Shakespeare's.

Will's posthumous "advice to the lovelorn" is less reanimation of its author than sanctification, "purifying" Shakespeare's writings and raising him to the level of cynosure and tutelary spirit of the age. No doubt the volume's value as nostalgia for a simpler, golden cultural past was intensified by its appearance in 1640, not long after the first rumblings of what was to become the English Civil War. Within two years, the theaters would close. Here as in the other verse collections, the portrait is offered both to confirm Shakespeare's identity and to displace it. The poet is no longer to be found in the corrupted physical body memorialized as it had been in life through the portrait, but can be located instead in the printed words that constitute the less ephemeral body of the book. Seventeenth-century memorial frontispieces are often decorated with cypresses, skulls, or other mementa mori that warn readers away from the lost physical presence of

Figure 6.6 Portrait frontispiece and title page to Shakespeare's *Poems* (1640)

POEMS:

VVRITTEN

BY

WIL. SHAKE-SPEARE.

Gent.

Printed at *London* by *Tho. Cotes*, and are
to be sold by *Iohn Benson*, dwelling in
St. *Dunstans* Church-yard. 1640.

the writer and toward the printed language that follows, through which the defunct author still speaks.[32]

John Milton's 1645 *Poems* offers a different mode of poetic embodiment. The anxiety about lost physical presence so often registered in seventeenth-century volumes of poems, plays, and sermons exists in this volume as well, but attached with more palpable immediacy to the figure of the author than to his potential readers. The portrait frontispiece of Milton and its accompanying verses have struck observers then and now as awkward and self-conscious, and indeed the frontispiece is not one of William Marshall's finest efforts (Figure 6.7). But its ungainliness may partly register the daring innovation of what it attempted rhetorically. At a time when poets' portrait frontispieces were still usually memorial in function, Milton's offers the image of a living man.

Of course, as Milton himself complained, the image is nothing like the "original." Perhaps through a lingering resonance of the linkage between printed portraiture and death, the frontispiece to the 1645 *Poems* presents its author as prematurely aged, much as *Hesperides* two or three years later was to show the author's head curiously mounted on a pre-memorial pedestal (Figure 6.1) and Moseley's 1656 edition of Abraham Cowley's *Poems* was to feature the author's self-description "as a *Dead*, or at least a *Dying Person*" present in the volume as though in attendance at his "own *Funeral*" (sig. (a)2r). Part of the fascination of the portrait frontispiece to Milton's 1645 *Poems* comes from the fact that we will never know certainly why it was included – at the instigation of the author or through the importunity of the publisher Humphrey Moseley? Other Moseley volumes often include frontispieces with similarly intricate messages, and Milton himself later blamed Moseley.[33] Either way, the quality of the engraver's work was outside the author's control. In the poem beneath the picture, we can watch Milton scrambling to cancel out the potential ill effects of the portrait's bad likeness. Nevertheless the visual image works along with other elements of the volume to infuse the *Poems* with an unprecedentedly strong aura of authorial presence, which operates in the expected fashion for the benefit of the book's invisible audience, but even more, we may sense, for the benefit of the poet, whose oxymoronic task in publishing his poems is to find intimate contact with kindred spirits across great distances through the forbiddingly impersonal medium of print.

Milton's was not the very first collection of English poems to feature the frontispiece portrait of a living as opposed to a deceased author, but it was surely one of the first. Drayton's folio volume preceded it; however, the only earlier examples I have found in small-format volumes come from Abraham Cowley, most notably his 1633 prodigy volume *Poetical Blossomes*, in which the usual miniaturesque oval displays a very young Cowley in his grammar-school garb with two cherubs holding a laurel crown above his head and the inscription "Vera Effigies Abra: Cowley Regii Alvmni Scolae

West:" Below the picture are verses by one of his schoolfellows warning the reader, according to the customary formula, against positing too direct an equivalence between image and verse:

> *Reader when first thou shalt behold this boyes*
> *Picture, perhaps thou'lt thinke his writings toyes*
> *Wrong not our* Cowley *so will nothing passe*
> *But gravity with thee* Apollo *was*
> *Beardlesse himselfe and for ought I can see*
> Cowley *may yongest sonne of* Phoebus *bee.*

There follow an obsequious dedicatory epistle by Cowley himself to "John [Williams] Lord Bishop of Lincolne. And Deane of *Westminster*," a second authorial poem "To the Reader" asking for tolerance toward the author's youthful "numbers," and short pieces by schoolfellows (one of them the same Benjamin Masters who wrote the frontispiece poem), congratulating Cowley on the magnitude of his poetic achievement at the tender age of thirteen, although he was actually fifteen rather than thirteen in 1633 when the volume was first published. Subsequent editions of Cowley's poems continued to present frontispiece portraits illustrating the *puer senex* motif, although the gap between chronological age and literary achievement gradually narrowed as the young poet matured.[34]

From its instant popularity, it would appear that this slender and seemingly inconsequential volume struck contemporaries as new and interesting, even audacious. It was prized for its evidence of Cowley's precocious brilliance as a versifier, but perhaps also for its strange, innovative frontispiece portrait of a living poet. After the introductory materials, Cowley's *Poetical Blossomes* do not show the internal devices for linking book and life of the poet that were to be mobilized two years later in the 1635 *Poems* of John Donne. Yet the Cowley volume and its enviably youthful portrait of the artist must have had a striking impact on Milton, who claimed the same early poetic vocation but was fully ten years Cowley's elder. Later, notoriously, Milton would place Cowley along with Spenser and Shakespeare among the premier English poets.[35] Milton's own volume of *Poems* doubtless owes much to earlier prodigy volumes like Cowley's and Thomas Randolph's, yet Milton's contributes important new elements to the construction of authorial presence. Earlier single-authored collections of poetry may have offered the image of the author for the reader's solace and contemplation, but the voice beneath the picture was another's. Milton's 1645 *Poems* offers readers a "living" picture of the author who *speaks* to readers – in the recondite language of Greek, to be sure, but in the author's "authentic" voice, so that the collection becomes a animate poetic *corpus* with the portrait frontispiece as its "head."

Figure 6.7 Portrait frontispiece and title page to Milton's *Poems* (1645)
Reproduced by permission of the Harry Ransom Humanities Research Center,
University of Texas, Austin

206

POEMS

OF

Mr. *John Milton*,

BOTH

ENGLISH and LATIN,

Compos'd at several times.

Printed by his true Copies.

The SONGS were set in Musick by
Mr. HENRY LAWES Gentleman of
the KINGS Chappel, and one
of His MAIESTIES
Private Musick.

———*Baccare frontem*
Cingite, ne vati noceat mala lingua futuro.
Virgil, Eclog. 7.

Printed and publish'd according to
ORDER.

LONDON,
Printed by *Ruth Raworth* for *Humphrey Moseley*,
and are to be sold at the signe of the Princes
Arms in S. *Pauls* Church-yard. 1645.

MILTON AS ORAL POET

We like to think of John Milton as a man of letters in our modern sense of the term: a man who functioned as poet and controversialist much as his twentieth-century counterparts might if thrust into the same historical circumstances. Unlike Shakespeare, who appears to have saved none of his literary works in manuscript and who, as a result, has been vulnerable to periodic attacks upon his authorial authenticity, Milton appears to have saved almost everything, more like a modern writer consciously construct-ing an archive than like the usual participant in seventeenth-century manuscript culture. Unlike Shakespeare, who was said to have composed without blotting a line, Milton blotted many as he revised and refined his work – witness the Trinity manuscript holdings that dealt such a blow to Charles Lamb's preferred conception of poetic genius as springing full born upon the world. Moreover, it is quite likely that Milton hand-corrected misprints in presentation copies of his printed poems.[36] But Milton was perhaps not so modern as we have thought. He was more an "oral" poet than we have liked to imagine; indeed, it is in part the profoundly oral quality of his literary production during a period of increasing emphasis on the visual potential of printed books that makes Milton appear a glorious throwback to the earlier days of European humanism. Yet he was one of the first English poets who apprehended fully the power of print to spread his work out to a vast, unseen multitude of potential readers. The title page of the 1645 *Poems* includes the Virgilian motto " – *Baccare frontem / Cingite, ne vati noceat mala lingua futuro*" – "Bind on your brow fragrant plants [or foxglove], so no evil tongue may harm the poet who is to be."[37] In the context of the Seventh Eclogue, from which Milton quotes, the "rising poet" Thyrsis utters the lines, fearing the envious tongue of Codrus as he conducts his singing-match with Corydon. Affixed to the title page of the *Poems* the Virgilian tag serves as a forceful reminder of the vulnerability of the *vates* who dares enter the ranks of published authors and subject himself to the wrath of an unknown sea of Codruses. Here as elsewhere, Milton links the prospect of publica-tion both with self-dispersal, as in the death of the paradigmatic poet Orpheus, and with the incantatory mana of the classical *vates* to summon and forge a community through the power of poetic voice.

Milton, like Machiavelli before him, thought of the perusal of printed volumes not as a purely visual activity but as a form of displaced orality – a conversation with kindred spirits who were long dead or at great distance. His description of the rhetorical force of *Eikon Basiliki* is startling in its conceptualization of the royal martyr's continuing presence. When the volume was printed, Charles I "as it were, rose from the grave, and in that book published after his death tried to cry himself up before the people with new verbal sleights and harlotries" (C 7:9 *First Defence*). Similarly,

Milton depicts the pamphlet warfare of the 1640s as a "troubl'd sea of noises and hoars disputes" – not writing, but oral disputation via the printed page (C 3.1: 241 *Reason of Church Government*). When Milton writes letters to friends, he can, as he told Thomas Young, "speak to you and behold you as if you were present" though the act of writing is a "cramped mode of speech" by contrast with the "Asiatic exuberance of words" Milton would offer if Young were at hand rather than at painful distance (Trans. C 12: 5, 7). Through printed books, other people speak to Milton and also harangue, rumble, bellow and murmur at him. Perusing the notes of Hugo Grotius for supporting arguments in the controversy over divorce, for example, Milton states that Grotius "whisper'd" to him "about the law of charity" – as though the earlier author were bent over the book alongside him (C 4: 11–15 *Judgement of Martin Bucer*).

Predictably for one who heard cries and murmurings as he read the printed page, Milton seems to have liked to absorb printed matter by the ear as much or more than by sight. John Aubrey describes the blind Milton's schedule as including several "reading sessions" each day: The poet rose early and

> had a man read to him: the first thing he read was the Hebrew Bible, and that was at 4 manè 4½+ [from four until past four-thirty]. Then he contemplated. At 7 his man came to him again and then read to him and wrote till dinner; the writing was as much as the reading. His daughter Deborah could read to him Latin, Italian, and French and Greek . . . [38]

But the use of readers here documented from the period of Milton's blindness was not just a late accommodation to his lack of sight. In *An Apology for Smectymnuus* (1642), long before he lost his vision, Milton describes his early hours similarly:

> Those morning haunts are where they should be, at home, not sleeping, or concocting the surfets of an irregular feast, but up, and stirring, in winter often ere the sound of any bell awake men to labour, or to devotion; in Summer as oft with the Bird that first rouses, or not much tardier, to reade good Authors, or cause them to be read, till the attention bee weary, or memory have his full fraught.
>
> (C 3.1: 298–99)

Cause them to be read. Many Miltonists have assumed that this unexpected use of the passive verbal form relates to the poet's work as a schoolteacher. But he is clearly referring rather to "aural" reading for his own edification by a relative, friend, or man hired for the purpose. Elsewhere he frequently describes poetry in strongly auditory terms – as "warbled wood-notes wild" or as song sung to imagined music of harp or viol.

209

Milton's listening to "good Authors" was anything but passive. As his description suggests, he used it systematically to replenish and augment the tables of his memory – the reading would continue until he tired or his memory was *full fraught*, unable to absorb any more. Aubrey states that his memory was "very good" but much helped by his "excellent method of thinking and disposing."[39] Although a Miltonic commonplace book has survived, it is unlikely that he entrusted a high percentage of his prodigious learning to codified written form. Rather, he consulted the book of memory. When, as was his lifelong habit, he gave copies of his own verses or orations to his available friends, he may have offered them orally, along with a written copy serving primarily to record and preserve the gift.[40] His academic prolusions were, of course, oratorical performances performed from memory aided by invention, but so, it would appear, were his poems, as his description of his visits to the Florentine academies specifies: In the "privat Academies of *Italy*, whither I was favor'd to resort" some "trifles which I had in memory, compos'd at under twenty or thereabout (for the manner is that every one must give some proof of his wit and reading there) met with acceptance above what was lookt for. . . . " (C 3.1: 235–36 *Reason of Church Government*). Though these poems were but trifles, he kept them filed away in his memory. If, as most scholars agree, *Paradise Lost* was largely composed after Milton's blindness became total, the poem was, at least in its origins, a memorial composition. Of course Milton made extensive use of books and writing throughout his life, but he trusted far more in a prodigious and well-trained memory than we moderns would dare. His mnemonic and auditory faculties continued to serve him well even after blindness deprived him of the ability to read for himself.

The process of composition, as Milton appears to have imagined it, did not move from the creative faculties straight to the hand, as it would for most of us, but (in the manner of John Marston, already quoted above (p. 162), or of Milton himself as implied in the letter to Young) from mind to voice and utterance, with the hand serving primarily as a recorder of voice, and writing conceptualized as an inferior mode of speech. Even before he became blind, Milton often wrote by dictation.[41] Most of his references to his own composition portray it as oral communication, not writing, and this oddity long predates his actual blindness. In *The Reason of Church Government* (1642) he becomes a latter-day Jeremiah, "speaking the truth" and "free" of speech, given his "tongue" by God so that He might "heare thy voice among his zealous servants" in defense of the church (C 3.1: 231–33). There and elsewhere he is a latter-day psalmist, taking up his "Harp" to "sing thee an elaborate Song to Generations" (C 3.1: 148 *Animadversions*); not always able to soar, sometimes confined to the "cool element of prose," but by preference a poet "soaring in the high region of his fancies with his garland and singing robes about him" (C 3.1: 235 *Reason of Church Government*). When he describes his acts of composition, he almost always presents them as voice or song: with "lofty strains . . . sounding forth through my parted lips" (Trans. C 1.1: 197 *Elegia Quinta*); or with water of Helicon rolling "in all its fulness, o'er my lips, to the end that, forgetting all humble strains, my Muse may rise on daring pinions . . ." (Trans. C 1.1: 269 *Ad Patrem*).

The language of orality is, of course, conventional in many areas of Western discourse: it survives even in academic prose of the end of the twentieth century, where we employ locutions based on speech acts to describe the course of written argument – we *speak* and *discuss* matters with our readers more often than we describe ourselves as *writing* to them. These locutions are no doubt vestiges of earlier times when academic disputation was still primarily oral. But for Milton, the language of orality was emphatically not yet vestigial. Much of his power as a writer, much of the mighty archaism that gives his discourse the flavor and impact of Old Testament prophecy or of classical epic song, comes out of his emphasis on voice and his ability, even within the most syntactically difficult language, to capture through his writings the quality of spoken or singing voice.

Indeed, for Milton, publication is oratory over vast distance. The stance is particularly obvious in *Areopagitica*, which the title page conceptualizes not as a written treatise but as the printed transcription of an oration before the Lords and Commons at Westminster. In *Areopagitica* Milton displays an almost preternatural sense of the capacity of print to preserve the "season'd life of man" and "as in a violl the purest efficacie and extraction of that living intellect that bred them" – to create an invisible public of like-minded readers who may "spring up armed men" to work violent alteration upon previously accepted truths (C 4: 298). Similarly if somewhat less militantly, in *An Apology for Smectymnuus*, he imagines his words as "well-order'd files" of servants enacting his commands (C 3.1: 362). By the time of the *Second Defense*, Milton had experienced the power of print firsthand. In that treatise, even more remarkably than in the early tracts, he situates himself not as a writer of controversial prose, but as an orator holding forth from his rostrum with all Europe as his audience:

> I confess it is with difficulty I restrain myself from soaring to a more daring height than is suitable to the purpose of an exordium, and from casting about for something of more grandeur, to which I may give utterance: for, to whatever degree I am surpassed (of which there can be little doubt) by the ancient, illustrious orators, not only as an orator, but also as a linguist (and particularly in a foreign tongue, which I employ of necessity, and in which I am often very far from satisfying myself) I shall surpass no less the orators of all ages in the nobleness and in the instructiveness of my subject. This it is, which has imparted such expectation, such celebrity to this theme,

that I now feel myself not in the forum or on the rostrum, surrounded by a single people only, whether Roman or Athenian, but,
as it were, by listening Europe, attending, and passing judgement.

The printed book allows him, as it were, magically to "set out upon my
travels" and

> behold from on high, tracts beyond the seas, and wide-extended
> regions; that I behold countenances strange and numberless, and
> all, in feelings of mind, my closest friends and neighbours. Here is
> presented to my eyes the manly strength of the Germans, disdainful
> of slavery; there the lively and generous impetuosity of the Franks,
> worthily so called; on this side, the considerate virtue of the
> Spaniards; on that, the sedate and composed magnanimity of the
> Italians.
>
> (Trans. C 8: 13, 15)

There could scarcely be a more forceful conceptualization of the power of
print to extend discourse over great distance. If Milton experienced the
estrangement from direct, face-to-face communication created by the
expansion of print culture and its creation of silent, invisible audiences, he
also imagined himself as possessing the technical means to overcome
that anonymity, extending the power of voice across heroic space. Unlike
the despised Salmasius, whom Milton derides as a mere writer–compiler,
stuffing his books with scraps of citation (C 8: 101), Milton is an orator with
the almost divine ability to reach all literate nations and peoples. In spite
of the surviving manuscript evidence that Milton could revise his work
elaborately in writing, almost everything he wrote down – whether poetry
or prose – he envisioned as more voiced than written – operating upon the
ear with the power of the biblical prophet-poet "with his singing robes
around him" or of the orators of Greece and Rome. As J. W. Saunders has
noted, Milton was one of the first English poets to use the printing press
to help finance the private transmission of his work to friends in far-flung
places: the contract for *Paradise Lost* specifies two hundred extra copies
that were no doubt the poet's own to distribute among his international
community of kindred spirits. We find him enlisting Andrew Marvell to
track down John Bradshaw with one of his pamphlets and sending off
copies of his printed works with friends like Henry Oldenberg to distribute
on the Continent.[42] Although the contract for the 1645 *Poems* is not known
to have survived, it may have carried a similar provision; indeed, there is
evidence from his early years onward that he made a practice of having
sheets of his occasional verses printed up privately for distribution to
friends and mentors. A very early octavo pamphlet version of *Epitaphium
Damonis* survives; another poem privately printed and included in a letter
to Alexander Gil has apparently been lost in that form.[43] Print technology

gave Milton the ability not only to reach his friends and acquaintances across great distances, but also to make invisible, unknown alliances through the power of his projected voice.

THE TREACHEROUS FRONTISPIECE

By now, readers will have noted a strong contrast between the present discussion of Milton and my earlier discussions of Shakespeare in terms of my willingness to attribute motivation to the artist. Milton has left sufficiently abundant self-reflective passages amidst his poetry and prose to allow critics like myself to pontificate with ease upon his personal qualities and preferences, while Shakespeare is sufficiently invisible in his work that editorially and critically posited versions of the author's subject-position tend to dissolve into uncertainty. In critical discourse at present, Milton continues to have a kind of agency that Shakespeare does not. "Shakespeare" in quotation marks is Shakespeare called into question, made to denote a set of shifting cultural functions rather than a known literary figure with an established historical identity. Despite recent inroads by poststructuralist criticism, Milton as we approach the year 2000 remains very largely Milton without the deauthorizing bracket of quotation marks, an identifiable historical figure seen against a landscape of significant historical developments in England but never allowed to meld into his or our own climate of ideas to the point that he loses his identity and becomes a set of cultural operations in the manner of "Shakespeare."

Part of the reason that Milton retains high visibility as an author is that he left so many traces of his authorship. As Chartier has noted, the History of the Book is a movement that revives authorial identity as a viable, if limited, concept – one among a number of competing and cooperating entities that give published materials the shape in which they reach their readership.[44] But Milton's voice, his self-presence in his writings, is somehow so powerful that many Miltonists have been mesmerized into uncritical acceptance of his self-constructions even when these fly in the face of other evidence: we convince ourselves that we know him because he projected such powerful images of himself. To say that Milton, even in late twentieth-century critical discourse, has not been turned into a set of cultural functions according to the Shakespearean model is not, however, to suggest that "Milton" fails to perform an important set of functions. Within the critical community today the name of Milton works to guarantee the continuation of a certain pervasive style of literary subjecthood that he himself has been credited with inventing and that Miltonists are reluctant to move out of. If Milton refuses to disappear under the rubric of history, or of deconstruction, or of the postmodernist "death of the author," that is because "Milton" to us has meant – quite precisely – resistance to all such decentering impulses. He, as much as any other single historical figure of the English Renaissance, has been credited with inaugurating a new way of situating the author within literary history, or rather, of asserting the author's resistance to or transcendence of the sometimes pressing local circumstances within which he created his work. Milton is not the first English "author" in the Foucaultian sense of the term, but he is the first English author to construct through his work a literary life in the modern sense of the phrase – a life in which artistic development is measured, documented, and presented to a significant degree as autonomous.

If we are to locate a specific inauguration point for the new view of literary subjecthood for which Milton is frequently given credit, that point may well be the 1645 *Poems of Mr.* John Milton, *Both English and Latin, Compos'd at several times* and printed, the title page tells us, "*by his true Copies.*" As Louis Martz has argued in his essay "The Rising Poet," Milton's volume, with its many Virgilian echoes and its scrupulous attention to genre, specifically asks us to view his achievement in terms of the development of his powers as a poet: "Milton's original arrangement creates the growing awareness of a guiding, central purpose that in turn gives the volume an impressive and peculiar sense of wholeness."[45] One of the volume's innovations is to locate many of the poems fairly precisely in terms of the author's life and artistic development. The title page itself refers to the rising poet through its Virgilian tag and directs attention to the "several times" at which the poems were "Compos'd"; within the volume, many of the individual poems designate the poet's age through a running commentary that repeatedly interweaves chronology and literary achievement.

The biographical evidence offered so plentifully in the 1645 *Poems* is not necessarily to be trusted: like Cowley's *Poetical Blossomes*, Milton's volume errs on the side of precocity in some of its datings. Nevertheless, the poems are ordered for the most part generically and/or chronologically, so that we can follow Milton's development as a poet through both the English and the Latin halves of the collection. Elsewhere, as on the title page of the 1645 *Poems*, Milton imagines an author as "born" through the act of printing and existing in a nebulous half-existence before then; the same conceit appears in the publisher Humphrey Moseley's preface to the reader, which lauds Milton as "*as true a Birth, as the Muses have brought forth since our famous* Spencer *wrote.*"[46] The very first English poem in the collection – "On the morning of Christs Nativity. Compos'd 1629." – was not the earliest written, but is presumably placed first as a suitable inaugural for a volume celebrating the birth of a poet. The association between *vates* and divinity is daring and potentially sacrilegious, but typically Miltonic in its intimations about the power of the artist. The psalm paraphrases that follow it are noted as composed earlier, "don by the Author at fifteen yeers old" (sig. [A6]v). Yet more revealingly, "The Passion" terminates abruptly with the note, "*This Subject the Author finding to be above the yeers he had, when he wrote it, and nothing satisfi'd with what was begun, left it unfinisht*" (sig. B2r). The failed poem is included along with the successes as important documentation of the poet's developing powers. After "The Passion" many of the English poems not explicitly dated are either dated internally – "How soon hath Time" (Sonnet VII), for example, refers to the theft of the poet's "three and twentith yeer" (sig. D[1]r) – or can be dated inferentially in terms of their occasion, usually a death, as in the poem on the Marchioness of Winchester and the two poems on the Cambridge carrier Hobson. "L'Allegro" and "Il Penseroso" are not dated (a highly interesting fact, in view of their universalization of competing elements of literary response) but the Italian sonnets that follow are contextualized through the author's editorializing placement of "How soon hath Time" immediately afterward – in context, a soberer 23-year-old's retrospective dismissal of his earlier Petrarchan frivolities.

Despite the close attention to chronology, it would be a mistake to characterize the volume's organization as governed by that element alone. Rather, the collection intermingles chronological, generic, and thematic principles of ordering. The Latin and Greek poems are furnished with their own full title page and can occasionally be found in copies that do not include the English half of the collection.[47] Constituting a separate "book" within the book, this part of the collection insists even more strongly than does the English on linkages to Milton's life, perhaps in part because the language reproduced is not the poet's native tongue. The title page of the Latin poems states that they were written "*Annum aetatis Vigesimum*" before the end of his twentieth year, and most of the individual poems also give the author's age at the time of composition. As in the English half of the volume, the author is willing to repudiate his own compositions while simultaneously offering them to the judgment of his readers. At the end of a group of seven Latin elegies (most of which are dated by the poet's age at the time of composition) are placed ten lines of verse separated by a horizontal rule and rejecting what has gone before as "idle trophies of my worthlessness" and "untaught youth" (sig. C4r, trans. C 1.1: 223). The final entry in the Latin and Greek half of the *Poems*, "Epitaphium Damonis," nicely balances the English half of the volume, whose main body ends with another pastoral elegy, "Lycidas," dated 1637 in its title.

Between the two halves of the volume in a category of its own but linked through its signature numbers with the English half, appears Milton's *Maske*, finally acknowledged by its author after its earlier anonymous publication and preceded by Henry Wotton's letter attesting to its literary excellence: "Wherin I should much commend the Tragical part, if the Lyrical did not ravish me with a certain Dorique delicacy in your Songs and Odes, whereunto I must plainly confess to have seen yet nothing parallel in our Language" (sig. E4). Wotton's letter echoes the publisher Moseley's innovative preface to the *Poems* in its insistence on the aesthetic as an appropriate category for evaluating the materials within. The volume's insistence upon the aesthetic as a category in itself, independent of time and occasion, was surely adopted at least in part to counterbalance Milton's known reputation as a left-wing controversialist – to temporarily shut out the babble of hoarse shouts and murmurs in the pamphlet wars in favor of a more harmonious image of the poet and his ravishing "Dorique delicacy." A year after the publication of the 1645 *Poems* Thomas Edwards offered a rather different public image of Milton by inscribing him among the monstrous heretics and grotesques of *Gangraena: Or A Catalogue and Discovery of many of the Errours, Heresies, Blasphemies and pernicious Practices of the Sectaries of this time, vented and acted in* England *in these four last years* (London, 1646). It is not this history that is highlighted in the Milton volume's format, but rather a personal history of artistic development that is presented as though totally separable from Milton's other history as pamphleteer. In addition to its other functions, the title page also neutralizes the obvious anti-Stuart slant of some of the included materials by asserting "The Songs were set in Musick by Mr. Henry Lawes Gentleman of the Kings Chappel, and one of His Maiesties Private Musick."

To us, with our post-Romantic inheritance of critical attention to the "growth of the poet's mind," the many aestheticizing features of the 1645 volume may appear rather unremarkable. We need to view them instead as milestones in the process by which the printed book became identified with the *corpus*, carrying the life and spirit of the author. By comparison with Milton's, earlier author-published volumes of poetry are positively reticent in communicating information about the poet. George Gascoigne's printed *Posies* (1575) anticipates a few of the features of Milton's volume, most notably its self-critical and quasi-autobiographical arrangement.[48] Similarly, in the 1616 *Workes* of Ben Jonson, derided in its own time for authorial puffery, the author dates some of his compositions and places them in a generic order that suggests poetic development, rewriting some of the materials in order to excise undesired topical references and non-authorial elements. Jonson's "Epigrams" offer subtle thematic hints of biographical ordering, but nothing so overt as Milton's repeated notes linking the author's life to the composition of individual poems. And in any case, Jonson's 1616 *Workes* is a body without a head: despite its elaborate and beautiful engraved title page, it lacks the frontispiece portrait and accompanying authorial "speech" that would make the volume distinctively an extension of the poet's physical presence.

Yet how can we be certain that it is *Milton* talking to us through the 1645 volume's many references to the poet's age and capacities? We tend to think of the poet as possessing full control over its publication – indeed, over all of his publications – even though the evidence by no means supports that point of view. The strong aestheticization of the author's life that is such an innovative feature of Milton's 1645 *Poems* may well owe as much or more to the publisher and printer than to the author himself; as comparison of the Milton volume with others in Humphrey Moseley's canon-making "English laureate" series suggests, Moseley himself was strongly interested in devices that communicated authorial presence. Much of the information attaching poems to specific years, even though it presumably derived from Milton's own data, could easily have been affixed by Moseley, whose admiring preface "to the Reader" asserts that he himself had solicited Milton's verses for publication. We cannot even rule out the less likely possibility that the notes could have been added by the volume's printer Ruth Raworth, whose deceased husband John Raworth had published *A Maske* in 1637 and had printed several books for Milton's friend and neighbor George Thomason. Both Ruth and John Raworth may have been personally acquainted with Milton.[49] As suggested earlier in our discussion of John Donne, seventeenth-century printers and publishers sometimes took an aggressive role in promoting the identification of author and *corpus* that was coming to be desired in poetry volumes of the period. But the main reason we identify the biographical commentary so readily with the voice of the author is, I would suggest, that that voice has been firmly established by the frontispiece, with its cryptic assemblage of the figure of Milton, a depiction of distant shepherds, and a sardonic Greek epigram offering us the "true" voice of the author.

The frontispiece to Milton's 1645 *Poems* has long intrigued readers because of its contradictory messages. The customary oval frame around the central portrait asserts Milton's age in the "effigy" to be twenty-one or in the twenty-first year (Figure 6.7). Yet many of the poems within the volume are dated considerably later – as much as eleven or twelve years later. Milton himself at the time of the volume's publication was thirty-seven years old – somewhat decayed by the standards of earlier prodigy volumes. And the effigy itself depicts a man who looks older even than that – perhaps as old as fifty. The figure in the oval is slightly turned toward the window, as though he has been observing the shepherds sporting below. They too are within the oval: might it be they, not the larger and more aged figure, who depict the author aged twenty-one? The suggestion receives support from Milton's own depiction of the volume in his later Latin dedication to John Rouse of the Bodleian Library: there the rising poet in English and Latin is described as having "played, foot-loose, now in the forest-shades of Ausonia and now on the lawns of England" and trifling "with his native lute."[50]

The frontispiece can be glossed by reference to the final lines of Milton's *Lycidas*, which is printed last in the main body of the English half of the volume and nicely balanced by the elegy on Charles Diodati at the end of the Latin and Greek half of the collection. Both parts, as well as *A Maske* in between them, make extensive use of traditional pastoral forms

217

and subjects. But in the final verse paragraph of *Lycidas*, the "uncouth" shepherd who has been singing almost without interruption to that point in the elegy is suddenly viewed from a distance, his voice replaced by a seemingly older and wiser voice who narrates the wandering youth's departure as something that has already taken place:

> Thus sang the uncouth Swain to th'Okes and rills,
> While the still morn went out with Sandals gray,
> He touch'd the tender stops of various Quills,
> With eager thought warbling his *Dorick* lay:
> And now the Sun had stretch'd out all the hills,
> And now was dropt into the Western bay;
> At last he rose, and twitch'd his Mantle blew:
> To morrow to fresh Woods, and Pastures new.
>
> (sig. E[1]r)

In the same way, the central figure in the frontispiece seems to gesture toward the distant shepherds as toward an earlier, and now superseded, version of himself – a self, perhaps, that had participated in a prewar world of pastoral mirth that must now be set behind him. The shepherds in the background are making rustic music, but the older figure in the foreground is surrounded by four muses in the corners outside the oval. He claims a higher art than the pastoral. The frontispiece can easily be read as a visualization of the familiar Virgilian *rota* by which the rising poet moves from the "low" form of pastoral through georgic and finally up to the "high" genre of epic; and that potential reading is reinforced by the Virgilian motto opposite, with its evocation of the rising poet.

But this interpretation of the frontispiece is still far too simple. Lest we be tempted to identify the more elderly figure with Milton in the present (1645) as opposed to a pastoral "Swain" from the past, the Greek verses beneath assure us that the portrait is no such thing. They read in David Masson's translation:

> That an unskilful hand had carved this print
> You'd say at once, seeing the living face;
> But, finding here no jot of me, my friends,
> Laugh at the botching artist's mis-attempt.[51]

Elsewhere, Milton referred to writing in Greek as "singing mostly to the deaf" (Trans. C 12: 17 Letter to Alexander Gill) but here it becomes a means for circumventing envious Codrus and establishing intimacy with an invisible audience of like-minded listeners. We are invited to recognize the "real" Milton here, in these verses, through language rather than picture, as he searches for a "fit audience though few" learned enough to comprehend the Greek. They are his honored "friends," "φίλοι"; they are invited, implicitly, to form a learned coterie in recognition of his artistic powers

– to compare the engraved face with his real, living face, and to laugh along with Milton at the artist's incompetence by contrast with the far greater competence of the poet and those who share his judgment. As in *Hamlet,* the voice of the poet sets up an implicit hierarchy which defines an elite group in terms of their shared derision for inferior art. But how is this group constituted? Masson's translation implies that readers will need to have seen Milton's real face in order to laugh at the counterfeit. The Greek is more equivocal, suggesting in a more literal rendering, "You would say that perhaps this image has been engraved by / A clumsy hand, if you were to look at the true appearance, / But since, friends, you do not recognize the man represented here / You laugh at this unskillful image by a worthless sculptor."[52] The epigram allows for both known and unknown readers: those who "recognize" Milton by sight and view the image will laugh because it doesn't look like him; those not acquainted with Milton's actual appearance may laugh because the image is ridiculous but cannot correct the "unskillful"copy except by recourse to the poems within. Part of Milton's anxiety in these lines surely relates to the disjunction between his known political affiliations and the predominantly Royalist company in which he is placed through his inclusion in Moseley's series of English laureates. Will readers who know his anti-prelatical leanings recognize him in the volume? Will those who do not know him be able to "find" his beliefs by reading his poems? If not, the poet's printed voice has failed as a surrogate for the liveliness of physical presence.

Traditionally, the epigram beneath the portrait frontispiece has been interpreted as a malicious jibe at William Marshall, who meticulously carved out the Greek letters with (we are asked to suppose) not the least knowledge of Greek or curiosity about what the lines might mean. English engravers were, by and large, less than skillful, at least if one compares them, as Milton surely did, with their more expert counterparts on the Continent. Milton himself later explained, in response to a squib by Salmasius, that

> my having consented, at the instance and from the importunity of the bookseller, to employ an unskillful engraver, because at that period of the war there was no other to be found in the city, argues not that I was over-solicitous, as you charge me, but that I was indifferent about the matter.
>
> (Trans. C 9: 125)

Through this disclaimer, Milton denies the appearance of authorial control over the volume that is set in motion through the verses beneath the picture and that enables us to read the miscellaneous editorial glosses throughout the volume as the author's more mature commentary upon his youthful achievement. The strong sense of authorial presence – even intimacy – communicated by the volume was very much a communal production, created in part through the accident of an ugly frontispiece.

We may wonder, though, whether William Marshall was either so incompetent or so ignorant a gull as Milton's verses imply. Other portrait frontispieces by him (like that of Donne in the 1635 *Poems* or Robert Herrick in his *Hesperides*) are considerably more appealing. It is far more likely that Marshall was well aware that his own artistry would be superseded by the higher claims of language as a vehicle for the spirit of the poet. Even if he had "small Greek," he carved a similar but less insultingly self-deprecatory message in English on the Donne frontispiece (1635) and in Latin on the frontispiece to Humphrey Moseley's edition of James Shirley's *Poems &c.* (1646). Milton's frontispiece needs to be read in terms of the long line of earlier English examples, discussed here and in the preceding chapter, that assert through one device or another the inadequacy of the visual and graphic by comparison with the verbal and oral in communicating authorial presence. Insofar as unhappy engravers of the period undertook frontispieces and title page portraits, they regularly condemned themselves to disparagement within the very volumes they helped to make more desirable for potential readers and purchasers.

Later re-engravers of Milton's 1645 image certainly understood the Greek verses beneath the portrait, and took care to mend Marshall's "botched attempt." Of the four copies of the 1645 *Poems* at the University of Texas, two have the original frontispiece intact. The other two, both bearing title pages in what was probably the first state of the printing, have frontispieces affixed later – possibly around 1700, as the cataloguer of the volumes has hypothesized. One of these later correctives to Marshall shows Milton's face with some of the lines smoothed out; the other, in addition, depicts him almost smiling (Figure 6.8). Might Milton have found these later renditions less unacceptable as likenesses than the original? In Restoration printings of Milton's works, William Marshall's image won out over Milton's complaint. The frontispiece to the 1645 *Poems* may have looked little enough like the Milton of 1645, but it is strikingly like the portraits of Milton in his sixties engraved by Faithorne and Dolle! Either the later engravers copied the 1645 image, or Milton in his sixties looked very much as Marshall had "aged" him earlier on.

Was Marshall incompetent enough to fail to capture Milton's youthful visage, or prescient enough to recognize through facial structure the visage that Milton would later become? The treacherous frontispiece may have been faithful to its subject after all, or at least no less unreliable than the later ones: John Aubrey was to testify that Milton's portrait frontispieces were "not at *all* like him."[53] Nevertheless, the 1645 volume offers a clever and highly original reworking of the usual set of disjunctions among competing figurations of the author. The aura of trustworthiness communicated by the poet's voice is produced out of its rejection of the two or more "false" portraits offered at the beginning of the volume – the effigy that is too old and unlike, the shepherds who are too distant and too generalized. The "real" Milton peers out at us only through the Greek of the inscription in a voice both engagingly intimate and self-referential, clearly established for knowing readers as the author's presence before the rest of his poetry is even encountered. The voice entices readers into a search for authenticity – a continuous measuring of Milton's past poetic powers against those of a nearer present. The reader's linear progress through the volume is simultaneously a survey of diverse generic types and an advance through the poet's waxing powers as an artist; the boundaries of the volume become coterminous with the author's individual identity, a metonym and container for his essential self. "Books," as Milton described them in *Areopagitica*, "are not absolutely dead things, but doe contain a potencie of life in them to be as active as that soule was whose progeny they are; nay, they do preserve as in a violl the purest efficacie and extraction of that living intellect that bred them" (C 4: 297–98). By instantiating this dictum, Milton's 1645 *Poems* helped to invent England literary subjecthood as we have traditionally been taught to understand it. The author is a category larger than history in that history, in the form of biography, is brought within the compass of the individual life marked out in the absence of the author by the boundaries of the book.

As the editors of the *OED* have noted, Milton provides the first recorded usage of several meanings for the word "individual" and its derivatives. Sometimes he used the word in its traditional sense of "indivisible," but he also inaugurated usages that emphasized the self-sameness of a discrete unit and its separateness from others. He documented his "individual" literary life by hanging on to early manuscript versions of many of his works, thereby making it possible for us to do something we can rarely do for writers before him, but can commonly do for writers who came after him – follow the process of a poem's alteration from first to later and usually more refined versions. As David Loewenstein and James Turner have noted, in his political pamphlets, Milton habitually aestheticizes his own history: not only does he offer himself as a "true poem" (as Jonson might have earlier) but he imagines that individual "poem" to be forged out of the crucible of contemporary events.[54] That is not to say that Milton failed to see himself as subject to contemporary history – only that he was constantly in process of constructing a literary vision of his own individual life that transcended contemporary history "as ever in my great task-Master's eye." Milton's ongoing "autobiographical literary history" is by no means static, but constantly in a process of stalemate, challenge, and reintegration. In fact, its vulnerability is part of its appeal. Poststructuralist approaches are threatening to many Miltonists who might otherwise find such approaches more sympathetic because they appear to assault the highly individualized "portrait of the artist" that Milton himself constructed so authoritatively and at such personal cost. Indeed, to adopt such approaches would be, seemingly, to deny Milton's authorial body and his

Figure 6.8 Later copies of the frontispiece to Milton's *Poems*
Reproduced by permission of the Harry Ransom Humanities Research Center,
University of Texas, Austin

ΕΤΑΗΣ.ΚΑ. ΙΟΑΝΝΗΣ

ΟΝΝΥ-ΣΙΟΙ ΕΓΓΙ GIES ANNO

Αμαβει γεγγαφθαιχειξι τίωδε μίν εἰκόνα
Φαίης ταχ᾽ ἄν, ωξὸς εἶδος ἀυτοφυες βλέπων
Τὸν δ᾽ ἐκτυπῶ7ον ὀκ ἐπηνγνόύντες φίλοι
Γελᾶτε φαύλ8 δυσμίμημα ζωγγάφ8.

M.V.d.Gucht Sc.   p.143.

223

authentic voice – his oft-asserted self-presence through "living intellect" within his writings.

Was Milton so insistent on preserving his personal and literary identity as some of his pronouncements have allowed us to believe? We need to remind ourselves that he also sometimes conceptualized "individual" in its more traditional sense to mean indivisible from some larger entity. The mighty voice of authorial agency that trumpets out "Milton!" with such strength and clarity from the 1645 *Poems* was constructed partly out of the process of publication, and out of the author's continuing need despite the print medium for the felt presence of a community of listeners in order to be fully himself. Milton only becomes fully "individual" as an author by making himself, as he terms himself in *An Apology*, a "member incorporate" into "truth" (C 3.1: 284) or into a larger collectivity of widely scattered "friends and neighbours" linked through his writings and collectively helping to reconstitute what Milton refers to in *Areopagitica* as the "scattered body of Truth."[55] Print individuates and disperses, but it also consolidates and re-members.

The need for reassuring visible marks of authorial presence that I have documented for collections of English poetry during the 1630s and 1640s was a relatively fleeting phenomenon. By the Restoration period, highly literate authors and readers appear to have acclimated themselves to the print medium and no longer needed frontispiece portraits quite so keenly as visual reminders of the physical body of an author behind the "dumb show" of the volume. That is not to suggest, of course, that frontispiece portraits of living poets ceased to exist – only that they quickly became sufficiently conventional in the experience of sophisticated readers to lose their seemingly preternatural status as surrogates for the physical presence of the author. The 1673 second edition of Milton's *Poems*, titled in full *Poems, &c. Upon Several Occasions*, does not reprint or replace the "speaking picture" from 1645: perhaps because the volume had a different publisher less interested in communicating the image of the poet, perhaps also because by 1673 the image had become dispensable – not only for sophisticated readers, but also for the author himself, who had been lionized for decades as England's eloquent champion in the *First* and *Second Defense* and no longer had the fledgling poet's anxieties about his ability to reach a sympathetic public. The second edition keeps Milton's poems in the same order as 1645 except for various additions, mostly of verses composed after the publication of the first edition. The 1673 text also preserves the first edition's internal markers of artistic "progress": indeed, several of the metrical psalms added at the end of the English half of the volume are dated even more precisely than any of the preceding – by day, month, and year of composition.

Milton did make some alterations to the poems themselves: most notably, for the second edition he corrected what Salmasius had derided as incorrect Latin in some of his youthful exercises.[56] But the 1673 volume is far less lively and performative than 1645, if only because of the loss of the earlier book's dense referentiality established through the contradictory messages of the frontispiece and the language and arrangement of the materials. In 1673, *A Mask* no longer has a separate title page, but is fully assimilated into the English and Italian half of the collection. The 1645 motif of poetic birth is abandoned for a more general emphasis on education: 1673 drops the Virgilian tag on the title page about the fledging poet and also the notice about Lawes' setting of the songs, offering instead the notice, "With a Small Tractate on Education *To Mr.* Hartlib." That tract appears after the end of the Latin and Greek poems, transforming the volume retroactively into an illustrative record of the poet's own education in language, poetry, and wisdom.

Here, I will spare readers a repetition of my earlier invectives against the shortcomings of modern editions. Suffice it to say that Milton's 1645 *Poems* is very seldom reprinted as a book – in a manner that allows us to read the subtle rhetoric of the volume as it was presented to early readers. Most frequently, editors ride roughshod over some elements of the 1645 arrangement of materials while insisting with fanatical precision on reproducing other elements. Merritt Hughes' widely used teaching edition (see n. 50), for example, obliterates the author's arrangement of materials out of a desire to present all of the Miltonic corpus in the precise conjectured order of composition, as a perfect reflection of the life. More recent editors, some of whom do preserve the ordering of the early editions, nevertheless characteristically omit or displace the 1645 front matter and "speaking picture" of the author, so that their many reverberations with the rest of the collection are lost. Few readers would wish to dispense altogether with the mediating scholarship that has made Milton's work intelligible and accessible. But many in recent decades have been repelled by the gargantuan, supercanonical monolith that Milton has become, in part as a result of the vast accretion of editorial tradition behind our standard editions. To revisit the 1645 *Poems* in their original printed "body" is to rediscover a Milton who is smaller, less ponderous, more approachable, yet paradoxically also harder to demarcate from the pressures of his time than the Milton we have inherited. In dispersing the 1645 volume's organization in favor of other principles of ordering, we have lost traces of a forgotten form of Miltonic authenticity: his strong self-depiction as an "oral" poet who preferred speech over writing as a poetic medium and published for readers who shared the same prejudice. Stanley Fish once suggested that Milton criticism is essentially over – it has all already happened in earlier forms. All that we can do, according to this highly conservative scenario, is reenact versions of past literary history: to destabilize hierarchy in *Paradise Lost* is to repeat Blake and Shelley, to deconstruct Milton is to rediscover Milton's own undermining of traditional generic categories, to intertextualize Milton is to rediscover the "multiple voices and traditions" inscribed within the text by the "editorial apparatus of the great eighteenth-century editions," and so on.[57] This version of Milton is always his own supplement, always already outside supplementarity. One of its most serious elisions is the poet's own eager, conflicted participation in the transition from orality to the printed book – not only as an extension of manuscript circulation to a circumscribed audience but also as a newly fixed form that could magically embody the poet's voice, sing forth across space and time.

Do we still believe, as Milton claimed in *Areopagitica*, that the spirit of the author is held within the printed volume as within a vial, ready to be reanimated each time the book is read with sympathy and understanding? For many of us, particularly as we move beyond the culture of the book into the the emerging world of the computerized network, Milton's formulations are beginning to sound rather odd, if only because the book as a self-contained, portable unit in three-dimensional space is no longer the only viable medium for the transmission of literary material. The computer does not delimit one author from another online with the book's crispness of definition, although it can print out "fixed" copies. The space on our shelves between one book and another is somehow more stable than the online space between one author's text and another's. Or is it simply that we who are not yet fully acclimated to the computer perceive the new medium as loosening the authority of authorship because we have not fully assimilated its distinctive conventions for demarcating authorship online? Online authorship has its own form of corporeality, but certainly not the form we are accustomed to. The tactile and auditory stimulation of the keyboard are very different from the near-silent turning of leaves of a book. As we move toward the computerization of literary texts we are in much the same position that Milton himself was during an earlier technological shift – full of heady enthusiasm for the possibilities opened up by a new medium but simultaneously uncertain about its effects on what we have previously understood as communication. The 1645 *Poems* are of particular interest just now because they mark an early instantiation of a form of textual embodiment we are beginning to perceive as transient.

Here at the end of the book, let me restate what I said at the beginning. In returning to Milton's 1645 "original" or the Shakespearean and Marlovian originals discussed earlier, we are not encountering our texts in some mythically pristine, unmediated form. Nor is that chimera the unspoken object of our secret desires. What we aim to accomplish in "Unediting the Renaissance" is to apply the same density and complexity of historical explanation to the early editions and manuscript materials as we have long applied to other elements of early modern culture. It should go without saying that anyone studying the impact of an author during any given period would do well to consult the material forms of the author's work generated during the time in question as well as in the standard modern editions. And yet, those of us who are willing to be numbered among the growing ranks of "new philologists" are often more interested in culture broadly defined and in the interactions among its diverse elements than in the writings of any single author. Here, as in my introduction, "unediting" the Renaissance is proposed not as a permanent condition or even as a possible condition, but rather as a process by which we recover and reconsider sixteenth and seventeenth-century printed materials in the uncouth, maladept, confusing, maddeningly or delightfully unstable, compelling bodies in which they circulated through their culture and reached readers who were part of the same culture. If we do not feel that our standard editions satisfactorily transmit the cultural imbeddedness and malleability we find in literary materials of the Renaissance or of any other era, we would do well to stop grousing about the shortcomings of past editors and become editors ourselves.

NOTES

1 INTRODUCTION

1 Frederick C. Crews, *The Pooh Perplex* (1963; reprinted New York: E. P. Dutton, 1965).

2 For work representative of the new currents mentioned here, see D. F. McKenzie, "Printers of the Mind: Some Notes on Bibliographical Theories and Printing-House Practices," *Studies in Bibliography* 22 (1969): 1–75; and his *Panizzi Lectures 1985: Bibliography and the Sociology of Texts* (London: British Library, 1986); Philip Gaskell, *From Writer to Reader: Studies in Editorial Method* (Oxford: Clarendon Press, 1978); Jerome J. McGann, *A Critique of Modern Textual Criticism* (1983; paperback edition Chicago and London: University of Chicago Press, 1985); his *The Beauty of Inflections: Literary Investigations in Historical Method and Theory* (1985; reprinted Oxford: Clarendon Press, 1988); and his *Black Riders: The Visible Language of Modernism* (Princeton: Princeton University Press, 1993); D. C. Greetham, *Textual Scholarship: An Introduction* (New York and London: Garland, 1992); his forthcoming *Theories of the Text* (Oxford: Oxford University Press); and Robert Darnton, "What Is the History of Books?" *Daedalus* 111 (1982): 65–83, and reprinted in his *The Kiss of Lamourette* (New York: W. W. Norton, 1990), pp. 107–35.

For the new work specifically in the field of Renaissance/early modern studies, see, for example, the Shakespearean studies by Steven Urkowitz, *Shakespeare's Revision of King Lear* (Princeton: Princeton University Press, 1980); Gary Taylor and Michael Warren, eds, *The Division of the Kingdoms: Shakespeare's Two Versions of King Lear* (Oxford: Clarendon Press, 1983); Stanley Wells, "The Unstable Image of Shakespeare's Text," in *Images of Shakespeare: Proceedings of the Third Congress of the International Shakespeare Association, 1986*, ed. Werner Habicht, D. J. Palmer, and Roger Pringle (Newark: University of Delaware Press; London and Toronto: Associated University Presses, 1988), pp. 305–13; Random Cloud [Randall McLeod], "The Marriage of Good and Bad Quartos," *Shakespeare Quarterly* 33 (1982): 421–31; Michael D. Bristol, *Shakespeare's America, America's Shakespeare* (London and New York: Routledge, 1990), especially chap. 4, "Editing the Text: The Deuteronomic Reconstruction of Authority," pp. 91–119; and the witty summation in Margreta de Grazia and Peter Stallybrass, "The Materiality of the Shakespearean Text," *Shakespeare Quarterly* 44 (1993): 255–83, which appeared after most of the present study was written but clearly anticipates a number of my arguments. For more general studies focussed on the period, see, for example, Elizabeth L. Eisenstein, *The Printing Press as an Agent of Change*, 2 vols (Cambridge: Cambridge University Press, 1979); Roger

Chartier, ed., *The Culture of Print: Power and the Uses of Print in Early Modern Europe*, trans. Lydia G. Cochrane (Princeton: Princeton University Press, 1989); and his very recent *The Order of Books*, trans. Lydia G. Cochrane (1992; English translation Cambridge: Polity Press; and Stanford: Stanford University Press, 1994).

3　Here and throughout, my quotations from the First Folio will be to Charlton Hinman's Norton Facsimile edition (London and New York: Paul Hamlyn, 1968), and indicated by Through Line Number in the text. Given that Hinman's facsimile combines "best" versions of each page of the First Folio rather than reproducing any single printed copy, it is, ironically from the point of view of the present study, far from being an "unedited" version of the Folio. As I will argue later on, the heuristic need to make use of an accessible standardized exemplar frequently overrides the need for absolute fidelity to any single printed text.

4　"Nugae Criticae," *London Magazine*, November, 1823; as cited in *Charles Lamb on Shakespeare*, ed. Joan Coldwell (London: Colin Smythe; New York: Barnes & Noble, 1978), pp. 62–64.

5　Cited respectively from *The Riverside Shakespeare*, ed. G. Blakemore Evans (Boston: Houghton Mifflin, 1974), p. 1615; *The Complete Works of Shakespeare*, ed. David Bevington, 4th edition (New York: Harper Collins, 1992), p. 1534; and *The Complete Signet Classic Shakespeare*, ed. Sylvan Barnet (New York and Chicago: Harcourt Brace Jovanovich, 1972), p. 1547.

6　See Frank Kermode, ed., *The Tempest*, The Arden Shakespeare, 6th edition (London: Methuen, 1958), p. 27 n.; George Lyman Kittredge, ed., *The Tempest* (Boston: Ginn, 1939), pp. 96–97; and Sir Arthur Quiller-Couch and John Dover Wilson, eds, *The Tempest* (Cambridge: Cambridge University Press; New York: Macmillan, 1921), p. 93. Most other twentieth-century single-play editions follow the standard formula, with Alfred Harbage and Northrop Frye's Pelican editions of *The Tempest* (Baltimore: Penguin, 1959; reprinted 1970) representing a prominent exception: the Pelican editors leave the line unglossed.

7　Paul Werstine, review of T. H. Howard-Hill, ed., *Shakespeare and Sir Thomas More: Essays on the Play and its Shakespearian Interest* (Cambridge: Cambridge University Press, 1989), in *Essays in Theatre* 9 (1990): 91–94.

8　Cited from the glossaries to *The Comedies of Shakespeare*, ed. W. J. Craig and Edward Dowden (London: Oxford University Press, 1932); and *The Temple Shakespeare: The Tempest*, ed. Israel Gollancz (London: J. M. Dent, 1910). Interestingly, Peter Alexander's editions, which do not have notes but do include a glossary, do not gloss the phrase.

9　William Aldis Wright, ed., *The Tempest*, The Clarendon Shakespeare (Oxford: Clarendon Press, 1874), pp. 91–92; see also Alexander Schmidt's supporting definition in his authoritative *Shakespeare-Lexicon: A Complete Dictionary of All the English Words, Phrases and Constructions in the Works of the Poet*, 2 vols (Berlin: Georg Reimer; London: Williams & Norgate, 1874–75), 1: 123.

10　Thomas Bowdler, ed., *The Family Shakespeare, in Ten Volumes* (London: Longman, 1818), title page.

11　See the survey of visual depictions of Caliban in Alden T. Vaughan and Virginia Mason Vaughan, *Shakespeare's Caliban: A Cultural History* (Cambridge: Cambridge University Press, 1991), pp. 215–51; and Howard Staunton, ed., *The Plays of Shakespeare*, vol. 3 (London and New York: Routledge, Warne & Routledge, 1860), pp. 12 and 23.

12　Daniel Wilson, *Caliban: The Missing Link* (London: Macmillan & Co., 1873), p. 227. For a history of nineteenth-century stage Calibans, see Stephen Orgel, ed., *The Tempest*, The Oxford Shakespeare (Oxford and New York: Oxford University Press, 1987; paperback reprint, 1991), pp. 71–75.

13 Cited respectively from "To J. H. Reynolds, Esq.," line 53, in *The Poetical Works of John Keats*, ed. H. W. Garrod, 2nd edition (Oxford: Clarendon Press, 1958), p. 485; *Prometheus Unbound* 2.1.114, in *Shelley's* Prometheus Unbound, *A Variorum Edition*, ed. Lawrence John Zillman (Seattle: University of Washington Press, 1959), p. 187; and "A Memory Picture," line 41, in *The Poems of Matthew Arnold*, ed. Kenneth Allott, 2nd edition, ed. Miriam Allott (London and New York: Longman, 1979), p. 115.

14 See J. Surtees Phillpotts, ed., *The Tempest*, The Rugby edition (London: Rivington's, 1876), as cited in Horace Howard Furness, ed., *A New Variorum Edition of Shakespeare*, vol. 9 *The Tempest* (Philadelphia and London: J. B. Lippincott, 1892), p. 61 n.; and Richard Grant White, *Studies in Shakespeare* (Boston and New York: Houghton Mifflin; Cambridge, Massachusetts: The Riverside Press, 1885), p. 324.

15 Charles and Mary Cowden Clarke, eds, *The Plays of William Shakespeare* (London, Paris, and New York: Cassell, Petter & Galpin, [1864–68]), vol. 3, *The Tragedies*, Preface, p. vii, and vol. 1, *The Comedies*, p. 10 n.

16 Furness, ed. (n. 14) 9: 62 n.

17 See *The Works of Geoffrey Chaucer*, ed. F. N. Robinson, 2nd edition (Boston: Houghton Mifflin, 1961), p. 18 (*General Prologue*, 152), p. 56 (*Reeve's Tale*, 3974); and John Skelton, *Philip Sparrow*, line 1014, in *The Complete Poems of John Skelton, Laureate*, ed. Philip Henderson 1931, revised edition (London and Toronto: J. M. Dent and Sons, 1948), p. 89.

18 Alexander Pope, *Epistles to Several Persons*, ed. F. W. Bateson, The Twickenham Edition of the Poems of Alexander Pope (London: Methuen; New Haven: Yale University Press, 1951; 2nd edition, 1961), vol. 3 part ii, p. 73.

19 See Stephen Booth, ed., *Shakespeare's Sonnets* (New Haven and London: Yale University Press, 1977), p. 111; and for other examples from among many, James Shirley's "To Odelia" and Sir John Suckling's Sonnet II as printed in *Ben Jonson and the Cavalier Poets*, ed. Hugh Maclean (New York: W. W. Norton, 1974), pp. 188 and 258.

20 See, for example, *The Poems of Henry Constable*, ed. Joan Grundy (Liverpool: Liverpool University Press, 1960), Sonnet Seven, p. 158.

21 *The Poetical Works of Edmund Spenser*, ed. J. C . Smith and E. de Selincourt (London and New York: Oxford University Press, 1929), pp. 565 (Sonnet XV) and 581 (*Epithalamion*, line 171). For another example, see the poem attributed to Thomas Lodge in *The Phoenix Nest 1593*, ed. Hyder Edward Rollins (Cambridge: Harvard University Press, 1931), p. 58. On the Petrarchan construction of beauty more generally, see Elizabeth Cropper, "The Beauty of Woman: Problems in the Rhetoric of Renaissance Portraiture," in *Rewriting the Renaissance: The Discourses of Sexual Difference in Early Modern Europe*, ed. Margaret W. Ferguson, Maureen Quilligan, and Nancy J. Vickers (Chicago and London: University of Chicago Press, 1986), pp. 175–90.

22 Cited from *The Poems of Sir Phillip Sidney*, ed. William A. Ringler, Jr (Oxford: Clarendon Press, 1962), p. 12.

23 See *Poems of Charles Cotton 1630–1687*, ed. John Beresford (New York: Boni & Liveright, n.d.), p. 124.

24 See George Chapman, trans., *The Iliads of Homer Prince of Poets* (London: for Nathaniell Butter [1612]), p. 20, line 24; p. 64, line 4; p. 66, line 18; p. 71, line 44; p. 96, line 17; p. 106, line 1, etc.; and Chapman, trans., *Homers Odysses* (London: for Nathaniell Butter [1614]), p. 4, line 31; p. 7, line 28; p. 83, line

48; p. 209, line 7, etc. Since Dryden never translated a Homeric epic in full, the examples are more scattered, and sometimes from Latin rather than Greek. But see his "Last Parting of Hector and Andromache," (*Examen Poeticum*, 1693), line 19 "blue-ey'd progeny of Jove"; *The Second Book of the Aeneis*, line 243 "blue-ey'd maid"; and *The Twelfth Book of Ovid His Metamorphoses*, line 208 "blue-ey'd maid"; all cited from *The Poetical Works of Dryden*, ed. George R. Noyes, new revised and enlarged edition (Cambridge, Massachusetts: The Riverside Press, 1950).

25 See in particular John Dryden, *The Tempest, or The Enchanted Island. A Comedy* (London: for Henry Herringman, 1670), available in George Robert Guffey's collection of facsimile editions, *After* The Tempest (Los Angeles: William Andrews Clark Memorial Library, 1969).

26 See T[homas] Duffett, *The Mock-Tempest or The Enchanted Castle* (London: for William Cademan, 1675), p. 52. This play is also available in the Guffey facsimile edition.

27 Orgel (n. 12), pp. 72, 189–90. On the play's classical echoes, see also Donna B. Hamilton, *Virgil and* The Tempest: *The Politics of Imitation* (Columbus: Ohio State University Press, 1990).

28 Martin Bernal, vol. 1 of *Black Athena: The Afroasiatic Roots of Classical Civilization*, entitled *The Fabrication of Ancient Greece 1785–1985* (London: Free Association Books; New Brunswick: Rutgers University Press, 1987).

29 See McGann, *Critique of Modern Textual Criticism* and *Beauty of Inflections* (n. 2).

30 See, for example, E. J. Kenney, *The Classical Text: Aspects of Editing in the Age of the Printed Book* (Berkeley and London: University of California Press, 1974), p. 94 and the sources he discusses.

31 Thomas L. Berger offered this interpretation at the beginning of his course on "The Book in the Renaissance," taught at the University of Texas, Austin, Spring, 1992. But see also W. W. Greg, *Collected Papers*, ed. J. C. Maxwell (Oxford: Clarendon Press, 1966), "The Function of Bibliography in Literary Criticism Illustrated in a Study of the Text of *King Lear*," pp. 267–97, which similarly suggests that the influence of the bibliographical outlook in criticism of the printed book was largely a phenomenon of the postwar years (p. 274).

32 *The Poems of John Donne*, ed. Herbert J. C. Grierson, 2 vols (Oxford: Clarendon Press, 1912), 2: v–vi.

33 E. K. Chambers, "The Disintegration of Shakespeare," Annual Shakespeare Lecture, 1924, in *Proceedings of the British Academy* 25 (1925): 89–108. See also the contextualization of the speech in terms of the anti-Stratfordian movement in Leah S. Marcus, *Puzzling Shakespeare: Local Reading and Its Discontents* (Berkeley and London: University of California Press, 1988), pp. 34–36.

34 See F. P. Wilson's description of the shift, "Shakespeare and the 'New Bibliography,'" in *The Bibliographical Society 1892–1942: Studies in Retrospect* (London: The Bibliographical Society, 1945), pp. 76–135, especially pp. 113–16. Wilson does not support my assessment of the dominance of the image of Shakespeare as reviser in the nineteenth century; he sees an equal division between those who saw the early texts as versions improved by Shakespeare and those who saw them as corrupt copies.

35 I am indebted to Loewenstein's Shakespeare Association of America paper, "Opening the Stationers Register: On the Origins of the New Bibliography" (Kansas City, 1992). The paper will be incorporated into his forthcoming book on the same subject.

36 For the formulation, I am indebted to Linda Brodkey, *Academic Writing as Social Practice* (Philadelphia: Temple University Press, 1987). For a more nuanced

account of twentieth-century Shakespearean criticism than that offered here, see Hugh Grady, *The Modernist Shakespeare: Critical Texts in a Material World* (Oxford: Clarendon Press, 1991), to which my own discussion of the paradigm shift is strongly indebted.

37 See Bernal (n. 28), and the articles critiquing *Black Athena* in a special issue of *Arethusa* 22 (Fall 1989), *The Challenge of* Black Athena, ed. Molly Myerowitz Levine.

38 See McGann, *Beauty of Inflections* (n. 2), pp. 69–89. Since writing this section of the book, I have discovered that my use of the label "new philology" has been anticipated by medievalists: see the special issue of *Speculum*, "The New Philology," ed. Stephen G. Nichols, 65. 1 (1990). Not all of the contributors to this special issue use the phrase in precisely the same way; nevertheless, most of them closely approximate my own sense of it as encompassing both re-editing and reconceptualization – a revisionary return to scholarly scrutiny of the local and material traces of previous cultures.

39 See, for example, Hugh Kenner's *The Mechanic Muse* (New York and Oxford: Oxford University Press, 1987), pp. 5–36; and Roland Barthes, "From Work to Text" (1971), reprinted in Josué V. Harari, ed. and trans., *Textual Strategies: Perspectives in Post-Structuralist Criticism* (Ithaca: Cornell University Press, 1979), pp. 73–81. I am also indebted to N. Katherine Hayles, *The Cosmic Web: Scientific Field Models and Literary Strategies in the Twentieth Century* (Ithaca: Cornell University Press, 1984), pp. 9–15.

40 See, for example, Marion Trousdale, "A Trip through the Divided Kingdoms," *Shakespeare Quarterly* 37 (1986): 218–23. More recently Grace Ioppolo's *Revising Shakespeare* (Cambridge and London: Harvard University Press, 1991) has shown a similar unwillingness to abandon traditional assumptions about authorship in the case of Shakespeare.

41 Barthes (n. 39), p. 78.

42 For the sample list of resources, I am indebted to Roy Flannagan, "The New Milton Reference Library: What is There Now and What is Coming," *Milton Quarterly* 25 (1991): 108–16; and his "Shakespeare Enters the Electronic Age," which he was kind enough to provide me with in manuscript.

43 See T. F. Dibdin, *The Library Companion; or, The Young Man's Guide, and the Old Man's Comfort, in the Choice of a Library* (London, 1824), p. 813; and Peter W. M. Blayney, *The First Folio of Shakespeare* (Washington: Folger Shakespeare Library, 1991), pp. 36–40.

44 *Ben Jonson: The Complete Masques*, ed. Stephen Orgel (New Haven: Yale University Press, 1969), p. 76.

45 See W. W. Greg, "The Rationale of Copy-Text," *Studies in Bibliography* 3 (1950–51): 19–36; and on the "blushing sins" of the author, his "Bibliography – an Apologia," (1932), reprinted in Greg, *Collected Papers* (n. 31), p. 252. This collection also contains a reprint of the essay on copytext. See also Fredson Bowers, "A Search for Authority: The Investigation of Shakespeare's Printed Texts," in *Print and Culture in the Renaissance: Essays on the Advent of Printing in Europe*, ed. Gerald P. Tyson and Sylvia S. Wagonheim (Newark: University of Delaware Press; London and Toronto: Associated University Presses, 1986), pp. 17–44; and Margreta de Grazia's "The Essential Shakespeare and the Material Book," *Textual Practice* 2 (1988): 69–86, which anticipates much of the argument of the present section.

46 G. Thomas Tanselle, *A Rationale of Textual Criticism* (Philadelphia: University of Pennsylvania Press, 1989), pp. 40, 81.

47 See his essay "One Hundred False Starts," first printed in the *Saturday Evening*

Post, March 4, 1933 and reprinted in F. Scott Fitzgerald, *Afternoon of an Author: A Selection of Uncollected Stories and Essays,* ed. Arthur Mizener (New York: Charles Scribner's Sons, 1957), p. 129.

48 On Fitzgerald's revision, see, for example, Matthew J. Bruccoli, "Some Transatlantic Texts: West to East," in O M Brack, Jr, and Warner Barnes, eds, *Bibliography and Textual Criticism: English and American Literature 1700 to the Present* (Chicago: University of Chicago Press, 1969), pp. 244–55; and the critique of editions of *Tender Is the Night* in John McClelland, "Text, Rhetoric, Meaning," *TEXT* 3 (1987): 11–26. For medieval books of memory, see Mary J. Carruthers, *The Book of Memory: A Study of Memory in Medieval Culture* (Cambridge: Cambridge University Press, 1990). The subject of memory will be taken up again below in chapters 5 and 6.

49 For pioneering work in this direction, see Steven Urkowitz, "Five Women Eleven Ways: Changing Images of Shakespearean Characters in the Earliest Texts," in *Images of Shakespeare* (n. 2), pp. 292–304; Barbara Hodgdon, *The End Crowns All: Closure and Contradiction in Shakespeare's History* (Princeton: Princeton University Press, 1991); and Phyllis Rackin, *Stages of History: Shakespeare's English Chronicles* (Ithaca: Cornell University Press, 1990), pp. 55–56 n.

50 Richard W. F. Kroll, *The Material Word: Literate Culture in the Restoration and Early Eighteenth Century* (Baltimore and London: Johns Hopkins University Press, 1991). There were also partial precursors much earlier in the seventeenth century: see Martin Elsky, *Authorizing Words: Speech, Writing, and Print in the English Renaissance* (Ithaca and London: Cornell, 1989); and Judith H. Anderson, *Words that Matter: Linguistic Perception in Renaissance English,* forthcoming from Stanford University Press.

2 TEXTUAL INSTABILITY AND IDEOLOGICAL DIFFERENCE

1 For a full spectrum of views, see Sylvan Barnet, ed., *Doctor Faustus* (1969; reprinted New York: New American Library, 1980); Fredson Bowers, ed., *The Complete Works of Christopher Marlowe,* vol. 2 (Cambridge: Cambridge University Press, 1973); and Bowers, "Marlowe's *Doctor Faustus:* The 1602 Additions," *Studies in Bibliography* 26 (1973): 1–18; Walter Cohen, *Drama of a Nation: Public Theater in Renaissance England and Spain* (Ithaca: Cornell University Press, 1985), pp. 23–25; Roy T. Eriksen, *"The Forme of Faustus Fortunes": A Study of* The Tragedie of Doctor Faustus, *1616* (Atlantic Highlands, New Jersey: Humanities Press, 1987); Roma Gill, Review of *The Complete Works of Christopher Marlowe,* ed. Fredson Bowers, *Review of English Studies* n.s. 25 (1974): 459–64; and Gill, ed., *Doctor Faustus,* vol. 2 of *The Complete Works of Christopher Marlowe* (Oxford: Clarendon Press, 1990); W. W. Greg, *A Bibliography of the English Printed Drama to the Restoration,* vol. 1 (London: Oxford University Press, 1939); and Greg, ed., *Marlowe's* Doctor Faustus, *1604–1616: Parallel Texts* (Oxford: Clarendon Press, 1950); John D. Jump, ed., *Doctor Faustus* (London: Methuen, 1962); Michael Keefer, ed., *Doctor Faustus: A 1604-version edition* (Peterborough, Ontario and Lewiston, New York: Broadview Press, 1991); Leo Kirschbaum, "The Good and Bad Quartos of *Doctor Faustus,*" *Library,* 4th series 26 (1945–46): 272–94; Constance Brown Kuriyama, "Dr. Greg and *Doctor Faustus:* The Supposed Originality of the 1616 Text," *English Literary Renaissance* 5 (1975): 171–97; and E. D. Pendry, ed., Christopher Marlowe, *Complete Plays and Poems* (London: Dent, 1976). On formulaic elements in both versions of the play, see also

Thomas Pettitt, "Formulaic Dramaturgy in *Doctor Faustus*," in Kenneth Friedenreich, Roma Gill, and Constance B. Kuriyama, eds, *"A Poet and a filthy Play-maker": New Essays on Christopher Marlowe* (New York: AMS, 1988), 167– 91.

Citations from *Doctor Faustus* in my text will be to line numbers from Greg's parallel text edition, since modern facsimiles of A and B are less than readily available. There are a few small errors but it offers a reasonably accurate transcription of the quarto texts.

2 W. W. Greg, ed., *The Tragical History of the Life and Death of Doctor Faustus: A Conjectural Reconstruction* (Oxford: Clarendon Press, 1950). It is noteworthy that this edition, despite its reliance on B, is more balanced than the parallel text edition in its assessment of A.

3 Michael J. Warren, "*Doctor Faustus*: The Old Man and the Text," *English Literary Renaissance* 11 (1981): 111–47.

4 See John Russell Brown, "Marlowe and the Actors," *Tulane Drama Review* 8.4 (1964): 155–73; E. K. Chambers, *The Elizabethan Stage* (Oxford: Clarendon Press, 1923), 3: 423–24; and Michael Goldman, "Marlowe and the Histrionics of Ravishment," in *Two Renaissance Mythmakers: Christopher Marlowe and Ben Jonson*, ed. Alvin Kernan, Selected Papers from the English Institute, 1975–76 (Baltimore: Johns Hopkins University Press, 1977), pp. 22–40.

5 Leah S. Marcus: *Puzzling Shakespeare: Local Reading and Its Discontents* (Berkeley and London: University of California Press, 1988), pp. 44–50, 156–59.

6 See Bowers, ed., *Doctor Faustus* (n. 1), pp. 142–43.

7 Kuriyama (n. 1), pp. 177–80.

8 Gill, ed., *Doctor Faustus* (n. 1), pp. xxii, 141. Gill represents a particularly interesting case in that she has altered textual allegiance over time. Her 1965 edition of *Doctor Faustus* (reprinted New York: Hill & Wang, 1966), followed Greg in preferring B as copytext; her new Oxford edition prefers A.

9 See Johannes H. Birringer, "Between Body and Language: 'Writing' the Damnation of Faustus," *Theatre Journal* 36 (1984): 335–55; quotation is from p. 351. Like Greg, G. K. Hunter also defends the artistry of the B text in his "Five-Act Structure in *Doctor Faustus*," *Tulane Drama Review* 8.4 (1964): 77–91. On Greg's at least implicit prejudice against Calvinist doctrine, see Keefer, ed. (n. 1), pp. lxiv–lxv.

10 See Warren (n. 3); Kuriyama (n. 1); and Stephen J. Greenblatt, "Marlowe and Renaissance Self-Fashioning," in Kernan, ed. (n. 4), p. 64 n. 2; and *Renaissance Self-Fashioning: From More to Shakespeare* (Chicago and London: University of Chicago Press, 1980), p. 290 n. 2. Edward A. Snow and C. L. Barber have expressed the same preference: see Snow, "Marlowe's *Doctor Faustus* and the Ends of Desire" in Kernan, ed. (n. 4), pp. 70–110; and Barber, "The Form of Faustus' Fortunes Good or Bad," *Tulane Drama Review* 8.4 (1964): 92–119, reprinted in somewhat different form in *Creating Elizabethan Tragedy: The Theater of Marlowe and Kyd*, ed. Richard P. Wheeler (Chicago: University of Chicago Press, 1988), pp. 87–130.

For the new editions, see David Ormerod and Christopher Wortham, eds, *Dr Faustus: The A-Text* (Nedlands: University of Western Australia Press, 1985); Keefer, ed. (n. 1); and David Bevington and Eric Rasmussen, eds, *Doctor Faustus: A- and B-texts (1604, 1616)* (Manchester and New York: Manchester University Press, 1993). I am grateful to the editors of the second and third of these for sending me welcome early copies of their work. Perhaps even more indicative of the recent shift is the fact that the most recent edition of *The Norton Anthology of World Masterpieces*, vol. 1, now uses the A text rather than

Boas's composite edition for its widely used teaching text of the play (New York and London: W. W. Norton, 1992).

In terms of both age and aesthetic preference, I too belong to the pro-A-text group. However, I am less interested in choosing between texts than in demonstrating relationships between them. To the extent that my work here displays the iconoclasm characteristic of my generation of scholars, I am directing it not against the B text, but against the idea that we can recover a genuine "Marlowe."

11 See Edward H. Sugden, *A Topographical Dictionary to the Works of Shakespeare and His Fellow Dramatists* (Manchester: Manchester University Press, 1925), p. 570. The traditional objection that "Wertenberg" is no more than a printinghouse error has recently been restated by Robert F. Fleissner in "'Wittenberg,' not 'Wertenberg': A Nominal Discrepancy in the A-text of *Doctor Faustus*," *Papers of the Bibliographical Society of America* 89 (1995):189–92; however, Fleissner offers no new evidence supporting the traditional view.

12 On the Duke and Württemberg, see William Brenchley Rye, *England as Seen by Foreigners in the Days of Elizabeth and James the First* (London: John Russell Smith, 1865), pp. lv–cvii, 7; H. J. Oliver, ed., *The Merry Wives of Windsor*, The Arden Shakespeare (London: Methuen, 1971), pp. xlvi–xlix; James Allen Vann, *The Making of a State: Württemberg 1593–1793* (Ithaca: Cornell University Press, 1984), p. 54; Gerald Strauss, *Law, Resistance, and the State: The Opposition to Roman Law in Reformation Germany* (Princeton: Princeton University Press, 1986), p. 265; A. W. Ward, *et al.*, *The Cambridge Modern History*, vols 2–3 (Cambridge: Cambridge University Press, 1903–04); and the account of the history and culture of Württemberg in Johannes Janssen's multi-volume study of the Reformation, *History of the German People at the Close of the Middle Ages*, trans. M. A. Mitchell and A. M. Christie, 17 vols (London: Kegan Paul, 1900–25), especially vols 2–9. Janssen's account is strongly anti-Reformation in its bias but wonderfully detailed. Since Württemberg was officially Lutheran rather than Calvinist the parallel between Marlowe's "Wertenberg" and the historical Württemburg obviously cannot be pressed too far. My argument here is more about English perceptions of kinship than it is about precise historical congruence.

13 On Wittenberg and Melanchthon, see Keefer, ed. (n. 1), pp. xxxiii–xlv; and William Empson, *Faustus and the Censor: The English Faust-book and Marlowe's Doctor Faustus*, ed. John Henry Jones (Oxford: Blackwell, 1987), pp. 6–14. Melanchthon himself had spent time at the University of Tübingen and taken the M.A. degree there, but later broke with it over theological matters: through most of the sixteenth century, Tübingen adhered to "heretical" doctrines that denied the sacrificial nature of the Eucharist (Janssen (n. 12), 7:74–77, 313).

For the topicality of *Merry Wives*, see Oliver, ed. (n. 12), p. 125 (*Merry Wives* 4.5.65–67); and the discussion of the Shakespearean scene in Patricia Parker, *Literary Fat Ladies: Rhetoric, Gender, Property* (London: Methuen, 1987), pp. 74–77. In a recent essay, Barbara Freedman has contested the dating that has enabled editorial identification of Shakespeare's stage character with the Duke of Württemberg. See her "Shakespearean Chronology, Ideological Complicity, and Floating Texts: Something Is Rotten in Windsor," *Shakespeare Quarterly* 45 (1994): 190–210. The matter will be taken up in greater detail in the next chapter, but whether or not the duke was satirized in Shakespeare, he was certainly a well-known figure in England during the 1590s.

14 *Historie of the Damnable Life and deserued death of Doctor Iohn Faustus*, trans. P. F. (London, 1592); facsimile edition (New York: Da Capo, 1969), p. 9.

15 Keefer, ed. (n. 1), p. lx. Keefer's edition appeared after the article on which the present chapter is based was first published. There are, however, many points of agreement between us, and I have profited by his work in making revisions here. Curiously enough, however, despite his opposition to Greg, Keefer shares with the New Bibliography a confidence that he can reconstruct a single Marlovian "original" of the play.

16 See, among many other discussions of the polarities, Christopher Hill, *Society and Puritanism in Pre-Revolutionary England*, 2nd edition (New York: Schocken, 1967); Patrick Collinson, *The Elizabethan Puritan Movement* (Berkeley: University of California Press, 1967); and J. Sears McGee, *The Godly Man in Stuart England: Anglicans, Puritans, and the Two Tables, 1620–1670* (New Haven: Yale University Press, 1976).

17 On the use of black-letter type, see Keith Thomas, "The Meaning of Literacy in Early Modern England," in Gerd Baumann, ed., *The Written Word: Literacy in Transition* (Oxford: Clarendon Press, 1986), pp. 97–131; and D. C. Greetham, *Textual Scholarship: An Introduction* (New York and London: Garland, 1992), pp. 228–36.

18 That is not to suggest that doctrinal difference was the only reason for the shift in title page; chapters 5 and 6 below will offer a more compelling explanation based on printers' desire to bring the public a lively sense of the milieu of performance as they read the printed page.

19 My argument here is dependent on Warren (n. 3), pp. 129–39; and on Robert G. Hunter, *Shakespeare and the Mystery of God's Judgments* (Athens: University of Georgia Press, 1976), pp. 39–66.

20 See Hunter (n. 19), p. 48.

21 In addition to Warren and Hunter, cited above (n. 19), see Lawrence Danson, "Christopher Marlowe: The Questioner," *English Literary Renaissance* 12 (1982): 3–29.

22 See Empson (n. 13); graduate students of mine at the University of Wisconsin who were exposed to both versions of the play independently recognized the same possibility, though not on the same grounds as his.

23 Marjorie Garber, "'Here's Nothing Writ': Scribe, Script, and Circumscription in Marlowe's Plays," *Theatre Journal* 36 (1984): 301–20, Barber, ed. Wheeler (n. 10), pp. 87–130.

24 For the suggestion about bodily fragmentation and the Eucharist, I am indebted to Sonja Weiner, personal communication, May, 1988. See also Roslyn L. Knutson, "Influence of the Repertory System on the Revival and Revision of *The Spanish Tragedy* and *Doctor Faustus*," *English Literary Renaissance* 18 (1988): 257–74, especially p. 273. For comparison of other instances of Faustus's apparent loss of body parts, see B 1412–45 (which has no counterpart in A) and compare the A and B versions of the "false leg" episode in Greg, ed., *Parallel Texts* (n. 1), pp. 260–61 and 270–73.

25 W. W. Greg, "The Damnation of Faustus," *Modern Language Review* 41 (1946): 97–107, reprinted in Clifford Leach, ed., *Marlowe: A Collection of Critical Essays* (Englewood Cliffs, New Jersey: Prentice Hall, 1964), pp. 92–107, and in Greg's *Collected Papers*, ed. J. C. Maxwell (Oxford: Clarendon Press, 1966), pp. 349–65.

26 Frederick S. Boas, ed., *The Tragical History of Doctor Faustus*, vol. 5 of R. H. Case, ed., *The Works and Life of Christopher Marlowe* (London: Methuen, 1932), pp. 163–64 n.

27 For the morality play, see Hunter (n. 19), pp. 26–36. For the point about engravings, I am indebted to Andrew D. Weiner, who cites the example of Jan Sadeler (1550–1600), whose engraving of the Almighty calling Adam in the

Garden was published in a Catholic version showing God in full figure, and in a Protestant version showing, instead of the figure of God, the divine name in Hebrew surrounded by a Glory.

28 Chambers (n. 4), 3: 423.

29 G. E. Bentley, *The Professions of Dramatist and Player in Shakespeare's Time, 1590–1642*, one-volume edition (Princeton: Princeton University Press, 1986), *Dramatist*, pp. 235–63. See also Greg, ed., *Parallel Texts* (n. 1), pp. l–14; and Chambers (n. 4), 3: 422–24.

30 Glynne Wickham, "*Exeunt to the Cave*: Notes on the Staging of Marlowe's Plays," *Tulane Drama Review* 8.4 (1964): 184–94.

31 See Birringer (n. 9), p. 351.

32 Editors have noted the topicality of Bruno's name, but I am indebted to my colleague Dolora Wojciehowski for pointing out the extent of the parallels.

33 See David Bevington, *Tudor Drama and Politics: A Critical Approach to Topical Meaning* (Cambridge: Harvard University Press, 1968), pp. 187–211; and Marcus (n. 5), pp. 51–105. For accounts of the historical situation, see R. B. Wernham, *After the Armada: Elizabethan England and the Struggle for Western Europe 1588–1595* (Oxford: Clarendon Press, 1984); and Charles Wilson, *Queen Elizabeth and the Revolt of the Netherlands* (Berkeley: University of California Press, 1970).

34 Cited among other examples in Lacey Baldwin Smith, *Treason in Tudor England: Politics and Paranoia* (Princeton: Princeton University Press, 1986), p. 114.

35 Arthur Freeman, "Marlowe, Kyd, and the Dutch Church Libel," *English Literary Renaissance* 3 (1973): 44–52.

36 For more parallels with the atmosphere of wartime, see Simon Shepherd, *Marlowe and the Politics of Elizabethan Theatre* (Brighton, UK: Harvester Wheatsheaf, 1986), pp. 137–41. Shepherd argues effectively that the play "speaks a discourse of English Protestantism," but does not distinguish between the two texts.

37 Editors have argued that the passage in A was deleted from B because of the tightening of censorship after the 1606 ordinance forbidding profanation of the name of God on stage. That may be so; on the other hand, it is equally likely that the passage was deleted from the play in the course of the 1602 revision, which toned down nearly every aspect of the play's religious language.

38 See Albert J. Loomie, *Toleration and Diplomacy: The Religious Issue in Anglo-Spanish Relations, 1603–05* (monograph), Transactions of the American Philosophical Society, n. s. 53.6 (Philadelphia: American Philosophical Society, 1963), p. 11; and Wilson (n. 33), pp. 120–22.

39 See Leslie M. Oliver, "Rowley, Foxe, and the *Faustus* Additions," *Modern Language Notes* 60 (1945): 391–94; John Foxe, *Acts and Monuments*, ed. Josiah Pratt (London: Seeley, 1870), 2: 192–95; and Frances A. Yates, *Astraea: The Imperial Theme in the Sixteenth Century* (London: Routledge, 1975), pp. 38–59.

40 See Loomie (n. 38), pp. 1–9, 15.

41 C. H. McIlwain, ed., *The Political Works of James I* (Cambridge: Harvard University Press, 1918), p. 274.

42 See Loomie (n. 38); and Marcus (n. 5), pp. 184–202.

43 This is a condensed and simplified summary of a number of issues which are widely discussed by historians. See, in particular, the essays in Kevin Sharpe, ed., *Faction and Parliament: Essays on Early Stuart History* (Oxford: Clarendon Press, 1978). Other plays of the same period as the revised *Doctor Faustus* also deal with the threat of empire. See the discussion of *Measure for Measure*, *Coriolanus*, and related issues in Marcus (n. 5), pp. 160–211. I am not, of course, suggesting any

absolute correlation between the religious climate of the B text and either Wittenberg itself or James I's own beliefs: for all his love of ceremony, he was firmly Calvinist in many points of doctrine, unlike the B text.

44 See Brown (n. 4), p. 167. It is possible, of course, that this is a description of *Faustus* as staged during the 1590s, as Bevington and Rasmussen (n. 10) have assumed (p. 49), rather than after the turn of the century, when Alleyn returned to the role. So garbed in the A version of the play, Faustus would defuse the "Marlowe effect" somewhat by diminishing its distinctly Puritan atmosphere; in the more ceremonial B text, such a "priestly" Faustus would be perfectly at home.

45 *The Tragicall History of the Life and Death of Doctor Faustus* (London: for W. Gilbertson, 1663). I am indebted to Thomas L. Berger for urging me to consider this version, and to Mike Steckel for sharing with me his paper on the 1663 revisions.

46 For the phrase I am indebted to D. P. Walker, *The Decline of Hell: Seventeenth-Century Discussions of Eternal Torment* (Chicago: University of Chicago Press, 1964).

47 For more detail, see Paul Rycaut, *The History of the Turkish Empire, from the Year 1623, to the Year 1677* (London: for Tho. Tasset, *et al.*, 1687); and Sir Edward S. Creasy, *History of the Ottoman Turks From the Beginning of the Empire to the Present Time*, new and revised edition (London: Bentley, 1877).

48 Quoted in Boas, ed. (n. 26), p. 50. Unlike most modern editors, Boas offers a useful discussion of the 1663 *Faustus*, though he makes no effort to place it in terms of its topical interest during the 1660s.

49 See Anne Barton, *Ben Jonson, Dramatist* (Cambridge: Cambridge University Press, 1984), pp. 13–28; Empson (n. 13), p. 195; and Knutson (n. 24).

50 Randall McLeod and Michael Warren, in "No more, the text is foolish" and "The Diminution of Kent," at least tacitly depart from most of the other essays in *The Division of the Kingdoms: Shakespeare's Two Versions of* King Lear, ed. Gary Taylor and Michael Warren (1983; reprinted Oxford: Clarendon Press, 1986), pp. 153–59, by not attributing both versions of *King Lear* to Shakespearean authorship. Philip C. McGuire makes a similar point about the various texts of *Hamlet* in his essay "Which Fortinbras, Which *Hamlet?*" in *The* Hamlet *First Published (Q1, 1603): Origins, Form, Intertextualities*, ed. Thomas Clayton (Newark: University of Delaware Press; London and Toronto: Associated University Presses, 1992), pp. 151–78. I am grateful to Philip McGuire for his kind willingness to share his work in manuscript. See also Stephen Orgel, "The Authentic Shakespeare," *Representations* 21 (1988): 1–25.

51 Quoted in John T. Shawcross, "Signs of the Times: Christopher Marlowe's Decline in the Seventeenth Century," in Friedenreich, *et al.* (n. 1), pp. 63–71. Quotation is from p. 64.

52 Various aspects of this fusion are discussed in Danson (n. 21), p. 11; Kenneth Friedenreich, "Marlowe's Endings" in Friedenreich, *et al.* (n. 1), pp. 361–68; William Urry, *Christopher Marlowe and Canterbury*, ed. Andrew Butcher (London: Faber & Faber, 1988), pp. 69–79; and in Barber (n. 10). But see also Lois Potter, "Marlowe in the Civil War and Commonwealth: Some Allusions and Parodies," in Friedenreich, *et al.* (n. 1), pp. 73–82: by the Civil War period, Marlowe's heroes had become detached from the name of the author in most contemporary references to the plays. The decline of Marlowe's visibility as a public personality may help to account for the failure of the 1663 revival, though there were others later in the century. See Bevington and Rasmussen's stage history (n. 10), p. 51.

3 PURITY AND DANGER IN THE MODERN EDITION

1 See James Fowler's study, "David Scott's *Queen Elizabeth Viewing the Performance of the 'Merry Wives of Windsor' in the Globe Theatre* (1840)," in Richard Foulkes, ed., *Shakespeare and the Victorian Stage* (Cambridge and New York: Cambridge University Press, 1986), pp. 23–38.

2 William Green, *Shakespeare's* Merry Wives of Windsor (Princeton: Princeton University Press, 1962), pp. 44, 62 n. 1.

3 H. J. Oliver, ed., *The Merry Wives of Windsor*, The Arden Shakespeare (London: Methuen, 1971), p. ix. Although I will offer various criticisms of this and other recent editions, the reader will note, and I would like to acknowledge, my strong dependence on them.

4 These numberings are approximate and vary slightly from edition to edition. The Bankside *Merry Wives*, for example, does not include the act and scene divisions (presumably supplied by the scrivener Ralph Crane) in its numbering, with the effect that its folio version has only 2701 lines. See *The Bankside Shakespeare*, ed. Appleton Morgan, vol. 1, *The Merry Wives of Windsor* (New York: Shakespeare Society of New York, 1888; reprinted New York: AMS Press, 1969).

5 See P. A. Daniel's introduction to William Griggs, *Shakespeare's Merry Wives of Windsor: The First Quarto, 1602* (London: W. Griggs, 1888); W. W. Greg, ed., *Shakespeare's Merry Wives of Windsor, 1602* (Oxford: Clarendon Press, 1910); and for detailed accounts of the editorial and critical reception of the play in both versions, the differing perspectives offered in Jeanne Addison Roberts, *Shakespeare's English Comedy:* The Merry Wives of Windsor *in Context* (Lincoln and London: University of Nebraska Press, 1979), pp. 1–40; and William Bracy's monograph, The Merry Wives of Windsor*: The History and Transmission of Shakespeare's Text*, The University of Missouri Studies, vol. 25, no. 1 (Columbia: University of Missouri Press, 1952), pp. 9–41. As will be noted later on, however, there has been a thin but steady current of opposition to the "memorial reconstruction" theory of the origins of Q that has not been reflected in the standard editions. This group includes Bracy and Hardin Craig, who reiterated many of Bracy's arguments in his *A New Look at Shakespeare's Quartos* (Stanford: Stanford University Press, 1961), pp. 65–75.

6 See J. M. Robertson, *The Problem of 'The Merry Wives of Windsor'* (London: Shakespeare Association, 1917); A. W. Pollard and J. Dover Wilson, "The 'Stolne and Surreptitious' Shakespearean Texts," *Times Literary Supplement* (August 7, 1919): 420; and Sir Arthur Quiller-Couch and John Dover Wilson, eds, *The Merry Wives of Windsor* (1921; first paperback edition Cambridge: Cambridge University Press, 1969).

7 See in particular Oliver's Arden edition (n. 3); Green (n. 2); Alfred Hart, *Stolne and Surreptitious Copies: A Comparative Study of Shakespeare's Bad Quartos* (Melbourne: Melbourne University Press and London: Oxford University Press, 1942), pp. 342–51; and E. K. Chambers' refutation of Pollard, Wilson, and Robertson in *William Shakespeare: A Study of Facts and Problems*, 2 vols (Oxford: Clarendon Press, 1930) 1: 425–38.

Although I will not treat their arguments in detail, it is worth noting from the outset that some of the so-called "memorial" errors in Q look much more like errors of transcription. Jeanne Addison Roberts (n. 5), herself an advocate of the memorial reconstruction theory, notes a salient example, pp. 18–19. One of Q's most obviously garbled passages is "I am cosened *Hugh*, and coy *Bardolfe*" (Q p. 574, [F4]v), where F has "Hue and cry, (villaine) goe: assist me Knight" (F TLN 2306). But even an oaf of the low mental capacities attributed to the memorial reconstructors would know the phrase "Hue and cry." The mistake is not one of mishearing, but of misreading and miscopying, or possibly compositorial error, since "Hugh" was a possible Renaissance spelling for "Hue" and "coy" is only one letter removed from "cry."

8　I am indebted to Steven Urkowitz, "'Do me the kindnes to looke vpon this' and 'Heere, read, read': An Invitation to the Pleasures of Textual/Sexual Di(Per)versity," read at the 1991 Shakespeare Association of America meeting in Seattle; Barbara Freedman, "*The Merry Wives of Windsor* Revisited, or George a Green," which the author was kind enough to send me in manuscript; Eric Sams, "Mistaken Methodology," *London Review of Books* (14 June, 1990): 4–5; Y. S. Bains, "Making Sense of Some Passages in the 1602 Quarto of Shakespeare's *The Merry Wives of Windsor*," *Notes and Queries* 237 (September, 1992): 322–26; Elizabeth Pittenger, "Dispatch Quickly: The Mechanical Reproduction of Pages," *Shakespeare Quarterly*, 42 (1991): 389–408; Grace Ioppolo, *Revising Shakespeare* (Cambridge and London: Harvard University Press, 1991), pp. 118–21; Kathleen O. Irace, *Reforming the "Bad" Quartos: Performance and Provenance of Six Shakespearean First Editions* (Newark: University of Delaware Press; London: Associated University Presses, 1994), which she was gracious enough to share with me in manuscript; see also the very brief discussion in Leah S. Marcus, "Levelling Shakespeare: Local Customs and Local Texts," *Shakespeare Quarterly* 42, special issue ed. Gail Kern Paster (1991): 168–78. Unlike the other critics represented here, Irace holds to the memorial reconstruction theory of Q's origins, but regards the text as considerably more interesting than did earlier advocates of the theory.

9　See John Sutherland's useful essay, "Publishing History: A Hole at the Centre of Literary Sociology," in Philippe Desan, Priscilla Parkhurst Ferguson, and Wendy Griswold, eds, *Literature and Social Practice* (Chicago and London: University of Chicago Press, 1989), pp. 267–82. But see also G. Thomas Tanselle's response, pp. 283–87.

10　Nearly every editor discusses the problem; for a useful summary, see Roberts (n. 5), pp. 41–50.

11　I am indebted to a seminar presentation by Thomas L. Berger, "The Book in the Renaissance," University of Texas at Austin, Spring, 1991. See also Lewis Mumford, "Emerson Behind Barbed Wire," *New York Review of Books* 10 (January 18, 1968): 3–5, as discussed in Edmund Wilson, "The Fruits of the MLA: I. 'Their Wedding Journey,'" *New York Review of Books* 11 (September 26, 1968): 7–10.

12　H. C. Hart, ed., *The Merry Wives of Windsor*, The Arden Shakespeare (London: Methuen, 1904), pp. xx–xxvi.

13　Mary Douglas, *Purity and Danger: An Analysis of the Concepts of Pollution and Taboo* (1966; reprinted London: ARK paperbacks, 1984).

14　[Henry L. Mansel], "Sensation Novels," *Quarterly Review* 113. 226 (1863): 481–514.

15　See Gary Taylor's "Textual and Sexual Criticism: A Crux in *The Comedy of Errors*," *Renaissance Drama*, n.s. 19 (1988): 195–225.

16　Green (n. 2), p. 75. For the Old-Spelling Shakespeare, see *The Merry Wives of Windsor*, ed. F. J. Furnivall and F. W. Clarke (New York: Duffield; London: Chatto & Windus, 1908). The other editions mentioned are cited above (nn. 3, 6, 12).

17　See, among other studies, Raymond Williams, *The Country and the City* (1973; reprinted New York: Oxford University Press, 1975); Christopher Hill, *Society and Puritanism in Pre-Revolutionary England*, 2nd edition (New York: Schocken,

1967); and Leah S. Marcus, *The Politics of Mirth: Jonson, Herrick, Milton, Marvell, and the Defense of Old Holiday Pastimes* (Chicago and London: University of Chicago Press, 1986).

18 See, for example, Appleton Morgan's introduction to the Bankside parallel-text edition of *Merry Wives* (n. 4), which begins with the startling assertion "William Shakespeare dearly loved a lord" but goes on to praise *Merry Wives* as almost the sole exception to the bard's association of magnanimity with nobility. See also Charles Knight, ed., *The Pictorial Edition of the Works of Shakespere*, 2nd edition, revised (London: Routledge, 1867), 1: 139–208.

19 Quiller-Couch and Wilson, eds (n. 6), pp. xxvii, xxxvii.

20 Fredson Bowers, ed., *The Merry Wives of Windsor*, The Pelican Shakespeare (1963; revised edition, New York: Viking Penguin Books, 1979), pp. 21–23.

21 See, in addition to the editions already cited, John Munro's arguments against a London locale for Q in "Some Matters Shakespearean – I," *Times Literary Supplement* (September 13, 1947): 472. Barbara Freedman (n. 8) makes the interesting observation that because of its suspect origins, the quarto word *Proctor* does not occur in the Harvard Shakespeare Concordance – yet another instance of the inbred connection between editorial practice and the standard reference materials.

22 Svetlana Alpers, *The Art of Describing: Dutch Art in the Seventeenth Century* (1983; paperback edition Chicago: University of Chicago Press, 1984), pp. 148–51.

23 I have noticed two others: "halfe *Windsor*" (Q p. 566, E[1]r), and "all *Windsor*" Q (p. 576, G3r). The presence of these few Windsor references in a text otherwise empty of them could be taken as evidence that the quarto is a revised version of the folio text; on the other hand, as will be shown below, there are ways in which the folio seems revised from the quarto – strong evidence that neither is the "original."

24 See Northrop Frye, *Anatomy of Criticism* (Princeton: Princeton University Press, 1957), p. 183; Jan Lawson Hinely, "Comic Scapegoats and the Falstaff of *The Merry Wives of Windsor*," *Shakespeare Studies* 15 (1982): 37–54; C. L. Barber, *Shakespeare's Festive Comedy: A Study in Dramatic Form and Its Relation to Social Custom* (1959; reprinted New York: Meridian Books, 1963), pp. 205–21; François Laroque, *Shakespeare's Festive World: Elizabethan Seasonal Entertainment and the Professional Stage*, trans. Janet Lloyd (1988; English version, Cambridge: Cambridge University Press, 1991), pp. 188–267 passim; and Roberts (n. 5), pp. 78–83.

25 On the Skimmington and related rituals, see David Underdown, "The Taming of the Scold: The Enforcement of Patriarchal Authority in Early Modern England," in Anthony Fletcher and John Stevenson, eds, *Order and Disorder in Early Modern England* (Cambridge: Cambridge University Press, 1985), pp. 116–36; Underdown, *Revel, Riot, and Rebellion: Popular Politics and Culture in England 1603–1660* (Oxford: Clarendon Press, 1985), pp. 102–11; and Buchanan Sharp, *In Contempt of All Authority: Rural Artisans and Riot in the West of England, 1586–1660* (Berkeley: University of California Press, 1980). For convenience in the present discussion, I will use the term "Skimmington" as my general term for the ritual even though, as Underdown argues, the Skimmington is properly understood as only one specific form of it.

26 See, in addition to Green's (n. 2) elaborate case for the topical reading, Leslie Hotson's *Shakespeare versus Shallow* (Boston: Little, Brown, 1931); and the alternative speculations in J. Crofts, *Shakespeare and the Post Horses: A New Study of The Merry Wives of Windsor*, University of Bristol Studies no. 5 (Bristol: J. W. Arrowsmith, 1937); and in Freedman (n. 8).

27 For garter interpretations of Falstaff's punishment, see Hinely (n. 24); and Peter Erickson's analysis in "The Order of the Garter, the Cult of Elizabeth, and Class-Gender Tensions in *The Merry Wives of Windsor*," in Jean E. Howard and Marion F. O'Connor, eds, *Shakespeare Reproduced: The Text in History and Ideology* (New York and London: Methuen, 1987), pp. 116–140. There are also, of course, mythological precedents for the scapegoating. See John M. Steadman, "Falstaff as Actaeon: A Dramatic Emblem," *Shakespeare Quarterly* 14 (1963): 231–44.

28 Andrew Gurr, "Intertextuality at Windsor," *Shakespeare Quarterly* 38 (1987): 189–200; see also Roslyn L. Knutson's "Rejoinder" and Gurr's reply, *Shakespeare Quarterly* 39 (1988): 391–98.

29 For this point I am indebted to Urkowitz (n. 8).

30 Folger ms. V.A. 73, dated circa 1660 in the Folger catalogue, but somewhat earlier by other sources. The manuscript was previously in the possession of James Halliwell, whose name along with the date of March, 1842 are written in on its title page. See his pamphlet *An Account of the Only Known Manuscript of Shakespeare's Plays* (London: John Russell Smith, 1843).

31 Erickson (n. 27), pp. 116–40. For other recent work on gender issues in the folio version, see Patricia Parker, *Literary Fat Ladies: Rhetoric, Gender, Property* (London and New York: Methuen, 1987); her new essay "*The Merry Wives of Windsor* and Shakespearean 'Translation,'" which she was kind enough to send me in manuscript; and Nancy Cotton's "Castrating (W)itches: Impotence and Magic in *The Merry Wives of Windsor*," *Shakespeare Quarterly* 38 (1987): 320–26.

32 See Bracy (n. 5); Craig (n. 5); Robert E. Burkhart, *Shakespeare's Bad Quartos: Deliberate Abridgements Designed for Performance by a Reduced Cast*, Studies in English Literature vol. 101 (The Hague and Paris: Mouton, 1975), pp. 83–95; and an early prototype for all such arguments, Madeleine Doran's Henry VI, Parts II and III: *Their Relation to the* Contention *and* True Tragedy, University of Iowa Humanistic Studies, vol. 4, no. 4 (Iowa City: The University, 1928). For revision of the usual assumption that touring was always a sign of financial crisis, see Alan Somerset, "'How Chances It They Travel?' Provincial Touring, Playing Places, and the King's Men," *Shakespeare Survey* 47 (1994): 45–60. Many advocates of the memorial reconstruction theory of Q *Merry Wives* have gone part way toward accepting the argument that it was the touring version of the play by contending for Q as a deliberately shortened version of a corrupt, pirated text of F.

    Bracy and Burkhart's arguments for 1602 as an abridged text have recently been challenged by Gerald D. Johnson in "*The Merry Wives of Windsor*, Q1: Provincial Touring and Adapted Texts," *Shakespeare Quarterly* 38 (1987): 154–65. Johnson argues that, by Greg's criteria for the doubling of characters, the cast of *Merry Wives* could not have been significantly smaller in Q than in F, as Bracy and Burkhart contend as part of their argument for Q as a touring version of the play. I would question, though, whether Greg's criteria are applicable to the stripped-down environment of touring. He does not allow an actor to appear as two separate characters in two consecutive scenes, on the grounds that there would not be time for a costume change. But the very speed of the changes might have been part of the fun of such productions. If the actors remained recognizable, and only altered hat and coat, they could appear in adjacent scenes, as is frequently practiced in modern productions, and the audience could enjoy their uncanny skill as they moved in and out of roles. As Johnson suggests at the end of his article, it is time for a thorough reevaluation of all of these issues.

33 Burkhart (n. 32), p. 94.
34 See Bracy (n. 5), pp. 98–104; and John H. Long, "Another Masque for *The Merry Wives of Windsor*," *Shakespeare Quarterly* 3 (1952): 39–43.

4 THE EDITOR AS TAMER

1 James Thurber, *Let Your Mind Alone! And Other More or Less Inspirational Pieces* (New York and London: Harper & Bros., 1937), p. 76. See also E. J. Kenney's discussion of the passage in *The Classical Text: Aspects of Editing in the Age of the Printed Book* (Berkeley and London: University of California Press, 1974), p. 23.
2 F. J. Furnivall, *The New Shakspere Society's Transactions*, series 1, no. 1 (London, 1874), pp. 95–103. See also William Benzie, *Dr. F. J. Furnivall: Victorian Scholar Adventurer* (Norman, Oklahoma: Pilgrim Books, 1983), pp. 194–96; and for the *Henry VI* plays, Leah S. Marcus, *Puzzling Shakespeare: Local Reading and Its Discontents* (Berkeley and London: University of California Press, 1988), pp. 51–52. For John Dover Wilson's opinions on *The Tempest*, see chapter 1 above and the New Shakespeare edition (chap. 1, n. 6), pp. 80–82.
3 Cited from Alfred Hart, *Stolne and Surreptitious Copies: A Comparative Study of Shakespeare's Bad Quartos* (Melbourne and London: Melbourne and Oxford University Presses, 1942), p. 104. The present chapter is part of a growing interrogation – and not only among feminist critics – of the gendering of traditional editorial practice. See, in addition to Gary Taylor's "Textual and Sexual Criticism" (chap. 3, n. 15), Betty T. Bennett, "Feminism and Editing Mary Wollstonecraft Shelley: The Editor And?/Or? the Text," in George Bornstein and Ralph G. Williams, eds, *Palimpsest: Editorial Theory in the Humanities* (Ann Arbor: University of Michigan Press, 1993), pp. 67–96; Donald H. Reiman, "Gender and Documentary Editing: A Diachronic Perspective," *TEXT* 4 (1988): 351–59; and Katie King, "Bibliography and a Feminist Apparatus of Literary Production," *TEXT* 5 (1991): 91–103.
4 Stephanie H. Jed, *Chaste Thinking: The Rape of Lucretia and the Birth of Humanism* (Bloomington and Indianapolis: Indiana University Press, 1989).
5 *The Tragidie of Ferrex and Porrex* [*Gorboduc*] (London, [1570]), sig. Aii.
6 Although I cite folio passages in the text by Through Line Numbers to the Norton Facsimile edition, I am also indebted to modern editors, especially to the New Cambridge *The Taming of the Shrew*, ed. Ann Thompson (Cambridge: Cambridge University Press, 1984); the Oxford *The Taming of the Shrew*, ed. H. J. Oliver (Oxford: Clarendon Press, 1982); and the Arden *The Taming of the Shrew*, ed. Brian Morris (London and New York: Methuen, 1981).
7 For discussion of recent performances, I am indebted to Tori Haring-Smith, *From Farce to Metadrama: A Stage History of* The Taming of the Shrew, *1594–1983* (Westport, Connecticut: Greenwood Press, 1985); to Barbara Hodgdon, "Katherina Bound; or, Play(K)ating the Strictures of Everyday Life," *PMLA* 107 (1992): 538–53; and to Graham Holderness, *The Taming of the Shrew*, Shakespeare in Performance Series (Manchester: Manchester University Press, 1989).
    Scattered earlier twentieth-century productions also brought back Sly. In 1958, for example, the director Margaret Webster wrote, "My own advice to the director is to raid the rest of the Sly material which is to be found in the other "*Shrew*" play, *The Taming of a Shrew*." See her commentary on her own production in the Laurel Shakespeare edition of *The Taming of the Shrew*, ed. Charles Jasper Sisson (New York: Dell Publishing, 1958), pp. 24–25.

8 Thompson ed. (n. 6), pp. 1–3; Morris ed. (n. 6), pp. 12–13.

9 Scholarly opinion differs as to whether Shakespeare himself was a member of Pembroke's Men and whether *A Shrew* was actually performed by that company or by the Lord Chamberlain's Men at Newington Butts. There are also marked differences of opinion over which of these early *Shrews* was *A Shrew* and which may have been *The Shrew*. For representative views, see E. K. Chambers, *William Shakespeare: A Study of Facts and Problems*, 2 vols (Oxford: Clarendon Press, 1930), 1: 324–28; *The Taming of the Shrew*, ed. Sir Arthur Quiller-Couch and John Dover Wilson (Cambridge: Cambridge University Press, 1928), pp. vii–xxv, 99–126; *The Taming of the Shrew*, ed. Oliver (n. 6), pp. 29–34; and David George, "Shakespeare and Pembroke's Men," *Shakespeare Quarterly* 32 (1981): 305–23.

10 Early editions I have consulted include Nicholas Rowe, ed., *The Works of Mr. William Shakespeare; In Six Volumes* (London: for Jacob Tonson, 1709); Alexander Pope, ed., *The Works of Shakespear . . . in Six Volumes* (London: for Jacob Tonson, 1720–25); Lewis Theobald, ed., *The Works of Shakespeare in Seven Volumes* (London: for Bettesworth, Hitch, *et al.*, 1733); Thomas Hanmer, ed., *The Works of Shakespear in Six Volumes* (Oxford: Oxford University Press, 1744); William Warburton, ed., *The Works of Shakespear in Eight Volumes* (London: for Kapton, Birt, *et al.*, 1747); Samuel Johnson, ed., *The Plays of William Shakespeare, in Eight Volumes* (London: for J. and R. Tonson, *et al.*, 1765); Edward Capell, ed., Mr. William Shakespeare *his COMEDIES, HISTORIES, AND TRAGEDIES* (London: for J. and R. Tonson, 1768); and Edmund Malone, ed., *The Plays and Poems of William Shakespeare in 10 Volumes* (London: for H. Baldwin, 1790). Capell represents a transitional case in that the Sly materials are included in the text of his London 1768 edition but branded as non-Shakespearean in the introduction and notes of his Dublin 1771 edition.

11 F. J. Furnivall, for example, held the opposite of modern opinion, finding *A Shrew* a pre-Shakespearean play and *The Shrew* an amalgam of several hands including Shakespeare's. See his facsimile edition of *The Taming of a Shrew. The First Quarto, 1594* (London: C. Praetorius, 1886), pp. iv–viii.

For more recent editors and critics contending for *A Shrew* as the earlier play, see F. S. Boas, ed., *The Taming of a Shrew* (London: Chatto & Windus; New York: Duffield and Company, 1908); R. Warwick Bond, ed., *The Works of Shakespeare: The Taming of the Shrew* (Indianapolis: Bobbs-Merrill, n.d.); Geoffrey Bullough, ed., *Narrative and Dramatic Sources of Shakespeare* vol. 1 (London: Routledge and Kegan Paul, 1966), p. 58; William J. Rolfe, ed., *Shakespeare's Comedy of* The Taming of the Shrew (New York: American Book Co., 1881; new edition 1898); W. J. Courthope, *A History of English Poetry* (London: Macmillan, 1895–1910), 4: 466–74; Eric Sams, "The Timing of the Shrews," *Notes and Queries* 230 (1985): 33–45; and, of course, William Aldis Wright, ed., *The Taming of the Shrew* (London and New York: Macmillan, 1894).

To their credit, Stanley Wells and Gary Taylor leave open the question of the relationship between *A Shrew* and *The Shrew* in *William Shakespeare: A Textual Companion* (Oxford: Clarendon Press, 1987). In their Oxford Shakespeare, the Sly materials are printed after the main text of the play, and in the same type, which is further than other editions have gone in associating the epilogue with the play in its canonical form. But see also their "No Shrew, A Shrew, and The Shrew: Internal Revision in *The Taming of the Shrew*," in Bernhard Fabian and Kurt Tetzeli von Rosador, eds, *Shakespeare: Text, Language, Criticism. Essays in Honour of Marvin Spevack* (Hildesheim, Zurich, and New York: Olms-Weidmann, 1987), pp. 351–70, which provisionally accepts the traditional argument regarding at least some "memorial elements" in *A Shrew*.

12 See Peter Alexander, "The Taming of a Shrew," *Times Literary Supplement* (September 16, 1926): 614; and also the companion articles "'II. Henry VI.' and the Copy for 'The Contention' (1594)," *TLS* (October 9, 1924): 629–30; and "'3 Henry VI' and 'Richard, Duke of York,'" *TLS* (November 13, 1924): 730. For recent refinements of the argument by which *A Shrew* is derived from *The Shrew* or from a common ancestor of both, see, for example, Raymond A. Houk, "The Evolution of *The Taming of the Shrew*," *PMLA*, 57 (1942): 1009–38; Henry David Gray, "*The Taming of a Shrew*," *Philological Quarterly* 20 (1941): 325–33; and G. I. Duthie, "*The Taming of a Shrew* and *The Taming of the Shrew*," *Review of English Studies* 19 (1943): 337–56. Similar arguments are made in almost every modern single-volume edition of the play.

13 Q p. xv; see also W. W. Greg, *The Shakespeare First Folio: Its Bibliographical and Textual History* (Oxford: Clarendon Press, 1955), pp. 210–16.

14 See Graham Holderness and Bryan Loughrey, eds, *A Pleasant Conceited Historie, Called The Taming of a Shrew* (Hemel Hempstead, UK: Harvester Wheatsheaf, 1992), as part of their series, "Shakespearean Originals: First Editions"; and Stephen Miller's forthcoming edition of the play for Oxford University Press. If the advance materials he has kindly supplied me with represent his anticipated editorial policy, Miller's edition will argue for memorial reconstruction in the case of *A Shrew* but portray the play as considerably more interesting than recent editors of *The Shrew* have found it.

15 For this point I am indebted to Margaret Downs-Gamble, "The Taming-school: *The Taming of the Shrew* as Lesson in Renaissance Humanism," in Jean R. Brink, ed., *Privileging Gender in Early Modern England*, Sixteenth Century Essays & Studies 23 (Kirksville, Missouri, 1993), pp. 65–80. See also Thompson, ed. (n. 6), pp. 13–14; Wayne Rebhorn's *The Emperor of Men's Minds: Literature and the Renaissance Discourse of Rhetoric* (Ithaca and London: Cornell University Press, 1995); his "Petruchio's 'Rope Tricks': *The Taming of the Shrew* and the Renaissance Discourse of Rhetoric," *Modern Philology* 92 (1995): 294–327; and Laurie E. Maguire's contextualization of the play in terms of militarism in "'Household Kates': Chez Petruchio, Percy, and Plantagenet," in *Gloriana's Face: Women, Public and Private, in the English Renaissance*, ed. S. P. Cerasano and Marion Wynne-Davies (Detroit: Wayne State University Press, 1992), pp. 129–65.

16 I am indebted to Professor Boose for giving me access to her essay "*The Taming of the Shrew*, Good Husbandry, and Enclosure" in several manuscript drafts.

17 See, for example, Oliver, ed. (n. 6), pp. 17–18.

18 Cited from sig. B3r of *A Pleasant Conceited Historie, called The taming of a Shrew* (London: for Cutbert Burbie, 1594); further citations will be indicated by signature number in the text. Given that facsimiles of the 1594 *A Shrew* are less than readily available, I will also include page numbers from the new Holderness–Loughrey edition (n. 14) (quoted passage is S p. 53). I am also indebted to Boas, ed. (n. 11). My thanks to Dan and Jean R. Brink for checking my quotations against the original once I was no longer in residence at the Huntington Library.

19 See Lawrence Stone, *The Family, Sex and Marriage in England, 1500–1800* (London: Weidenfeld, 1977); Joan Kelly, "Did Women Have a Renaissance?" (1977), reprinted in *Women, History and Theory: The Essays of Joan Kelly* (Chicago: University of Chicago Press, 1984), pp. 19–50; Susan Dwyer Amussen, *An Ordered Society: Gender and Class in Early Modern England* (Oxford: Basil Blackwell, 1988); and David Underdown's critique of Alice Clark's *Working Life of Women in the Seventeenth Century*, 2nd edition, with new introduction by M. Chaytor and J. Lewis (London: Routledge, 1982), in Underdown's "The

Taming of the Scold: The Enforcement of Patriarchal Authority in Early Modern England," in *Order and Disorder in Early Modern England*, ed. Anthony Fletcher and John Stevenson (Cambridge: Cambridge University Press, 1985), pp. 116–36. Underdown accepts the theory of a general decline in the independence of women during the period, but argues that increased attention to the scold may signal increased opportunities for women in some segments of sixteenth and seventeenth-century culture.

20 Furnivall (n. 2), p. 104. See also Morris, ed. (n. 6), pp. 62–63. John Russell Brown uses the appeal to realism in *The Shrew* to build a broad argument about increasing naturalism in acting styles during the age of Shakespeare, "On the Acting of Shakespeare's Plays," (1953), reprinted in *The Seventeenth-Century Stage: A Collection of Critical Essays*, ed. G. E. Bentley (Chicago: University of Chicago Press, 1968), pp. 41–54.

21 John Harington, *The Metamorphosis of Ajax*, ed. Elizabeth Donno (London, 1962), pp. 153–54; cited in Oliver, ed. (n. 6), p. 34.

22 See, for example, John C. Bean, "Comic Structure and the Humanizing of Kate in *The Taming of the Shrew*," in *The Woman's Part: Feminist Criticism of Shakespeare*, ed. Carolyn Ruth Swift Lenz, Gayle Greene, and Carol Thomas Neely (Urbana: University of Illinois Press, 1980; reprinted 1983), pp. 65–78; and Peter Berek, "Text, Gender, and Genre in *The Taming of the Shrew*," in *"Bad" Shakespeare: Revaluations of the Shakespearean Canon*, ed. Maurice Charney (London and Toronto: Associated University Presses; Rutherford, Madison, and Teaneck: Farleigh Dickinson University Press, 1988), pp. 91–104, both of which consistently misread *A Shrew* out of a desire to demonstrate Shakespeare's greater tolerance and humanity. For use of Kate's submission speech from *A Shrew* see Ann Thompson's fine edition (n. 6), pp. 28–29.

Other interpretive articles with which I may not agree but to which my own thinking is indebted include Lynda E. Boose, "Scolding Brides and Bridling Scolds: Taming the Woman's Unruly Member," *Shakespeare Quarterly* 42 (1991): 179–213; Richard A. Burt, "Charisma, Coercion, and Comic Form in *The Taming of the Shrew*," *Criticism* 26 (1984): 295–311; Joel Fineman, "The Turn of the Shrew," in *Shakespeare and the Question of Theory*, ed. Patricia Parker and Geoffrey Hartman (London: Methuen, 1985), pp. 138–59; Thelma Nelson Greenfield, "The Transformation of Christopher Sly," *Philological Quarterly* 33 (1954): 34–42; Robert B. Heilman, "The *Taming* Untamed, or, The Return of the Shrew," *Modern Language Quarterly* 27 (1966): 147–61; Richard Hosley, "Was There a 'Dramatic Epilogue' to *The Taming of the Shrew?*" *Studies in English Literature 1500–1900* 1 (1961): 17–34; Sears Jayne, "The Dreaming of *The Shrew*," *Shakespeare Quarterly* 17 (1966): 41–56; Ernest P. Kuhl, "Shakespeare's Purpose in Dropping Sly," *Modern Language Notes* 36 (1921): 321–29; Karen Newman, "Renaissance Family Politics and Shakespeare's *The Taming of the Shrew*," *English Literary Renaissance* 16 (1986): 86–100; Marianne L. Novy, "Patriarchy and Play in *The Taming of the Shrew*," *English Literary Renaissance* 9 (1979): 264–80; Marion D. Perrit, "Petruchio: The Model Wife," *Studies in English Literature 1500–1900* 23 (1983): 223–35; Michael W. Shurgot, "From Fiction to Reality: Character and Stagecraft in *The Taming of the Shrew*," *Theatre Journal* 33 (1981): 327–40; Edward Tomarken's forthcoming essay "The Discipline of Criticism: Samuel Johnson on Shakespeare," which he was kind enough to send me in manuscript; Valerie Wayne, "Refashioning the Shrew," *Shakespeare Studies* 17 (1985): 159-87; and Karl P. Wentersdorf, "The Original Ending of *The Taming of the Shrew*: A Reconsideration," *Studies in English Literature 1500–1900* 18 (1978): 201–15.

23 See G. E. Bentley, *The Professions of Dramatist and Player in Shakespeare's Time, 1590–1642*, one-volume paperback edition (1971 and 1984; reprinted Princeton: Princeton University Press, 1986); and Muriel C. Bradbrook, "The Status Seekers: Society and the Common Player in the Reign of Elizabeth I" (1961), reprinted in Bentley, ed. (n. 20), pp. 55–69.

24 Wilson, citing, as nearly all discussions of the problem do, Samuel Hickson, "Marlowe and the Old 'Taming of a Shrew,' " *Notes and Queries*, 1 (1850): 194, 226–27, in Quiller-Couch and Wilson, ed. (n. 9), p. 179.

25 Wilson (again citing Hickson), ibid., p. 168.

26 See in particular, Susan Amussen's argument (n. 19).

27 See, for example, Duthie (n. 12), pp. 338–42.

28 See, for example, Simon Latham, *Lathams Falconry or The Faulcons Lure, and Cure: In Two Books* (London: for Roger Iackson, 1614), sig. c [1]r; and George Turbervile, *The Booke of Falconrie or Hawking . . . newly reviued, corrected, and augmented* (London: by Thomas Purfoot, 1611), sig. Aiiv. In *An Approved Treatise of Hawkes and Hawking* (London: for Richard Moore, 1619), however, Edmund Bert advocates that the newly caught hawk be kept on the hawker's fist night and day. As Turbervile remarks, hawks and falcons are of "sundry natures and properties, and therefore they must be diuersly gouerned and enticed, which is the cause that it is hard to giue generall Rules" (sig. [G3]v).

29 Alexander (n. 12), p. 614. All editorial argument about Marlovian borrowings rests ultimately on Hickson's work from the 1850s, cited above (n. 24). On Marlovian borrowings, see also Boas, ed (n. 11), pp. xxx–xxxii and 91–98, and nearly every modern edition of the play. My own argument that the Marlovian passages work as successful burlesque has been anticipated in part by a few editors, most prominently Quiller-Couch in Quiller-Couch and Wilson, eds (n. 9), pp. xxi–xxii; and Holderness and Loughrey (n. 14), pp. 23–25.

    The matter of Marlovian borrowings from *A Shrew* has an importance for advocates of the theory of memorial construction beyond the instance of *The Shrew*, since the case for the A text of *Doctor Faustus* as a corrupt copy of B rests on the editorial judgment that Marlovian echoes in *A Shrew* parallel the B version rather than A, proving that B was extant before 1594, when *A Shrew* was published. But most of the parallels are too generally Marlovian to be precise quotations of either A or B. Only one example of those offered in Boas – *A Shrew*'s "gloomie shaddow of the night" – resembles the B text more than it does the A text, since B reads "night" while A reads "earth." However, that one-word correspondence is evidence too slender to carry the point about B's temporal priority. As I have suggested in chapter 2, the Marlovian text was unstable, and stage echoes of it can be expected to reflect minor variations in language that no doubt existed from performance to performance even within the same stage run.

30 Quiller-Couch and Wilson, eds (n. 9), p. 126.

31 See Arthur Marotti, " 'Love Is Not Love': Elizabethan Sonnet Sequences and the Social Order," *ELH* 49 (1982): 396–428; and Jonathan Goldberg, *James I and the Politics of Literature: Jonson, Shakespeare, Donne, and Their Contemporaries* (Baltimore and London: Johns Hopkins University Press, 1983), pp. 210–19. The same tendency is more pronounced in later Cavalier poetry than in the John Donne writings discussed by Goldberg.

32 On signs of revision in the folio version, see Florence Huber Ashton, "The Revision of the Folio Text of *The Taming of the Shrew*," *Philological Quarterly* 6 (1927): 151–60; Wells and Taylor, "No Shrew, A Shrew, and The Shrew" (n. 11); Sams (n. 11); and Bullough (n. 11), pp 65–68.

33 Johnson, ed. (n. 10), 3: 99. For discussion of eighteenth-century adaptations, see Haring-Smith (n. 7), pp. 9–22; and Oliver, ed. (n. 6), pp. 65–69.

34 See, for an example of women's response, Marianne Novy's Introduction to *Women's Re-Visions of Shakespeare*, ed. Novy (Urbana: University of Illinois Press, 1990), p. 7.

35 See Irene G. Dash's discussion of Garrick and nineteenth-century productions, *Wooing, Wedding, and Power: Women in Shakespeare's Plays* (New York: Columbia University Press, 1981), pp. 41–64.

36 For all of these and other examples, see Haring-Smith (n. 7), pp. 43–64. See also Susan J. Wolfson, "Explaining to Her Sisters: Mary Lamb's *Tales from Shakespear*," in Novy, ed. (n. 34), pp. 16–40, especially pp. 23–27.

37 D. C. Greetham, *Textual Scholarship: An Introduction* (New York and London: Garland, 1992), pp. 323–25.

38 See, for example, the postcards reproduced in Elspeth King, *The Hidden History of Glasgow's Women: The Thenew Factor* (Edinburgh: Mainstream Publishing, 1993), p. 29. I am indebted to the kindness of Lynda Boose for this reference.

39 Thompson, ed. (n. 6), p. 21.

40 See Alexander, "The Taming of a Shrew" (n. 12), p. 614. See also the more recent sources cited in n. 12 above.

41 Quiller-Couch and Wilson, eds (n. 9), p. xxvi. For another similar view, see A. L. Rowse, ed., *The Annotated Shakespeare, Vol. I: The Comedies* (New York: C. N. Potter, 1978), pp. 119–21.

42 See, for example, Shirley Garner, "*The Taming of the Shrew*: Inside or Outside of the Joke?" in "*Bad*" *Shakespeare* (n. 22), pp. 105–19.

43 See, for example, Valerie Wayne, ed., *The Matter of Difference: Materialist Feminist Criticism of Shakespeare* (Ithaca: Cornell University Press, 1991), particularly Catherine Belsey's "Afterword: A Future for Materialist Feminist Criticism?" pp. 257–70.

44 Oliver, ed. (n. 6), p. 64.

45 See the new Oxford Shakespeare and, for yet a more flexible array of texts, Michael Warren, ed., *The Complete King Lear: 1608–1623* (Berkeley and London: University of California Press, 1989).

5 BAD TASTE AND BAD *HAMLET*

1 For the purpose of this anecdote, I offer my own edited version of the first quarto of *Hamlet*, with modernized spelling and punctuation; see also Albert B. Weiner, ed., *Hamlet: The First Quarto 1603* (Great Neck, New York: Barron's Educational Series, 1962), pp. 104–05.

2 The most electrifying recent production has been Sam Walter's 1985 Q1 *Hamlet* for the Orange Tree Theatre, Richmond, which several reviewers considered the theatrical highpoint of the year in the London area. For descriptions of that and other recent productions, see the accounts in Thomas Clayton, ed., *The* Hamlet *First Published (Q1, 1603): Origins, Form, Intertextualities* (Newark: University of Delaware Press; London and Toronto: Associated University Presses, 1992), pp. 59–60 and 123–36; and Graham Holderness and Bryan Loughrey, eds, *The Tragicall Historie of Hamlet Prince of Denmarke*, Shakespearean Originals: First Editions (Hemel Hempstead, UK: Harvester Wheatsheaf, 1992), pp. 13–29. Q1 has also aroused interest on the Polish stage: see Clayton's introduction, p. 18 and n. 2. See also Marvin Rosenberg's "The First Modern English Staging of *Hamlet* Q1," in Clayton, ed., pp. 241–48, for William Poel's less successful effort in 1881.

3 New Cambridge *Hamlet*, ed. Philip Edwards (Cambridge and New York: Cambridge University Press, 1985), p. 8. See also two important recent articles: Paul Werstine, "The Textual Mystery of *Hamlet*," *Shakespeare Quarterly* 39 (1988): 1–26; and Barbara Mowat, "The Form of *Hamlet*'s Fortunes," *Renaissance Drama*, n.s. 19 (1988): 97–126.

4 See Stanley Wells and Gary Taylor, *William Shakespeare: A Textual Companion* (Oxford: Clarendon Press, 1987), p. 402; and G. R. Hibbard's single-volume *Hamlet* for the Oxford Shakespeare (Oxford: Clarendon Press, 1987). As usual, for all my disagreements with them, my own thinking is strongly indebted to recent editions of the play, in particular Wells and Taylor's Oxford Shakespeare (*Textual Companion*); Edwards' New Cambridge *Hamlet* (n. 3); G. R. Hibbard's *Hamlet*; and Harold Jenkins' Arden edition, *Hamlet* (London and New York: Routledge, 1982; reprinted 1987 and 1989). For readers interested in working with the second quarto and the first folio versions concurrently in a convenient pocket edition, the New Folger Library *Hamlet*, ed. Barbara Mowat and Paul Werstine (New York and London: Washington Square Press, 1992), which conflates the two texts but marks all passages unique to Q2 and all passages unique to F1, is particularly valuable. There is also a useful discussion of Q1 variants in Grace Ioppolo, *Revising Shakespeare* (Cambridge and London: Harvard University Press, 1991), pp. 134–46, which vacillates between memorial reconstruction and authorial revision as explanations for the origins of Q1.

5 See in particular, Jenkins, ed. (n. 4); and Marga Munkelt's analysis of editorial practice, "Traditions of Emendation in *Hamlet*: The Handling of the First Quarto," in Clayton, ed. (n. 2), pp. 211–40.

6 See Charles Knight, *William Shakspere: A Biography*, 3rd edition (London: Routledge & Sons, 1867), p. 361. The theory of Q1 as an inept reconstruction of some sort was articulated during the nineteenth century, most notably by John Payne Collier, but was not dominant then. See the surveys of opinion in Hibbard, ed. (n. 4), pp. 75–76; and in George Ian Duthie, *The "Bad" Quarto of Hamlet: A Critical Study*, Shakespeare Problems VI (Cambridge: Cambridge University Press, 1941), pp. 90–91.

7 See A. C. Bradley, *Shakespearean Tragedy* (1904; reprinted New York: Meridian, 1955), p. 111, n. 2; and John Dover Wilson, *What Happens in Hamlet* (1935; reprinted Cambridge and New York: Cambridge University Press, 1990), p. 120. For Wilson's earlier views of Q1, see his "The Copy for 'Hamlet,' 1603," *Library*, 3rd series 9 (1918): 153–85; and "The 'Hamlet' Transcript, 1593" in the same volume, pp. 217–47. See also the discussion of his theories in Duthie (n. 6).

In 1919 T. S. Eliot notoriously agreed with the "disintegrator" J. M. Robertson that *Hamlet* was a palimpsest and an artistic failure – a philosophical tragedy uneasily grafted upon a much simpler and cruder revenge play closely resembling Q1. But in the case of *Hamlet*, yet once more, E. K. Chambers and the anti-disintegrationists won the day during the 1920s; thereafter, the image of the Bard "as a patcher of other men's plays" became intolerable for the twentieth-century critical mainstream. See J. M. Robertson, *The Problem of "Hamlet"* (London: George Allen & Unwin, 1919); T. S. Eliot, *The Sacred Wood* (1920; reprinted London: Methuen, 1972), pp. 95–103; his *Selected Essays, 1917–1932* (New York: Harcourt, Brace, 1932), pp. 121–26; and the contextualization of Eliot's opinion in William H. Quillian, *Hamlet and the New Poetic: James Joyce and T. S. Eliot*, Studies in Modern Literature, no. 13 (Ann Arbor, Michigan: UMI Research Press, 1983, 1975), pp. 49–77; Terence Hawkes, *Meaning by Shakespeare* (London and New York: Routledge, 1992), pp. 93–96; and his *That Shakespeherian Rag: Essays on a Critical Process* (London and New York: Methuen, 1986), pp. 92–119.

8 One recent exception is Holderness and Loughrey's edition (n. 2), an early copy of which was kindly supplied by Bryan Loughrey. For other recent work "rehabilitating" Q1 *Hamlet*, see especially Steven Urkowitz, "'Well-sayd olde Mole': Burying Three *Hamlet*s in Modern Editions," in Georgianna Ziegler, ed., *Shakespeare Study Today* (New York: AMS Press, 1986), pp. 37–70; his "Good News about 'Bad' Quartos," in Maurice Charney, ed., *"Bad" Shakespeare: Revaluations of the Shakespeare Canon* (Rutherford: Farleigh Dickinson University Press, 1988), pp. 189–206; and "Back to Basics: Thinking about the *Hamlet* First Quarto," in Clayton, ed. (n. 2), pp. 257–91. See also Philip C. McGuire's essay in the same volume, "Which Fortinbras, Which *Hamlet?*" pp. 151–78, which the author kindly sent me in manuscript; and Kathleen O. Irace's discussion in *Reforming the "Bad" Quartos: Performance and Provenance of Six Shakespearean First Editions* (Newark: University of Delaware Press; London: Associated University Presses, 1994), which argues for Q1 as memorially reconstructed but still worthy of perusal.

9 See in particular their *Textual Companion* (n. 4), pp. 23–31 and 398. The Norton Shakespeare currently in preparation will, in using the Oxford text, presumably keep its hypothesis of memorial reconstruction for Q1; similarly, Kathleen Irace's forthcoming Cambridge edition of Q1 will posit it as memorially reconstructed. But the critical landscape is gradually changing. See, in addition to Holderness and Loughrey's edition of Q1 (n. 2), two recent editions that leave open the matter of Q1's origins: the Folger edition, ed. Mowat and Werstine (n. 4), and the new *Three-Text Hamlet*, ed. Paul Bertram and Bernice W. Kliman (New York: AMS Press, 1991), cited in the present study as H. The *New Variorum Hamlet*, ed. Bernice Kliman and William Hutchings, with anticipated completion in 2001, will appear in both computerized hypertext and in print format, and will enormously facilitate textual work on the play.

10 Cited from T. M. Raysor, ed., *Coleridge's Shakespearean Criticism* (London: Constable, 1930), 1: 21.

11 See Barbara Herrnstein Smith, *Contingencies of Value: Alternative Perspectives for Critical Theory* (Cambridge and London: Harvard University Press, 1988); Pierre Bourdieu, *Distinction: A Social Critique of the Judgment of Taste*, trans. Richard Nice (Cambridge and London: Harvard University Press, 1984); and Terry Eagleton, *The Ideology of the Aesthetic* (Oxford: Basil Blackwell, 1990).

12 Cited from Boswell's *Malone's Shakespeare* 1: 134–35, in J. D. Wilson, *The Manuscript of Shakespeare's* Hamlet, *and the Problems of Its Transmission: An Essay in Critical Bibliography*, 2 vols (New York: Macmillan; Cambridge: Cambridge University Press, 1934), 1: 2.

13 W. W. Greg, *Two Elizabethan Stage Abridgements: The Battle of Alcazar & Orlando Furioso*, Malone Society Extra Volume, 1922 (Oxford: Frederick Hall, 1923), p. 256.

14 Although I am skeptical about the technological determinism of some of the arguments in the first two authors in the following list, my speculations in this chapter are strongly indebted to: Walter J. Ong, *Orality and Literacy: The Technologizing of the Word* (London and New York: Methuen, 1982); Jack Goody, *The Interface between the Written and the Oral*, Studies in Literacy, Family, Culture and the State (Cambridge and New York: Cambridge University Press, 1987); his earlier book in the same series, *The Logic of Writing and the Organization of Society* (Cambridge and New York: Cambridge University Press, 1986); and Ruth Finnegan's extension and critique in *Literacy and Orality: Studies in the Technology of Communication* (Oxford: Basil Blackwell, 1988).

15 Cited from Jenkins, ed. (n. 4), p. 13.

16 For recent editorial discussion and attenuation of this hypothetical scenario, see Jenkins, ed. (n. 4), pp. 13–18; Hibbard, ed. (n. 4), pp. 67–71; and Edwards, ed. (n. 3), pp. 9–10.

17 See Gerald D. Johnson, "Nicholas Ling, Publisher 1580–1607," *Studies in Bibliography* 38 (1985): 203–14, and his "John Trundle and the Book-Trade 1603–1626," *Studies in Bibliography* 39 (1986): 177–99. Despite Trundle's poor reputation among modern editors, some of his publications were highly interesting. He was, for example, the publisher of *Hic Mulier* and *Haec-Vir*.

18 Wilson (n. 12), 1: 20; other scholars (also with Claudius in mind?) refer to the play as a patchwork: see in particular Duthie's definitive dismissal of Q1 (n. 6).

19 Here and throughout, the *Hamlet* texts are cited from *The Three-Text Hamlet*. I have also checked all Q1 citations either against the Huntington Library copy of Q1 or against Q, and have checked Q2 citations against Q. For the convenience of readers not in possession of the parallel-text edition, my citations include signature numbers for substantive quotations in addition to the page numbers from H.

20 For recent readings of Q1 Gertred, see, for example, Steven Urkowitz, "Five Women Eleven Ways: Changing Images of Shakespearean Characters in the Earliest Texts," in *Images of Shakespeare*, Proceedings of the Third Congress of the International Shakespeare Association, 1986, ed. Werner Habicht, D. J. Palmer, and Roger Pringle (Newark: University of Delaware Press; London and Toronto: Associated University Presses, 1988), pp. 292–304; Kathleen Irace, "Adapting *Hamlet* Q1 to Zeffirelli," paper presented at the Shakespeare Association of America seminar on text, 1992; and Dorothea Kehler, "The First Quarto of *Hamlet*: Reforming the Lusty Widow," paper presented at the SAA seminar on text, 1994.

21 Ernest Jones, *Hamlet and Oedipus* (1949; reprinted New York: Norton, 1976), written, according to Jones, "as an exposition of a footnote in Freud's 'Traumdeutung' (1900), p. 9."

22 Quoted from Peter Guinness in Brian Loughrey, "Q1 in Recent Performance: An Interview," in Clayton, ed. (n. 2), p. 128.

23 See Loughrey (n. 22) and the current of minority opinion represented in Frank G. Hubbard, ed., *The First Quarto Edition of Shakespeare's Hamlet*, University of Wisconsin Studies in Language and Literature no. 8 (Madison: [University of Wisconsin], 1920), pp. 32–35; Weiner, ed. (n. 1); Maxwell E. Foster, *The Play behind the Play*: Hamlet *and Quarto One*, ed. Anne Shiras (Pittsburgh: Privately published by the Foster Executors, 1991); Hardin Craig, *A New Look at Shakespeare's Quartos* (Stanford: Stanford University Press, 1961), pp. 78–82; Urkowitz (n. 20); and Holderness and Loughrey, eds (n. 2), pp. 13–29.

24 Bradley (n. 7), pp. 112–13, nn.

25 Nashe and Lodge are cited from Geoffrey Bullough, ed., *Narrative and Dramatic Sources of Shakespeare*, vol. 7 (London: Routledge & Kegan Paul; New York: Columbia University Press, 1973), pp. 15, 24.

26 Eric Sams, "Taboo or Not Taboo? The Text, Dating and Authorship of *Hamlet*, 1589–1623," *Hamlet Studies* 10 (1988): 12–46.

27 Robert Greene, *Groats-worth of Wit* . . . (London: for Richard Oliue, 1596), [E3]v–[E4]r.

28 *The Dramatic Works of Thomas Dekker*, 4 vols, ed. Fredson Bowers (Cambridge: Cambridge University Press, 1953), 1: 351.

29 See in particular Peter Guinness's comments on Q1 in Loughrey (n. 22), p. 124.

30 See Trevor Howard-Hill's speculation in "The Author as Scribe or Reviser? Middleton's Intentions in *A Game at Chess*," *TEXT* 3 (1987): 305–18.

31 Eric S. Mallin, *Inscribing the Time: Shakespeare and the End of Elizabethan England* (Berkeley, Los Angeles, and London: University of California Press, 1995). The hypothesis that Shakespeare wrote Q2 while the theaters were closed during plaguetime conflicts with Leeds Barroll's stimulating recent argument that he tended to do his writing for the stage when the theaters were open, and also with my speculations below about the orality of the Shakespearean theater. See Barroll's *Politics, Plague, and Shakespeare's Theater: The Stuart Years* (Ithaca and London: Cornell University Press, 1991).

32 For the doubling of roles, see Loughrey (n. 22), p. 127, and Scott McMillin's differing view in "Casting the *Hamlet* Quartos. The Limit of Eleven," in Clayton, ed. (n. 2), pp. 179–94.

33 See Craig (n. 23), pp. 78–82. His arguments are refined and amplified in Robert E. Burkhart, *Shakespeare's Bad Quartos* (The Hague and Paris: Mouton, 1975), pp. 96–113.

34 Howard-Hill (n. 30); see also Ioppolo (n. 4), pp. 70–76.

35 See David Ward, "The King and *Hamlet*," *Shakespeare Quarterly* 43 (1992): 280–302; and, for a sense of the continuing malleability of the chronological arrangement of the texts, G. R. Hibbard's revision of the argument made in his Oxford Shakespeare *Hamlet* edition, "The Chronology of the Three Substantive Texts of Shakespeare's *Hamlet*," in Clayton, ed. (n. 2), pp. 79–89.

36 Quoted in Loughrey (n. 22), p. 124.

37 Ibid., pp. 124 and 126. Following Foucaultian theory of the origins of the "author," David Wiles has made a cogent argument for the demands of censorship as precipitating a more fixed, "literary" view of the playtexts in the late sixteenth century. See in particular his discussion of the role of the clown and fool in *Shakespeare's Clown: Actor and Text in the Elizabethan Playhouse* (Cambridge, London, New York, etc.: Cambridge University Press, 1987), pp. 11–15.

38 See, for example, Ursula Schaefer's essay, "Hearing from Books: The Rise of Fictionality in Old English Poetry," in A. N. Doane and Carol Braun Pasternack, eds, *Vox intexta: Orality and Textuality in the Middle Ages* (Madison and London: University of Wisconsin Press, 1991), pp. 117–36. Like my own discussion to follow, Shaefer's is dependent on Ong and Goody (n. 14).

39 See Goody, *Interface* (n. 14), pp. 263–89; and Finnegan's critique (n. 14), pp. 59–85.

40 For the "invisibility" of versification on stage, see George T. Wright, *Shakespeare's Metrical Art* (Berkeley and London: University of California Press, 1988), pp. 91–107. As Wright points out, even "good" Shakespearean dramatic verse is metrically rough. Indeed, consistently end-stopped and metrically correct lines might well have proved unsuccessful on stage. See also his "An Almost Oral Art: Shakespeare's Language on Stage and Page," *Shakespeare Quarterly* 43 (1992): 159–69.

41 Andrew Gurr, *The Shakespearean Stage 1574–1642*, 3rd edition (Cambridge, New York, and Melbourne: Cambridge University Press, 1992), p. 209. However, Gurr himself would presumably not extend his generalizations about performance to the playtext itself, which he portrays in the usual way as polished by the author from its inception.

42 *Histrio-Mastix. Or, The Player whipt* ([London]: for Th. Thorp, 1610), sig. [C1]v.

43 I am indebted to Rita Copeland's work on Lollard pedagogy, forthcoming from Cambridge University Press as *Criticism and Dissent in the Middle Ages*.

44 See G. E. Bentley, *The Professions of Dramatist and Player in Shakespeare's Time, 1590–1642*, one-volume paperback edition (Princeton and Guildford, UK: Princeton University Press, 1986), *Dramatist*, pp. 76–79 and *Player*, pp. 38–41. That is not to suggest that actors never asked to read the parts themselves, rather than have them read by the playwright. Bentley suggests there must have been some sort of preliminary culling out of materials, otherwise the readings would have taken up too much of the company's time. See the example from *The Hog Hath Lost His Pearl* in David Mann, *The Elizabethan Player: Contemporary Stage Representation* (London and New York: Routledge, 1991), pp. 183–86.

45 See Mann (n. 44), pp. 183–85: the author Haddit is loath to give the actor more than a few minutes with a new jig lest the actor carry away enough of the plot to have the company poet recreate it. In this scene, however, it is clear that the actor actually reads a text rather than having it read aloud to him. He is not reading to the company, but canvassing for works to be read to the company later on.

46 For *Orlando Furioso*, see Bentley, *Player* (n. 44), p. 83 n., citing W. W. Greg, *Dramatic Documents from the Elizabethan Playhouses*, 1: 176–81. See also "The Part of 'Poore,'" ed. N. W. Bawcutt, *Collections Volume XV* (Oxford: The Malone Society, 1993), pp. 111–69.

47 Cited from *The Return from Parnassus*, ed. John S. Farmer, Tudor Facsimile Texts (1912; reprinted New York: AMS, 1970), sig. G3r.

48 My thanks to Guy Hamel for this point, personal communication, April, 1994. See also *Histrio-Mastix* (n. 42); Bentley's citation of a letter from Robert Shaw to Henslowe (*Dramatist* (n. 44), p. 77) in which Shaw reports that "we have heard their book and like it"; Wells and Taylor (n. 4), p. 3; Gurr (n. 41), p. 173; and on "hearing" plays more generally, Andrew Gurr, *Playing in Shakespeare's London* (Cambridge, New York, etc.: Cambridge University Press, 1987; reprinted 1989), pp. 85–97.

49 See William B. Long, "Stage Directions: A Misinterpreted Factor in Determining Textual Provenance," *TEXT* 2 (1985): 121-37. I am also indebted to the recent research, primarily on *Two Merry Milkmaids*, presented by Long, Leslie Thomson, and Alan C. Dessen at the Shakespeare Association of America session on "Annotated Quartos and Elizabethan Staging Practices," Albuquerque, New Mexico, 1994. Long's contribution is printed in reduced form as "Bookkeepers and Playhouse Manuscripts: A Peek at the Evidence," *Shakespeare Newsletter* 44 (1994): 3.

These scholars sometimes suggest that the prompter did no actual prompting of actors; however, there are several references to prompting in our sense of the term from the early to mid-seventeenth century. See Bentley, *Player* (n. 44), pp. 80–82. Given that most of Bentley's examples are from the 1620s and 1630s, it may be that prompting actors was becoming an increasingly significant aspect of the Bookkeeper's job as the desire for precise rendition of the language of the playtext as licensed became more prominent among the acting companies.

50 Mary Carruthers, *The Book of Memory: A Study of Memory in Medieval Culture* (1990; reprinted Cambridge and New York: Cambridge University Press, 1992), pp. 86–91.

51 See Mann (n. 44), pp. 5–6 and 54–73. On Shakespeare as actor and the redefinition of theater, I am indebted also to Gurr (n. 41); and to Meredith Anne Skura, *Shakespeare the Actor and the Purposes of Playing* (Chicago and London: University of Chicago Press, 1993), pp. 1–63.

52 For more examples, see Jenkins' discussion (n. 4), p. 62.

53 *Pericles* represents a prominent exception, since it existed in several "bad" quartos published before 1623, the first-known of which appeared in 1609. Since it was not included by Heminge and Condell in the First Folio it is sufficiently anomalous to constitute a case unto itself that merits further study.

54 If "vttered" is not taken in its oral sense, the most plausible meaning is the *OED*'s obsolete usage c: "To produce or yield, to send out, supply, or furnish," which still preserves some of the aura of the marketplace. On the playhouse as a miniature market, see Barroll (n. 31); and Douglas Bruster, *Drama and the Market in the Age of Shakespeare*, Cambridge Studies in Renaissance Literature and Culture 1 (Cambridge and New York: Cambridge University Press, 1992).

55 John Marston, *The Malcontent* (London: for William Aspley, 1604). On humanist theorization of the relationship between thought and speech, see the early chapters of Martin Elsky, *Authorizing Words: Speech, Writing, and Print in the English Renaissance* (Ithaca and London: Cornell University Press, 1989).

56 As E. A. J. Honigmann notes in *The Stability of Shakespeare's Text* (London: Edward Arnold, 1965), pp. 47–77, a similar penchant for revision in the process of copying has been characteristic even of more recent authors operating much more squarely within the assumptions of print culture.

57 For instances of scribal publication of theatrical documents, see Harold Love, *Scribal Publication in Seventeenth-Century England* (Oxford: Clarendon Press, 1993), pp. 65–70. In *Textual Companion* (n. 4), p. 19, Wells and Taylor cite Humphrey Moseley's assertion that when the actors' friends "desir'd a Copy, then they (and justly too) transcribed what they *Acted*," but while Wells and Taylor argue that this transcription was legitimized by being made from a written copy (presumably the "promptbook"), I would argue that actors' transcription could well have been mnemonic (copied from the book of memory) and nevertheless legitimate. The resulting copy would be the play as acted with all the alterations for the stage, but still, as Moseley contends, in a form that carried the "*Authour's* consent." See the Beaumont and Fletcher folio *Comedies and Tragedies* (London: for Humphrey Robinson and Humphrey Moseley, 1647), "The Stationer to the Readers."

58 Nearly all pedagogical treatises of the period mention memory as highly important, but see in particular John Brinsley's discussion of the "places" in *Lvdvs Literarivs: or, The Grammar Schoole* (London: for Thomas Man, 1612), pp. 182, 253–58.

59 See Dante, *The New Life*, trans. William Anderson (Baltimore: Penguin, 1964), p. 37; and "The Life of St. Thomas Aquinas" by Bernardo Gui and Bartholomew of Capua, trans. Kenelm Foster, in *Biographical Documents for the Life of St. Thomas Aquinas* (Oxford: Blackfriars, 1949), all as cited in Carruthers (n. 50), p. 3. For Elizabeth I, see Sir John Harington, *Nugae Antiquae* (London: for W. Frederick, 1769), pp. 117–19, which records both the letter the queen is said to have written and the one she is said to have dictated. Similar mnemonic powers were attributed to Julius Caesar (Carruthers, p. 7).

60 Love (n. 57), pp. 52–53. On our reluctance to consider Shakespeare's oral sources, see Linda Woodbridge, "Patchwork: Piecing the Early Modern Mind in England's First Century of Print Culture," *English Literary Renaissance* 23 (1993): 5–45. For Jonson's comment, see *Discoveries* in *Ben Jonson*, ed. C. H. Herford, Percy and Evelyn Simpson, vol. 8 (Oxford: Clarendon, 1947), pp. 583–84.

61 Frances Yates, *The Art of Memory* (Chicago: University of Chicago Press; London: Routledge & Kegan Paul, 1966), pp. 342–67.

62 See D. F. McKenzie, "Speech-Manuscript-Print," in *New Directions in Textual*

Studies, ed. Dave Oliphant and Robin Bradford with an introduction by Larry Carver (Austin: Harry Ransom Humanities Research Center of the University of Texas at Austin, 1990), pp. 86–109. In a recent lecture at the University of Texas, the art historian Joan Holladay offered several medieval examples, among them the Wilhelm Ms. of Heinrich II, Landgrave of Hesse, in which the patron as projected author is shown in miniature as part of a decorative capital at the beginning of the text as a way of suggesting that the words that follow are to be imagined as possessing the "truth" of oral communication.

63 See *The Malcontent*, sig. [A4]r; and for Armin, Wiles (n. 37), p. 140. On sermons and other religious materials, see McKenzie (n. 62); Keith Thomas, "The Meaning of Literacy in Early Modern England," in Gerd Baumann, ed., *The Written Word: Literacy in Transition* (Oxford: Clarendon Press, 1988), pp. 97–131; and Tessa Watt, *Cheap Print and Popular Piety, 1550–1640*, Cambridge Studies in Early Modern British History (Cambridge: Cambridge University Press, 1991).

64 For a reading of the portrait and front matter, see Leah S. Marcus, *Puzzling Shakespeare: Local Reading and Its Discontents* (Berkeley and London: University of California Press, 1988), pp. 2–25. In the 1620s and 1630s, as Thomas L. Berger has pointed out to me, such title-page illustrations became very common on playbooks, no doubt for the same reason: they reduced the distance between the play as staged and the play as read.

I am reminded of a similar instance from our own technologically semi-literate age: the newest version of Norton Disk Doctor displays a grave moving image of a doctor at work while the software analyzes the disk. Surely, for us, the purpose is similar: to reassure us that something personal, healing, careful, and clinically sound is being accomplished even though we can't see it happening.

65 T. S. Eliot, *The Waste Land and Other Poems* (in Oriya translation) (India: Prafalla Ch., by arrangement with Faber & Faber, 1956).

66 Ong and Goody (n. 14). See also Wiles (n. 37), pp. 109–10, which applies Basil Bernstein's theory of "restricted codes" and "elaborated codes" to precisely the transition under discussion here.

67 See Jenkins, ed. (n. 4), p. 305, where the word is given as "pajock" and glossed as a "base contemptible fellow" (n.); Wiles (n. 37), p. 59, glosses the term as "patched or motley fool." My argument here is indebted to Wiles' interpretation of the aftermath of the play-within-a-play scene in *Hamlet* as full of allusions to Kemp's departure from the company, pp. 57–60.

68 See Wiles' biography of Kemp (n. 37), pp. 24–42.

69 See Jenkins, ed. (n. 4), who offers a useful discussion of the many ways in which F constitutes a more "literary" text than Q2, pp. 61–62; Joseph Loewenstein, "Plays Agonistic and Competitive: The Textual Approach to Elsinore," *Renaissance Drama*, n.s. 19 (1988): 63–96, which discounts Q1 but offers interesting analysis of the differences between Q2 and F; and Wilson, "The Copy for 'Hamlet,' 1603" (n. 7), pp. 161–62.

70 Q1 calls the play a "Tragicall Historie" on the title page and head title, but a "Tragedy" or "Tragedie" in the running titles; Q2 calls it a "Tragicall Historie" on the title page but a "Tragedie" in the head title and running titles; in the First Folio, the play is fully invested with the dignity of "Tragedie" as a generic designation.

71 Alfred Hart, *Stolne and Surreptitious Copies: A Comparative Study of Shakespeare's Bad Quartos* (Melbourne and London: Melbourne and Oxford University Presses, 1942), p. 104.

72 See Wilson, "'Hamlet' Transcript" (n. 7), pp 240–41. Wilson cites not the original 1613 edition, but James Halliwell's reprint, *Tarlton's Jests, and News Out of Purgatory* (London: Shakespeare Society, 1844), which expurgates some of the material. Since Tarleton died in 1588, for Wilson at this early stage of his thinking about *Hamlet* the presence of the jests indicated a very early date for this segment of the play – a view I find highly plausible. More recent memorial reconstructionists, with almost the same degree of plausibility, see the passage as "castigating the Tarlton tradition which had become outworn in the hands of his successors," Duthie (n. 6), pp. 232–34.

6 JOHN MILTON'S VOICE

1 Cited from the *London Magazine* in Alfred W. Pollard, "The Bibliography of Milton," *Library*, n.s. 37, vol. 10 (1909): 1–33.

2 See the recent discussions of the poem's occasion in David Norbrook, *Poetry and Politics in the English Renaissance* (London, Boston, Melbourne, and Henley: Routledge & Kegan Paul, 1984), pp. 269–85; and John Leonard, "'Trembling ears': The Historical Moment of *Lycidas*," *Journal of Medieval and Renaissance Studies* 21 (1991): 59–81.

3 In the 1637 edition, the work belongs to John Earl of Bridgewater, Lord President of Wales and his family. The title page carries no reference to Milton, but identifies the work as "A Maske Presented at Ludlow Castle, 1634: *On Michaelmasse night, before the* Right Honorable, Iohn *Earle of Bridgewater, Vicount* Brackly, *Lord Praesident of* Wales, And one of His Maiesties most honorable Privie Counsell." Lawes' dedicatory preface to Bridgewater's eldest son mentions an anonymous author who has not "*openly acknowledg'd*" the work, but redirects its authorship to the Bridgewater family, through whom the "Poem . . . *receiv'd its first occasion of birth*."

In the 1645 *Poems*, "A Maske" is set apart from the rest of Milton's works by a separate title page, but the title page clearly identifies it as Milton's, "A Mask Of the same Author Presented At *Ludlow*-Castle, 1634. Before The Earl of Bridgewater Then President of Wales." Both the Michaelmas occasion and Bridgewater's status as a Privy Counsellor disappear from this version, which also includes "The Copy of a Letter Writt'n by Sir Henry Wootton, To the Author" praising the poem and its author.

By the time of the 1673 *Poems*, the maske has lost its separate title page and become assimilated into the body of Milton's works. It bears the same title as the head title from the earlier editions, "A Mask presented at Ludlow-Castle, 1634. &c." Even its connection with the Council of Wales and the Earl and his family who had "birthed" the masque has disappeared in this version.

Of course, by 1645 "A Maske" had already lost other elements of its occasion that would have been evident in the performance. As C. W. R. D. Moseley remarks in *The Poetic Birth: Milton's Poems of 1645* (Aldershot, UK: Scolar Press, 1991), p. 201, "The complexity and richness of presentation of the masque, and the peculiar relationship of an audience to people they know acting a part, necessarily disappears in *Poems* (1645)."

4 For differing interpretations, see Pollard (n. 1); William Riley Parker, *Milton: A Biography* (Oxford: Clarendon Press, 1968), 2: 1108–12; Hugh Amory, "Things Unattempted Yet: A Bibliography of the First Edition of *Paradise Lost*," *Book Collector* 32 (1983): 41–66; John Barnard, "Bibliographical Context and the Critic," *TEXT* 3 (1987): 27–46; and Peter Lindenbaum, "The Poet in the

Marketplace: Milton and Samuel Simmons," in Paul G. Stanwood, ed., *Of Poetry and Politics: New Essays on Milton and His World*, Medieval and Renaissance Texts and Studies vol. 126 (Binghamton, New York: MRTS, 1995), pp. 249–62. See also Lindenbaum's "Milton's Contract," *Cardozo Arts and Entertainment Law Journal* 10 (1992): 439–54; and his "John Milton and the Republican Mode of Literary Production," *Yearbook of English Studies* 21 (1991): 121–36. My thanks to the author, who was kind enough to send me his work in manuscript.

5 See R. G. Moyles, *The Text of* Paradise Lost: *A Study in Editorial Procedure* (Toronto, Buffalo, and London: University of Toronto Press, 1985).

6 See Stephen B. Dobranski, "*Samson Agonistes* and the "Omissa," presented at MLA, San Diego, 1994, and forthcoming in *Studies in English Literature: 1500–1900*; similar material will appear in his University of Texas dissertation, "The Labor of Book-Writing: A Critical and Textual Analysis of John Milton and the Seventeenth-Century Book Trade," scheduled for completion during 1995 or 1996.

7 Harold Love, *Scribal Publication in Seventeenth-Century England* (Oxford: Clarendon Press, 1993); and Arthur F. Marotti, *Manuscript, Print, and the English Renaissance Lyric* (Ithaca and London: Cornell University Press, 1995). I am grateful to Professor Marotti for sending me an early copy of his book just as I was finishing the present chapter.

8 See, for example, the discussion of *sparagmos* in Michael Lieb, *Milton and the Culture of Violence* (Ithaca: Cornell University Press, 1994).

9 Mary Nyquist and Margaret W. Ferguson, eds, *Re-membering Milton* (New York and London: Methuen, 1987).

10 In addition to Love and Marotti (n. 7), I am strongly indebted to my student Margaret Downs-Gamble, whose dissertation on "John Donne's Monstrous Body," Department of English, University of Texas, 1993, got me thinking about authorial embodiment. She is presently working on a book about answer poems in manuscript.

11 See in particular, the volume editor's essay on Herbert in Randall McLeod, ed., *Crisis in Editing: Texts of the English Renaissance: Papers given at the Twenty-Fourth Annual Conference on Editorial Problems University of Toronto 4–5 November 1988* (New York: AMS Press, 1994), pp. 61–172; and more generally, Marotti's discussion (n. 7), p. 289; Martin Elsky, *Authorizing Words: Speech, Writing, and Print in the English Renaissance* (Ithaca and London: Cornell University Press, 1989), pp. 147–68; Jonathan Goldberg, *Voice Terminal Echo: Postmodernism and English Renaissance Texts* (New York and London: Methuen, 1986), pp. 101–23; and the broader discussion of poetic patterning in Neil Fraistat, *The Poem and the Book: Interpreting Collections of Romantic Poetry* (Chapel Hill and London: University of North Carolina Press, 1985), pp. 3–21.

12 The discussion to follow is indebted both to L. C. Martin, ed., *The Poetical Works of Robert Herrick* (Oxford: Clarendon Press, 1956); and to J. Max Patrick, ed., *The Complete Poetry of Robert Herrick* (1963; reprinted New York: W. W. Norton, 1968).

13 See Martin, ed. (n. 12); and the discussion of some of the variants in Leah S. Marcus, "Robert Herrick," in Thomas N. Corns, ed., *The Cambridge Companion to English Poetry, Donne to Marvell* (Cambridge and New York: Cambridge University Press, 1993), pp. 171–81.

14 *Quarterly Review* 4 (August, 1810), Article XII, pp. 171–72. See also the more elaborate discussion in Leah S. Marcus, *Childhood and Cultural Despair: A Theme and Variations in Seventeenth-Century Literature* (Pittsburgh: University of Pittsburgh Press, 1978).

15 *Discoveries* in *Ben Jonson*, ed. C. H. Herford and Percy and Evelyn Simpson, vol. 8 (Oxford: Clarendon Press, 1947; reprinted 1954), p. 625. For orality in the earlier humanists and Jonson see Elsky (n. 11), pp. 35–85. I am also indebted to Richard B. Wollman's 1994 Renaissance Society of America talk in Dallas, Texas, "'Speak that I may see thee': Manuscript Culture and Ben Jonson's Print Poetry."

16 See Louise Schleiner, *The Living Lyre in English Verse from Elizabeth through the Restoration* (Columbia: University of Missouri Press, 1984), pp. 72–84. As Schleiner notes, there were many other Herrick lyrics in circulation that the poet apparently chose to exclude from *Hesperides*. Although some lyrics become more complex in their revised *Hesperides* versions, others retain their "oral" quality – are deliberately left conceptually bare and undeveloped to "leave a composer room to work" (p. 77).

17 Roger Chartier, *The Order of Books*, trans. Lydia G. Cochrane (1992; reprinted Stanford: Stanford University Press, 1994), p. 55. See also Elizabeth L. Eisenstein's indispensable *The Printing Press as an Agent of Change* (Cambridge, New York, etc.: Cambridge University Press, 1979), 2 vols; and her abridgement, *The Printing Revolution in Early Modern Europe* (Cambridge University Press, 1983), in which some of the author's arguments are more clearly drawn.

18 My treatment of corpse and *corpus* is indebted to Margaret Downs-Gamble (n. 10) and to earlier conversations with Alan Liu.

19 Or perhaps the manuscript itself, like some others from the period, contained a portrait miniature of the author as medieval manuscripts frequently had. If such a manuscript of *Metempsycosis* existed, however, it has apparently not survived. For examples of such miniatures in contemporary manuscripts, see Esther Inglis's self-portraits as discussed and reproduced in Jonathan Goldberg, *Writing Matter: From the Hands of the English Renaissance* (Stanford: Stanford University Press, 1990), pp. 146–53 and figs 19 and 20; and George Gascoigne's frontispiece to *The Tale of Hemetes the Heremyte* as reproduced from British Library Royal ms. 18 A xlviii in *The Complete Works of George Gascoigne*, 2 vols, ed. John W. Cunliffe (Cambridge: Cambridge University Press, 1907–10; reprinted Grosse Pointe, Michigan: Scholarly Press, 1969), 2: [472]. My thanks to Ernest Sullivan and other editors of the *Donne Variorum* for helpful information on the range of manuscript copies of *Metempsycosis*.

20 For this and all other bibliographical details I have not observed myself, I am indebted to Sir Geoffrey Keynes, *A Bibliography of Dr. John Donne Dean of Saint Paul's*, 4th edition (Oxford: Clarendon Press, 1973).

21 For verification of the signature, I am indebted to the collective wisdom of members of the John Donne Society, before whom portions of the present argument were presented in an early version. For the Harvard copy, see Ann Arbor University Microfilms, STC reel 881. I am grateful to Ted-Larry Pebworth for confirming its present location. This copy is "sophisticated" in that it has a frontispiece portrait added from a later edition. The signature on the title page, however, appears genuine.

22 On connections between the portrait miniature and poetry in manuscript, see Patricia Fumerton, *Cultural Aesthetics: Renaissance Literature and the Practice of Social Ornament* (Chicago and London: University of Chicago Press, 1991), pp. 67–110.

23 I am indebted to Catherine Creswell's contextualization of the motto in "Giving a Face to an Author: Reading Donne's Portraits and the 1635 Edition," *Texas Studies in Literature and Language* 37 (1995): 1–15. Although I read her article after most of the present chapter was written, I am happy to acknowledge

affinities between her discussion of the 1633 and 1635 Donne poems and my own briefer discussion here.

24 Cited from John King, *Lectures upon Jonas Delivered at Yorke* (Oxford, 1597), at p. 113 of Keith Thomas, "The Meaning of Literacy in Early Modern England," in Gerd Baumann, ed., *The Written Word: Literacy in Transition* (Oxford: Clarendon Press, 1986), pp. 97–131.

25 On associations between writing and/or print and death more generally, see Walter J. Ong, *Orality and Literacy: The Technologizing of the Word* (London and New York: Methuen, 1982), p. 81.

26 See, for example, Marotti (n. 7), p. 240; I am indebted to David L. Gants, Research Associate at the University of Virginia, who has seen many more copies than I of Jonson's 1616 *Workes* and assures me that those with the portrait frontispiece have indeed been altered after the fact. Similarly, Marotti publishes an illustration (p. 249) of the Huntington Library copy of Herbert's 1633 *The Temple* along with a facing frontispiece portrait that has evidently been pasted in from a much later edition – the 1670s at the earliest. See F. E. Hutchinson, ed., *The Works of George Herbert* (1941; reprinted Oxford: Clarendon Press, 1945), pp. lvi–lxii. Marotti's argument about the rhetoric of the 1633 frontispiece is invalidated by the fact that there was no such animal. The ease with which such errors can be made is an object lesson in the continuing importance of consulting the standard bibliographical descriptions even as we quarrel with some of the methodology behind them.

27 My thanks to Jean R. Brink for reminding me of the Drayton example, reproduced as frontispiece and jacket design for her volume *Michael Drayton Revisited* in the Twayne's English Authors Series (Boston: Twayne, 1990). See also her helpful discussion of the volume, pp. 97–111.

28 Walter Benjamin, "The Work of Art in the Age of Mechanical Reproduction," trans. Harry Zohn in *Illuminations* (New York: Schocken, 1969), pp. 217–51. Benjamin's "aura," which was carried, he contends, by works of art in the pre-modern period before commodification caused them to lose it, in some ways parallels my use of the concept of authorial "presence," which had to be built into books in order to replace the loss of the actual presence of the originator of the discourse. I would contend, however, that any such aura is temporary, produced retroactively by the unfamiliarity of a new medium rather than by commodification per se.

29 The translation is that of Niccolò Machiavelli, *The Prince and The Discourses*, ed. Max Lerner (New York: Modern Library, 1950), p. xxix. For Peter Burke's point about residual orality and the Renaissance dialogue, particularly as represented in Castiglione's *Courtier*, I am indebted to his presentation in April, 1995 at CUNY Graduate School in New York under the auspices of its Center for Renaissance Studies. See also D. F. McKenzie, "Speech–Manuscript–Print," in *New Directions in Textual Studies*, ed. Dave Oliphant and Robin Bradford, with an introduction by Larry Carver (Austin: Harry Ransom Humanities Research Center, 1990), pp. 86–109.

30 Cited from John Ramsey's Commonplace Book, Bodleian ms. Douce 280, fol. 91v, in Marotti (n. 7), p. 21.

31 See Margreta de Grazia, *Shakespeare Verbatim* (Oxford: Clarendon Press, 1991), pp. 163–72; and William A. Jackson's commentary on the volume in *The Carl H. Pforzheimer Library: English Literature 1475–1700* (New York: privately printed, 1940), 3: 908–09. Even Milton's publisher Humphrey Moseley was a prolific publisher of "self-help" miscellanies resembling the Shakespeare 1640 *Poems;*

the Shakespeare volume turns up on Moseley's 1656 catalogue. For Moseley as popular publisher, see Ann Baynes Coiro, "Milton and Class Identity: The Publication of *Areopagitica* and the 1645 *Poems*," *Journal of Medieval and Renaissance Studies* 22 (1992): 261–89.

32 See, for example, Humphrey Moseley's posthumous edition of *The Last Remains of Sr John Suckling* (London, 1659), which shows the poet's bust on a monument flanked by cypress trees: reading the book is figured as equivalent to visiting the poet's physical "remains" at a gravesite!

33 *The Works of John Milton*, Columbia edition, ed. Frank Allen Patterson, 18 vols in 21 (New York: Columbia University Press, 1931–38), 9: 125, cited in the present study as C. In addition to the examples of frontispiece rhetoric already discussed above, Moseley's posthumous edition of the writings of William Cartwright (1651) provides yet further evidence that the publisher was interested in the rhetoric of the frontispiece, since in this instance the engraver was not William Marshall. The frontispiece shows Cartwright as university proctor, seated with his head leaning on one arm which rests on an open copy of the works of Aristotle, whom the accompanying verses characterize as a chief mainstay of the author. Moseley's epistles dedicatory and much other useful information is collected in John Curtis Reed's monograph, *Humphrey Moseley, Publisher*, Oxford Bibliographical Society Proceedings and Papers vol. 2 Part 2, 1928 (Oxford: Oxford University Press, 1929).

34 I have seen the 1633 Cowley volume only in microfilm copy, but its frontispiece is reproduced and discussed in *The Collected Works of Abraham Cowley*, vol. 1, ed. Thomas O. Calhoun, Laurence Heyworth, and Allan Pritchard (Newark: University of Delaware Press; London and Toronto: Associated University Presses, 1989), p. [12] and notes. The second and third editions of 1636 and 1637 respectively have cruder portrait frontispieces and anticipate Milton's 1645 *Poems* by including an epistle from the author apologizing for their poor quality. Interestingly enough, Humphrey Moseley's 1656 folio edition of Cowley's writings does not include a portrait frontispiece. By that late point in his career, Cowley was adopting the more usual seventeenth-century posture of reluctant author forced into print.

35 That is, according to early biographical sources: see David Masson, *The Life of John Milton* (Gloucester, Massachusetts: Peter Smith, 1965), 6: 682 n.; and J. Milton French, *The Life Records of John Milton* (New Brunswick, New Jersey: Rutgers University Press, 1949–58), 5: 123, 322–23.

36 For possible examples, see M. H. Black's notice of the Cambridge University Library copy of the 1638 *Lycidas*, which inserts an omitted line, probably in Milton's own hand, *Cambridge University Press 1584–1984* (Cambridge and New York: Cambridge University Press, 1984), p. 70. A British Library copy shows similar corrections: see Pollard (n. 1), p. 6; as does the Bridgewater copy of the 1637 edition of *A Maske* presently in the Pforzheimer Collection at the University of Texas. See Jackson's commentary on the Bridgewater copy of *A Maske, Pforzheimer Library* (n. 31), 2: 724. Since the corrections imitate the typography of the words they are correcting, it is impossible to know certainly whether any of these hands is Milton's. In addition, there are many printed copies of Milton's prose tracts from the period before his blindness showing corrections that may be in his own hand. See French (n. 35) 2: 36, 98, 114–15.

37 Translation by C. W. R. D. Moseley (n. 3), p. 82. See also E. V. Rieu, trans., Penguin Classics edition of Virgil, *The Pastoral Poems* (Harmondsworth, UK: Penguin, 1949).

38 Cited from Helen Darbishire, ed., *The Early Lives of Milton* (New York: Barnes and

Noble; London, Constable and Co., 1932), p. 6. I have expanded abbreviations.
39 Ibid., p. 4.
40 See the list of such copies in J. W. Saunders, *The Profession of English Letters* (London: Routledge & Kegan Paul; Toronto: University of Toronto Press, 1964), pp. 88–89; other examples of his circulation of his own work in manuscript or printed form are recorded in French (n. 35), 1: 93 (Letter to Thomas Young); 1: 172 (Letter to Alexander Gill); 1: 290 (Letter to Alexander Gill); 2: 24 (Letter to Carlo Dati); 2: 35 (*Of Reformation* presented to Thomason); 2: 56 (*Reason of Church Government* presented to Thomason); 2: 59 (*Apology* presented to Thomason); 2: 113 (*Areopagitica* presented to Thomason); 2: 114 (*Areopagitica* presented to an unknown friend); 2: 125 (copies of ten tracts sent bound together with a dedicatory inscription to Patrick Young); 2: 140 (*Poems* and eleven prose works presented along with a dedicatory poem to John Rouse for the library of Oxford University); 2: 190 (promises to send Latin part of *Poems* to Charles Dati); 2: 282–83 (*Eikonoklastes* presented to the Earl of Carbery, to John Dury, and by Milton's nephew to John Barker); 2: 355–56 and 3: 66 (*Defensio* presented to several friends); 4: 101 (*Eikonoklastes* presented to Bodleian Library); 4: 109 (*Poems* presented to Peter Heimbach along with dedicatory inscription); and 4: 166 (reference to previous sending of one of the *Defenses* to Saumur).
41 See Edward Phillips's testimony, Darbishire (n. 38), p. 61.
42 Saunders (n. 40), pp. 88–90. More recently, in "Milton's Contract" and "The Poet in the Marketplace," Peter Lindenbaum has contested Saunders' interpretation of the contract for *Paradise Lost*, basing himself on William Riley Parker's statistics in *Biography* 2: 1109 and note and 1116, n. 40, showing that fully a fourth of the first edition of *Paradise Lost* survives. Parker assumes that many of these must have been presentation copies although they are not so marked. Lindenbaum contends that if they were not marked they could not have been presentation copies, but there are many other examples of Milton presentation copies that are not so inscribed by the author, even from the period before Milton's blindness. Many of the presentation copies of other Milton books listed in the previous note were either not inscribed at all or inscribed by the recipient. It seems unlikely that Milton would have been able to supply impromptu visitors and distant friends so readily if he did not have his own stock of copies of his works at hand.
43 French (n. 35), 1: 171–72 (Letter to Alexander Gill refers to an included copy of Milton's commencement verses "committed to type," "Haec quidem Typis donata ad te misi"; and 2: 19; in French, the early printed version of *Epitaphium Damonis* is listed as British Library ms. C.57.d.48.
44 Chartier (n. 17), pp. 27–32.
45 Louis L. Martz, "The Rising Poet," in *The Lyric and Dramatic Milton: Selected Papers from the English Institute*, ed. Joseph H. Summers (New York and London: Columbia University Press, 1965), 3–33. The citation is from p. 4. As readers will readily observe, my own reading of the 1645 volume is strongly indebted to Martz's important article and also to C. W. R. D. Moseley's extension and reworking of Martz in *The Poetic Birth* (n. 3); to John K. Hale, "Milton's Self-Presentation in *Poems . . . 1645*," *Milton Quarterly* 25 (1991): 37–48; and more generally, to Saunders (n. 40), pp. 85–92.
46 See Coiro's discussion of the trope (n. 31); and, for another instance, Milton's letter to Lucas Holstenius (1639), which refers to the as yet unprinted classical manuscripts in the Vatican Library as souls waiting in a deep valley to be born into the world above through the hands of the printer (C 12: 39, 41).

47 See Harris Francis Fletcher, ed., *John Milton's Complete Poetical Works Reproduced in Photographic Facsimile*, 4 vols (Urbana: University of Illinois Press, 1943–48), 1: 150. Similarly, Fletcher notes a few copies of the English half without the Latin and Greek poems, and occasional copies in which the Latin "book" is bound before the English.

48 My thanks to Janel Mueller for pointing this out in a personal communication; see also Marotti's discussion of Gascoigne (n. 7), pp. 219–26; and Richard C. Newton, "Making Books from Leaves: Poets become Editors," in *Print and Culture in the Renaissance: Essays on the Advent of Printing in Europe*, ed. Gerald P. Tyson and Sylvia S. Wagonheim (Newark: University of Delaware Press; London and Toronto: Associated University Presses, 1986), pp. 246-64.

49 Fletcher, ed. (n. 47), 1: 149. On the rhetoric of textual annotation more generally, see Stephen A. Barney, ed., *Annotation and Its Texts* (New York and Oxford: Oxford University Press, 1991); and Evelyn B. Tribble, *Margins and Marginality: The Printed Page in Early Modern England* (Charlottesville and London: University Press of Virginia, 1993).

50 Since this translation is seriously botched in the Columbia Milton, I cite the standard version offered in Merritt Y. Hughes, ed., *Paradise Regained, The Minor Poems, and Samson Agonistes* (New York: Odyssey Press, 1937), p. 353.

51 Masson (n. 35), 3: 459.

52 I am indebted to my colleague Elizabeth Richmond-Garza for confirming my sense of the ambiguity of the lines and supplying me with this literal translation.

53 Darbishire (n. 38), p. 3.

54 See David Loewenstein, *Milton and the Drama of History: Historical Vision, Iconoclasm, and the Literary Imagination* (Cambridge: Cambridge University Press, 1990); and Loewenstein and James Grantham Turner, eds, *Politics, Poetics, and Hermeneutics in Milton's Prose* (Cambridge: Cambridge University Press, 1990).

55 On Milton and collectivity, see in particular William Kolbrener, "'Plainly Partial': The Liberal *Areopagitica*," *ELH* 60 (1993): 57–79; and Stanley Fish, "Wanting a Supplement: The Question of Interpretation in Milton's Early Prose," in Loewenstein and Turner (n. 54), pp. 41–68.

56 See the excerpts from Salmasius's posthumous *Responsio* (1660) reproduced in French (n. 35), 4: 346–48; and Masson (n. 35), 6: 205–11.

57 Stanley Fish, "Milton's Career and the Career of Theory," delivered at the Modern Language Association, New Orleans, 1988; see also his "Wanting a Supplement" (n. 55), which considerably complicates Fish's earlier position by demonstrating Milton's contradictory motions toward selfhood/autonomy and membership in larger collectivities.

INDEX